Great Issues

in American

History

*

From Reconstruction to the
Present Day, 1864-1969

* * *
* *
*
* *
*

GREAT ISSUES IN AMERICAN HISTORY

From Reconstruction to the
Present Day, 1864-1969

✳ EDITED BY ✳

Richard Hofstadter

VINTAGE BOOKS
A DIVISION OF RANDOM HOUSE
New York

*

To My Father

*

Preface

THESE documentary selections are intended to provide a generous sampling from the major political controversies in American history. I hope that the general introductions, together with the headnotes supplied for each selection, will serve to set the documents in their historical context in such a way as to make it possible for a reader with a modest knowledge of American history to read them profitably and without further supplement. But the volumes have been planned with special concern for the interests and needs of undergraduates who will have occasion to use them in connection with a textbook or a general survey of American history. With this in mind, I have not tried to make my general introductions into a collective history of American politics, nor even into histories of the particular issues I have chosen to illustrate; they are simply brief glosses on a few issues of central importance. They will serve their purpose if they refresh the memory of the general reader and assist the student in establishing the links between these sources and his other readings.

It has been my purpose to concentrate on political controversy. I have not tried to include the texts of statutes, which are available in reference books and are usually well summarized for the student's purposes in general books; nor have I—except in the cases of a few documents whose special importance seemed to demand their inclusion —reprinted purely illustrative materials. Almost everything in these volumes can be described as argumentative. These documents reproduce the words of major actors of American political history—whether judges, statesmen, legislative bodies, or private individuals of influence—engaged in debating issues of central importance. It has not been possible to include all the historical issues that may be considered important. To achieve such inclusiveness seems less desirable than that every issue selected should be discussed in some depth in the chosen documents, and that opposing views should be adequately represented.

Of necessity, the documents have been edited, and the ellipses indicate omitted portions. But I have tried to avoid snippets. Where severe selection from a larger text has been necessary, enough has been included in each case to give a coherent sample of the original argument at the point at which the author was stating the novel or essential portions of his case. Some small amount of modernization has been imposed on most documents written before about 1815.

I am grateful to my wife, Beatrice Kevitt Hofstadter, who generously took time from her own work in progress to help me collate and edit these documents and prepare the commentaries; and to Gerald and Dorothy Stearn for editorial assistance at every stage in the preparation of the manuscript.

March, 1958   R. H.

PREFACE TO THE REVISED EDITION

In bringing this final volume up to date I had to select rigorously from a multitude of issues in order to keep the work within a manageable length. I found it best to concentrate on six focal matters: 1) the epoch-making development of the American economy under the guidance of the "new economics"; 2) the attempt to extend the welfare state and to wage war on the dangerous and dessicating poverty that persisted amid affluence; 3) the Supreme Court's decisions on reapportionment, which promise to reshape our representative institutions; 4) the Cuban missile crisis of 1962, upon whose outcome the survival of the world depended; 5) the debate over the war in Vietnam, which among all the foreign policy issues was the most symptomatic and the most decisive; and 6) the profound, divisive issue of racial injustice. I am obliged to Michael Wallace for help in the selection of new materials.

March, 1969   R. H.

Contents

PART I: RECONSTRUCTION AND AFTER

PART II: INDUSTRIALISM AND SOCIAL REFORM

PART III: AGRARIAN PROTEST

PART IV: IMPERIALISM AND WAR

PART V: PROGRESSIVISM

PART VII: WORLD WAR II AND THE POST-WAR WORLD

PART VIII: A TIME OF TROUBLES: THE 1960's

Great Issues
in American
History

*

From Reconstruction to the
Present Day, 1864-1969

★ PART I ★

Reconstruction and After

INTRODUCTION

THE defeat of the Confederacy in 1865 settled for all time
the issue of disunion that had agitated the Republic through
most of its history. But the question of how to treat those
states that had in fact seceded was to prove nearly as
thorny and bitter as had been the issue of their right to do
so. What was the present constitutional status of the defeated states? Had they ever been legally out of the Union?
Were they, for the time being, still members of the federal
government, but in some sort of political suspension? Or
were they a conquered territory, subject to the will of the
conqueror? Was the President or Congress to decide
what their legal status was, and how and when they should
be fully reinstated in the Union? Should the terms of re-
instatement be harsh or lenient? Inseparable from these
issues was the new problem of the freedmen. What demands could and should be made upon the Southern
states in their behalf? What place were they to have in the
new South? Who would give them the guidance and control they must have to make the transition from depend-
ence to civic responsibility?

Long before the war was over, the President and
Congress began to differ over their respective powers in
reconstructing the South. The Constitution gave very little
explicit guidance for such a situation. Northern legal
theory had been based on the idea that secession was
legally impossible; but if, then, the Southern states had

never been out of the Union, could they now be treated as though they were new *territories* to be governed by Congress? Lincoln took the initiative as early as December 1863, by announcing a program of generous amnesty, and promising recognition—by the President, not Congress—of the governments of states where emancipation would be accepted and where as few as ten percent of the voters of 1860 would take oaths of loyalty to the Union. The first important move made by Lincoln's Congressional opponents was the harsh Wade-Davis Bill of July 4, 1864, which demanded sweeping oaths of past as well as future loyalty from a *majority* of the electorate, as a condition of restoration to the Union. Since this bill was passed at the end of a Congressional session, Lincoln was able to kill it by a pocket veto. But this did not satisfy him; he chose to issue a proclamation (Document 1) in which he stated his opinion of the bill. Although Lincoln meant his statement to be conciliatory, the Congressional Radicals took it as the opening shot in a struggle between themselves and the President. Senator Benjamin F. Wade of Ohio and Representative Henry Winter Davis of Maryland, co-sponsors of the contested bill, issued a manifesto (Document 2) against executive tyranny, in which they claimed that the authority to determine the legally constituted government of a state was "exclusively vested in Congress by the Constitution." But the President imperturbably continued to argue for a mild policy and tried to avoid legalisms in determining the South's position. In a speech (Document 3) delivered shortly before his death, he tried again to conciliate the Radicals, but insisted firmly that attempts to decide whether or not the Southern states had ever been out of the Union served no purpose but to distract policy-makers with "a merely pernicious abstraction."

Not long after Lincoln's death the Radicals realized that Andrew Johnson would oppose them even more intransigently than Lincoln had. During the summer of 1865, acting on Lincoln's plan, Johnson recognized the four Southern state governments that Lincoln had set up. He also began to organize provisional governments for the remaining seven states. When Congress convened in the winter, Thaddeus Stevens, the Radical leader, delivered

a speech (Document 4) assailing the President's conception of Reconstruction. The Southern states were not states
of the Union, he announced, but "conquered provinces
subject to the will of Congress." Congress then set up its
own agency, the Joint Committee on Reconstruction,
which Stevens dominated. In the summer of 1866 this
committee delivered a report (Document 5) which restated Stevens' views of Southern status, and set harsh,
punitive terms for readmission. The freedmen also entered
the struggle. In some places they found articulate leaders
who were able to argue eloquently for action that would
safeguard their new freedom (Document 6). Nor were
Southern whites, chafing under the deprivations they were
suffering even under the governments established by
President Johnson, willing to remain silent (Document 7).
Men like Alexander Stephens appeared before the Joint
Committee on Reconstruction (Document 8) to protest
making the acceptance of Negro suffrage or the Fourteenth
Amendment a condition of restoration to the Union.

   During this time, the Fourteenth Amendment (*Great
Issues in American History from Revolution to the Civil
War, 1765–1865,* Part II, Document 4) had been enacted
by Congress and was in the process of being ratified by the
states. It declared that Negroes were citizens of the United
States and also of the states in which they lived; it attempted to secure to Negroes all the rights and privileges
of citizenship; and it provided that any state which denied
Negroes the right to vote would then have its representation in Congress reduced proportionately to the number of
persons so deprived. The Joint Committee on Reconstruction recommended that no state be readmitted until it had
accepted this amendment. Thus the Radicals hoped to
guarantee a large electorate of ex-slaves, whose support of
the Republican party could be counted on. Many Radicals
were, of course, also genuinely concerned with the welfare
of the ex-slaves.

   While Johnson and the Radicals were battling in
Washington, white Southerners were struggling to regain
local supremacy, and to devise new institutions which
would nullify the effects of the changes that were being
imposed on them. In 1865 the first of the notorious Black
Codes was passed. These laws gave some rights to Negroes

and withheld others, but on the pretense of preventing what was called "vagrancy," set limitations upon the behavior and movements of Negro labor that seemed to many Northerners to have the effect of enforcing involuntary servitude. To protect the Negro, and to provide other ways of managing the chaotic Southern labor market, Congress passed the Freedman's Bureau bill in March 1865. A year later Johnson vetoed a bill extending the Bureau's life. But in April 1866 such a bill passed over another veto. The same month, again over a veto, Congress passed a Civil Rights Act, to extend civil rights to all citizens; but constitutional doubts led Congress two months later to put some of its terms in the Fourteenth Amendment.

As the Congressional elections of 1866 approached, Johnson decided to take his case against the Radicals to the people. In August and September he made his famous "swing around the circle"—his unfortunate speaking tour of the Middle West. Johnson's ineptness, however (Document 9), only weakened his case, and the Republicans re-soundingly beat him, winning two-thirds of both houses. The Radicals now held full control of Reconstruction policy. The following spring the newly elected Congress passed the First Reconstruction Act, over an elaborate veto (Document 10) in which Johnson reviewed in detail his case against Congressional Reconstruction.

In 1867 and 1868, in the shadow of military governments set up by the First Reconstruction Act, Radical-dominated Southern state conventions wrote new constitutions under which were begun the famous "carpet bag" governments, whose reign aroused bitter and long-lasting resentments among Southern whites. Senators and representatives satisfactory to the Congressional Radicals began to be elected, and were allowed to take their seats in Congress. A number of Negroes were sent both to state legislatures and to Congress. Corruption and disorder were widespread under the carpet bag regimes, but in the midst of much misgovernment some real reforms were effected.

In Washington, meanwhile, Johnson and the Radicals were fighting each other at every possible point. The Radicals passed a Tenure of Office Act in March 1867, forbidding the President to remove any federal officer to

whose appointment the Senate had consented, unless the
Senate also consented to the removal. Johnson dismissed
Secretary of War Stanton to test the Act, which was am-
biguous on vital points. The Radicals promptly impeached
him on eleven charges, eight of which dealt with Stanton's
removal. From March 30 to May 16 a bitter impeachment
trial went on (Documents 11 and 12). Johnson's defenders maintained, with considerable effect, that whatever his failings, the President was hardly guilty of the
"high crimes and misdemeanors" which the Constitution
specifies as the grounds for removal from office. On this
issue even the Republicans divided, and the Radicals fell
just one vote short of the two-thirds necessary for con
viction.

After this narrow escape, Johnson remained isolated
and ineffectual, but the Radicals did not possess the presidency. To maintain their control the Radicals also needed
broader popular support in the South, which they were
trying to govern against the wishes of the majority of its
politically effective population. The white South, growing
in strength, and convinced that it had been victimized
by a superior force (Document 13) without moral authority, was determined to expel the Northerners and subordinate the freedmen. During the 1870's the Southern
states one by one restored conservative governments.
Spokesmen for the Negro cause pointed in vain to the
prevalence of violence or fraud in state elections (Document 14).

The efforts being made by militant advocates of white
supremacy to defy Congress and to reduce the social and
political gains made by Negroes after the war, in time
gathered further strength from a number of Supreme Court
decisions. In 1873, the Supreme Court in the *Slaughter-
house Cases* (Document 15), distinguished between citizenship in a state and in the United States. The Court thus
deprived Negroes of much of the intended protection of
the Fourteenth Amendment, because only their rights as
citizens of the United States could now be protected under
its terms. In the *Civil Rights Cases* of 1883 (Document
16), from which Justice John Marshall Harlan fervently
dissented (Document 17), the court invalidated legislation
Congress had enacted to try to guarantee to Negroes

equal rights in inns, public conveyances, and theaters. In 1896, when the position of the Southern Negro was lower than at any time since emancipation, the Supreme Court's decision in *Plessy v. Ferguson* (Document 18) gave the *coup de grâce* to whatever hopes for civil equality might still have been held. By accepting the doctrine that "separate but equal" facilities met the requirements of the Constitution, the Court laid a firm legal basis for subsequent segregation. Again Justice Harlan dissented (Document 19), and this time his dissent proved to be remarkably prophetic. The great social strides taken by the Negro in the twentieth century made the ultimate acceptance of Harlan's views inescapable, and in a momentous decision of 1954, *Brown v. Board of Education of Topeka* (Document 20), the Supreme Court declared segregation in public schools unconstitutional. Southern response to this decision was intense (Document 21), but, more important, the issue of race was posed, North and South, with a sharpness never before equaled. For later race relations, see Part VIII, Documents 13, 14, 17, 18, and 19.

DOCUMENT 1

ABRAHAM LINCOLN, PROCLAMATION ON THE WADE-DAVIS BILL,
JULY 8, 1864

Since the Wade-Davis Bill was passed during the closing hours of a Congressional session, Lincoln could have disposed of it silently by "pocket veto," that is, by failing to sign it within ten days. However, he felt the bill raised issues too important to be merely "swallowed"; in order to indicate his reasons for the veto, but also to show which parts of the act he would accept, he took the unprecedented step of issuing this proclamation (revised in minor details by his Attorney–General, Edward Bates). But the Radicals did not react as Lincoln had hoped to the conciliatory aspects of his proclama-

*tion. "What an infamous proclamation!" exclaimed
Thaddeus Stevens. "The idea of pocketing a bill and
then issuing a proclamation as to how far he will conform to it. . . ."*

Whereas, at the late Session, Congress passed a Bill, "To
guarantee to certain States, whose governments have been
usurped or overthrown, a republican form of Government," a copy of which is hereunto annexed:

And whereas, the said Bill was presented to the President of the United States, for his approval, less than one
hour before the *sine die* adjournment of said Session, and
was not signed by him:

And whereas, the said Bill contains, among other
things, a plan for restoring the States in rebellion to their
proper practical relation in the Union, which plan expresses the sense of Congress upon that subject, and which
plan it is now thought fit to lay before the people for their
consideration:

Now, therefore, I, Abraham Lincoln, President of the
United States, do proclaim, declare, and make known,
that, while I am, (as I was in December last, when by
proclamation I propounded a plan for restoration) unprepared, by a formal approval of this Bill, to be inflexibly
committed to any single plan of restoration; and, while
I am also unprepared to declare, that the free-state constitutions and governments, already adopted and installed
in Arkansas and Louisiana, shall be set aside and held for
nought, thereby repelling and discouraging the loyal citizens
who have set up the same, as to further effort; or to declare a constitutional competency in Congress to abolish
slavery in States, but am at the same time sincerely hoping
and expecting that a constitutional amendment, abolishing
slavery throughout the nation, may be adopted, nevertheless, I am fully satisfied with the system for restoration
contained in the Bill, as one very proper plan for the loyal
people of any State choosing to adopt it; and that I am,
and at all times shall be, prepared to give the Executive
aid and assistance to any such people, so soon as the military resistance to the United States shall have been suppressed in any such State, and the people thereof shall have
sufficiently returned to their obedience to the Constitution

and the laws of the United States,—in which cases, military Governors will be appointed, with directions to proceed according to the Bill.

DOCUMENT 2

THE WADE-DAVIS MANIFESTO,

AUGUST 5, 1864

This document answered Lincoln's Proclamation with a ringing assertion of Congressional supremacy over Reconstruction. Although there was much sympathy in the North for the Radicals, it was, as a Harper's Weekly editorial said, "simply impossible to make the American People believe that the President is a wily despot or a political gambler." A few days after this manifesto was published, Lincoln told Gideon Welles that he had not read it and had no intention of doing so.

We have read without surprise, but not without indignation, the Proclamation of the President of the 8th of July. . . .

The President, by preventing this bill from becoming a law, holds the electoral votes of the Rebel States at the dictation of his personal ambition.

If those votes turn the balance in his favor, is it to be supposed that his competitor, defeated by such means, will acquiesce?

If the Rebel majority assert their supremacy in those States, and send votes which elect an enemy of the Government, will we not repel his claims?

And is not that civil war for the Presidency, inaugurated by the votes of Rebel States?

Seriously impressed with these dangers, Congress, *"the proper constitutional authority,"* formally declared that there are no State Governments in the Rebel States, and provided for their erection at a proper time; and both the Senate and the House of Representatives rejected the Senators and Representatives chosen under the authority of what the President calls the Free Constitution and Government of Arkansas.

The President's proclamation *"holds for naught"* this judgment, and discards the authority of the Supreme Court, and strides headlong toward the anarchy his Proclamation of the 8th of December inaugurated.

If electors for President be allowed to be chosen in either of those States, a sinister light will be cast on the motives which induced the President to "hold for naught" the will of Congress rather than his Government in Louisiana and Arkansas.

That judgment of Congress which the President defies was the exercise of an authority exclusively vested in Congress by the Constitution to determine what is the established Government in a State, and in its own nature and by the highest judicial authority binding on all other departments of the Government. . . .

A more studied outrage on the legislative authority of the people has never been perpetrated.

Congress passed a bill; the President refused to approve it, and then by proclamation puts as much of it in force as he sees fit, and proposes to execute those parts by officers unknown to the laws of the United States and not subject to the confirmation of the Senate!

The bill directed the appointment of Provisional Governors by and with the advice and consent of the Senate.

The President, after defeating the law, proposes to appoint without law, and without the advice and consent of the Senate, *Military* Governors for the Rebel States!

He has already exercised this dictatorial usurpation in Louisiana, and he defeated the bill to prevent its limitation. . . .

The President has greatly presumed on the forbearance which the supporters of his Administration have so long practiced, in view of the arduous conflict in which we are engaged, and the reckless ferocity of our political opponents.

But he must understand that our support is of a cause and not of a man; that the authority of Congress is paramount and must be respected; that the whole body of the Union men of Congress will not submit to be impeached by him of rash and unconstitutional legislation; and if he wishes our support, he must confine himself to his executive duties—to obey and execute, not make the laws—to suppress by arms armed Rebellion, and leave political reorganization to Congress.

If the supporters of the Government fail to insist on this, they become responsible for the usurpations which they fail to rebuke, and are justly liable to the indignation of the people whose rights and security, committed to their keeping, they sacrifice.

Let them consider the remedy for these usurpations, and, having found it, fearlessly execute it.

DOCUMENT 3

ABRAHAM LINCOLN, SPEECH,
APRIL 11, 1865

This selection is from Lincoln's last speech, in which he set his views of Reconstruction before the public. It was a moment of triumph; the news of Appomattox had just arrived, and a large, enthusiastic crowd came to serenade the President. Lincoln began to read his carefully prepared message on the White House balcony, holding in one hand its text and in the other a candle, which his friend, the journalist Noah Brooks, presently took from him. After finishing, Lincoln remarked to Brooks: "That was a pretty fair speech, I think, but you threw some light on it." To those who disagreed with Lincoln about Reconstruction, the speech was no occasion for humor. Charles Sumner wrote: "The President's speech and other things augur confusion and uncertainty in the future, with hot controversy. Alas! Alas!"

By these recent successes the re-inauguration of the national authority—reconstruction—which has had a large share of thought from the first, is pressed much more closely upon our attention. It is fraught with great difficulty. Unlike the case of a war between independent nations, there is no authorized organ for us to treat with.

No one man has authority to give up the rebellion for any other man. We simply must begin with, and mould from, disorganized and discordant elements. Nor is it a small additional embarrassment that we, the loyal people, differ among ourselves as to the mode, manner, and means of reconstruction.

As a general rule, I abstain from reading the reports of attacks upon myself, wishing not to be provoked by that to which I can not properly offer an answer. In spite of this precaution, however, it comes to my knowledge that I am much censured for some supposed agency in setting up, and seeking to sustain, the new State Government of Louisiana. In this I have done just so much as, and no more than, the public knows. In the Annual Message of Dec. 1863 and accompanying Proclamation, I presented *a* plan of re-construction (as the phrase goes) which, I promised, if adopted by any State, should be acceptable to, and sustained by, the Executive government of the nation. I distinctly stated that this was not the only plan which might possibly be acceptable; and I also distinctly protested that the Executive claimed no right to say when, or whether members should be admitted to seats in Congress from such States. This plan was, in advance, submitted to the then Cabinet, and distinctly approved by every member of it. . . . The Message went to Congress, and I received many commendations of the plan, written and verbal; and not a single objection to it, from any professed emancipationist, came to my knowledge, until after the news reached Washington that the people of Louisiana had begun to move in accordance with it. . . .

I have been shown a letter on this subject, supposed to be an able one, in which the writer expresses regret that my mind has not seemed to be definitely fixed on the question whether the seceded States, so called, are in the Union or out of it. It would perhaps, add astonishment to his regret, were he to learn that since I have found professed Union men endeavoring to make that question, I have *purposely* forborne any public expression upon it. As appears to me that question has not been, nor yet is, a practically material one, and that any discussion of it, while it thus remains practically immaterial, could have no effect other than the mischievous one of dividing our friends. As yet, whatever it may hereafter become, that question is bad, as the basis of a controversy, and good for nothing at all—a merely pernicious abstraction.

We all agree that the seceded States, so called, are out of their proper practical relation with the Union; and that the sole object of the government, civil and military, in regard to those States is to again get them into that proper practical relation. I believe it is not only possible, but in fact, easier, to do this, without deciding, or even considering, whether these states have even been out of the Union, than with it. Finding themselves safely at home, it would be utterly immaterial whether they had ever been abroad. Let us all join in doing the acts necessary to restoring the proper practical relations between these states and the Union; and each forever after, innocently indulge his own opinion whether, in doing the acts, he brought the States from without, into the Union, or only gave them proper assistance, they never having been out of it. . . .

And yet so great peculiarities pertain to each state; and such important and sudden changes occur in the same state; and, withal, so new and unprecedented is the whole case, that no exclusive, and inflexible plan can safely be prescribed as to details and colatterals. Such exclusive, and inflexible plan, would surely become a new entanglement. Important principles may, and must, be inflexible.

DOCUMENT 4

THADDEUS STEVENS, SPEECH,
DECEMBER 18, 1865

The speech excerpted here, in which Stevens argues that the Southern states are simply conquered provinces and can be treated accordingly, was one of the longest and most elaborately prepared of his career. It was inspired by Andrew Johnson's message to Congress, December 5, 1865, in which the President argued against treating the Southern states as conquered territory and remarked that military govern-

ments in these states "would have envenomed hate
rather than have restored affection."

The President assumes, what no one doubts, that the late
rebel States have lost their constitutional relations to the
Union, and are incapable of representation in Congress,
except by permission of the Government. It matters but
little, with this admission, whether you call them States
out of the Union, and now conquered territories, or assert
that because the Constitution forbids them to do what
they did do, that they are therefore only dead as to all
national and political action, and will remain so until the
Government shall breathe into them the breath of life anew
and permit them to occupy their former position. In other
words, that they are not out of the Union, but are only
dead carcasses lying within the Union. In either case, it is
very plain that it requires the action of Congress to enable
them to form a State government and send representatives
to Congress. Nobody, I believe, pretends that with their old
constitutions and frames of government they can be permitted to claim their old rights under the Constitution.
They have torn their constitutional States into atoms, and
built on their foundations fabrics of a totally different
character. Dead men cannot raise themselves. Dead States
cannot restore their existence "as it was." Whose especial
duty is it to do it? In whom does the Constitution place the
power? Not in the judicial branch of Government, for it
only adjudicates and does not prescribe laws. Not in the
Executive, for he only executes and cannot make laws.
Not in the Commander-in-Chief of the armies, for he can
only hold them under military rule until the sovereign
legislative power of the conqueror shall give them law.
Unless the law of nations is a dead letter, the late war
between two acknowledged belligerents severed their original compacts and broke all the ties that bound them together. The future condition of the conquered power depends on the will of the conqueror. They must come in
as new states or remain as conquered provinces. Congress . . . is the only power that can act in the matter.
Congress alone can do it. . . . Congress must create
States and declare when they are entitled to be represented.
Then each House must judge whether the members pre-

senting themselves from a recognized State possess the requisite qualifications of age, residence, and citizenship; and whether the election and returns are according to law. . . .

It is obvious from all this that the first duty of Congress is to pass a law declaring the condition of these outside or defunct States, and providing proper civil governments for them. Since the conquest they have been governed by martial law. Military rule is necessarily despotic, and ought not to exist longer than is absolutely necessary. As there are no symptoms that the people of these provinces will be prepared to participate in constitutional government for some years, I know of no arrangement so proper for them as territorial governments. There they can learn the principles of freedom and eat the fruit of foul rebellion. Under such governments, while electing members to the territorial Legislatures, they will necessarily mingle with those to whom Congress shall extend the right of suffrage. In Territories Congress fixes the qualifications of electors; and I know of no better place nor better occasion for the conquered rebels and the conqueror to practice justice to all men, and accustom themselves to make and obey equal laws. . . .

They ought never to be recognized as capable of acting in the Union, or of being counted as valid States, until the Constitution shall have been so amended as to make it what its framers intended; and so as to secure perpetual ascendency to the party of the Union; and so as to render our republican Government firm and stable forever. The first of those amendments is to change the basis of representation among the States from Federal numbers to actual voters. . . . With the basis unchanged the 83 Southern members, with the Democrats that will in the best times be elected from the North, will always give a majority in Congress and in the Electoral college. . . . I need not depict the ruin that would follow. . . .

But this is not all that we ought to do before inveterate rebels are invited to participate in our legislation. We have turned, or are about to turn, loose four million slaves without a hut to shelter them or a cent in their pockets. The infernal laws of slavery have prevented them from acquiring an education, understanding the common laws of contract, or of managing the ordinary business of life. This Congress is bound to provide for them until they can take care of themselves. If we do not furnish them with homesteads, and hedge them around with protective laws; if we leave them to the legislation of their late masters, we had better have left them in bondage. . . .

If we fail in this great duty now, when we have the power, we shall deserve and receive the execration of history and of all future ages.

DOCUMENT 5

REPORT OF THE JOINT COMMITTEE ON RECONSTRUCTION,
JUNE 20, 1866

At the instance of Thaddeus Stevens, the Joint Committee on Reconstruction, consisting of nine members from the House and six from the Senate, was created to make recommendations on all bills and resolutions pertaining to Reconstruction. Of the fifteen, only one senator and two congressmen were Democrats, and the outstanding figure was Stevens himself. A committee so constituted reflected Radical views, as is shown here by the committee's characterization of the status of the South.

A claim for the immediate admission of senators and representatives from the so-called Confederate States has been urged, which seems to your committee not to be founded either in reason or in law, and which cannot be passed without comment. Stated in a few words, it amounts to this: That inasmuch as the lately insurgent States had no legal right to separate themselves from the Union, they still retain their positions as States, and consequently the people thereof have a right to immediate representation in Congress without the imposition of any conditions whatever. . . . It has even been contended that until such admission all legislation affecting their interests is, if not unconstitutional, at least unjustifiable and oppressive.

It is believed by your Committee that these propositions are not only wholly untenable, but, if admitted, would tend to the destruction of the government. . . .

It must not be forgotten that the people of these States, without justification or excuse, rose in insurrection against the United States. They deliberately abolished their State governments so far as the same connected them politically with the Union. . . . They opened hostilities and levied war against the government. They continued this war for four years with the most determined and malignant spirit. . . . Whether legally and constitutionally or not, they did, in fact, withdraw from the Union and made themselves subjects of another government of their own creation. And they only yielded when . . . they were compelled by utter exhaustion to lay down their arms . . . expressing no regret, except that they had no longer the power to continue the desperate struggle.

It cannot, we think, be denied by any one, having a tolerable acquaintance with public law, that the war thus waged was a civil war of the greatest magnitude. The people waging it were necessarily subject to all the rules which, by the law of nations, control a contest of that character, and to all the legitimate consequences following it. One of those consequences was that, within the limits prescribed by humanity, the conquered rebels were at the mercy of the conquerors. That a government thus outraged had a most perfect right to exact indemnity for the injuries done, and security against the recurrence of such outrages in the future, would seem too clear for dispute. . . .

Your committee came to the consideration of the subject referred to them with the most anxious desire to ascertain what was the condition of the people of the States recently in insurrection, and what, if anything, was necessary to be done before restoring them to the full enjoyment of all their original privileges. It was undeniable that the war into which they had plunged the country had materially changed their relations to the people of the loyal States. Slavery had been abolished by constitutional amendment. A large proportion of the population had become, instead of mere chattels, free men and citizens. Through all the past struggle these had remained true and loyal, and had, in large numbers, fought on the side of the Union. It was impossible to abandon them, without securing them their rights as free men and citizens. . . . Hence it became important to inquire what could be done to secure their rights, civil and political. It was evident to your committee that adequate security could only be found in appropriate constitutional provisions. By an original provision of the Constitution, representation is based on the whole number of free persons in each State, and three–fifths of all other persons. When all become free, representation for all necessarily follows. As a consequence the inevitable effect of the rebellion would be to increase the political power of the insurrectionary States, whenever they should be allowed to resume their position as States of the Union. . . . It did not seem just or proper that all the political advantages derived from their becoming free should be confined to their former masters, who had fought against the Union, and withheld from themselves, who had always been loyal. . . . Doubts were entertained whether Congress had power, even under the amended Constitution, to prescribe the qualifications of voters in a State, or could act directly on the subject. It was doubtful . . . whether the States would consent to surrender a power they had always exercised, and to which they were attached. As the best if not the only method of surmounting the difficulty, and as eminently just and proper in itself, your committee came to the conclusion that political power should be possessed in all the States exactly in proportion as the right of suffrage should be granted, without distinction of color or race. This it was thought would leave the whole question with the people of each State, holding out to all the advantage of increased political power as an inducement to allow all to participate in its exercise. Such a provision would be in its nature gentle and persuasive, and would lead, it was hoped, at no distant day, to an equal participation of all, without distinction, in all the rights and privileges of citizenship, thus affording a full and adequate protection to all classes of citizens, since all would have, through the ballot-box, the power of self-protection. . . .

With such evidence before them, it is the opinion of your committee—

I. That the States lately in rebellion were, at the close of the war, disorganized communities, without civil government, and without constitutions or other forms, by virtue of which political relations could legally exist between them and the federal government.

II. That Congress cannot be expected to recognize as valid the election of representatives from disorganized communities, which, from the very nature of the case, were unable to present their claim to representation under those established and recognized rules, the observance of which has been hitherto required.

III. That Congress would not be justified in admitting such communities to a participation in the government of the country without first providing such constitutional or other guarantees as will tend to secure the civil rights of all citizens of the republic; a just equality of representation; protection against claims founded in rebellion and crime; a temporary restoration of the right of suffrage to those who had not actively participated in the efforts to destroy the Union and overthrow the government, and the exclusion from positions of public trust of, at least, a portion of those whose crimes have proved them to be enemies to the Union, and unworthy of public confidence.

DOCUMENT 6

AN ADDRESS TO THE LOYAL CITIZENS AND CONGRESS OF THE UNITED STATES OF AMERICA,
AUGUST 1865

During 1865 and 1866 Negroes in a number of Southern cities held conventions in which they discussed their problems and formulated appeals for support and protection from the people of the nation. This address was adopted by a convention held in Alexandria, Virginia, from August 2 to 5, 1865.

We, the undersigned members of a Convention of colored
citizens of the State of Virginia, would respectfully
represent that, although we have been held as slaves, and
denied all recognition as a constituent of your nationality
for almost the entire period of the duration of your
Government, and that by *your permission* we have been
denied either home or country, and deprived of the dearest
rights of human nature: yet when you and our immediate
oppressors met in deadly conflict upon the field of battle
—the one to destroy and the other to save your Government and nationality, *we,* with scarce an exception, in our
inmost souls espoused your cause, and watched, and
prayed, and waited, and labored for your success. . . .

When the contest waxed long, and the result hung
doubtfully, you appealed to us for help, and how well we
answered is written in the rosters of the two hundred
thousand colored troops now enrolled in your service; and
as to our undying devotion to your cause, let the uniform
acclamation of escaped prisoners, "whenever we saw a
black face we felt sure of a friend," answer.

Well, the war is over, the rebellion is "put down,"
and we are *declared* free! Four fifths of our enemies are
paroled or amnestied, and the other fifth are being pardoned, and the President has, in his efforts at the reconstruction of the civil government of the States, late in
rebellion, left us entirely at the mercy of these subjugated
but unconverted rebels, in *everything* save the privilege
of bringing us, our wives and little ones, to the auction
block. . . . We *know* these men—know them *well*—and
we assure you that, with the majority of them, loyalty is
only "lip deep," and that their professions of loyalty are
used as a cover to the cherished design of getting restored
to their former relations with the Federal Government,
and then, by all sorts of "unfriendly legislation," to render
the freedom you have given us more intolerable than the
slavery they intended for us.

We warn you in time that our only safety is in keeping them under Governors of the *military persuasion* until
you have so amended the Federal Constitution that it will
prohibit the States from making any distinction between
citizens on account of race or color. In one word, the only
salvation for us besides the power of the Government, is

in the *possession of the ballot*. Give us this, and we will protect ourselves. . . . But, 'tis said we are ignorant. Admit it. Yet who denies we *know* a traitor from a loyal man, a gentleman from a rowdy, a friend from an enemy? The twelve thousand colored votes of the State of New York sent Governor Seymour home and Reuben E. Fenton to Albany. Did not they know who to vote for? . . . All we ask is an *equal chance* with the white *traitors* varnished and japanned with the oath of amnesty. Can you deny us this and still keep faith with us? . . .

We are "sheep in the midst of wolves," and nothing but the military arm of the Government prevents us and all the *truly* loyal white men from being driven from the land of our birth. Do not then, we beseech you, give to one of these "wayward sisters" the rights they abandoned and forfeited when they rebelled until you have secured *our* rights by the aforementioned amendment to the Constitution. . . .

Trusting that you will not be deaf to the appeal herein made, nor unmindful of the warnings which the malignity of the rebels are constantly giving you, and that you will rise to the height of being just for the sake of justice, we remain yours for our flag, our country and humanity.

DOCUMENT 7

WADE HAMPTON ON RECONSTRUCTION, 1866

Wade Hampton of South Carolina gave his great prestige among fellow Southerners to the support of Andrew Johnson's plan of Reconstruction. But in this letter to the President he voices his discontent with the state of affairs as they stood in 1866.

Having acceded to the terms laid down by your Excellency, they supposed that they would be restored to all their rights as citizens of the U. S. and they believed fully— whether justly or not—that they were entitled to receive

these rights, their allegiance to the Government being
renewed and all their duties to it being . . . exacted, but
the construction which the South placed upon the covenant
which had been made, seems not to have been the one
received by the authorities at Washington, for no sooner
had the South conformed to the terms of your Proclamation than other conditions were imposed. . . . First, she
found all her state authorities set aside—her Governors
imprisoned—her legislatures broken up—her Judiciary
suppressed—her press muzzled—her Temples closed—all
by the arbitrary hand of military power. Then came the
appointment of Presidential Governors, an anomaly heretofore unknown in a Government composed of states
which were once supposed to possess some at least of the
attributes of sovereignty. By the exercise of an authority . . . —whence derived has never been clearly explained—these Presidential Governors called conventions
in their several states and new Legislatures were ordered
to be chosen. These conventions, once the highest tribunals
recognized by sovereign states, the great High Courts of
a free people—met, registered the decrees framed at
Washington and disappeared. After an existence as in-
glorious as it was brief, "unwept, unhonored and un-
sung" each convention was followed by its own bastard
offspring, the Legislature of its creation, a political
"nullius filius"—a body somewhat "after the order of
Melchesidec, without father, without mother, without
descent," fit successors of most unhonored predecessors. I
speak of these bodies in their political and collective
capacity, not of the individuals composing them, for that
these latter were actuated in most instances by the highest
patriotism is evidenced by the fact that for the sake of
the country, they consented to serve in Mr. Seward's
Legislatures. When these Legislatures met in what was
literally "extraordinary session" what a spectacle was
presented! In these halls where once the free representatives of sovereign states were wont to discuss the highest
questions of polity, all subjects were strictly tabooed save
such as were dictated from Washington, and it required
no great stretch of imagination to fancy that one heard in
the votes but the echoes of Mr. Seward's "little bell." The
telegraph lines offered a ready means by which that

manipulator could use to its fullest extent his "judicious admixture of pressure and persuasion," and under this new but convenient system the proceedings of the Legislatures consisted solely in recording the dicta of the Supreme Justice in Washington.

DOCUMENT 8

ALEXANDER STEPHENS ON RECONSTRUCTION, APRIL 11, 1866

The Joint Committee on Reconstruction heard a great deal of testimony on conditions and attitudes in the South. On April 11, the former Vice-President of the Confederacy appeared to testify. Stephens made these comments in answer to the question posed by the ardent Radical George S. Boutwell, whether Georgia would accept restoration to the Union either on the basis of granting suffrage to Negroes or accepting a diminution in her representation in Congress proportionate to the number of those to whom suffrage was denied. These were, of course, the terms of the Fourteenth Amendment (Volume I, Part II, Document 4) which had recently passed Congress and stood before the states for ratification. Stephens did not feel that such terms should be put to the Southern states as "conditions precedent" of restoration to the Union.

I think the people of the State would be unwilling to do more than they have done for restoration. Restricted or limited suffrage would not be so objectionable as general or universal. But it is a matter that belongs to the State to regulate. The question of suffrage, whether universal or restricted, is one of State policy exclusively, as they believe. Individually I should not be opposed to a proper system of restricted or limited suffrage to this class of our population. . . . The only view in their opinion that could possibly justify the war that was carried on by the federal government against them was the idea of the indissolubleness of the Union; that those who held the administration for the time were bound to enforce the execution of the laws and the maintenance of the integrity of the country under the Constitution. . . . They expected as soon as the confederate cause was abandoned that immediately the States would be brought back into their practical relations with the government as previously constituted. That is what they looked to. They expected that the States would immediately have their representatives in the Senate and in the House; and they expected in good faith, as loyal men, as the term is frequently used— loyal to law, order, and the Constitution—to support the government under the Constitution. . . . Towards the Constitution of the United States the great mass of our people were always as much devoted in their feelings as any people ever were towards any laws or people . . . they resorted to secession with a view of more securely maintaining these principles. And when they found they were not successful in their object in perfect good faith, as far as I can judge from meeting with them and conversing with them, looking to the future development of their country . . . their earnest desire and expectation was to allow the past struggle . . . to pass by and to co-operate with . . . those of all sections who earnestly desire the preservation of constitutional liberty and the perpetuation of the government in its purity. They have been . . . disappointed in this, and are . . . patiently waiting, however, and believing that when the passions of the hour have passed away this delay in representation will cease. . . .

My own opinion is, that these terms ought not to be offered as conditions precedent. . . . It would be best for the peace, harmony, and prosperity of the whole country that there should be an immediate restoration, an immediate bringing back of the States into their original practical relations; and let all these questions then be discussed in common council. Then the representatives from the south could be heard, and you and all could judge much better of the tone and temper of the people than you could from the opinions given by any individuals. . . . My judgment, therefore, is very decided, that it would have been better as soon as the lamentable conflict was over, when the people of the south abandoned their cause and agreed to accept the issue, desiring as they do to resume their places for the future in the Union, and to look to the arena of reason and justice for the protection of their rights in the Union—it would have been better to have allowed that result to take place, to follow under the policy adopted by the administration, than to delay or hinder it by propositions to amend the Constitution in respect to suffrage. . . . I think the people of all the southern States would in the halls of Congress discuss these questions calmly and deliberately, and if they did not show that the views they entertained were just and proper, such as to control the judgment of the people of the other sections and States, they would quietly . . . yield to whatever should be constitutionally determined in common council. But I think they feel very sensitively the offer to them of propositions to accept while they are denied all voice . . . in the discussion of these propositions. I think they feel very sensitively that they are denied the right to be heard.

DOCUMENT 9

ANDREW JOHNSON, CLEVELAND SPEECH, SEPTEMBER 3, 1866

The speech represented here was one of the unfortunate speeches Johnson gave during his "swing around the circle." Not only were his remarks undignified, but he permitted himself to be drawn into exchanges with hecklers, probably planted in the audience by Radical leaders. Cleveland's Radical newspaper, the Leader, *gleefully pronounced this speech "the most disgraceful ever delivered by any president of the United States."*

And let me say to-night that my head has been threatened. It has been said that my blood was to be shed. Let me say to those who are still willing to sacrifice my life [derisive laughter and cheers], if you want a victim and my country requires it, erect your altar, and the individual who addresses you tonight, while here a visitor, ["No," "No," and laughter,] erect your altar if you still thirst for blood, and if you want it, take out the individual who now addresses you and lay him upon your altar, and the blood that now courses his veins and warms his existence shall be poured out as a last libation to Freedom. I love my country, and I defy any man to put his finger upon anything to the contrary. Then what is my offence? [Voices, "You ain't a radical," "New Orleans," "Veto."] Somebody says "Veto." Veto of what? What is called the Freedmen's Bureau bill, and in fine, not to go into any argument here to-night, if you do not understand what the Freedmen's Bureau bill is, I can tell you. [Voice, "Tell us."] Before the rebellion there were 4,000,000 called colored persons held as slaves by about 340,000 people living in the South. That is, 340,000 slave owners paid expenses, bought land, and worked the negroes, and at the expiration of the year when cotton, tobacco, and rice were gathered and sold, after all paying expenses, these slave owners put the money in their pockets— [slight interruption]—your attention—they put the property in their pocket. In many instances there was no profit, and many came out in debt. Well that is the way things stood before the rebellion. The rebellion commenced and the slaves were turned loose. Then we come to the Freedmen's Bureau bill. And what did the bill propose? It proposed to appoint agents and sub-agents in all the cities, counties, school districts, and parishes, with power to make contracts for all the slaves, power to control, and power to hire them out—dispose of them, and in addition to that the whole military power of the government applied to carry it into execution.

Now [clamor and confusion] I never feared clamor. I have never been afraid of the people, for by them I have always been sustained. And when I have all the truth, argument, fact and reason on my side, clamor nor affront, nor animosities can drive me from my purpose.

Now to the Freedmen's Bureau. What was it? Four million slaves were emancipated and given an equal chance and fair start to make their own support—to work and produce; and having worked and produced, to

have their own property and apply it to their own support. But the Freedmen's Bureau comes and says we must
take charge of these 4,000,000 slaves. The bureau comes
along and proposes, at an expense of a fraction less than
$12,000,000 a year, to take charge of these slaves. You
had already expended $3,000,000,000 to set them free
and give them a fair opportunity to take care of themselves
—then these gentlemen, who are such great friends of the
people, tell us they must be taxed $12,000,000 to sustain
the Freedmen's Bureau. [Great confusion.] I would
rather speak to 500 men that would give me their attention that to 100,000 that would not. [With all this mass
of patronage he said he could have declared himself
dictator.]

The Civil Rights bill was more enormous than the
other. I have exercised the veto power, they say. Let me
say to you of the threats from your Stevenses, Sumners,
Phillipses, and all that class, I care not for them. As they
once talked about forming a "league with hell and a
covenant with the devil," I tell you, my countrymen,
here to-night, though the power of hell, death and Stevens
with all his powers combined, there is no power that can
control me save you the people and the God that spoke
me into existence. In bidding you farewell here to-night, I
would ask you with all the pains Congress has taken to
calumniate and malign me, what has Congress done?
Has it done anything to restore the Union of the States?
But, on the contrary, has it not done everything to prevent
it?

And because I stand now as I did when the rebellion
commenced, I have been denounced as a traitor. My
countrymen here to-night, who has suffered more than
I? Who has run greater risk? Who has borne more than
I? But Congress, factious, domineering, tyrannical Congress has undertaken to poison the minds of the American
people, and create a feeling against me in consequence of
the manner in which I have distributed the public patronage.

While this gang—this common gang of cormorants
and bloodsuckers, have been fattening upon the country
for the past four of five years—men never going into
the field, who growl at being removed from their fat

offices, they are great patriots! Look at them all over your district? Everybody is a traitor that is against them. I think the time has come when those who stayed at home and enjoyed fat offices for the last four or five years —I think it would be more than right for them to give way and let others participate in the benefits of office. Hence you can see why it is that I am traduced and assaulted. I stood by these men who were in the field, and I stand by them now.

I have been drawn into this long speech, while I intended simply to make acknowledgments for the cordial welcome; but if I am insulted while civilities are going on I will resent it in a proper manner, and in parting here to-night I have no anger nor revengeful feelings to gratify. All I want now, peace has come and the war is over, is for all patriotic men to rally round the standard of their country, and swear by their altars and their God, that all shall sink together but what this Union shall be supported. Then in parting with you to-night, I hang over you this flag, not of 25 but of 36 stars; I hand over to you the Constitution of my country, though imprisoned, though breaches have been made upon it, with confidence hoping that you will repair the breaches; I hand it over to you, in whom I have always trusted and relied, and, so far, I have never deserted—and I feel confident, while speaking here to-night, for heart responds to heart of man, that you agree to the same great doctrine.

DOCUMENT 10

ANDREW JOHNSON, VETO OF THE FIRST RECONSTRUCTION ACT,

MARCH 2, 1867

Andrew Johnson rejected the premise upon which the First Reconstruction Act was based—that there were no lawful governments in the seceded states. This was the main argument of his veto, which was drafted principally by the distinguished Pennsylvania lawyer Jeremiah S. Black, later one of Johnson's counsel in

*the impeachment trial. The bill, however, was quickly
passed over Johnson's veto, by a vote of 135 to 48
in the House and 38 to 10 in the Senate.*

The bill places all the people of the ten States therein
named under the absolute domination of military rulers;
and the preamble undertakes to give the reason upon
which the measure is based and the ground upon which
it is justified. It declares that there exists in those States
no legal governments and no adequate protection for life
or property, and asserts the necessity of enforcing peace
and good order within their limits. Is this true as matter
of fact?

It is not denied that the States in question have each
of them an actual government, with all the powers—
executive, judicial, and legislative—which properly belong to a free state. They are organized like the other
States of the Union, and, like them, they make, administer,
and execute the laws which concern their domestic affairs.
An existing *de facto* government, exercising such functions as these, is itself the law of the state upon all
matters within its jurisdiction. To pronounce the supreme
law-making power of an established state illegal is to say
that law itself is unlawful.

The provisions which these governments have made
for the preservation of order, the suppression of crime,
and the redress of private injuries are in substance and
principle the same as those which prevail in the Northern States and in other civilized countries. . . .

The bill, however, would seem to show upon its face
that the establishment of peace and good order is not its
real object. The fifth section declares that the preceding
sections shall cease to operate in any State where certain
events shall have happened. . . . All these conditions
must be fulfilled before the people of any of these States
can be relieved from the bondage of military domination;
but when they are fulfilled, then immediately the pains
and penalties of the bill are to cease, no matter whether
there be peace and order or not, and without any reference
to the security of life or property. The excuse given for
the bill in the preamble is admitted by the bill itself not
to be real. The military rule which it establishes is plainly

to be used, not for any purpose of order or for the prevention of crime, but solely as a means of coercing the people into the adoption of principles and measures to which it is known that they are opposed, and upon which they have an undeniable right to exercise their own judgment.

I submit to Congress whether this measure is not in its whole character, scope, and object without precedent and without authority, in palpable conflict with the plainest provisions of the Constitution, and utterly destructive to those great principles of liberty and humanity for which our ancestors on both sides of the Atlantic have shed so much blood and expended so much treasure.

The ten States named in the bill are divided into five districts. For each district an officer of the Army, not below the rank of a brigadier-general, is to be appointed to rule over the people; and he is to be supported with an efficient military force to enable him to perform his duties and enforce his authority. Those duties and that authority, as defined by the third section of the bill, are "to protect all persons in their rights of person and property, to suppress insurrection, disorder, and violence, and to punish or cause to be punished all disturbers of the public peace or criminals." The power thus given to the commanding officer over all the people of each district is that of an absolute monarch. His mere will is to take the place of all law. The law of the States is now the only rule applicable to the subjects placed under his control, and that is completely displaced by the clause which declares all interference of State authority to be null and void. He alone is permitted to determine what are rights of person or property, and he may protect them in such way as in his discretion may seem proper. It places at his free disposal all the lands and goods in his district, and he may distribute them without let or hindrance to whom he pleases. Being bound by no State law, and there being no other law to regulate the subject, he may make a criminal code of his own; and he can make it as bloody as any recorded in history, or he can reserve the privilege of acting upon the impulse of his private passions in each case that arises. He is bound by no rules of evidence; there is, indeed, no provision by which he is authorized or required to take any evidence at all. Everything is a crime which he chooses to call so, and all persons are condemned whom he pronounces to be guilty. He is not bound to keep and record or make any report of his proceedings. He may arrest his victims wherever he finds them, without warrant, accusation, or proof of probable cause. If he gives them a trial before he inflicts the punishment, he gives it of his grace and mercy, not because he is commanded so to do. . . .

It is plain that the authority here given to the military officer amounts to absolute despotism. But to make it still more unendurable, the bill provides that it may be delegated to as many subordinates as he chooses to appoint, for it declares that he shall "punish or cause to be punished." Such a power has not been wielded by any monarch in England for more than five hundred years. In all that time no people who speak the English language have borne such servitude. It reduces the whole population of the ten States—all persons, of every color, sex, and condition, and every stranger within their limits—to the most abject and degrading slavery. No master ever had a control so absolute over the slaves as this bill gives to the military officers over both white and colored persons. . . .

I come now to a question which is, if possible, still more important. Have we the power to establish and carry into execution a measure like this? I answer, Certainly not, if we derive our authority from the Constitution and if we are bound by the limitations which it imposes.

This proposition is perfectly clear, that no branch of the Federal Government—executive, legislative, or judicial —can have any just powers except those which it derives through and exercises under the organic law of the Union. Outside of the Constitution we have no legal authority more than private citizens, and within it we have only so much as that instrument gives us. This broad principle limits all our functions and applies to all subjects. It protects not only the citizens of States which are within the Union, but it shields every human being who comes or is brought under our jurisdiction. We have no right to do in one place more than in another that which the Constitution says we shall not do at all. If, therefore, the Southern States were in truth out of the Union, we could not treat their people in a way which the fundamental law forbids.

Some persons assume that the success of our arms in crushing the opposition which was made in some of the States to the execution of the Federal laws reduced those States and all their people—the innocent as well as the guilty—to the condition of vassalage and gave us a power over them which the Constitution does not bestow or define or limit. No fallacy can be more transparent than this. Our victories subjected the insurgents to legal obedience, not to the yoke of an arbitrary despotism. . . .

Invasion, insurrection, rebellion, and domestic violence were anticipated when the Government was framed, and the means of repelling and suppressing them were wisely provided for in the Constitution; but it was not thought necessary to declare that the States in which they might occur should be expelled from the Union. Rebellions, which were invariably suppressed, occurred prior to that out of which these questions grow; but the States continued to exist and the Union remained unbroken. In Massachusetts, in Pennsylvania, in Rhode Island, and in New York, at different periods in our history, violent and armed opposition to the United States was carried on; but the relations of those States with the Federal Government were not supposed to be interrupted or changed thereby after the rebellious portions of their population were defeated and put down. It is true that in these earlier cases there was no formal expression of a determination to withdraw from the Union, but it is also true that in the Southern States the ordinances of secession were treated by all the friends of the Union as mere nullities and are now acknowledged to be so by the States themselves. If we admit that they had any force or validity or that they did in fact take the States in which they were passed out of the Union, we sweep from under our feet all the grounds upon which we stand in justifying the use of Federal force to maintain the integrity of the Government. . . .

I need not say to the representatives of the American people that their Constitution forbids the exercise of judicial power in any way but one—that is, by the ordained and established courts. It is equally well known that in all criminal cases a trial by jury is made indispensable by the express words of that instrument. . . . An act of Congress is proposed which, if carried out, would deny a trial by the lawful courts and juries to 9,000,000 American citizens and to their posterity for an indefinite period. It seems to be scarcely possible that anyone should seriously believe this consistent with a Constitution which declares in simple, plain, and unambiguous language that all persons shall have that right and that no person shall ever in any case be deprived of it. The Constitution also forbids the arrest of the citizen without judicial warrant, founded on probable cause. This bill authorizes an arrest without warrant, at the pleasure of a military commander. The Constitution declares that "no person shall be held to answer for a capital or otherwise infamous crime unless on presentment by a grand jury." This bill holds every person not a soldier answerable for all crimes and all charges without any presentment. The Constitution declares that "no person shall be deprived of life, liberty, or property without due process of law." This bill sets aside all process of law, and makes the citizen answerable in his person and property to the will of one man, and as to his life to the will of two. . . .

The United States are bound to guarantee to each State a republican form of government. Can it be pretended that this obligation is not palpably broken if we carry out a measure like this, which wipes away every vestige of republican government in ten States and puts the life, property, liberty, and honor of all the people in each of them under the domination of a single person clothed with unlimited authority? . . .

The purpose and object of the bill—the general intent which pervades it from beginning to end—is to change the entire structure and character of the State governments and to compel them by force to the adoption of organic laws and regulations which they are unwilling to accept if left to themselves. The negroes have not asked for the privilege of voting; the vast majority of them have no idea what it means. This bill not only thrusts it into their hands, but compels them, as well as the whites, to use it in a particular way. If they do not form a constitution with prescribed articles in it and afterwards elect a legislature which will act upon certain measures in a prescribed way, neither blacks nor whites can be relieved from the slavery which the bill imposes upon them. Without pausing here to consider the policy or impolicy of Africanizing the southern part of our territory, I would simply ask the attention of Congress to that manifest, well-known, and universally acknowledged rule of constitutional law which declares that the Federal Government has no jurisdiction, authority, or power to regulate such subjects for any State. To force the right of suffrage out of the hands of the white people and into the hands of the negroes is an arbitrary violation of this principle. . . .

The bill also denies the legality of the governments of ten of the States which participated in the ratification of the amendment to the Federal Constitution abolishing slavery forever within the jurisdiction of the United States and practically excludes them from the Union. If this assumption of the bill be correct, their concurrence can not be considered as having been legally given, and the important fact is made to appear that the consent of three-fourths of the States—the requisite number—has not been constitutionally obtained to the ratification of that amendment, thus leaving the question of slavery where it stood before the amendment was officially declared to have become a part of the Constitution.

That the measure proposed by this bill does violate the Constitution in the particulars mentioned and in many other ways which I forbear to enumerate is too clear to admit of the least doubt. . . .

DOCUMENT 11

CHARLES SUMNER, OPINION ON THE TRIAL OF ANDREW JOHNSON, 1868

Senator Sumner of Massachusetts took a leading role in Johnson's impeachment. Eighteen of the thirty-five senators who voted for conviction filed opinions in

the case. Sumner's, part of which appears here, was
the longest and most bitter of all.

This is one of the last great battles with slavery. Driven from these legislative chambers, driven from the field of war, this monstrous power has found a refuge in the Executive Mansion, where, in utter disregard of the Constitution and laws, it seeks to exercise its ancient far-reaching sway. . . . Andrew Johnson is the impersonation of the tyrannical slave power. In him it lives again. He is the lineal successor of John C. Calhoun and Jefferson Davis; and he gathers about him the same supporters. Original partisans of slavery north and south; habitual compromisers of great principles; maligners of the Declaration of Independence; politicians without heart; lawyers, for whom a technicality is everything, and a promiscuous company who at every stage of the battle have set their faces against equal rights; these are his allies. It is the old troop of slavery, with a few recruits, ready as of old for violence—cunning in device, and heartless in quibble. With the President at their head, they are now entrenched in the Executive Mansion.

Not to dislodge them is to leave the country a prey to one of the most hateful tyrannies of history. Especially is it to surrender the Unionists of the rebel States to violence and bloodshed. Not a month, not a week, not a day should be lost. *The safety of the Republic requires action at once.* The lives of innocent men must be rescued from sacrifice.

I would not in this judgment depart from that moderation which belongs to the occasion; but God forbid that, when called to deal with so great an offender, I should affect a coldness which I cannot feel. Slavery has been our worst enemy, assailing all, murdering our children, filling our homes with mourning, and darkening the land with tragedy; and now it rears its crest anew, with Andrew Johnson as its representative. Through him it assumes once more to rule the Republic and to impose its cruel law. The enormity of his conduct is aggravated by his barefaced treachery. He once declared himself the Moses of the colored race. Behold him now the Pharaoh. With such treachery in such a cause there can be no parley.

Every sentiment, every conviction, every vow against slavery must now be directed against him. Pharaoh is at the bar of the Senate for judgment. . . .

There is nothing of usurpation which he has not attempted. Beginning with an assumption of all power in the rebel States, he has shrunk from nothing in the maintenance of this unparalleled assumption. . . . Timid at first, he grew bolder and bolder. He saw too well that his attempt to substitute himself for Congress in the work of reconstruction was sheer usurpation, and, therefore, by his Secretary of State, did not hesitate to announce that "it must be distinctly understood that the restoration will be *subject to the decision of Congress*." On two separate occasions, in July and September, 1865, he confessed the power of Congress over the subject; but when Congress came together in December, this confessor of congressional power found that he alone had this great prerogative. According to his new-fangled theory, Congress had nothing to do but admit the States with the governments which had been instituted through his will alone. It is difficult to measure the vastness of this usurpation, involving as it did a general nullification. Strafford was not bolder, when, speaking for Charles I, he boasted that "the little finger of prerogative was heavier than the loins of the law;" but these words helped the proud minister to the scaffold. No monarch, no despot, no Sultan, could claim more than an American President; for he claimed all. By his edict alone governments were organized, taxes were levied, and even the franchises of the citizens were determined.

Had this assumption of power been incidental, for the exigency of the moment, as under the pressure of war, and especially to serve the cause of human rights, to which before his elevation the President had professed such vociferous devotion, it might have been pardoned. It would have passed into the chapter of unauthorized acts which a patriot people had condoned. But it was the opposite in every particular. Beginning and continuing in usurpation, it was hateful beyond pardon, because it sacrificed the rights of Unionists, white and black, and was in the interest of the rebellion and of those very rebels who had been in arms against their country. . . .

More than one person was appointed provisional governor who could not take the oath of office required by act of Congress. Other persons in the same predicament were appointed in the revenue service. The effect of these appointments was disastrous. They were in the nature of notice to rebels everywhere, that participation in the rebellion was no bar to office. If one of their number could be appointed governor, if another could be appointed to a confidential position in the Treasury Department, then there was nobody on the long list of blood who might not look for preferment. And thus all offices from governor to constable were handed over to a disloyal scramble. Rebels crawled forth from their retreats. Men who had hardly ventured to expect their lives were now candidates for office, and the rebellion became strong again. The change was felt in all the gradations of government, whether in States, counties, towns, or villages. Rebels found themselves in places of trust, while the true-hearted Unionists, who had watched for the coming of our flag and ought to have enjoyed its protecting power, were driven into hiding-places. All this was under the auspices of Andrew Johnson. It was he who animated the wicked crew. He was at the head of the work. Loyalty everywhere was persecuted. White and black, whose only offence was that they had been true to their country, were insulted, abused, murdered. . . .

The Freedmen's Bureau, that sacred charity of the Republic, was despoiled of its possessions for the sake of rebels, to whom their forfeited estates were given back after they had been vested by law in the United States. The proceeds of captured and abandoned property, lodged under the law in the national treasury, were ravished from their place of deposit and sacrificed. Rebels were allowed to fill the ante-chambers of the Executive Mansion and to enter into his counsels. The pardoning power was prostituted, and pardons were issued in lots to suit rebels, thus grossly abusing that trust whose discreet exercise is so essential to the administration of justice. The powers of the Senate over appointments were trifled with and disregarded by reappointing persons who had been already rejected, and by refusing to communicate the names of others appointed by him during the recess. The veto power conferred by the Constitution as a remedy for ill-considered legislation, was turned by him into a weapon of offence against Congress and into an instrument to beat down the just opposition which his usurpation had aroused. The power of removal, which patriot Presidents had exercised so sparingly, was seized as an engine of tyranny and openly employed to maintain his wicked purposes by the sacrifice of good citizens who would not consent to be his tools. Incompetent and dishonest creatures, whose only recommendation was that they echoed his voice, were appointed to office, especially in the collection of the internal revenue, through whom a new organization, known as the "Whiskey Ring," has been able to prevail over the government and to rob the treasury of millions at the cost of tax-paying citizens, whose burdens are thus increased. Laws enacted by Congress for the benefit of the colored race, including that great statute for the establishment of the Freedmen's Bureau, and that other great statute for the establishment of Civil Rights, were first attacked by his veto, and, when finally passed by the requisite majority over his veto, were treated by him as little better than dead letters, while he boldly attempted to prevent the adoption of a constitutional amendment, by which the right of citizens and the national debt were placed under the guarantee of irrepealable law. During these successive assumptions, usurpations, and tyrannies, utterly without precedent in our history, this deeply guilty man ventured upon public speeches, each an offence to good morals, where, lost to all shame, he appealed in coarse words to the coarse passions of the coarsest people, scattering firebrands of sedition, inflaming anew the rebel spirit, insulting good citizens, and with regard to office-holders, announcing in his own characteristic phrase that he would "kick them out"—the whole succession of speeches being from their brutalities and indecencies in the nature of a "criminal exposure of his person," indictable at common law, for which no judgment can be too severe. But even this revolting transgression is aggravated, when it is considered that through these utterances the cause of justice was imperiled and the accursed demon of civil feud was lashed again into vengeful fury. All these things from beginning to end are plain facts, already recorded in history and known to all. And it is further recorded in history and known to all, that, through these enormities, any one of which is enough for condemnation, while all together present an aggregation of crime, untold calamities have been brought upon our country; disturbing business and finance; diminishing the national revenues; postponing specie payments; dishonoring the Declaration of Independence in its grandest truths; arresting the restoration of the rebel States; reviving the dying rebellion, and instead of that peace and reconciliation so much longed for, sowing strife and wrong, whose natural fruit is violence and blood.

DOCUMENT 12

JAMES W. GRIMES, OPINION ON THE TRIAL OF ANDREW JOHNSON, 1868

Senator Grimes of Iowa disapproved of many of President Johnson's acts, but feeling that they could not be classed as "high crimes and misdemeanors," he opposed impeachment. This excerpt represents his views. During the trial Grimes suffered a stroke, and had to be carried into the Senate chamber to register his vote of "Not guilty."

It is clear to my mind that the *proviso* [of the Tenure of Office Act of 1867] does not include, and was not intended to include, Mr. Stanton's case. It is not possible to apply to his case the language of the proviso unless we suppose it to have been intended to legislate him out of office; a conclusion, I consider, wholly inadmissible. He was appointed by President Lincoln during his first term of office. He cannot hereafter go out of office at the end of the term of the President by whom he was appointed. That term was ended before the law was passed. The proviso, therefore, cannot have been intended to make a rule for his case; and it is shown that it was not intended. This was plainly declared in debate by the conference committee, both in the Senate and in the House of Representatives, when the proviso was introduced and its effect explained. The meaning and effect of the *proviso* were then explained and understood to be that the only tenure of the Secretaries provided for by this law was a tenure to end with the term of service of the President by whom they were appointed, and as this new tenure could not include Mr. Stanton's case, it was here explicitly declared that it did not include it. . . .

I come now to the question of intent. Admitting that the President had no power under the law to issue the order to remove Mr. Stanton and appoint General Thomas Secretary for the Department of War *ad interim*, did he issue those orders with a manifest *intent* to violate the laws and "the Constitution of the United States," as charged in the articles, or did he issue them, as he says he did, with a view to have the constitutionality of the tenure-of-office act judicially decided?

It is apparent to my mind that the President thoroughly believed the tenure-of-office act to be unconstitutional and void. He was so advised by every member of his cabinet when the bill was presented to him for his approval in February, 1867 . . . including the Attorney General, whose duty it is made by law to give legal advice to him, including the Secretary for the Department of War, also an eminent lawyer and an Attorney General of the United States under a former administration. . . . The question [is] whether Mr. Stanton's case is included in the provisions of that act. If it was not, as I think it clearly was not, then the question of intent is not in issue, for he did no unlawful act. If it was included, then I ask whether, in view of those facts, the President's *guilty intent* to do an unlawful act "shines with such a clear and certain light" as to justify, to require us to pronounce him guilty of a high constitutional crime or misdemeanor? . . .

It is not denied, I think, that the constitutional validity of this law could not be tested before the courts unless a case was made and presented to them. No such case could be made unless the President made a removal. That act of his would necessarily be the basis on which the case would rest. He is sworn to "preserve, protect, and defend the Constitution of the United States." He must *defend* it against all encroachments, from whatever quarter. A question arose between the legislative and executive departments as to their relative powers in the matter of removals and appointments to office. That question was, Does the Constitution confer on the President the power which the tenure-of-office act seeks to take away? It was a question manifestly of construction and interpretation. The Constitution has provided a common arbiter in such cases of controversy—the Supreme Court of the United States. Before that tribunal can take jurisdiction a removal must be made. The President attempted to give the court jurisdiction in that way. For doing so he is impeached, and for the reason, as the Managers say, that—

> He has no authority under the Constitution, or by any law, to enter into any schemes or plans for the purpose of testing the validity of the laws of the country, either judicially or otherwise.

If this be true, then if the two Houses of Congress should pass by a two-thirds vote over the President's veto an act depriving the President of the right to exercise the pardoning power, and he should exercise that power nevertheless, or if he should exercise it only in a single case for the purpose of testing the constitutionality of the law, he would be guilty of a high crime and misdemeanor and impeachable accordingly. The Managers' theory establishes at once the complete supremacy of Congress over the other branches of government. I can give my assent to no such doctrine.

This was a *punitive* statute. It was directed against the President alone. It interfered with the prerogatives of his department as recognized from the foundation of the Government. It wrested from him powers which, according to the legislative and judicial construction of 80 years, had been bestowed upon him by the Constitution itself. In my opinion it was not only proper, but it was his duty to cause the disputed question to be determined in the manner and by the tribunal established for such purposes. This Government can only be preserved and the liberty of the people maintained by preserving intact the co-ordinate branches of it—legislative, executive, judicial—alike. I am no convert to any doctrine of the omnipotence of Congress. . . .

I cannot agree to destroy the harmonious working of the Constitution for the sake of getting rid of an unacceptable President.

DOCUMENT 13

ATLANTA *NEWS*, "MEET BRUTE FORCE WITH BRUTE FORCE,"

SEPTEMBER 10, 1874

This militant editorial shows how the most ardent advocates of white supremacy felt during the years when they were trying to regain their pre-war position in the Southern states.

Let there be White Leagues formed in every town, village and hamlet of the South, and let us organize for the great struggle which seems inevitable. If the October elections which are to be held at the North are favorable to the radicals, the time will have arrived for us to prepare for the very worst. The radicalism of the republican party must be met by the radicalism of white men. We have no war to make against the United States Government, but against the republican party our hate must be unquenchable, our war interminable and merciless. Fast fleeting away is the day of wordy protests and idle appeals to the magnanimity of the republican party. By brute force they are endeavoring to force us into acquiescence to their hideous programme. We have submitted long enough to indignities, and it is time to meet brute-force with brute-force. Every Southern State should swarm with White Leagues, and we should stand ready to act the moment Grant signs the civil-rights bill. It will not do to wait till radicalism has fettered us to the car of social equality before we make an effort to resist it. The signing of the bill will be a declaration of war against the southern whites. It is our duty to ourselves, it is our duty to our children, it is our duty to the white race whose prowess subdued the wilderness of this continent, whose civilization filled it with cities and towns and villages, whose mind gave it power and grandeur, and whose labor imparted to it prosperity, and whose love made peace and happiness dwell within its homes, to take the gage of battle the moment it is thrown down. If the white democrats of the North are men, they will not stand idly by and see us borne down by northern radicals and half-barbarous negroes. But no matter what they may do, it is time for us to organize. We have been temporizing long enough. Let northern radicals understand that military supervision of southern elections and the civil-rights bill mean war, and that war means bloodshed, and that we are terribly in earnest, and even they, fanatical as they are, may retrace their steps before it is too late.

DOCUMENT 14

BLANCHE K. BRUCE, SPEECH IN THE SENATE,

MARCH 31, 1876

Blanche K. Bruce, a Negro leader in Mississippi, was elected to the Senate in 1874 and served from 1875 to 1881. He spent a good deal of his time as senator in debates on election frauds and disorders in the South. This speech shows that his views were moderate, even at a time when white supremacy was rapidly being restored in the South.

The conduct of the late election in Mississippi affected not merely the fortunes of partisans—as the same were necessarily involved in the defeat or success of the respective parties to the contest—but put in question and jeopardy the sacred rights of the citizen; and the investigation contemplated in the pending resolution has for its object not the determination of the question whether the offices shall be held and the public affairs of that State be administered by democrats or republicans, but the higher and more important end, the protection in all their purity and significance of the political rights of the people and the free institutions of the country. . . .

The evidence in hand and accessible will show beyond peradventure that in many parts of the State corrupt and violent influences were brought to bear upon the registrars of voters, thus materially affecting the character of the voting or poll lists; upon the inspectors of election, prejudicially and unfairly thereby changing the number of votes cast; and, finally, threats and violence were practiced directly upon the masses of voters in such measures and strength as to produce grave apprehensions for their personal safety and as to deter them from the exercise of their political franchises. . . .

It will not accord with the laws of nature or history to brand colored people a race of cowards. On more than one historic field, beginning in 1776 and coming down to this centennial year of the Republic, they have attested in blood their courage as well as a love of liberty. I ask Senators to believe that no consideration of fear or personal danger has kept us quiet and forbearing under the provocations and wrongs that have so sorely tried our souls. But feeling kindly toward our white fellow-citizens, appreciating the good purposes and offices of the better classes, and, above all, abhoring a war of races, we determined to wait until such time as an appeal to the good sense and justice of the American people could be made. . . .

The sober American judgment must obtain in the South as elsewhere in the Republic, that the only distinctions upon which parties can be safely organized and in harmony with our institutions are differences of opinion relative to principles and policy of government, and that differences of religion, nationality, or race can neither with safety nor propriety be permitted for a moment to enter into the party contests of the day. The unanimity with which the colored voters act with a party is not referable to any race prejudice on their part. On the contrary, they invite the political co-operation of their white brethren, and vote as a unit because proscribed as such. They deprecate the establishment of the color line by the opposition, not only because the act is unwise and wrong in principle, but because it isolates them from the white men of the South, and forces them, in sheer self-protection and against their inclination, to act seemingly upon the basis of a race prejudice that they neither respect nor entertain. As a class they are free from prejudices, and have no uncharitable suspicions against their white fellow-citizens, whether native born or settlers from the Northern States. They not only recognize the equality of citizenship and the right of every man to hold, without proscription any position of honor and trust to which the confidence of the people may elevate him; but owing nothing to race, birth, or surroundings, they, above all other classes in the community, are interested to see prejudices drop out of both politics and the business of the country, and success in life proceed only upon the integrity and merit of the man who seeks it. . . . But withal, as they progress in intelligence and appreciation of the dignity of their prerogatives as citizens, they, as an evidence of growth begin to realize the significance of the proverb, "When thou doest well for thyself, men shall praise thee;" and are disposed to exact the same protection and concession of rights that are conferred upon other citizens by the Constitution, and that, too, without the humiliation involved in the enforced abandonment of their political convictions. . . .

I have confidence, not only in my country and her institutions, but in the endurance, capacity, and destiny of my people. We will, as opportunity offers and ability serves, seek our places, sometimes in the field of letters, arts, sciences, and the professions. More frequently mechanical pursuits will attract and elicit our efforts; more still of my people will find employment and livelihood as the cultivators of the soil. The bulk of this people—by surroundings, habits, adaptation, and choice—will continue to find their homes in the South, and constitute the masses of its yeomanry. We will there probably, of our own volition and more abundantly than in the past, produce the great staples that will contribute to the basis of foreign exchange, aid in giving the nation a balance of trade, and minister to the wants and comfort and build up the prosperity of the whole land. Whatever our ultimate position in the composite civilization of the Republic and whatever varying fortunes attend our career, we will not forget our instincts for freedom nor our love of country.

DOCUMENT 15

SLAUGHTERHOUSE CASES,
1873

*This case, the first interpretation by the Supreme
Court of the Fourteenth Amendment, largely nullified
the "privileges and immunities" clause of that Amendment (Volume I, Part II, Document 4) within five
years of its ratification. After this decision, Negroes
were unable to invoke that clause to protect their
civil rights against acts of the states. The case arose
from a measure passed by the legislature of Louisiana
in 1869, giving what amounted to a monopoly grant
of the business of slaughtering livestock in New Orleans to one company of that city. The other butchers
appealed to the Supreme Court on the ground that
the law, by taking away their businesses, deprived
them of their privileges and immunities as citizens of
the United States, guaranteed under the Fourteenth Amendment. The Court rejected their appeal
by a five to four vote. Speaking through Justice
Samuel Miller, it took the position, quite as disastrous
to the legal position of Negroes as to the appeal of the
New Orleans butchers, that there is a distinction between citizenship of the United States and citizenship of a state. The Fourteenth Amendment, the
Court found, banned the impairment by states of
privileges and immunities enjoyed by persons as citizens of the United States; but the Amendment did
not speak of their rights as citizens of the states. Most
of the civil rights of the individual, the Court argued,
were in fact derived from his state citizenship, not
his federal citizenship, and thus could not be protected against state action under the Fourteenth
Amendment.*

MILLER, J. . . . The first section of the fourteenth
article, . . . opens with a definition of citizenship—

not only citizenship of the United States, but citizenship of the States. No such definition was previously found in the Constitution, nor had any attempt been made to define it by act of Congress. . . . It had been said by eminent judges that no man was a citizen of the United States, except as he was a citizen of one of the States composing the Union. Those, therefore, who had been born and resided always in the District of Columbia or in the Territories, though within the United States, were not citizens. Whether this proposition was sound or not had never been judicially decided. But it had been held by this court, in the celebrated Dred Scott Case, only a few years before the outbreak of the civil war, that a man of African descent whether a slave or not, was not and could not be a citizen of a State or of the United States. This decision, while it met the condemnation of some of the ablest statesmen and constitutional lawyers of the country, had never been overruled; and if it was to be accepted as a constitutional limitation of the right of citizenship, then all the negro race who had recently been made freemen, were still, not only not citizens, but were incapable of becoming so by anything short of an amendment to the Constitution.

To remove this difficulty primarily, and to establish a clear and comprehensive definition of citizenship which should declare what should constitute citizenship of the United States, and also citizenship of a State, the first clause of the first section was framed.

"All persons born or naturalized in the United States, and subject to the jurisdiction thereof, are citizens of the United States and of the State wherein they reside." . . .

It is quite clear, then, that there is a citizenship of the United States, and a citizenship of a State, which are distinct from each other, and which depend upon different characteristics or circumstances in the individual.

We think this distinction and its explicit recognition in this amendment of great weight in this argument, because the next paragraph of this same section, which is the one mainly relied on by the plaintiffs in error, speaks only of privileges and immunities of citizens of the United States, and does not speak of those of citizens of the several States. The argument, however, in favor of the plaintiffs rests wholly on the assumption that the citizenship is the same, and the privileges and immunities guaranteed by the clause are the same.

The language is, "No State shall make or enforce any law which shall abridge the privileges or immunities of citizens of *the United States.*" It is a little remarkable, if this clause was intended as a protection to the citizen of a State against the legislative power of his own State, that the word citizen of the State should be left out when it is so carefully used, and used in contradistinction to citizens of the United States, in the very sentence which precedes it. It is too clear for argument that the change in phraseology was adopted understandingly and with a purpose.

Of the privileges and immunities of the citizen of the United States, and of the privileges and immunities of the citizen of the State, and what they respectively are, we will presently consider; but we wish to state here that it is only the former which are placed by this clause under the protection of the federal Constitution, and that the latter, whatever they may be, are not intended to have any additional protection by this paragraph of the amendment.

If, then, there is a difference between the privileges and immunities belonging to a citizen of the United States as such, and those belonging to the citizen of the State as such, the latter must rest for their security and protection where they have heretofore rested; for they are not embraced by this paragraph of the amendment. . . .

Was it the purpose of the Fourteenth Amendment, by the simple declaration that no State should make or enforce any law which shall abridge the privileges and immunities of *citizens of the United States,* to transfer the security and protection of all the civil rights which we have mentioned, from the States to the federal government? And where it is declared that Congress shall have the power to enforce that article, was it intended to bring within the power of Congress the entire domain of civil rights heretofore belonging exclusively to the States?

All this and more must follow, if the proposition of the plaintiffs in error be sound. . . .

Having shown that the privileges and immunities

relied on in the argument are those which belong to citizens of the States as such, and that they are left to the state governments for security and protection, and not by this article placed under the special care of the federal government, we may hold ourselves excused from defining the privileges and immunities of citizens of the United States which no State can abridge, until some case involving those privileges may make it necessary to do so. . . .

DOCUMENT 16

CIVIL RIGHTS CASES,
1883

In the Second Civil Rights Act of 1875, the Radicals in Congress attempted to protect the civil equality of Negroes by making it a punishable offense to deprive them of accommodations and advantages in inns, public conveyances, and theaters. In the Civil Rights Cases, *the Court, speaking through Justice Joseph P. Bradley, made it impossible to enforce this law, which was held to have no Constitutional basis in either the Fourteenth or the Fifteenth Amendment.*

BRADLEY, J. [Argues first that the Fourteenth Amendment provides no basis for the "plenary power" of Congress to protect individual rights.]

But the power of Congress to adopt direct and primary, as distinguished from corrective legislation, on the subject in hand, is sought in the second place, from the Thirteenth Amendment, which abolishes slavery. . . .

It is true that slavery cannot exist without law any more than property in lands and goods can exist without law, and therefore the Thirteenth Amendment may be regarded as nullifying all state laws which establish or uphold slavery. But it has a reflex character also, establishing and decreeing universal civil and political freedom throughout the United States; and it is assumed that the power vested in Congress to enforce the article by appropriate legislation, clothes Congress with power to pass all laws necessary and proper for abolishing all badges and incidents of slavery in the United States; and upon this assumption it is claimed that this is sufficient authority for declaring by law that all persons shall have equal accommodations and privileges in all inns, public conveyances, and places of public amusement; the argument being that the denial of such equal accommodations and privileges is in itself a subjection to a species of servitude within the meaning of the amendment. Conceding the major proposition to be true, that Congress has a right to enact all necessary and proper laws for the obliteration and prevention of slavery with all its badges and incidents, is the minor proposition also true, that the denial to any person of admission to the accommodations and privileges of an inn, a public conveyance, or a theatre, does subject that person to any form of servitude, or tend to fasten upon him any badge of slavery? If it does not, then power to pass the law is not found in the Thirteenth Amendment. . . .

But is there any similarity between such servitudes and a denial by the owner of an inn, a public conveyance, or a theatre, of its accommodations and privileges to an individual, even though the denial be founded on the race or color of that individual? Where does any slavery or servitude, or badge of either, arise from such an act of denial? Whether it might not be a denial of a right which, if sanctioned by the state law, would be obnoxious to the prohibitions of the Fourteenth Amendment, is another question. But what has it to do with the question of slavery? . . .

The long existence of African slavery in this country gave us very distinct notions of what it was, and what were its necessary incidents. Compulsory service of the slave for the benefit of the master, restraint of his movements except by the master's will, disability to hold property, to make contracts, to have a standing in court, to be a witness against a white person, and such like burdens and incapacities were the inseparable incidents of the institution. . . . Can the act of a mere individual, the owner of the inn, the public conveyance, or place of amusement, refusing the accommodation, be justly regarded as imposing any badge of slavery or servitude upon the applicant, or only as inflicting an ordinary civil injury, properly cognizable by the laws of the State, and presumably subject to redress by those laws until the contrary appears?

After giving to these questions all the consideration which their importance demands, we are forced to the conclusion that such an act of refusal has nothing to do with slavery or involuntary servitude, and that if it is violative of any right of the party, his redress is to be sought under the laws of the State; or, if those laws are adverse to his rights and do not protect him, his remedy will be found in the corrective legislation which Congress has adopted, or may adopt, for counteracting the effect of state laws, or state action, prohibited by the Fourteenth Amendment. It would be running the slavery argument into the ground to make it apply to every act of discrimination which a person may see fit to make as to the guests he will entertain, or as to the people he will take into his coach or cab or car, or admit to his concert or theatre, or deal with in other matters of intercourse or business. . . .

When a man has emerged from slavery, and by the aid of beneficient legislation has shaken off the inseparable concomitants of that state, there must be some stage in the progress of his elevation when he takes the rank of a mere citizen, and ceases to be the special favorite of the laws, and when his rights as a citizen, or a man, are to be protected in the ordinary modes by which other men's rights are protected. There were thousands of free colored people in this country before the abolition of slavery, enjoying all the essential rights of life, liberty and property the same as white citizens; yet no one, at that time, thought that it was any invasion of his personal status as a freeman because he was not admitted to all the privileges enjoyed by white citizens, or because he was subjected to discriminations in the enjoyment of accommodations in inns, public conveyances and places of amusement. Mere discriminations on account of race or color were not regarded as badges of slavery. If, since that time, the enjoyment of equal rights in all these respects has become established by constitutional enactment, it is not by force of the Thirteenth Amendment (which merely abolishes slavery), but by force of the Fourteenth and Fifteenth Amendments.

On the whole we are of the opinion that no countenance of authority for the passage of the law in question can be found in either the Thirteenth or Fourteenth Amendment of the Constitution. . . .

DOCUMENT 17

JOHN MARSHALL HARLAN, DISSENTING
OPINION IN *CIVIL RIGHTS CASES*,
1883

The vigorous Kentucky jurist, John Marshall Harlan, was a strong defender of civil rights, and wrote a number of notable dissents in this area. He himself considered this opinion to be his best, though the eloquence of his dissent (Document 19) in Plessy v. Ferguson *has been much admired, especially in recent years.*

MR. JUSTICE HARLAN dissenting. The opinion in these cases proceeds, it seems to me, upon grounds entirely too narrow and artificial. I cannot resist the conclusion that the substance and spirit of the recent amendments of the Constitution have been sacrificed by a subtle and ingenious verbal criticism. . . . Constitutional provisions, adopted in the interest of liberty, and for the purpose of securing, through national legislation, if need be, rights inhering in a state of freedom, and belonging to American citizenship, have been so construed as to defeat the ends the people desired to accomplish, and which they supposed they had accomplished by changes in their fundamental law. . . .

I do not contend that the Thirteenth Amendment invests Congress with authority, by legislation, to define and regulate the entire body of civil rights which citizens enjoy, in the several states. But I hold that since slavery, as the court has repeatedly declared, . . . was the moving or principal cause of the adoption of that amendment, and since that institution rested wholly upon the inferiority, as a race, of those held in bondage, their freedom necessarily involved immunity from, and protection against, all discrimination against them, because of their race, in respect of such civil rights as belong to freemen of other races. Congress, therefore, under its express power to enforce that amendment, by appropriate legislation, may enact laws to protect that people against the deprivation, *because of their race,* of any civil rights granted to other freemen in the same State; and such legislation may be of a direct and primary character, operating upon States, their officers and agents, and, also, upon, at least, such individuals and corporations as exercise public functions and wield power and authority under the State. . . .

No State can sustain her denial to colored citizens of other States, while within her limits, of privileges or immunities, fundamental in republican citizenship, upon the ground that she accords such privileges or immunities only to her white citizens and withholds them from her colored citizens. The colored citizens of other States, within the jurisdiction of that State, could claim . . . every privilege and immunity which that State secures to her white citizens. . . . A colored citizen of Ohio or Indiana, while in the jurisdiction of Tennessee, is entitled to enjoy any privilege or immunity, fundamental in citizenship, which is given to citizens of the white race in the latter state. It is not to be supposed that any one will controvert this proposition. . . .

It was perfectly well known that the great danger to the equal enjoyment by citizens of their rights, as citizens, was to be apprehended not altogether from unfriendly state legislation, but from the hostile action of corporations and individuals in the States. And it is to be presumed that it was intended, by that section, to clothe Congress with power and authority to meet that danger. . . .

DOCUMENT 18

PLESSY v. *FERGUSON,*
1896

This decision approved segregation of the races as being consistent with the Fourteenth Amendment and formulated the doctrine of "separate but equal" facilities. It served as a legal basis for segregation in education. The case arose when one Homer A. Plessy, who was seven-eighths Caucasian and one-eighth Negro, was arrested for entering a railroad coach reserved for whites and refusing to sit in a segregated coach for Negroes established in accordance with a Louisiana law of 1890. The Court, speaking through Justice Henry B. Brown, found that these "separate but equal accommodations" satisfied the demands of the Fourteenth Amendment.

BROWN, J. . . . The constitutionality of this act is attacked upon the ground that it conflicts both with the Thirteenth Amendment of the Constitution, abolishing slavery, and the Fourteenth Amendment, which prohibits certain restrictive legislation on the part of the States.

1. That it does not conflict with the Thirteenth Amendment, which abolishes slavery and involuntary servitude, except as a punishment for crime, is too clear for argument. Slavery implies involuntary servitude—a state of bondage. . . .

2. . . . The object of the [Fourteenth] amendment was undoubtedly to enforce the absolute equality of the two races before the law, but in the nature of things it could not have been intended to abolish distinctions based upon color, or to enforce social, as distinguished from political equality, or a commingling of the two races upon terms unsatisfactory to either. Laws permitting, and even requiring, their separation in places where they are liable to be brought into contact do not necessarily imply the inferiority of either race to the other, and have been gen-

erally, if not universally, recognized as within the competency of the state legislatures in the exercise of their police power. The most common instance of this is connected with the establishment of separate schools for white and colored children, which has been held to be a valid exercise of the legislative power even by courts of States where the political rights of the colored race have been longest and most earnestly enforced. . . .

Laws forbidding the intermarriage of the two races may be said in a technical sense to interfere with the freedom of contract, and yet have been universally recognized as within the police power of the State. . . .

So far, then, as a conflict with the Fourteenth Amendment is concerned, the case reduces itself to the question whether the statute of Louisiana is a reasonable regulation, and with respect to this there must necessarily be a large discretion on the part of the legislature. In determining the question of reasonableness it is at liberty to act with reference to the established usages, customs and traditions of the people, and with a view to the promotion of their comfort, and the preservation of the public peace and good order. Gauged by this standard, we cannot say that a law which authorizes or even requires the separation of the two races in public conveyances is unreasonable, or more obnoxious to the Fourteenth Amendment than the acts of Congress requiring separate schools for colored children in the District of Columbia, the constitutionality of which does not seem to have been questioned, or the corresponding acts of state legislatures.

We consider the underlying fallacy of the plaintiff's argument to consist in the assumption that the enforced separation of the two races stamps the colored race with a badge of inferiority. If this be so, it is not by reason of anything found in the act, but solely because the colored race chooses to put that construction upon it. The argument necessarily assumes that if, as has been more than once the case, and is not unlikely to be so again, the colored race should become the dominant power in the state legislature, and should enact a law in precisely similar terms, it would thereby relegate the white race to an inferior position. We imagine that the white race, at least, would not acquiesce in this assumption. The argument also assumes that social prejudices may be overcome by legislation, and that equal rights cannot be secured to the negro except by an enforced commingling of the two races. We cannot accept this proposition. If the two races are to meet upon terms of social equality, it must be the result of natural affinities, a mutual appreciation of each other's merits and a voluntary consent of individuals. . . . Legislation is powerless to eradicate racial instincts or to abolish distinctions based upon physical differences, and the attempt to do so can only result in accentuating the difficulties of the present situation. If the civil and political rights of both races be equal one cannot be inferior to the other civilly or politically. If one race be inferior to the other socially, the Constitution of the United States cannot put them upon the same plane.

DOCUMENT 19

JOHN MARSHALL HARLAN, DISSENTING
OPINION IN *PLESSY* v. *FERGUSON,*
1896

Justice Harlan stood alone in this opinion when he wrote it, but he foreshadowed the views that were to be expressed by the Court fifty-eight years later when, in Brown v. Board of Education (*Document 20*), *it overruled* Plessy v. Ferguson.

Mr. Justice Harlan dissenting. . . . In respect of civil rights, common to all citizens, the Constitution of the United States does not, I think, permit any public authority to know the race of those entitled to be protected in the enjoyment of such rights. Every true man has pride of race, and under appropriate circumstances when the rights of others, his equals before the law, are not to be affected, it is his privilege to express such pride and to take such action based upon it as to him seems proper. But I deny that any legislative body or judicial tribunal may have regard to the race of citizens when the civil rights of those citizens are involved. Indeed, such legislation, as that here in question, is inconsistent not only with that equality of rights which pertains to citizenship, National and State, but with the personal liberty enjoyed by every one within the United States. . . .

The white race deems itself to be the dominant race in this country. And so it is, in prestige, in achievements, in education, in wealth and in power. So, I doubt not, it will continue to be for all time, if it remains true to its great heritage and holds fast to the principles of constitutional liberty. But in view of the Constitution, in the eye of the law, there is in this country no superior, dominant, ruling class of citizens. There is no caste here. Our Constitution is color-blind, and neither knows nor tolerates classes among citizens. In respect of civil rights, all citizens are equal before the law. The humblest is the peer of the most powerful. The law regards man as man, and takes no account of his surroundings or of his color when his civil rights as guaranteed by the supreme law of the land are involved. It is, therefore, to be regretted that this high tribunal, the final expositor of the fundamental law of the land, has reached the conclusion that it is competent for a State to regulate the enjoyment by citizens of their civil rights solely upon the basis of race. . . .

The arbitrary separation of citizens, on the basis of race, while they are on a public highway, is a badge of servitude wholly inconsistent with the civil freedom and the equality before the law established by the Constitution. It cannot be justified upon any legal grounds.

If evils will result from the commingling of the two races upon public highways established for the benefit of all, they will be infinitely less than those that will surely come from state legislation regulating the enjoyment of civil rights upon the basis of race. We boast of the freedom enjoyed by our people above all other peoples. But it is difficult to reconcile that boast with a state of the law which, practically, puts the brand of servitude and degradation upon a large class of our fellow-citizens, our equals before the law. The thin disguise of "equal" accommodations for passengers in railroad coaches will not mislead any one, nor atone for the wrong this day done. . . .

DOCUMENT 20

BROWN v. BOARD OF EDUCATION OF TOPEKA,
1954

For some time before 1954 the "separate but equal" doctrine was under attack, and in two cases, Sweatt v. Painter (1950) and McLaurin v. Oklahoma State Regents (1950), the Court had unanimously outlawed segregation in professional and graduate education. In 1954 a number of cases came before it bearing upon the status of segregation in grade and high schools. Here again, Chief Justice Warren spoke for a unanimous Court in one of the most momentous judicial decisions in American history.

WARREN, C. J., These cases come to us from the States of Kansas, South Carolina, Virginia, and Delaware. They are premised on different facts and different local conditions, but a common legal question justifies their consideration together in this consolidated opinion.

In each of the cases, minors of the Negro race, through their legal representatives, seek the aid of the courts in obtaining admission to the public schools of their community on a nonsegregated basis. In each instance, they had been denied admission to schools attended by white children under laws requiring or permitting segregation according to race. This segregation was alleged to deprive the plaintiffs of the equal protection of the laws under the Fourteenth Amendment. In each of the cases other than the Delaware case, a three-judge federal district court denied relief to the plaintiffs on the so-called "separate but equal" doctrine announced by this Court in *Plessy* v. *Ferguson,* 163 U.S. 537. Under that doctrine, equality of treatment is accorded when the races are provided substantially equal facilities, even though these facilities be separate. In the Delaware case, the Supreme Court of Delaware adhered to that doctrine, but ordered

PART I: *Reconstruction and After*   60

that the plaintiffs be admitted to the white schools because
of their superiority to the Negro schools.

The plaintiffs contend that segregated public schools
are not "equal" and cannot be made "equal," and that
hence they are deprived of the equal protection of the laws.
Because of the obvious importance of the question presented, the Court took jurisdiction. Argument was heard
in the 1952 Term, and reargument was heard this Term
on certain questions propounded by the Court.

Reargument was largely devoted to the circumstances
surrounding the adoption of the Fourteenth Amendment
in 1868. It covered exhaustively consideration of the
Amendment in Congress, ratification by the states, then
existing practices in racial segregation, and the views of
proponents and opponents of the Amendment. This discussion and our own investigation convince us that, although these sources cast some light, it is not enough to
resolve the problem with which we are faced. At best,
they are inconclusive. The most avid proponents of the
post-War Amendments undoubtedly intended them to remove all legal distinctions among "all persons born or
naturalized in the United States." Their opponents, just
as certainly, were antagonistic to both the letter and the
spirit of the Amendments and wished them to have the
most limited effect. What others in Congress and the state
legislatures had in mind cannot be determined with any
degree of certainty.

An additional reason for the inconclusive nature of
the Amendment's history, with respect to segregated
schools, is the status of public education at that time. In
the South, the movement toward free common schools,
supported by general taxation, had not yet taken hold.
Education of white children was largely in the hands of
private groups. Education of Negroes was almost non-
existent, and practically all of the race were illiterate. In
fact, any education of Negroes was forbidden by law in
some states. Today, in contrast, many Negroes have
achieved outstanding success in the arts and sciences as
well as in the business and professional world. It is true
that public school education at the time of the Amendment had advanced further in the North, but the effect
of the Amendment on Northern States was generally ig-

nored in the congressional debates. Even in the North, the conditions of public education did not approximate those existing today. The curriculum was usually rudimentary; ungraded schools were common in rural areas; the school term was but three months a year in many states; and compulsory school attendance was virtually unknown. As a consequence, it is not surprising that there should be so little in the history of the Fourteenth Amendment relating to its intended effect on public education.

In the first cases in this Court construing the Fourteenth Amendment, decided shortly after its adoption, the Court interpreted it as proscribing all state-imposed discriminations against the Negro race. The doctrine of "separate but equal" did not make its appearance in this Court until 1896 in the case of *Plessy* v. *Ferguson, supra,* involving not education but transportation. American courts have since labored with the doctrine for over half a century. In this Court, there have been six cases involving the "separate but equal" doctrine in the field of public education. In *Cumming* v. *County Board of Education,* 175 U.S. 528, and *Gong Lum* v. *Rice,* 275 U.S. 78, the validity of the doctrine itself was not challenged. In more recent cases, all on the graduate school level, inequality was found in that specific benefits enjoyed by white students were denied to Negro students of the same educational qualifications. *Missouri ex rel. Gaines* v. *Canada,* 305 U.S. 337; *Sipuel* v. *Oklahoma,* 332 U.S. 631; *Sweatt* v. *Painter,* 339 U.S. 629; *McLaurin* v. *Oklahoma State Regents,* 339 U.S. 637. In none of these cases was it necessary to re-examine the doctrine to grant relief to the Negro plaintiff. And in *Sweatt* v. *Painter, supra,* the Court expressly reserved decision on the question whether *Plessy* v. *Ferguson* should be held inapplicable to public education.

In the instant cases, that question is directly presented. Here, unlike *Sweatt* v. *Painter,* there are findings below that the Negro and white schools involved have been equalized, or are being equalized, with respect to buildings, curricula, qualifications and salaries of teachers, and other "tangible" factors. Our decision, therefore, cannot turn on merely a comparison of these tangible factors in the Negro and white schools involved in each of the cases.

We must look instead to the effect of segregation itself on public education.

In approaching this problem, we cannot turn the clock back to 1868 when the Amendment was adopted, or even to 1896 when *Plessy* v. *Ferguson* was written. We must consider public education in the light of its full development and its present place in American life throughout the Nation. Only in this way can it be determined if segregation in public schools deprives these plaintiffs of the equal protection of the laws.

Today, education is perhaps the most important function of state and local governments. Compulsory school attendance laws and the great expenditures for education both demonstrate our recognition of the importance of education to our democratic society. It is required in the performance of our most basic public responsibilities, even service in the armed forces. It is the very foundation of good citizenship. Today it is a principal instrument in awakening the child to cultural values, in preparing him for later professional training, and in helping him to adjust normally to his environment. In these days, it is doubtful that any child may reasonably be expected to succeed in life if he is denied the opportunity of an education. Such an opportunity, where the state has undertaken to provide it, is a right which must be made available to all on equal terms.

We come then to the question presented: Does segregation of children in public schools solely on the basis of race, even though the physical facilities and other "tangible" factors may be equal, deprive the children of the minority group of equal educational opportunities? We believe that it does.

In *Sweatt* v. *Painter, supra,* in finding that a segregated law school for Negroes could not provide them equal educational opportunities, this Court relied in large part on "those equalities which are incapable of objective measurement but which make for greatness in a law school." In *McLaurin* v. *Oklahoma State Regents, supra,* the Court, in requiring that a Negro admitted to a white graduate school be treated like all other students, again resorted to intangible considerations: ". . . his ability to study, to engage in discussions and exchange views with other students, and, in general, to learn his profession." Such considerations apply with added force to children in grade and high schools. To separate them from others of similar age and qualifications solely because of their race generates a feeling of inferiority as to their status in the community that may affect their hearts and minds in a way unlikely ever to be undone. The effect of this separation on their educational opportunities was well stated by a finding in the Kansas case by a court which nevertheless felt compelled to rule against the Negro plaintiffs:

> "Segregation of white and colored children in public schools has a detrimental effect upon the colored children. The impact is greater when it has the sanction of the law; for the policy of separating the races is usually interpreted as denoting the inferiority of the negro group. A sense of inferiority affects the motivation of a child to learn. Segregation with the sanction of law, therefore has a tendency to [retard] the educational and mental development of negro children and to deprive them of some of the benefits they would receive in a racial[ly] integrated school system."

Whatever may have been the extent of psychological knowledge at the time of *Plessy* v. *Ferguson*, this finding is amply supported by modern authority. Any language in *Plessy* v. *Ferguson* contrary to this finding is rejected. We conclude that in the field of public education the doctrine of "separate but equal" has no place. Separate educational facilities are inherently unequal. Therefore, we hold that the plaintiffs and others similarly situated for whom the actions have been brought are, by reason of the segregation complained of, deprived of the equal protection of the laws guaranteed by the Fourteenth Amendment. This disposition makes unnecessary any discussion whether such segregation also violates the Due Process Clause of the Fourteenth Amendment.

Because these are class actions, because of the wide applicability of this decision, and because of the great variety of local conditions, the formulation of decrees in these cases presents problems of considerable complexity. On reargument, the consideration of appropriate relief was necessarily subordinated to the primary question—the constitutionality of segregation in puᴏⅼⅰc education. We have now announced that such segregation is a denial of the equal protection of the laws. In order that we may have the full assistance of the parties in formulating decrees, the cases will be restored to the docket, and the parties are requested to present further argument on Questions 4 and 5 [dealing with detailed implementation of the decision] previously propounded by the Court for the reargument of this Term.

DOCUMENT 21

DECLARATION OF NINETY-SIX SOUTHERN CONGRESSMEN ON INTEGRATION,

MARCH 11, 1956

By the time this statement of the segregationist case was released to the press by a large Southern bloc in Congress, it had become clear that many Southerners would resist desegregation as long as they could, and that much remained to be done before the decision in Brown v. Board of Education of Topeka (*Document 20*) *could be generally enforced.*

We regard the decision of the Supreme Court in the school cases as clear abuse of judicial power. It climaxes a trend in the Federal judiciary undertaking to legislate, in derogation of the authority of Congress, and to encroach upon the reserved rights of the states and the people.

The original Constitution does not mention education. Neither does the Fourteenth Amendment nor any other amendment. The debates preceding the submission of the Fourteenth Amendment clearly show that there was no intent that it should affect the systems of education maintained by the states.

The very Congress which proposed the amendment subsequently provided for segregated schools in the District of Columbia.

When the amendment was adopted in 1868, there were thirty-seven states of the Union. Every one of the twenty-six states that had any substantial racial differences among its people either approved the operation of segregated schools already in existence or subsequently established such schools by action of the same law-making body which considered the Fourteenth Amendment.

As admitted by the Supreme Court in the public school case (*Brown* v. *Board of Education*), the doctrine of separate but equal schools "apparently originated in *Roberts* v. *City of Boston* (1849), upholding school segregation against attack as being violative of a state constitutional guarantee of equality." This constitutional doctrine began in the North—not in the South—and it was followed not only in Massachusetts but in Connecticut, New York, Illinois, Indiana, Michigan, Minnesota, New Jersey, Ohio, Pennsylvania and other northern states until they, exercising their rights as states through the constitutional processes of local self-government, changed their school systems.

In the case of *Plessy* v. *Ferguson* in 1896 the Supreme Court expressly declared that under the Fourteenth Amendment no person was denied any of his rights if the states provided separate but equal public facilities. This decision has been followed in many other cases. It is notable that the Supreme Court, speaking through Chief Justice Taft, a former President of the United States, unanimously declared in 1927 in *Lum* v. *Rice* that the "separate but equal" principle is ". . . within the discretion of the state in regulating its public schools and does not conflict with the Fourteenth Amendment."

This interpretation, restated time and again, became a part of the life of the people of many of the states and confirmed their habits, customs, traditions and way of life. It is founded on elemental humanity and common sense, for parents should not be deprived by Government of the right to direct the lives and education of their own children.

Though there has been no constitutional amendment or act of Congress changing this established legal principle almost a century old, the Supreme Court of the United States, with no legal basis for such action, undertook to exercise their naked judicial power and substituted their personal political and social ideas for the established law of the land.

This unwarranted exercise of power by the court, contrary to the Constitution, is creating chaos and confusion in the states principally affected. It is destroying the amicable relations between the white and Negro races that have been created through ninety years of patient effort by the good people of both races. It has planted hatred and suspicion where there has been heretofore friendship and understanding.

Without regard to the consent of the governed, outside agitators are threatening immediate and revolutionary changes in our public school systems. If done, this is certain to destroy the system of public education in some of the states.

With the gravest concern for the explosive and dangerous condition created by this decision and inflamed by outside meddlers:

We reaffirm our reliance on the Constitution as the fundamental law of the land.

We decry the Supreme Court's encroachments on rights reserved to the states and to the people, contrary to established law and to the Constitution.

We commend the motives of those states which have declared the intention to resist forced integration by any lawful means.

We appeal to the states and people who are not directly affected by these decisions to consider the constitutional principles involved against the time when they too, on issues vital to them, may be the victims of judicial encroachment.

Even though we constitute a minority in the present Congress, we have full faith that a majority of the American people believe in the dual system of government which has enabled us to achieve our greatness and will in time demand that the reserved rights of the states and of the people be made secure against judicial usurpation.

We pledge ourselves to use all lawful means to bring about a reversal of this decision which is contrary to the Constitution and to prevent the use of force in its implementation.

In this trying period, as we all seek to right this wrong, we appeal to our people not to be provoked by the agitators and troublemakers invading our states and to scrupulously refrain from disorder and lawless acts.

✳ PART II ✳

Industrialism and Social Reform

INTRODUCTION

IN THE years from the Civil War to the end of the nine-teenth century, bold new men of industry, primitive in morals but mature in the techniques of exploitation, re-made the United States both physically and socially. The triumphs of industrialism were magnificently visible. The continent was settled, railroads crossed and recrossed it; great new industries, whole new cities appeared. The entire nation marveled at the new developments in oil, coal, steel, railroads, electric power, streetcar systems. But at the same time the ravages of industry were pain-fully evident. Two major depressions struck the country, threatening businessmen with the terrors of bankruptcy and workers with unrelieved poverty. The heterogeneous mil-lions of immigrants who streamed in to fill the need for a new labor force were not welcomed by the native popu-lation and often found only the most dismal living condi-tions. Strikes, though infrequent, were at times bloody and violent. The farmer (see Part III), especially in the West and South, was finding himself at an increasing dis-advantage in the economy; his life was plagued by the steady decline in the price level, the exactions made on him by the railroads, difficulties in obtaining credit, and speculative uncertainties.

Before remedies could be prescribed for these social evils, it was necessary to diagnose them. This was an age, not of practical reform, but of social speculation, of argument and counter-argument over the merits and demerits, the past and the future, of the capitalist order. Daring social critics were not new to America; before the Civil War there had been Utopians and Transcendentalists, Jacksonian theorists and philosophical anarchists, abolitionists and currency reformers. But maturing industrialism created new social issues so various and so pressing that solutions were demanded with a wholly new urgency.

Certainly the most colorful and probably the most effective of the new group of social critics was Henry George, the Prophet of San Francisco. His *Progress and Poverty* (Document 1), published in 1879, was not merely a tract for the times but a major text in American social criticism. George named the central problem of the age: industrial progress was unmistakably accompanied by searing poverty. Out of a deep Christian passion for mankind, George protested eloquently in this and subsequent books against the suffering brought on by industrialism; and even those who did not accept his economic argument and his panacea for social ills—a single tax on land values—were moved by his account of that suffering.

What George was trying to do by long, closely textured, economic argument, his contemporary Edward Bellamy tried to do in the novel. In his *Looking Backward* (1888) (Document 2), Bellamy indicted the irrationality of capitalist society by describing a future Utopia which had gradually replaced the disorderly world of the Gilded Age with a rationalized system of labor and distribution and a nationalized system of production. Still another, and more direct, technique of social criticism was developed by Henry Demarest Lloyd, who attacked the powerful monopolists by criticizing the methods they had used to beat their competitors. His assault on Standard Oil, *Wealth against Commonwealth* (Document 5), which appeared in 1894, foreshadowed the work of the muckrakers of the next decade. Lloyd was concerned about the small producers who had been forced out of business by Rockefeller and his associates, and about the consumers now at the mercy of the emerging monopolies. But the working man had his spokesmen, too, in the new kind of labor leader represented here by Samuel Gompers, head of the rapidly growing American Federation of Labor. In answer to the legal attack against the Pullman strike of 1894, Gompers wrote a stirring letter (Document 6) indicting the callousness shown by many conservatives toward the working classes, and defending the rising trade unionism against criticism by spokesmen of the vested interests.

The status quo had able defenders, though none of them wrote anything so impressive as *Progress and Poverty* or *Looking Backward*. Andrew Carnegie, who was himself a hero of the new industrial order, praised those spurs to achievement provided by competitive capitalism, but also insisted that the rich must behave responsibly toward the community if they would vindicate their system (Document 3). But William Graham Sumner, an economist and professor at Yale famous for his adaptations of Darwinian conceptions of natural strife to the social system, categorically repudiated all reforms as futile efforts to interfere with the natural order (Document 4).

In practical politics and in the courts, as in the economy at large, all the advantages lay with the proponents of conservatism. Politicians were willing to make gestures to meet the demands of the discontented—an Interstate Commerce Act, a Sherman Anti-Trust Act, an income tax—but most of them were not interested in passing laws that were truly effective. Just as the farmers and businessmen who sought effective federal regulation of railroads found themselves frustrated by executive inaction or unfavorable court decisions (Part III, Document 3), so those who looked for legislative action to remedy unfair business practices and monopoly or to modify social injustices were at a disadvantage. The Supreme Court made conservative law out of the social philosophy of men like Sumner, in decisions that were imposing reminders of the difficulties facing reformers. Two decisions of 1895, coming at a time of widespread discontent, were especially provocative. Congress had included in the Wilson-Gorman Tariff of 1894 a two percent tax on incomes over $4,000. Sentiment for such a measure had been growing for several years, especially in the West and South, and a demand for such a tax had appeared in the Populist platform of 1892

(Part III, Document 4). But the Court, in one of its most criticized decisions (Documents 7 and 8), nullified the income tax by a five to four vote. In the same year the Court's decision in *U.S.* v. *E. C. Knight and Co.* (Documents 9 and 10), imposed serious obstacles to enforcement of the Sherman Anti-Trust Act. At the close of the century, with agrarian reform defeated and conservatives in firm control of all three divisions of the federal government, few men could have foreseen the immense burst of successful reform legislation which was to come in the Progressive era (Part V).

DOCUMENT 1

HENRY GEORGE, *PROGRESS AND POVERTY*, 1879

George started the book from which this excerpt is taken in San Francisco during 1877 and finished it in March 1879 after eighteen months of arduous work. He submitted it to D. Appleton and Co., who rejected it with a pleasant note on the "great clearness and force" with which it was written, but who also found it "very aggressive" and too commercially unpromising for them to publish. George turned to a printer friend William Hinton, who let George use his shop. On May 17, 1879 George wrote in his diary: "Commenced to set type on book. Set first two sticks myself." His son and some printer friends helped complete the plates for a small author's edition of 500 copies, which at $3 a copy sold well enough to pay for the plates. With a set of plates in hand, George was able to persuade Appleton to reconsider, and in the following year, 1880, they brought out a commercial edition. At first the book sold slowly, but before long it began to evoke that interest which was to make Henry George a nationwide and a worldwide influence. Within fourteen months five large editions were published, and in 1882 Lovell's Library brought out an edition at twenty cents. Soon it had

been translated into ten languages. Neither its in-
fluence nor its sales can be completely measured; but
Frank Luther Mott, in his study of best-sellers, finds
credible a worldwide estimate of two million copies
sold and thinks that an estimate of the American sales
to 1947 of 700,000 or 800,000 is "conservative."

This association of poverty with progress is the great
enigma of our times. It is the central fact from which
spring industrial, social, and political difficulties that per-
plex the world, and with which statesmanship and philanthropy and education grapple in vain. From it come the
clouds that overhang the future of the most progressive
and self-reliant nations. It is the riddle which the Sphinx
of Fate puts to our civilization, and which not to answer
is to be destroyed. So long as all the increased wealth
which modern progress brings goes but to build up great
fortunes, to increase luxury and make sharper the contrast between the House of Have and the House of Want,
progress is not real and cannot be permanent. The reaction
must come. The tower leans from its foundations, and
every new story but hastens the final catastrophe. To educate men who must be condemned to poverty, is but to
make them restive; to base on a state of most glaring
social inequality political institutions under which men
are theoretically equal, is to stand a pyramid on its apex.

All-important as this question is, pressing itself from
every quarter painfully upon attention, it has not yet received a solution which accounts for all the facts and
points to any clear and simple remedy. This is shown by
the widely varying attempts to account for the prevailing
depression. They exhibit not merely a divergence between
vulgar notions and scientific theories, but also show that
the concurrence which should exist between those who
avow the same general theories breaks up upon practical
questions into an anarchy of opinion. Upon high economic
authority we have been told that the prevailing depression
is due to over-consumption; upon equally high authority,
that it is due to over-production; while the wastes of war,
the extension of railroads, the attempts of workmen to
keep up wages, the demonetization of silver, the issues
of paper money, the increase of labor-saving machinery,

the opening of shorter avenues to trade, etc., are separately pointed out as the cause, by writers of reputation.

And while professors thus disagree, the ideas that there is a necessary conflict between capital and labor, that machinery is an evil, that competition must be restrained and interest abolished, that wealth may be created by the issue of money, that it is the duty of government to furnish capital or to furnish work, are rapidly making way among the great body of the people, who keenly feel a hurt and are sharply conscious of a wrong. Such ideas, which bring great masses of men, the repositories of ultimate political power, under the leadership of charlatans and demagogues, are fraught with danger; but they cannot be successfully combated until political economy shall give some answer to the great question which shall be consistent with all her teachings, and which shall commend itself to the perceptions of the great masses of men. . . .

I propose in the following pages to attempt to solve by the methods of political economy the great problem I have outlined. I propose to seek the law which associates poverty with progress, and increases want with advancing wealth; and I believe that in the explanation of this paradox we shall find the explanation of those recurring seasons of industrial and commercial paralysis which, viewed independently of their relations to more general phenomena, seem so inexplicable. . . .

What constitutes the rightful basis of property? What is it that enables a man justly to say of a thing, "It is mine"? From what springs the sentiment which acknowledges his exclusive right as against all the world? Is it not, primarily, the right of a man to himself, to the use of his own powers, to the enjoyment of the fruits of his own exertions? Is it not this individual right, which springs from and is testified to by the natural facts of individual organization—the fact that each articular pair of hands obey a particular brain and are related to a particular stomach; the fact that each man is a definite, coherent, independent whole—which alone justifies individual ownership? As a man belongs to himself, so his labor when put in concrete form belongs to him. . . .

Now, this is not only the original source from which all ideas of exclusive ownership arise—as is evident from

the natural tendency of the mind to revert to it when the
idea of exclusive ownership is questioned, and the manner in which social relations develop—but it is necessarily
the only source. There can be to the ownership of anything no rightful title which is not derived from the
title of the producer and does not rest upon the natural
right of the man to himself. There can be no other rightful
title, because (1st) there is no other natural right from
which any other title can be derived, and (2d) because
the recognition of any other title is inconsistent with and
destructive of this.

For (1st) what other right exists from which the
right to the exclusive possession of anything can be
derived, save the right of a man to himself? With what
other power is man by nature clothed, save the power of
exerting his own faculties? How can he in any other way
act upon or affect material things or other men? Paralyze
the motor nerves, and your man has no more external
influence or power than a log or stone. From what else,
then, can the right of possessing and controlling things
be derived? If it spring not from man himself, from
what can it spring? Nature acknowledges no ownership
or control in man save as the result of exertion. In no
other way can her treasures be drawn forth, her powers
directed, or her forces utilized or controlled. She makes
no discriminations among men, but is to all absolutely
impartial. She knows no distinction between master and
slave, king and subject, saint and sinner. All men to her
stand upon an equal footing and have equal rights. She
recognizes no claim but that of labor, and recognizes that
without respect to the claimant. If a pirate spread his
sails, the wind will fill them as well as it will fill those of
a peaceful merchantman or missionary bark; if a king
and a common man be thrown overboard, neither can
keep his head above water except by swimming; birds
will not come to be shot by the proprietor of the soil
any quicker than they will come to be shot by the
poacher; fish will bite or will not bite at a hook in utter
disregard as to whether it is offered them by a good little
boy who goes to Sunday-school, or a bad little boy who
plays truant; grain will grow only as the ground is prepared and the seed is sown; it is only at the call of labor

that ore can be raised from the mine; the sun shines and the rain falls, alike upon just and unjust. The laws of nature are the decrees of the Creator. There is written in them no recognition of any right save that of labor; and in them is written broadly and clearly the equal right of all men to the use and enjoyment of nature; to apply to her by their exertions, and to receive and possess her reward. Hence, as nature gives only to labor, the exertion of labor in production is the only title to exclusive possession.

2d. This right of ownership that springs from labor excludes the possibility of any other right of ownership. If a man be rightfully entitled to the produce of his labor, then no one can be rightfully entitled to the ownership of anything which is not the produce of his labor, or the labor of some one else from whom the right has passed to him. If production give to the producer the right to exclusive possession and enjoyment, there can rightfully be no exclusive possession and enjoyment of anything not the production of labor, and the recognition of private property in land is a wrong. For the right to the produce of labor cannot be enjoyed without the right to the free use of the opportunities offered by nature, and to admit the right of property in these is to deny the right of property in the produce of labor. When non-producers can claim as rent a portion of the wealth created by producers, the right of the producers to the fruits of their labor is to that extent denied.

There is no escape from this position. To affirm that a man can rightfully claim exclusive ownership in his own labor when embodied in material things, is to deny that any one can rightfully claim exclusive ownership in land. To affirm the rightfulness of property in land, is to affirm a claim which has no warrant in nature, as against a claim founded in the organization of man and the laws of the material universe.

What most prevents the realization of the injustice of private property in land is the habit of including all the things that are made the subject of ownership in one category, as property, or, if any distinction is made, drawing the line, according to the unphilosophical distinction of the lawyers, between personal property and real estate, or things movable and things immovable. The real and natural distinction is between things which are the produce of labor and things which are the gratuitous offerings of nature; or, to adopt the terms of political economy, between wealth and land.

These two classes of things are in essence and relations widely different, and to class them together as property is to confuse all thought when we come to consider the justice or the injustice, the right or the wrong of property.

A house and the lot on which it stands are alike property, as being the subject of ownership, and are alike classed by the lawyers as real estate. Yet in nature and relations they differ widely. The one is produced by human labor, and belongs to the class in political economy styled wealth. The other is a part of nature, and belongs to the class in political economy styled land.

The essential character of the one class of things is that they embody labor, are brought into being by human exertion, their existence or non-existence, their increase or diminution, depending on man. The essential character of the other class of things is that they do not embody labor, and exist irrespective of human exertion and irrespective of man; they are the field or environment in which man finds himself; the storehouse from which his needs must be supplied, the raw material upon which and the forces with which alone his labor can act.

The moment this distinction is realized, that moment is it seen that the sanction which natural justice gives to one species of property is denied to the other; that the rightfulness which attaches to individual property in the produce of labor implies the wrongfulness of individual property in land; that, whereas the recognition of the one places all men upon equal terms, securing to each the due reward of his labor, the recognition of the other is the denial of the equal rights of men, permitting those who do not labor to take the natural reward of those who do.

Whatever may be said for the institution of private property in land, it is therefore plain that it cannot be defended on the score of justice.

The equal right of all men to the use of land is as

clear as their right to breathe the air—it is a right pro-claimed by the fact of their existence. For we cannot suppose that some men have a right to be in this world and others no right. . . .

The wide-spreading social evils which everywhere oppress men amid an advancing civilization spring from a great primary wrong—the appropriation, as the exclusive property of some men, of the land on which and from which all must live. From this fundamental injustice flow all the injustices which distort and endanger modern development, which condemn the producer of wealth to poverty and pamper the non-producer in luxury, which rear the tenement house with the palace, plant the brothel behind the church, and compel us to build prisons as we open new schools.

There is nothing strange or inexplicable in the phenomena that are now perplexing the world. It is not that material progress is not in itself a good; it is not that nature has called into being children for whom she has failed to provide; it is not that the Creator has left on natural laws a taint of injustice at which even the human mind revolts, that material progress brings such bitter fruits. That amid our highest civilization men faint and die with want is not due to the niggardliness of nature, but to the injustice of man. Vice and misery, poverty and pauperism, are not the legitimate results of increase of population and industrial development; they only follow increase of population and industrial development because land is treated as private property—they are the direct and necessary results of the violation of the supreme law of justice, involved in giving to some men the exclusive possession of that which nature provides for all men. . . .

Whether in the present drifts of opinion and taste there are as yet any indications of retrogression, it is not necessary to inquire; but there are many things about which there can be no dispute, which go to show that our civilization has reached a critical period, and that unless a new start is made in the direction of social equality, the nineteenth century may to the future mark its climax. These industrial depressions, which cause as much waste and suffering as famines or wars, are like the twinges and shocks which precede paralysis. Everywhere is it evident that the tendency to inequality, which is the necessary result of material progress where land is monopolized, cannot go much further without carrying our civilization into that downward path which is so easy to enter and so hard to abandon. Everywhere the increasing intensity of the struggle to live, the increasing necessity for straining every nerve to prevent being thrown down and trodden under foot in the scramble for wealth, is draining the forces which gain and maintain improvements. In every civilized country pauperism, crime, insanity, and suicides are increasing. In every civilized country the diseases are increasing which come from overstrained nerves, from insufficient nourishment, from squalid lodgings, from unwholesome and monotonous occupations, from premature labor of children, from the tasks and crimes which poverty imposes upon women. In every highly civilized country the expectation of life, which gradually rose for several centuries, and which seems to have culminated about the first quarter of this century, appears to be now diminishing.

It is not an advancing civilization that such figures show. It is a civilization which in its undercurrents has already begun to recede. When the tide turns in bay or river from flood to ebb, it is not all at once; but here it still runs on, though there it has begun to recede. When the sun passes the meridian, it can be told only by the way the short shadows fall; for the heat of the day yet increases. But as sure as the turning tide must soon run full ebb; as sure as the declining sun must bring darkness, so sure is it, that though knowledge yet increases and invention marches on, and new states are being settled, and cities still expand, yet civilization has begun to wane when, in proportion to population, we must build more and more prisons, more and more almshouses, more and more insane asylums. It is not from top to bottom that societies die; it is from bottom to top.

But there are evidences far more palpable than any that can be given by statistics, of tendencies to the ebb of civilization. There is a vague but general feeling of disappointment; an increased bitterness among the working classes; a widespread feeling of unrest and brooding revolution. If this were accompanied by a definite idea of how relief is to be obtained, it would be a hopeful sign; but it is not. Though the schoolmaster has been abroad some time, the general power of tracing effect to cause does not seem a whit improved. The reaction toward protectionism, as the reaction toward other exploded fallacies of government, shows this. And even the philosophic free-thinker cannot look upon that vast change in religious ideas that is now sweeping over the civilized world without feeling that this tremendous fact may have most momentous relations, which only the future can develop. For what is going on is not a change in the form of religion, but the negation and destruction of the ideas from which religion springs. Christianity is not simply clearing itself of superstitions, but in the popular mind it is dying at the root, as the old paganisms were dying when Christianity entered the world. And nothing arises to take its place. The fundamental ideas of an intelligent Creator and of a future life are in the general mind rapidly weakening. Now, whether this may or may not be in itself an advance, the importance of the part which religion has played in the world's history shows the importance of the change that is now going on. Unless human nature has suddenly altered in what the universal history of the race shows to be its deepest characteristics, the mightiest actions and reactions are thus preparing. Such stages of thought have heretofore always marked periods of transition. On a smaller scale and to a less depth (for I think any one who will notice the drift of our literature, and talk upon such subjects with the men he meets, will see that it is sub-soil and not surface plowing that materialistic ideas are now doing), such a state of thought preceded the French Revolution. But the closest parallel to the wreck of religious ideas now going on is to be found in that period in which ancient civilization began to pass from splendor to decline. What change may come, no mortal man can tell, but that some great change must come, thoughtful men begin to feel. The civilized world is trembling on the verge of a great movement. Either it must be a leap upward, which will open the way to advances yet undreamed of, or it must be a plunge downward which will carry us back toward barbarism.

DOCUMENT 2

EDWARD BELLAMY, *LOOKING BACKWARD,* 1888

Bellamy later recalled that "Looking Backward *began in earnest to be written in the fall or winter of 1886, and was substantially finished in the following six or eight months . . . It went to the publishers in August or September 1887, . . . and . . . did not appear till January 1888. Although it made a stir among the critics, up to the close of 1888 the sales had not exceeded ten thousand, after which they leaped into the hundred thousands." Its total sales are now well over half a million copies. The book was the mainspring of a "Nationalist" movement started to realize Bellamy's ideas, and it inspired a score of imitators. In the sections excerpted here, Julian West, the hero, who has fallen asleep in 1887 and awakened in the year 2000, learns how the social order of 1887 was replaced by a better one, and how the rational new order organizes its labor force.*

"You have not yet told me what was the answer to the riddle which you found," I said. "I am impatient to know by what contradiction of natural sequence the peace and prosperity which you now seem to enjoy could have been the outcome of an era like my own."

"Excuse me," replied my host, "but do you smoke?" It was not till our cigars were lighted and drawing well that he resumed. "Since you are in the humor to talk rather than to sleep, as I certainly am, perhaps I cannot do better than to try to give you enough idea of our modern industrial system to dissipate at least the impression that there is any mystery about the process of its evolution. The Bostonians of your day had the reputation of being great askers of questions, and I am going to show my descent by asking you one to begin with. What should you name as the most prominent feature of the labor troubles of your day?"

"Why, the strikes, of course," I replied.

"Exactly; but what made the strikes so formidable?"

"The great labor organizations."

"And what was the motive of these great organizations?"

"The workmen claimed they had to organize to get their rights from the big corporations," I replied.

"That is just it," said Dr. Leete; "the organization of labor and the strikes were an effect, merely, of the concentration of capital in greater masses than had ever been known before. Before this concentration began, while as yet commerce and industry were conducted by innumerable petty concerns with small capital, instead of a small number of great concerns with vast capital, the individual workman was relatively important and independent in his relations to the employer. Moreover, when a little capital or a new idea was enough to start a man in business for himself, workingmen were constantly becoming employers and there was no hard and fast line between the two classes. Labor unions were needless then, and general strikes out of the question. But when the era of small concerns with small capital was succeeded by that of the great aggregations of capital, all this was changed. The individual laborer, who had been relatively important to the small employer, was reduced to insignificance and powerlessness over against the great corporation, while at the same time the way upward to the grade of employer was closed to him. Self-defense drove him to union with his fellows.

"The records of the period show that the outcry against the concentration of capital was furious. Men believed that it threatened society with a form of tyranny more abhorrent than it had ever endured. They believed that the great corporations were preparing for them the yoke of a baser servitude than had ever been imposed on the race, servitude not to men but to soulless machines incapable of any motive but insatiable greed. Looking back, we cannot wonder at their desperation, for certainly humanity was never confronted with a fate more sordid and hideous than would have been the era of corporate tyranny which they anticipated.

"Meanwhile, without being in the smallest degree checked by the clamor against it, the absorption of business by ever larger monopolies continued. In the United States there was not, after the beginning of the last quarter of the century, any opportunity whatever for individual enterprise in any important field of industry, unless backed by a great capital. During the last decade of the century, such small businesses as still remained were fast-failing survivals of a past epoch, or mere parasites on the great corporations, or else existed in fields too small to attract the great capitalists. Small businesses, as far as they still remained, were reduced to the condition of rats and mice, living in holes and corners, and counting on evading notice for the enjoyment of existence. . . .

"The fact that the desperate popular opposition to the consolidation of business in a few powerful hands had no effect to check it proves that there must have been a strong economical reason for it. The small capitalists, with their innumerably petty concerns, had in fact yielded the field to the great aggregations of capital, because they belonged to a day of small things and were totally incompetent to the demands of an age of steam and telegraphs and the gigantic scale of its enterprises. To restore the former order of things, even if possible, would have involved returning to the day of stagecoaches. Oppressive and intolerable as was the regime of the great consolidations of capital, even its victims, while they cursed it, were forced to admit the prodigious increase of efficiency which had been imparted to the national industries, the vast economies effected by concentration of management and unity of organization, and to confess that since the new system had taken the place of the old the wealth of the world had increased at a rate before undreamed of. To be sure this vast increase had gone chiefly to make the rich richer, increasing the gap between them and the poor; but the fact remained that, as a means merely of producing wealth, capital had been proved efficient in proportion to its consolidation. The restoration of the old system with the subdivision of capital, if it were possible, might indeed bring back a greater equality of conditions, with more individual dignity and freedom, but it would be at the price of general poverty and the arrest of material progress.

"Was there, then, no way of commanding the services of the mighty wealth-producing principle of consolidated capital without bowing down to a plutocracy like that of Carthage? As soon as men began to ask themselves these questions, they found the answer ready for them. The movement toward the conduct of business by larger and larger aggregations of capital, the tendency toward monopolies, which had been so desperately and vainly resisted, was recognized at last, in its true significance, as a process which only needed to complete its logical evolution to open a golden future to humanity.

"Early in the last century the evolution was completed by the final consolidation of the entire capital of the nation. The industry and commerce of the country, ceasing to be conducted by a set of irresponsible corporations and syndicates of private persons at their caprice and for their profit, were intrusted to a single syndicate representing the people, to be conducted in the common interest for the common profit. The nation, that is to say, organized as the one great business corporation in which all other corporations were absorbed; it became the one capitalist in the place of all other capitalists, the sole employer, the final monopoly in which all previous and lesser monopolies were swallowed up, a monopoly in the profits and economies of which all citizens shared. The epoch of trusts had ended in The Great Trust. In a word, the people of the United States concluded to assume the conduct of their own business, just as one hundred odd years before they had assumed the conduct of their own government, organizing now for industrial purposes on precisely the same grounds that they had then organized for political purposes. . . ."

"Such a stupendous change as you describe," said I, "did not, of course, take place without great bloodshed and terrible convulsions."

"On the contrary," replied Dr. Leete, "there was absolutely no violence. The change had been long foreseen. Public opinion had become fully ripe for it, and the whole mass of the people was behind it. There was no more possibility of opposing it by force than by argument. On the other hand the popular sentiment toward the great corporations and those identified with them had ceased to be one of bitterness, as they came to realize their necessity as a link, a transition phase, in the evolution of the true industrial system. The most violent foes of the great private monopolies were now forced to recognize how invaluable and indispensable had been their office in educating the people up to the point of assuming control of their own business. Fifty years before, the consolidation of the industries of the country under national control would have seemed a very daring experiment to the most sanguine. But by a series of object lessons, seen and studied by all men, the great corporations had taught the people an entirely new set of ideas on this subject. They had seen for many years syndicates handling revenues greater than those of states, and directing the labors of hundreds of thousands of men with an efficiency and economy unattainable in smaller operations. It had come to be recognized as an axiom that the larger the business the simpler the principles that can be applied to it; that, as the machine is truer than the hand, so the system, which in a great concern does the work of the master's eye in a small business, turns out more accurate results. Thus it came about that, thanks to the corporations themselves, when it was proposed that the nation should assume their functions, the suggestion implied nothing which seemed impracticable even to the timid. To be sure it was a step beyond any yet taken, a broader generalization, but the very fact that the nation would be the sole corporation in the field would, it was seen, relieve the undertaking of many difficulties with which the partial monopolies had contended." . . .

Dr. Leete ceased speaking, and I remained silent, endeavoring to form some general conception of the changes in the arrangements of society implied in the tremendous revolution which he had described.

Finally I said, "The idea of such an extension of the functions of government is, to say the least, rather overwhelming."

"Extension!" he repeated, "where is the extension?"

"In my day," I replied, "it was considered that the proper functions of government, strictly speaking, were limited to keeping the peace and defending the people against the public enemy, that is, to the military and police powers."

"And, in heaven's name, who are the public enemies?" exclaimed Dr. Leete. "Are they France, England, Germany, or hunger, cold, and nakedness? In your day governments were accustomed, on the slightest international misunderstanding, to seize upon the bodies of citizens and deliver them over by hundreds of thousands to death and mutilation, wasting their treasures the while like water; and all this oftenest for no imaginable profit to the victims. We have no wars now, and our governments no war powers, but in order to protect every citizen against hunger, cold, and nakedness, and provide for all his physical and mental needs, the function is assumed of directing his industry for a term of years. No, Mr. West, I am sure on reflection you will perceive that it was in your age, not in ours, that the extension of the functions of governments was extraordinary. Not even for the best ends would men now allow their governments such powers as were then used for the most maleficent."

"Leaving comparisons aside," I said, "the demagoguery and corruption of our public men would have been considered, in my day, insuperable objections to any assumption by government of the charge of the national industries. We should have thought that no arrangement could be worse than to entrust the politicians with control of the wealth-producing machinery of the country. Its material interests were quite too much the football of parties as it was."

"No doubt you were right," rejoined Dr. Leete, "but all that is changed now. We have no parties or politicians, and as for demagoguery and corruption, they are words having only an historical significance."

"Human nature itself must have changed very much," I said.

"Not at all," was Dr. Leete's reply, "but the conditions of human life have changed, and with them the motives of human action. The organization of society with you was such that officials were under a constant temptation to misuse their power for the private profit of themselves or others. Under such circumstances it seems almost strange that you dared entrust them with any of your affairs. Nowadays, on the contrary, society is so constituted that there is absolutely no way in which an official, however ill-disposed, could possibly make any profit for himself or any one else by a misuse of his power. Let him be as bad an official as you please, he cannot be a corrupt one. There is no motive to be. The social system no longer offers a premium on dishonesty. But these are matters which you can only understand as you come, with time, to know us better."

"But you have not yet told me how you have settled the labor problem. It is the problem of capital which we have been discussing," I said. "After the nation had assumed conduct of the mills, machinery, railroads, farms, mines, and capital in general of the country, the labor question still remained. In assuming the responsibilities of capital the nation had assumed the difficulties of the capitalist's position."

"The moment the nation assumed the responsibilities of capital those difficulties vanished," replied Dr. Leete. "The national organization of labor under one direction was the complete solution of what was, in your day and under your system, justly regarded as the insoluble labor problem. When the nation became the sole employer, all the citizens, by virtue of their citizenship, became employees, to be distributed according to the needs of industry."

"That is," I suggested, "you have simply applied the principle of universal military service, as it was understood in our day, to the labor question."

"Yes," said Dr. Leete, "that was something which followed as a matter of course as soon as the nation had become the sole capitalist. The people were already accustomed to the idea that the obligation of every citizen, not physically disabled, to contribute his military services to the defense of the nation was equal and absolute. That it was equally the duty of every citizen to contribute his quota of industrial or intellectual services to the maintenance of the nation was equally evident, though it was not until the nation became the employer of labor that citizens were able to render this sort of service with any pretense either of universality or equity. No organization of labor was possible when the employing power was divided among hundreds or thousands of individuals and corporations, between which concert of any kind was neither desired, nor indeed feasible. It constantly happened then that vast numbers who desired to labor could find no opportunity, and on the other hand, those who desired to evade a part or all of their debt could easily do so."

"Service, now, I suppose, is compulsory upon all," I suggested.

"It is rather a matter of course than of compulsion," replied Dr. Leete. "It is regarded as so absolutely natural and reasonable that the idea of its being compulsory has ceased to be thought of. He would be thought to be an incredibly contemptible person who should need compulsion in such a case. Nevertheless, to speak of service being compulsory would be a weak way to state its absolute inevitableness. Our entire social order is so wholly based upon and deduced from it that if it were conceivable that a man could escape it, he would be left with no possible way to provide for his existence. He would have excluded himself from the world, cut himself off from his kind, in a word, committed suicide."

"Is the term of service in this industrial army for life?"

"Oh, no; it both begins later and ends earlier than the average working period in your day. Your workshops were filled with children and old men, but we hold the period of youth sacred to education, and the period of maturity, when the physical forces begin to flag, equally sacred to ease and agreeable relaxation. The period of industrial service is twenty-four years, beginning at the close of the course of education at twenty-one and terminating at forty-five. After forty-five, while discharged from labor, the citizen still remains liable to special calls, in case of emergencies causing a sudden great increase in the demand for labor, till he reaches the age of fifty-five, but such calls are rarely, in fact almost never, made. The fifteenth day of October of every year is what we call Muster Day, because those who have reached the age of twenty-one are then mustered into the industrial service, and at the same time those who, after twenty-four years' service, have reached the age of forty-five, are honorably mustered out. It is the great day of the year with us, whence we reckon all other events, our Olympiad, save that it is annual."

DOCUMENT 3

ANDREW CARNEGIE, "WEALTH,"

JUNE 1889

Unlike many millionaires, Andrew Carnegie had a passionate desire to understand and justify in deeds the enormous fortunes that he and a few other tycoons had made. He believed fervently in the social value of conditions that encouraged individual wealth, but he also believed that equally large social responsibilities went with it. The appearance of this essay in the North American Review *aroused a great deal of interest, and it was reprinted in a British periodical as "The Gospel of Wealth," a title which was later attached to a collection of Carnegie's essays. Carnegie's observations on the responsibilities of the rich man intrigued many of his contemporaries, and became one of the chief texts of a kind of socially minded conservatism.*

Objections to the foundations upon which society is based are not in order, because the condition of the race is better with these than with any others which have been tried. Of the effect of any new substitutes proposed we cannot be sure. The Socialist or Anarchist who seeks to overturn present conditions is to be regarded as attacking the foundation upon which civilization itself rests, for civilization took its start from the day when the capable, industrious workman said to his incompetent and lazy fellow, "If thou dost not sow, thou shalt not reap," and thus ended primitive Communism by separating the drones from the bees. One who studies this subject will soon be brought face to face with the conclusion that upon the sacredness of property civilization itself depends— the right of the laborer to his hundred dollars in the savings bank, and equally the legal right of the millionaire to his millions. To those who propose to substitute Communism for this intense Individualism, the answer therefore is: The race has tried that. All progress from that barbarous day to the present time has resulted from its displacement. Not evil, but good, has come to the race from the accumulation of wealth by those who have had the ability and energy to produce it. But even if we admit for a moment that it might be better for the race to discard its present foundation, Individualism,—that it is a nobler ideal that man should labor, not for himself alone, but in and for a brotherhood of his fellows, and share with them all in common . . . even admit all this, and a sufficient answer is, This is not evolution, but revolution. It necessitates the changing of human nature itself—a work of eons, even if it were good to change it, which we cannot know. It is not practicable in our day or in our age. Even if desirable theoretically, it belongs to another and long-succeeding sociological stratum. Our duty is with what is practicable now. . . . It is criminal to waste our energies in endeavoring to uproot, when all we can profitably or possibly accomplish is to bend the universal tree of humanity a little in the direction most favorable to the production of good fruit under existing circumstances. We might as well urge the destruction of the highest existing type of man because he failed to reach our ideal as to favor the destruction of Individualism, Private Property, the Law of Accumulation of Wealth, and the Law of Competition; for these are the highest result of human experience, the soil in which society so far has produced the best fruit. Unequally or unjustly, perhaps, as these laws sometimes operate, and imperfect as they appear to the Idealist, they are, nevertheless, like the highest type of man, the best and most valuable of all that humanity has yet accomplished.

We start, then, with a condition of affairs under which the best interests of the race are promoted, but which inevitably gives wealth to the few. Thus far, accepting conditions as they exist, the situation can be surveyed and pronounced good. The question then arises, —and, if the foregoing be correct, it is the only question with which we have to deal,—What is the proper mode of administering wealth after the laws upon which civilization is founded have thrown it into the hands of the few? And it is of this great question that I believe I offer the true solution. It will be understood that *fortunes* are here spoken of, not moderate sums saved by many years of effort, the returns from which are required for the comfortable maintenance and education of families. This is not *wealth,* but only competence, which it should be the aim of all to acquire.

There are but three modes in which surplus wealth can be disposed of. It can be left to the families of the decedents; or it can be bequeathed for public purposes; or finally, it can be administered during their lives by its possessors. Under the first and second modes most of the wealth of the world that has reached the few has hitherto been applied. Let us in turn consider each of these modes. The first is the most injudicious. In monarchical countries, the estates and the greatest portion of the wealth are left to the first son, that the vanity of the parent may be gratified by the thought that his name and title are to descend to succeeding generations unimpaired. The condition of this class in Europe today teaches the futility of such hopes or ambitions. The successors have become impoverished through their follies, or from the fall in the value of land. Even in Great Britain the strict law of entail has been found inadequate to maintain the status of an hereditary class. Its soil is rapidly passing into the hands of the stranger. Under republican institutions the division of property among the children is much fairer, but the question which forces itself upon thoughtful men in all lands is: Why should men leave great fortunes to their children? If this is done from affection, is it not misguided affection? Observation teaches that, generally speaking, it is not well for the children that they should be so burdened. Neither is it well for the state. Beyond providing for the wife and daughters moderate sources of income, and very moderate allowances indeed, if any, for the sons, men may well hesitate, for it is no longer questionable that great sums bequeathed often work more for the injury than for the good of the recipients. Wise men will soon conclude that, for the best interests of the members of their families, and of the state, such bequests are an improper use of their means.

It is not suggested that men who have failed to educate their sons to earn a livelihood shall cast them adrift in poverty. If any man has seen fit to rear his sons with a view to their living idle lives, or, what is highly commendable, has instilled in them the sentiment that they are in a position to labor for public ends without reference to pecuniary considerations, then, of course, the duty of the parent is to see that such are provided for *in moderation*. There are instances of millionaires' sons unspoiled by wealth, who, being rich, still perform great services in the community. Such are the very salt of the earth, as valuable as, unfortunately, they are rare. It is not the exception, however, but the rule, that men must regard; and, looking at the usual result of enormous sums conferred upon legatees, the thoughtful man must shortly say, "I would as soon leave my son a curse as the almighty dollar," and admit to himself that it is not the welfare of the children, but family pride, which inspires these enormous legacies.

As to the second mode, that of leaving wealth at death for public uses, it may be said that this is only a means for the disposal of wealth, provided a man is content to wait until he is dead before he becomes of much good in the world. Knowledge of the results of legacies bequeathed is not calculated to inspire the brightest hopes of much posthumous good being accomplished. The cases are not few in which the real object sought by the testator is not attained, nor are they few in which his real wishes are thwarted. In many cases the bequests are so used as to become only monuments of his folly. It is well to remember that it requires the exercise of not less ability than that which acquired the wealth to use it so as to be really beneficial to the community. Besides this, it may fairly be said that no man is to be extolled for doing what he cannot help doing, nor is he to be thanked by the community to which he only leaves wealth at death. Men who leave vast sums in this way may fairly be thought men who would not have left it at all, had they been able to take it with them. The memories of such cannot be held in grateful remembrance, for there is no grace in their gifts. It is not to be wondered at that such bequests seem so generally to lack the blessing.

The growing disposition to tax more and more heavily large estates left at death is a cheering indication of the growth of a salutary change in public opinion. The State of Pennsylvania now takes—subject to some exceptions—one tenth of the property left by its citizens. The budget presented in the British Parliament the other day proposes to increase the death-duties; and, most significant of all, the new tax is to be a graduated one. Of all forms of taxation, this seems the wisest. Men who continue hoarding great sums all their lives, the proper use of which for public ends would work good to the community, should be made to feel that the community, in the form of the state, cannot thus be deprived of its proper share. By taxing estates heavily at death the state marks its condemnation of the selfish millionaire's unworthy life.

It is desirable that nations should go much further in this direction. Indeed, it is difficult to set bounds to the share of a rich man's estate which should go at his death to the public through the agency of the state, and by all means such taxes should be graduated, beginning at nothing upon moderate sums to dependents, and increasing rapidly as the amounts swell. . . . This policy would work powerfully to induce the rich man to attend to the administration of wealth during his life, which is the end that society should always have in view, as being by far the most fruitful for the people. Nor need it be feared that this policy would sap the root of enterprise and render men less anxious to accumulate, for, to the class whose ambition it is to leave great fortunes and be talked about after their death, it will attract even more attention, and, indeed, be a somewhat nobler ambition to have enormous sums paid over to the state from their fortunes.

There remains, then, only one mode of using great fortunes; but in this we have the true antidote for the temporary unequal distribution of wealth, the reconciliation of the rich and the poor—a reign of harmony—another ideal, differing, indeed, from that of the Communist in requiring only the further evolution of existing conditions, not the total overthrow of our civilization. It is founded upon the present most intense individualism, and the race is prepared to put it in practice by degrees whenever it pleases. Under its sway we shall have an ideal state, in which the surplus wealth of the few will become, in the best sense, the property of the many, because administered for the common good; and this wealth, passing through the hands of the few, can be made a much more potent force for the elevation of our race than if it had been distributed in small sums to the people themselves. Even the poorest can be made to see this, and to agree that great sums gathered by some of their fellow-citizens and spent for public purposes, from which the masses reap the principal benefit, are more valuable to them than if scattered among them through the course of many years in trifling amounts.

DOCUMENT 4

WILLIAM GRAHAM SUMNER, "THE ABSURD EFFORT TO MAKE THE WORLD OVER,"

MARCH 1894

Sumner was one of the most outspoken and belligerent apologists of the status quo during the Gilded Age. In 1894, he published in the Forum *the article reprinted here in large part. In this article he dogmatically told dissenters and critics that their hopes and schemes were all fruitless because they flew in the face of nature.*

It will not probably be denied that the burden of proof is on those who affirm that our social condition is utterly diseased and in need of radical regeneration. My task at present, therefore, is entirely negative and critical: to examine the allegations of fact and the doctrines which are put forward to prove the correctness of the diagnosis and to warrant the use of the remedies proposed. . . .

When anyone asserts that the class of skilled and unskilled manual laborers of the United States is worse off now in respect to diet, clothing, lodgings, furniture, fuel, and lights; in respect to the age at which they can marry; the number of children they can provide for; the start in life which they can give to their children, and their chances of accumulating capital, than they ever have been at any former time, he makes a reckless assertion for which no facts have been offered in proof. Upon an appeal to facts, the contrary of this assertion would be clearly established. It suffices, therefore, to challenge those who are responsible for the assertion to make it good.

Nine-tenths of the socialistic and semi-socialistic, and sentimental or ethical, suggestions by which we are overwhelmed come from failure to understand the phenomena of the industrial organization and its expansion. It controls us all because we are all in it. It creates the conditions of our existence, sets the limits of our social activity, regulates the bonds of our social relations, determines our conceptions of good and evil, suggests our life-philosophy, molds our inherited political institutions, and reforms the oldest and toughest customs, like marriage and property. I repeat that the turmoil of heterogeneous and antagonistic social whims and speculations in which we live is due to the failure to understand what the industrial organization is and its all-pervading control over human life, while the traditions of our school of philosophy lead us always to approach the industrial organization, not from the side of objective study, but from that of philosophical doctrine. Hence it is that we find that the method of measuring what we see happening by what are called ethical standards, and of proposing to attack the phenomena by methods thence deduced, is so popular.

The advance of a new country from the very simplest social coordination up to the highest organization is a most interesting and instructive chance to study the development of the organization. It has of course been attended all the way along by stricter subordination and higher discipline. All organization implies restriction of liberty. The gain of power is won by narrowing individual range. The methods of business in colonial days were loose and slack to an inconceivable degree. The movement of industry has been all the time toward promptitude, punctuality, and reliability. It has been attended all the way by lamentations about the good old times; about the decline of small industries; about the lost spirit of comradeship between employer and employee; about the narrowing of the interests of the workman; about his conversion into a machine or into a "ware," and about industrial war. These lamentations have all had reference to unquestionable phenomena attendant on advancing organization. In all occupations the same movement is discernible—in the learned professions, in schools, in trade, commerce, and transportation. It is to go on faster than ever, now that the continent is filled up by the first superficial layer of population over its whole extent and the intensification of industry has begun. The great inventions both make the intension of the organization possible and make it inevitable, with all its consequences, whatever they may be. I must expect to be told here, according to the current fashions of thinking, that we ought to control the development of the organization. The first instinct of the modern man is to get a law passed to forbid or prevent what, in his wisdom, he disapproves. A thing which is inevitable, however, is one which we cannot control. We have to make up our minds to it, adjust ourselves to it, and sit down to live with it. Its inevitableness may be disputed, in which case we must reexamine it; but if our analysis is correct, when we reach what is inevitable we reach the end, and our regulations must apply to ourselves, not to the social facts.

Now the intensification of the social organization is what gives us greater social power. It is to it that we owe our increased comfort and abundance. We are none of us ready to sacrifice this. On the contrary, we want more of it. We would not return to the colonial simplicity and the colonial exiguity if we could. If not, then we must pay the price. Our life is bounded on every side by conditions. We can have this if we will agree to submit to that. In the case of industrial power and product the great condition is combination of force under discipline and strict coordination. Hence the wild language about wage-slavery and capitalistic tyranny. . . .

The movement of the industrial organization which has just been described has brought out a great demand for men capable of managing great enterprises. Such have been called "captains of industry." The analogy with military leaders suggested by this name is not misleading. The great leaders in the development of the industrial organization need those talents of executive and administrative skill, power to command, courage, and fortitude, which were formerly called for in military affairs and scarcely anywhere else. The industrial army is also as dependent on its captains as a military body is on its generals. One of the worst features of the existing system is that the employees have a constant risk in their employer. If he is not competent to manage the business with success, they suffer with him. Capital also is dependent on the skill of the captain of industry for the certainty and magnitude of its profits. Under these circumstances there has been a great demand for men having the requisite ability for this function. As the organization has advanced, with more impersonal bonds of coherence and wider scope of operations, the value of this functionary has rapidly increased. The possession of the requisite ability is a natural monopoly. Consequently, all the conditions have concurred to give to those who possessed this monopoly excessive and constantly advancing rates of remuneration.

Another social function of the first importance in an intense organization is the solution of those crises in the operation of it which are called the conjuncture of the market. It is through the market that the lines of relation run which preserve the system in harmonious and rhythmical operation. The conjuncture is the momentary sharper misadjustment of supply and demand which indicates that a redistribution of productive effort is called for. The industrial organization needs to be insured against these conjunctures, which, if neglected, produce a crisis and catastrophe; and it needs that they shall be anticipated and guarded against as far as skill and foresight can do it. The rewards of this function for the bankers and capitalists who perform it are very great. The captains of industry and the capitalists who operate on the conjuncture, therefore, if they are successful, win, in these days, great fortunes in a short time. There are no earnings which are more legitimate or for which greater services are rendered to the whole industrial body. The popular notions about this matter really assume that all the wealth accumulated by these classes of persons would be here just the same if they had not existed. They are supposed to have appropriated it out of the common stock. This is so far from being true that, on the contrary, their own wealth would not be but for themselves; and besides that, millions more of wealth, many-fold greater than their own, scattered in the hands of thousands, would not exist but for them. . . .

But it is repeated until it has become a commonplace which people are afraid to question, that there is some social danger in the possession of large amounts of wealth by individuals. I ask, Why? I heard a lecture two years ago by a man who holds perhaps the first chair of political economy in the world. He said, among other things, that there was great danger in our day from great accumulations; that this danger ought to be met by taxation, and he referred to the fortune of the Rothschilds and to the great fortunes made in America to prove his point. He omitted, however, to state in what the danger consisted or to specify what harm has ever been done by the Rothschild fortunes or by the great fortunes accumulated in America. It seemed to me that the assertions he was making, and the measures he was recommending, ex-cathedra, were very serious to be thrown out so recklessly. It is hardly to be expected that novelists, popular magazinists, amateur economists, and politicians will be more responsible. It would be easy, however, to show what good is done by accumulations of capital in a few hands—that is, under close and direct management, permitting prompt and accurate application; also to tell what harm is done by loose and unfounded denunciations of any social component or any social group. In the recent debates on the income tax the assumption that great accumulations of wealth are socially harmful and ought to be broken down by taxation was treated as an axiom, and we had direct proof how dangerous it is to fit out the average politician with such unverified and unverifiable dogmas as his warrant for his modes of handling the direful tool of taxation.

Great figures are set out as to the magnitude of certain fortunes and the proportionate amount of the national wealth held by a fraction of the population, and eloquent exclamation-points are set against them. If the figures were beyond criticism, what would they prove? Where is the rich man who is oppressing anybody? If there was one, the newspapers would ring with it. The facts about the accumulation of wealth do not constitute a plutocracy, as I will show below. Wealth, in itself considered, is only power, like steam, or electricity, or knowledge. The question of its good or ill turns on the question how it will be used. To prove any harm in aggregations of wealth it must be shown that great wealth is, as a rule, in the ordinary course of social affairs, put to a mischievous use. This cannot be shown beyond the very slightest degree, if at all. . . .

Although we cannot criticise democracy profitably, it may be said of it, with reference to our present subject, that up to this time democracy never has done anything, either in politics, social affairs, or industry, to prove its power to bless mankind. If we confine our attention to the United States, there are three difficulties with regard to its alleged achievements, and they all have the most serious bearing on the proposed democratization of industry.

1. The time during which democracy has been tried in the United States is too short to warrant any inferences. A century or two is a very short time in the life of political institutions, and if the circumstances change rapidly during the period the experiment is vitiated.

2. The greatest question of all about American democracy is whether it is a cause or a consequence. It is popularly assumed to be a cause, and we ascribe to its beneficent action all the political vitality, all the easiness of social relations, all the industrial activity and enterprise which we experience and which we value and enjoy. I submit, however, that, on a more thorough examination of the matter, we shall find that democracy is a consequence. There are economic and sociological causes

for our political vitality and vigor, for the ease and elasticity of our social relations, and for our industrial power and success. Those causes have also produced democracy, given it success, and have made its faults and errors innocuous. . . .

3. It is by no means certain that democracy in the United States has not, up to this time, been living on a capital inherited from aristocracy and industrialism. We have no pure democracy. Our democracy is limited at every turn by institutions which were developed in England in connection with industrialism and aristocracy, and these institutions are of the essence of our system. While our people are passionately democratic in temper and will not tolerate a doctrine that one man is not as good as another, they have common sense enough to know that he is not; and it seems that they love and cling to the conservative institutions quite as strongly as they do to the democratic philosophy. They are, therefore, ruled by men who talk philosophy and govern by the institutions. Now it is open to Mr. Bellamy to say that the reason why democracy in America seems to be open to the charge made in the last paragraph, of responsibility for all the ill which he now finds in our society, is because it has been infected with industrialism (capitalism); but in that case he must widen the scope of his proposition and undertake to purify democracy before turning industry over to it. The socialists generally seem to think that they make their undertakings easier when they widen their scope, and make them easiest when they propose to re-make everything; but in truth social tasks increase in difficulty in an enormous ratio as they are widened in scope.

The question, therefore, arises, if it is proposed to reorganize the social system on the principles of American democracy, whether the institutions of industrialism are to be retained. If so, all the virus of capitalism will be re-tained. It is forgotten, in many schemes of social reforma-tion in which it is proposed to mix what we like with what we do not like, in order to extirpate the latter, that each must undergo a reaction from the other, and that what we like may be extirpated by what we do not like. We may find that instead of democratizing capitalism we

have capitalized democracy—that is, have brought in
plutocracy. Plutocracy is a political system in which the
ruling force is wealth. . . .

If this poor old world is as bad as they say, one more
reflection may check the zeal of the headlong reformer.
It is at any rate a tough old world. It has taken its trend
and curvature and all its twists and tangles from a long
course of formation. All its wry and crooked gnarls and
knobs are therefore stiff and stubborn. If we puny men by
our arts can do anything at all to straighten them, it will
only be by modifying the tendencies of some of the forces
at work, so that, after a sufficient time, their action may
be changed a little and slowly the lines of movement may
be modified. This effort, however, can at most be only
slight, and it will take a long time. In the meantime spon-
taneous forces will be at work, compared with which our
efforts are like those of a man trying to deflect a river,
and these forces will have changed the whole problem
before our interferences have time to make themselves
felt. The great stream of time and earthly things will
sweep on just the same in spite of us. It bears with it now
all the errors and follies of the past, the wreckage of all
the philosophies, the fragments of all the civilizations,
the wisdom of all the abandoned ethical systems, the debris
of all the institutions, and the penalties of all the mistakes.
It is only in imagination that we stand by and look at and
criticize it and plan to change it. Everyone of us is a child
of his age and cannot get out of it. He is in the stream
and is swept along with it. All his sciences and philosophy come to him out of it. Therefore the tide will not be
changed by us. It will swallow up both us and our experiments. It will absorb the efforts at change and take them
into itself as new but trivial components, and the great
movement of tradition and work will go on unchanged by
our fads and schemes. The things which will change it
are the great discoveries and inventions, the new reactions
inside the social organism, and the changes in the earth
itself on account of changes in the cosmical forces. These
causes will make of it just what, in fidelity to them, it
ought to be. The men will be carried along with it and
be made by it. The utmost they can do by their cleverness
will be to note and record their course as they are carried

along, which is what we do now, and is that which leads us to the vain fancy that we can make or guide the movement. That is why it is the greatest folly of which a man can be capable, to sit down with a slate and pencil to plan out a new social world.

DOCUMENT 5

HENRY DEMAREST LLOYD, *WEALTH AGAINST COMMONWEALTH,* 1894

Lloyd, a Chicago editor and reformer, began his career as perhaps the leading critic of monopoly of his day in an article attacking the railroads and Standard Oil published in the Atlantic Monthly *in 1881. His long book,* Wealth against Commonwealth, *on which he began work in 1889, was largely an exposure and criticism of the business methods of Standard Oil; the passages here illustrate his conclusions about the social consequences of these methods. While the work was in progress, Lloyd wrote to his mother: "It keeps me poking about and scavenging in piles of filthy human greed and cruelty almost too nauseous to handle. Nothing but the sternest sense of duty and the conviction that men must understand the vices of our present system before they will be able to rise to a better, drives me back to my desk every day."*

Nature is rich; but everywhere man, the heir of nature, is poor. Never in this happy country or elsewhere—except in the Land of Miracle, where "they did all eat and were filled"—has there been enough of anything for the people. Never since time began have all the sons and daughters of men been all warm, and all filled, and all shod and roofed. Never yet have all the virgins, wise or foolish, been able to fill their lamps with oil.

The world, enriched by thousands of generations of toilers and thinkers, has reached a fertility which can give every human being a plenty undreamed of even in the Utopias. But between this plenty ripening on the boughs of our civilization and the people hungering for it step the "cornerers," the syndicates, trusts, combinations, with the cry of "over-production"—too much of everything. Holding back the riches of earth, sea, and sky from their fellows who famish and freeze in the dark, they declare to them that there is too much light and warmth and food. They assert the right, for their private profit, to regulate the consumption by the people of the necessaries of life, and to control production, not by the needs of humanity, but by the desires of a few for dividends. The coal syndicate thinks there is too much coal. There is too much iron, too much lumber, too much flour—for this or that syndicate.

The majority have never been able to buy enough of anything; but this minority have too much of everything to sell.

Liberty produces wealth, and wealth destroys liberty. "The splendid empire of Charles V.," says Motley, "was erected upon the grave of liberty." Our bignesses—cities, factories, monopolies, fortunes, which are our empires, are the obesities of an age gluttonous beyond its powers of digestion. Mankind are crowding upon each other in the centres, and struggling to keep each other out of the feast set by the new sciences and the new fellowships. Our size has got beyond both our science and our conscience. The vision of the railroad stockholder is not far-sighted enough to see into the office of the General Manager; the people cannot reach across even a ward of a city to rule their rulers; Captains of Industry "do not know" whether the men in the ranks are dying from lack of food and shelter; we cannot clean our cities nor our politics; the locomotive has more man-power than all the ballot-boxes, and millwheels wear out the hearts of workers unable to keep up beating time to their whirl. If mankind had gone on pursuing the ideals of the fighter, the time would necessarily have come when there would have been only a few, then only one, and then none left. This is what we are witnessing in the world of livelihoods. Our ideals of livelihood are ideals of mutual deglutition. We are rapidly reaching the stage where in each province only a few are left; that is the key to our times. Beyond the deep is another deep. This era is but a passing phase in the evolution of industrial Caesars, and these Caesars will be of a new type—corporate Caesars.

For those who like the perpetual motion of a debate in which neither of the disputants is looking at the same side of the shield, there are infinite satisfactions in the current controversy as to whether there is any such thing as "monopoly." "There are none," says one side. "They are legion," says the other. "The idea that there can be such a thing is absurd," says one, who with half a dozen associates controls the source, the price, the quality, the quantity of nine-tenths of a great necessary of life. But "There will soon be a trust for every production, and a master to fix the price for every necessity of life," said the Senator who framed the United States Anti-Trust Law. This difference as to facts is due to a difference in the definitions through which the facts are regarded. Those who say "there are none" hold with the Attorney-General of the United States and the decision he quotes from the highest Federal court which had then passed on this question that no one has a monopoly unless there is a "disability" or "restriction" imposed by law on all who would compete. A syndicate that had succeeded in bottling for sale all the air of the earth would not have a monopoly in this view, unless there were on the statute books a law forbidding every one else from selling air. No others could get air to sell; the people could not get air to breathe, but there would be no monopoly because there is no "legal restriction" on breathing or selling the atmosphere.

Excepting in the manufacture of postage-stamps, gold dollars, and a few other such cases of a "legal restriction," there are no monopolies according to this definition. It excludes the whole body of facts which the people include in their definition, and dismisses a great public question by a mere play on words. The other side of the shield was described by Judge Barrett, of the Supreme Court of New York. A monopoly he declared to be "any combination the tendency of which is to prevent competition in its broad and general sense, and to control and thus at will enhance prices to the detriment of the public. . . . Nor need it be permanent or complete. It is enough that it may be even temporarily and partially successful. The question in the end is, Does it inevitably tend to public injury?"

Those who insist that "there are none" are the fortunate ones who came up to the shield on its golden side. But common usage agrees with the language of Judge Barrett, because it exactly fits a fact which presses on common people heavily, and will grow heavier before it grows lighter.

The committee of Congress investigating trusts in 1889 did not report any list of these combinations to control markets, "for the reason that new ones are constantly forming, and that old ones are constantly extending their relations so as to cover new branches of the business and invade new territories."

It is true that such a list, like a dictionary, would begin to be wrong the moment it began to appear. But though only an instantaneous photograph of the whirlwind, it would give an idea, to be gained in no other way, of a movement shadowing two hemispheres. In an incredible number of the necessaries and luxuries of life, from meat to tombstones, some inner circle of the "fittest" has sought, and very often obtained, the sweet power which Judge Barrett found the sugar trust had: It "can close every refinery at will, close some and open others, limit the purchases of raw material (thus jeopardizing, and in a considerable degree controlling, its production), artificially limit the production of refined sugar, enhance the price to enrich themselves and their associates at the public expense, and depress the price when necessary to crush out and impoverish a foolhardy rival." . . .

Laws against these combinations have been passed by Congress and by many of the States. There have been prosecutions under them by the State and Federal governments. The laws and the lawsuits have alike been futile.

In a few cases names and form of organization have been changed, in consequence of legal pursuit. The whiskey, sugar, and oil trusts had to hang out new signs. But the thing itself, the will and the power to control markets, livelihoods, and liberties, and the toleration of this by the public—this remains unimpaired; in truth, facilitated by the greater secrecy and compactness which have been the only results of the appeal to law.

The Attorney-General of the national government gives a large part of his annual report for 1893 to showing "what small basis there is for the popular impression" "that the aim and effect of this statute" (the Anti-Trust Law) "are to prohibit and prevent those aggregations of capital which are so common at the present day, and which sometimes are on so large a scale as to practically control all the branches of an extensive industry." This executive says of the action of the "co-ordinate" Legislature: "It would not be useful, even if it were possible, to ascertain the precise purposes of the framers of the statute." He is the officer charged with the duty of directing the prosecutions to enforce the law; but he declares that since, among other reasons, "all ownership of property is a monopoly, . . . any literal application of the provisions of the statute is out of the question." Nothing has been accomplished by all these appeals to the legislatures and the courts, except to prove that the evil lies deeper than any public sentiment or public intelligence yet existent, and is stronger than any public power yet at call.

What we call Monopoly is Business at the end of its journey. The concentration of wealth, the wiping out of the middle classes, are other names for it. To get it is, in the world of affairs, the chief end of man. . . .

If our civilization is destroyed, as Macaulay predicted, it will not be by his barbarians from below. Our barbarians come from above. Our great money-makers have sprung in one generation into seats of power kings do not know. The forces and the wealth are new, and have been the opportunity of new men. Without restraints of culture, experience, the pride, or even the inherited caution of class or rank, these men, intoxicated, think they are the wave instead of the float, and that they have created the business which has created them. To them science is but a never-ending repertoire of investments stored up by nature for the syndicates, government but a fountain of franchises, the nations but customers in squads, and a million the unit of a new arithmetic of wealth written for them. They claim a power without control, exercised through forms which make it secret, anonymous, and perpetual. The possibilities of its gratification have been widening before them without interruption since they began, and even at a thousand millions they will feel no satiation and will see no place to stop. They are gluttons of luxury and power, rough, unsocialized, believing that mankind must be kept terrorized. Powers of pity die out of them, because they work through agents and die in their agents, because what they do is not for themselves. . . .

By their windfall of new power they have been forced into the position of public enemies. Its new forms make them seem not to be within the jurisdiction of the social restraints which many ages of suffering have taught us to bind about the old powers of man over man. A fury of rule or ruin has always in the history of human affairs been a characteristic of the "strong men" whose fate it is to be in at the death of an expiring principle. The leaders who, two hundred years ago, would have been crazy with conquest, to-day are crazy with competition. To a dying era some man is always born to enfranchise it by revealing it to itself. Men repay such benefactors by turning to rend them. Most unhappy is the fate of him whose destiny it is to lead mankind too far in its own path. Such is the function of these men, such will be their lot, as that of those for whom they are building up these wizard wealths. . . .

Business motived by the self-interest of the individual runs into monopoly at every point it touches the social life—land monopoly, transportation monopoly, trade monopoly, political monopoly in all its forms, from contraction of the currency to corruption in office. The society in which in half a lifetime a man without a penny can become a hundred times a millionaire is as over-ripe, industrially, as was, politically, the Rome in which the most popular bully could lift himself from the ranks of the legion on to the throne of the Caesars. Our rising issue is with business. Monopoly is business at the end of its journey. It has got there. The irrepressible conflict is now as distinctly with business as the issue so lately met was with slavery. Slavery went first only because it was the cruder form of business.

Against the principles, and the men embodying them and pushing them to extremes—by which the powers of government, given by all for all, are used as franchises for personal aggrandizement; by which, in the same line, the common toil of all and the common gifts of nature, lands, forces, mines, sites, are turned from service to selfishness, and are made by one and the same stroke to give gluts to a few and impoverishment to the many—we must plan our campaign. The yacht of the millionaire incorporates a million days' labor which might have been given to abolishing the slums, and every day it runs the labor of hundreds of men is withdrawn from the production of helpful things for humanity, and each of us is equally guilty who directs to his own pleasure the labor he should turn to the wants of others. Our fanatic of wealth reverses the rule that serving mankind is the end and wealth an incident, and has made wealth the end and the service an accident, until he can finally justify crime itself if it is a means to the end—wealth—which has come to be the supreme good; and we follow him.

It is an adjudicated fact of the business and social life of America that to receive the profits of crime and cherish the agents who commit it does not disqualify for fellowship in the most "solid" circles—financial, commercial, religious, or social. It illustrates what Ruskin calls the "morbid" character of modern business that the history of its most brilliant episodes must be studied in the vestibules of the penitentiary. The riches of the combinations are the winnings of a policy which, we have seen, has certain constant features. Property to the extent of uncounted millions has been changed from the possession of the many who owned it to the few who hold it:

1. Without the knowledge of the real owners.
2. Without their consent.
3. With no compensation to them for the value taken.
4. By falsehood, often under oath.
5. In violation of the law.

Our civilization is builded on competition, and competition evolves itself crime—to so acute an infatuation has the lunacy of self-interest carried our dominant opinion. We are hurried far beyond the point of not listening to the new conscience which, pioneering in moral exploration, declares that conduct we think right because called "trade" is really lying, stealing, murder. "The definite result," Ruskin preaches, "of all our modern haste to be rich is assuredly and constantly the murder of a certain number of persons by our hands every year." To be unawakened by this new voice is bad enough, but we shut our ears even against the old conscience. . . .

Two social energies have been in conflict, and the energy of reform has so far proved the weaker. We have chartered the self-interest of the individual as the rightful sovereign of conduct; we have taught that the scramble for profit is the best method of administering the riches of earth and the exchange of services. Only those can attack this system who attack its central principle, that strength gives the strong in the market the right to destroy his neighbor. Only as we have denied that right to the strong elsewhere have we made ourselves as civilized as we are. And we cannot make a change as long as our songs, customs, catchwords, and public opinions tell all to do the same thing if they can. Society, in each person of its multitudes, must recognize that the same principles of the interest of all being the rule of all, of the strong serving the weak, of the first being the last—"I am among you as one that serves"—which have given us the home where the weakest is the one surest of his rights and of the fullest service of the strongest, and have given us the republic in which all join their labor that the poorest may be fed, the weakest defended, and all educated and prospered, must be applied where men associate in common toil as wherever they associate. Not until then can the forces be reversed which generate those obnoxious persons—our fittest.

Our system, so fair in its theory and so fertile in its happiness and prosperity in its first century, is now, following the fate of systems, becoming artificial, technical, corrupt; and, as always happens in human institutions, after noon, power is stealing from the many to the few. Believing wealth to be good, the people believed the wealthy to be good. But, again in history, power has intoxicated and hardened its possessors, and Pharaohs are bred in counting-rooms as they were in palaces. Their furniture must be banished to the world-garret, where lie the out-worn trappings of the guilds and slavery and other old lumber of human institutions.

DOCUMENT 6

SAMUEL GOMPERS, LETTER ON LABOR IN INDUSTRIAL SOCIETY,

SEPTEMBER 1894

Samuel Gompers was one of the founders of the American Federation of Labor in 1886 and, except for one year, its president until his death in 1924. Gompers wrote this letter to Judge Peter Grosscup. Grosscup was one of the federal judges who issued an injunction against Eugene V. Debs and the American Railway Union to restrain them from interfering with interstate commerce or the transportation of mail during the strike against the Pullman Company in 1894. When the injunction was violated, Grosscup joined with the district attorney and others in a telegram to President Cleveland calling for federal troops. At the same time he summoned a grand jury to hear charges against Debs. In his charge to the jury, which commanded much attention, Grosscup stated the classic anti-labor thesis that union organizing was a conspiracy and defended the use of injunctions to restrain such "conspiracies." Gompers here criticizes Grosscup for his charge to the jury and affirms the larger social need for union organization.

You say that as you stated in your charge to the Grand Jury, you believe in labor organizations within such lawful and reasonable limits as will make them a service to the laboring man, and not a menace to the lawful institutions of the country.

I have had the pleasure of reading your charge to the Grand Jury, and have only partially been able to discover how far you believe in labor organizations. You would certainly have no objection officially or personally to workingmen organizing, and in their meetings discuss perhaps "the origin of man," benignly smiling upon each other, and declaring that all existing things are right, going to their wretched homes to find some freedom in sleep from gnawing hunger. You would have them extol the virtues of monopolists and wreckers of the people's welfare. You would not have them consider seriously the fact that more than two millions of their fellows are unemployed, and though willing and able, cannot find the opportunity to work, in order that they may sustain themselves, their wives and their children. You would not have them consider seriously the fact that Pullman who has grown so rich from the toil of his workingmen, that he can riot in luxury, while he heartlessly turns these very workmen out of their tenements into the streets and leave to the tender mercies of corporate greed. Nor would you have them ponder upon the hundreds of other Pullmans of different names.

You know, or ought to know, that the introduction of machinery is turning into idleness thousands, faster than new industries are founded, and yet, machinery certainly should not be either destroyed or hampered in its full development. The laborer is a man, he is made warm by the same sun and made cold—yes, colder—by the same winter as you are. He has a heart and brain, and feels and knows the human and paternal instinct for those depending upon him as keenly as do you.

What shall the workers do? Sit idly by and see the vast resources of nature and the human mind be utilized and monopolized for the benefit of the comparative few? No. The laborers must learn to think and act, and soon, too, that only by the power of organization, and common concert of action, can either their manhood be maintained, their rights to life (work to sustain it) be recognized, and liberty and rights secured.

Since you say that you favor labor organizations within certain limits, will you kindly give to thousands of your anxious fellow citizens what you believe the workers could and should do in their organizations to solve this great problem? Not what they should not do. You have told us that.

I am not one of those who regards the entire past as a failure. I recognize the progress made and the improved conditions of which nearly the entire civilized world are the beneficiaries. I ask you to explain, however, that if the wealth of the whole world is, as you say, "pre-eminently and beneficially the nation's wealth," how is it that thousands of able-bodied, willing, earnest men and women are suffering the pangs of hunger? We may boast of our wealth and civilization, but to the hungry man and woman and child our progress is a hollow mockery, our civilization a sham, and our "national wealth" a chimera.

You recognize that the industrial forces set in motion by steam and electricity have materially changed the structure of our civilization. You also admit that a system has grown up where the accumulations of the individual have passed from his control into that of representative combinations and trusts, and that the tendency in this direction is on the increase. How, then, can you consistently criticize the workingmen for recognizing that as individuals they can have no influence in deciding what the wages, hours of toil and conditions of employment shall be?

You evidently have observed the growth of corporate wealth and influence. You recognize that wealth, in order to become more highly productive, is concentrated into fewer hands, and controlled by representatives and directors, and yet you sing the old siren song that the workingman should depend entirely upon his own "individual effort."

The school of *laissez faire,* of which you seem to be a pronounced advocate, has produced great men in advocating the theory of each for himself, and his Satanic Majesty taking the hindermost, but the most pronounced advocates of your school of thought in economics have, when practically put to the test, been compelled to admit that combination and organization of the toiling masses are essential both to prevent the deterioration and to secure an improvement in the condition of the wage earners.

If, as you say, the success of commercial society depends upon the full play of competition, why do not you and your confreres turn your attention and direct the shafts of your attacks against the trusts and corporations, business wreckers and manipulators in the food products —the necessities of the people. Why garland your thoughts in beautiful phrase when speaking of these modern vampires, and steep your pen in gall when writing of the laborers' efforts to secure some of the advantages accruing from the concentrated thought and genius of the ages? . . .

One becomes enraptured in reading the beauty of your description of modern progress. Could you have had in mind the miners of Spring Valley or Pennsylvania, or the clothing workers of the sweat shops of New York or Chicago when you grandiloquently dilate, "Who is not rich to-day when compared with his ancestors of a century ago? The steamboat and the railroad bring to his breakfast table the coffees of Java and Brazil, the fruits from Florida and California, and the steaks from the plains. The loom arrays him in garments and the factories furnish him with a dwelling that the richest contemporaries of his grandfather would have envied. With health and industry he is a prince."

Probably you have not read within the past year of babies dying of starvation at their mothers' breasts. More than likely the thousands of men lying upon the bare stones night after night in the City Hall of Chicago last winter escaped your notice. You may not have heard of the cry for bread that was sounded through this land of plenty by thousands of honest men and women. But should these and many other painful incidents have passed you by unnoticed, I am fearful that you may learn of them with keener thoughts with the coming sleets and blasts of winter.

You say that "labor cannot afford to attack capital." Let me remind you that labor has no quarrel with capital, as such. It is merely the possessors of capital who refuse to accord to labor the recognition, the right, the justice which is the laborers' due, with whom we contend.

See what is implied by your contemptuous reference to the laborer when you ask, "Will the conqueror destroy his trophy?" Who ever heard of a conqueror marching unitedly with his *trophy*, as you would have them? But if by your comparison you mean that the conqueror is the corporation, the trust, the capitalist class, and ask then whether they would destroy their *trophy*, I would have you ask the widows and orphans of the thousands of men killed annually through the avarice of railroad corporations refusing to avail themselves of modern appliances in coupling and other improvements on their railroads.

Inquire from the thousands of women and children whose husbands or fathers were suffocated or crushed in the mines through the rapacious greed of stockholders clamoring for more dividends. Investigate the sweating dens of the large cities. Go to the mills, factories, through the country. Visit the modern tenement houses or hovels in which thousands of workers are compelled to eke out an existence. Ask these whether the conqueror (monopoly) cares whether his trophy (the laborers) is destroyed or preserved. Ascertain from employers whether the laborer is not regarded the same as a machine, thrown out as soon as all the work possible has been squeezed out of him.

Are you aware that all the legislation ever secured for the ventilation or safety of mines, factory or workshop is the result of the efforts of organized labor? Do you know that the trade unions were the shield for the seven-year-old children from being the conqueror's trophy until they become somewhat older? And that the reformatory laws now on the statute books, protecting or defending the trophies of both sexes, young and old, from the fond care of the conquerors, were wrested from Congresses, legislatures and parliaments despite the Pullmans, the Jeffries, the Ricks, the Tafts, the Williams, the Woods, or the Grosscups.

By what right, sir, do you assume that the labor organizations do not conduct their affairs within lawful limits, or that they are a menace to the lawful institutions of the country? Is it because some thoughtless or over-zealous member at a time of great excitement and smarting under a wrong may violate under a law or commit an improper act? Would you apply the same rule to the churches, the other moral agencies and organizations that you do to the organizations of labor? If you did, the greatest moral force of life to-day, the trade unions, would certainly stand out the clearest, brightest and purest. Because a certain class (for which you and a number of your colleagues on the bench seem to be the special pleaders) have a monopoly in their lines of trade, I submit that this is no good reason for their claim to have a monopoly on true patriotism or respect for the lawful institutions of the country. . . .

Year by year man's liberties are trampled under foot at the bidding of corporations and trusts, rights are invaded and law perverted. In all ages wherever a tyrant has shown himself he has always found some willing judge to clothe that tyranny in the robes of legality, and modern capitalism has proven no exception to the rule.

You may not know that the labor movement as represented by the trades unions, stands for right, for justice, for liberty. You may not imagine that the issuance of an injunction depriving men of a legal as well as a natural right to protect themselves, their wives and little ones, must fail of its purpose. Repression or oppression never yet succeeded in crushing the truth or redressing a wrong.

In conclusion let me assure you that labor will organize and more compactly than ever and upon practical lines, and despite relentless antagonism, achieve for humanity a nobler manhood, a more beautiful womanhood and a happier childhood.

DOCUMENT 7

POLLOCK v. FARMERS' LOAN AND TRUST CO.,
1895

When a two percent tax on incomes over $4,000 was incorporated in the Wilson–Gorman Tariff of 1894, a test case was quickly arranged to bring the constitutionality of the measure before the Court. An income tax had been passed during the Civil War and had been retained for some years afterward; its constitutionality, never attacked while it was in effect, had later been firmly asserted by the Court in Springer v. United States (1881). *Nonetheless, the* Pollock *case, coming at a time of social upheaval, and when an extraordinarily conservative body of justices sat on the Court, took a new and surprising*

*tack which made this, after the Dred Scott case, the
most widely criticized decision in the Court's history.
The tone of the opposition to the tax was struck by
Joseph H. Choate, who appealed to the justices to
halt the "communist march"—as he called the current
demand for social reform.*

*The case was heard twice. In its first presenta-
tion, the issue was whether a tax upon rents or income issuing out of lands was constitutional, in the
light of the clauses of the Constitution—Article I,
section 2, clause 3, and section 9, clause 4—which
provide that "direct taxes" be apportioned among the
states according to their population as established for
representation in the House, and which prohibit any
"capitation, or other direct, tax" unless levied in proportion to the census enumeration. On the first hearing, the Court, by a vote of six to two, found that a
tax on income from land, in order to be constitutional,
must be apportioned according to population.*

*The question remained whether a tax on other
forms of income was also to fall under the Court's
ban. Justice Howell E. Jackson, who had been ill
during the first argument of the case, returned; and
the entire Court, which had been divided four to
four on important questions raised by this case, now
heard a reargument. By a five to four vote, the Court
decided that taxes on income from personal property
were direct taxes, precisely as were taxes on income
from land, and were therefore also unconstitutional.
A roar of indignation went up throughout the country,
though many conservatives were happy at what they
considered a blow to "Populism." Because of this decision, the Sixteenth Amendment had to be passed in
1913 before income taxes could be levied.*

FULLER, C. J. . . .

Our previous decision was confined to the consideration of the validity of the tax on the income from real
estate, and on the income from municipal bonds. . . .

We are now permitted to broaden the field of inquiry,

and to determine to which of the two great classes a tax upon a person's entire income, whether derived from rents, or products, or otherwise, of real estate, or from bonds, stocks, or other forms of personal property, belongs; and we are unable to conclude that the enforced subtraction from the yield of all the owner's real or personal property, in the manner prescribed, is so different from a tax upon the property itself, that it is not a direct, but an indirect, tax in the meaning of the Constitution. . .

We know of no reason for holding otherwise than that the words "direct taxes," on the one hand, and "duties, imposts and excises," on the other, were used in the Constitution in their natural and obvious sense. Nor, in arriving at what those terms embrace, do we perceive any ground for enlarging them beyond, or narrowing them within, their natural and obvious import at the time the Constitution was framed and ratified. . . .

The reasons for the clauses of the Constitution in respect of direct taxation are not far to seek. . . .

The founders anticipated that the expenditures of the States, their counties, cities, and towns, would chiefly be met by direct taxation on accumulated property, while they expected that those of the Federal government would be for the most part met by indirect taxes. And in order that the power of direct taxation by the general government should not be exercised, except on necessity; and, when the necessity arose, should be so exercised as to leave the States at liberty to discharge their respective obligations, and should not be so exercised, unfairly and discriminatingly, as to particular States or otherwise, by a mere majority vote, possibly of those whose constituents were intentionally not subjected to any part of the burden, the qualified grant was made.

Those who made it knew that the power to tax involved the power to destroy, and that, in the language of Chief Justice Marshall, in *McCulloch* v. *Maryland*, "the only security against the abuse of this power is found in the structure of the government itself." . . . And they retained this security by providing that direct taxation and representation in the lower house of Congress should be adjusted on the same measure.

Moreover, whatever the reasons for the constitutional provisions, there they are, and they appear to us to speak in plain language.

It is said that a tax on the whole income of property is not a direct tax in the meaning of the Constitution, but a duty, and, as a duty, leviable without apportionment, whether direct or indirect. We do not think so. Direct taxation was not restricted in one breath, and the restriction blown to the winds in another. . . .

The Constitution prohibits any direct tax, unless in proportion to numbers as ascertained by the census; and, in the light of the circumstances to which we have referred, is it not an evasion of that prohibition to hold that a general unapportioned tax, imposed upon all property owners as a body for or in respect of their property, is not direct, in the meaning of the Constitution, because confined to the income therefrom?

Whatever the speculative views of political economists or revenue reformers may be, can it be properly held that the Constitution, taken in its plain and obvious sense, and with due regard to the circumstances attending the formation of the government, authorizes a general unapportioned tax on the products of the farm and the rents of real estate, although imposed merely because of ownership and with no possible means of escape from payment, as belonging to a totally different class from that which includes the property from whence the income proceeds?

There can be but one answer, unless the constitutional restriction is to be treated as utterly illusory and futile, and the object of its framers defeated. We find it impossible to hold that a fundamental requisition, deemed so important as to be enforced by two provisions, one affirmative and one negative, can be refined away by forced distinctions between that which gives value to property, and the property itself.

Nor can we perceive any ground why the same reasoning does not apply to capital in personalty held for the purpose of income or ordinarily yielding income, and to the income therefrom. . . .

Personal property of some kind is of general distribution; and so are incomes, though the taxable range thereof might be narrowed through large exemptions. . . .

Nor are we impressed with the contention that, because in the four instances in which the power of direct taxation has been exercised, Congress did not see fit, for reasons of expediency, to levy a tax upon personalty, this amounts to such a practical construction of the Constitution that the power did not exist, that we must regard ourselves bound by it. We should regret to be compelled to hold the powers of the general government thus restricted, and certainly cannot accede to the idea that the Constitution has become weakened by a particular course of inaction under it. . . .

Admitting that this act taxes the income of property irrespective of its source, still we cannot doubt that such a tax is necessarily a direct tax in the meaning of the Constitution. . . .

The power to tax real and personal property and the income from both, there being an apportionment, is conceded; that such a tax is a direct tax in the meaning of the Constitution has not been, and, in our judgment, cannot be successfully denied; and yet we are thus invited to hesitate in the enforcement of the mandate of the Constitution, which prohibits Congress from laying a direct tax on the revenue from property of the citizen without regard to state lines, and in such manner that the States cannot intervene by payment in regulation of their own resources, lest a government of delegated powers should be found to be, not less powerful, but less absolute, than the imagination of the advocate had supposed.

We are not here concerned with the question whether an income tax be or be not desirable, nor whether such a tax would enable the government to diminish taxes on consumption and duties on imports, and to enter upon what may be believed to be a reform of its fiscal and commercial system. Questions of that character belong to the controversies of political parties, and cannot be settled by judicial decision. In these cases our province is to determine whether this income tax on the revenue from property does or does not belong to the class of direct taxes. If it does, it is, being unapportioned, in violation of the Constitution, and we must so declare. . . .

Our conclusions may, therefore, be summed up as follows:

First. We adhere to the opinion already announced, that, taxes on real estate being indisputably direct taxes, taxes on the rents or income of real estate are equally direct taxes.

Second. We are of opinion that taxes on personal property, or on the income of personal property, are likewise direct taxes.

Third. The tax imposed by sections twenty-seven to thirty-seven, inclusive, of the act of 1894, so far as it falls on the income of real estate and of personal property, being a direct tax within the meaning of the Constitution, and, therefore, unconstitutional and void because not apportioned according to representation, all those sections, constituting one entire scheme of taxation, are necessarily invalid.

DOCUMENT 8

JOHN MARSHALL HARLAN, DISSENTING OPINION IN *POLLOCK* v. *FARMERS' LOAN AND TRUST CO.*,

1895

Justice Harlan, along with three of his brethren, dissented from the decision in the Pollock *case. The New York Sun, reporting the event, said that in delivering his dissent, Justice Harlan "pounded the desk, shook his finger under the noses of the Chief Justice and Mr. Justice Field, turned more than once almost angrily upon his colleagues in the majority, and expressed his dissent from their conclusions in a tone and language more appropriate to a stump address at a Populist barbecue than to an opinion on a question of law before the Supreme Court of the United States." Whatever Harlan's manner, his dissent, of which only a small part appears here, was a long and learned discussion of the historical and legal issues raised by the "direct tax" question. Not only the Court's precedents, but the records of the Federal Convention of 1787 bore out his arguments; for the direct tax clauses had been intended to apply only to the taxation of land and of persons, having been passed to meet the demands of Southerners in the Convention who were concerned lest their land be taxed by its area and their slaves be taxed by their numbers. In the* Hylton *case of 1796 (to which Justice Harlan refers), the Court, two of whose justices had been members of the Convention and had actually taken part in the writing of the direct tax clause, had passed clearly upon its historic meaning. Subsequent historians of the Court have generally agreed with the argument of this heated dissent, and a later Chief Justice, Charles Evans Hughes, once referred to the majority decision in the case as "a self-inflicted wound."*

Let us examine the grounds upon which the decision of the majority rests, and look at some of the consequences that may result from the principles now announced. I have a deep, abiding conviction, which my sense of duty compels me to express, that it is not possible for this court to have rendered any judgment more to be regretted than the one just rendered. . . .

In my judgment a tax on *income* derived from real property ought not to be, and until now has never been, regarded by any court as a direct tax on such property within the meaning of the Constitution. As the great mass of lands in most of the States do not bring any rents, and as incomes from rents vary in the different States, such a tax cannot possibly be apportioned among the States on the basis merely of numbers with any approach to equality of right among taxpayers, any more than a tax on carriages or other personal property could be so apportioned. And, in view of former adjudications, beginning with the *Hylton case* and ending with the *Springer case,* a decision now that a tax on income from real property can be laid and collected only by apportioning the same among the States, on the basis of numbers, may, not improperly, be regarded as a judicial revolution, that may sow the seeds of hate and distrust among the people of different sections of our common country. . . .

But the court, by its judgment just rendered, goes far

in advance not only of its former decisions, but of any decision heretofore rendered by an American court. . . .

In my judgment—to say nothing of the disregard of the former adjudications of this court, and of the settled practice of the government—this decision may well excite the gravest apprehensions. It strikes at the very foundations of national authority, in that it denies to the general government a power which is, or may become, vital to the very existence and preservation of the Union in a national emergency, such as that of war with a great commercial nation, during which the collection of all duties upon imports will cease or be materially diminished. It tends to reëstablish that condition of helplessness in which Congress found itself during the period of the Articles of Confederation, when it was without authority, by laws operating directly upon individuals, to lay and collect, through its own agents, taxes sufficient to pay the debts and defray the expenses of government, but was dependent, in all such matters, upon the good will of the States, and their promptness in meeting requisitions made upon them by Congress.

Why do I say that the decision just rendered impairs or menaces the national authority? The reason is so apparent that it need only be stated. In its practical operation this decision withdraws from national taxation not only all incomes derived from real estate, but tangible personal property, *"invested* personal property, bonds, stocks, investments of all kinds," and the income that may be derived from such property. This results from the fact that by the decision of the court, all such personal property and all incomes from real estate and personal property, are placed beyond national taxation otherwise than by *apportionment* among the States *on the basis* simply *of population.* No such apportionment can possibly be made without doing gross injustice to the many for the benefit of the favored few in particular States. Any attempt upon the part of Congress to apportion among the States, upon the basis simply of their population, taxation of personal property or of incomes, would tend to arouse such indignation among the freemen of America that it would never be repeated. . . .

The decree now passed dislocates—principally, for

reasons of an economic nature—a sovereign power expressly granted to the general government and long recognized and fully established by judicial decisions and legislative actions. It so interprets constitutional provisions, originally designed to protect the slave property against oppressive taxation, as to give privileges and immunities never contemplated by the founders of the government. . . .

I cannot assent to an interpretation of the Constitution that impairs and cripples the just powers of the National Government in the essential matter of taxation, and at the same time discriminates against the greater part of the people of our country.

The practical effect of the decision to-day is to give to certain kinds of property a position of favoritism and advantage inconsistent with the fundamental principles of our social organization, and to invest them with power and influence that may be perilous to that portion of the American people upon whom rests the larger part of the burdens of the government, and who ought not to be subjected to the dominion of aggregated wealth any more than the property of the country should be at the mercy of the lawless.

DOCUMENT 9

U.S. v. E. C. KNIGHT AND CO.,
1895

The American Sugar Refining Company, by buying the stock of four Philadelphia sugar refining companies, had acquired a virtual monopoly of the manufacture of refined sugar in the United States. Attorney-General Richard Olney, who never respected the Sherman Anti-Trust Act, nonetheless brought suit for a court order cancelling the agreements under which the stock had been acquired, on the ground that these agreements created a monopoly. The question before the Court was whether a monopoly in the manufacture of a product, which presumably

afforded control of supply and prices, involved interstate commerce *to the extent that it could be brought
under the provisions of the Anti-Trust Act and controlled under the Constitution's commerce clause.
The government's case was badly presented by Olney,
who neglected to establish the close relation between
a monopoly in manufacture (which was local) and sales
and distribution (which were interstate). Hence the
Court ruled that "commerce succeeds to manufacture,
and is not a part of it." The resulting decision of the
Court, with its powerful blow at enforcement of the
Sherman Act, hardly displeased Olney, who wrote to
his Secretary: "You will observe that the government
has been defeated. . . . I have always supposed it
would and have taken the responsibility of not
prosecuting [other possible cases] under a law I believed to be no good."*

FULLER, C. J. . . . The fundamental question is, whether
conceding that the existence of a monopoly in manufacture
is established by the evidence, that monopoly can be
directly suppressed under the act of Congress in the mode
attempted by this bill. . . .

The argument is that the power to control the manufacture of refined sugar is a monopoly over a necessary of
life, to the enjoyment of which by a large part of the
population of the United States interstate commerce is
indispensable, and that, therefore, the general government
in the exercise of the power to regulate commerce may
repress such monopoly directly and set aside the instruments which have created it. But this argument cannot be
confined to necessaries of life merely, and must include all
articles of general consumption. Doubtless the power to
control the manufacture of a given thing involves in a
certain sense the control of its disposition, but this is a
secondary and not the primary sense; and although the
exercise of that power may result in bringing the operation of commerce into play it does not control it and affects
it only incidentally and indirectly. Commerce succeeds
to manufacture, and is not a part of it. The power to
regulate commerce is the power to prescribe the rule by
which commerce shall be governed, and is a power inde-

pendent of the power to suppress monopoly. But it may operate in repression of monopoly whenever that comes within the rules by which commerce is governed or whenever the transaction is itself a monopoly of commerce.

It is vital that the independence of the commercial power and of the police power, and the delimitation between them, however sometimes perplexing, should always be recognized and observed, for while the one furnishes the strongest bond of union, the other is essential to the preservation of the autonomy of the States as required by our dual form of government; and acknowledged evils, however grave and urgent they may appear to be, had better be borne, than the risk be run, in the effort to suppress them, of more serious consequences by resort to expedients of even doubtful constitutionality.

It will be perceived how far-reaching the proposition is that the power of dealing with a monopoly directly may be exercised by the general government whenever interstate or international commerce may be ultimately affected. The regulation of commerce applies to the subjects of commerce and not to matters of internal police. Contracts to buy, sell, or exchange goods to be transported among the several States, the transportation and its instrumentalities, and articles bought, sold, or exchanged for the purposes of such transit among the States, or put in the way of transit, may be regulated, but this is because they form part of interstate trade or commerce. The fact that an article is manufactured for export to another State does not of itself make it an article of interstate commerce, and the intent of the manufacturer does not determine the time when the article or product passes from the control of the State and belongs to commerce. . . .

Contracts, combinations, or conspiracies to control domestic enterprise in manufacture, agriculture, mining, production in all its forms, or to raise or lower prices or wages, might unquestionably tend to restrain external as well as domestic trade, but the restraint would be an indirect result, however inevitable and whatever its extent, and such result would not necessarily determine the object of the contract, combination, or conspiracy.

Again, all the authorities agree that in order to vitiate a contract or combination it is not essential that its result should be a complete monopoly; it is sufficient if it really tends to that end and to deprive the public of the advantages which flow from free competition. Slight reflection will show that if the national power extends to all contracts and combinations in manufacture, agriculture, mining, and other productive industries, whose ultimate result may affect external commerce, comparatively little of business operations and affairs would be left for state control.

It was in the light of well-settled principles that the act of July 2, 1890 [the Sherman Act] was framed. Congress did not attempt thereby to assert the power to deal with monopoly directly as such; or to limit and restrict the rights of corporations created by the States or the citizens of the States in the acquisition, control, or disposition of property; or to regulate or prescribe the price or prices at which such property or the products thereof should be sold; or to make criminal the acts of persons in the acquisition and control of property which the States of their residence or creation sanctioned or permitted. Aside from the provisions applicable where Congress might exercise municipal power, what the law struck at was combinations, contracts, and conspiracies to monopolize trade and commerce among the several States or with foreign nations; but the contracts and acts of the defendants related exclusively to the acquisition of the Philadelphia refineries and the business of sugar refining in Pennsylvania, and bore no direct relation to commerce between the States or with foreign nations. The object was manifestly private gain in the manufacture of the commodity, but not through the control of interstate or foreign commerce. It is true that the bill alleged that the products of these refineries were sold and distributed among the several States, and that all the companies were engaged in trade or commerce with the several States and with foreign nations; but this was no more than to say that trade and commerce served manufacture to fulfill its function. . . . There was nothing in the proofs to indicate any intention to put a restraint upon trade or commerce, and the fact, as we have seen, that trade or commerce might be indirectly affected was not enough to entitle complainants to a decree. . . .

DOCUMENT 10

JOHN MARSHALL HARLAN, DISSENTING OPINION IN U.S. v. E. C. KNIGHT AND CO.,
1895

Alone among the justices, Harlan found that a monopoly operating within a single state but trading across state lines must be considered as engaged in interstate commerce; and that the federal power to regulate commerce must be extended to cover it, if the control of monopoly was to be meaningful. His powerful dissent, and the protest in the country at large against the Court's decision may have impelled the Court to change its view in later cases, which gave some encouragement to enforcement of the Sherman Act. In Addystone Pipe and Steel Company v. U.S. (1899), for instance, the Court, though it did not specifically reverse the Knight decision, allowed the Sherman Act to be applied against an industrial combination. The implications of Harlan's dissent were later followed by the Court in Swift and Co. v. U.S. (1905), in which Justice Holmes found that, where a combination to control sales was demonstrated, a monopoly within a single state had an effect that was not "accidental, secondary, remote, or merely probable."

The power of Congress covers and protects the absolute freedom of such intercourse and trade among the States as may or must succeed manufacture and precede transportation from the place of purchase. This would seem to be conceded; for, the court in the present case expressly declare that "*contracts to buy, sell, or exchange goods to be transported among the several States,* the transportation and its instrumentalities, and articles bought, sold, or exchanged for the purpose of such transit among the States, or put in the way of transit, *may be regulated,* but this is *because they form part of interstate trade or commerce.*" Here is a direct admission—one which the settled doctrines of this court justify—that contracts to buy and the purchasing of goods *to be transported from one State to another,* and transportation, with its instrumentalities, are all *parts* of interstate trade or commerce. Each part of such trade is then under the protection of Congress. And yet, by the opinion and judgment in this case, if I do not misapprehend them, Congress is without power to protect the commercial intercourse that such purchasing necessarily involves against the restraints and burdens arising from the existence of *combinations* that meet purchasers, from whatever State they come, with the threat—for it is nothing more nor less than a threat—that they *shall not* purchase what they desire to purchase, *except at the prices fixed by such combinations.* A citizen of Missouri has the right to go in person, or send orders, to Pennsylvania and New Jersey for the purpose of purchasing refined sugar. But of what value is that right if he is confronted in those States by a vast *combination* which absolutely controls the price of that article by reason of its having acquired all the sugar refineries in the United States in order that they may fix prices in their own interest exclusively?

In my judgment, the citizens of the several States composing the Union are entitled, of right, to buy goods in the State where they are manufactured, or in any other State, without being confronted by an illegal combination whose business extends throughout the whole country, which by the law everywhere is an enemy to the public interests, and which prevents such buying, except at prices arbitrarily fixed by it. I insist that the free course of trade among the States cannot coexist with such combinations. When I speak of trade I mean the buying and selling of articles of every kind that are recognized articles of interstate commerce. Whatever improperly obstructs the free course of interstate intercourse and trade, as involved in the buying and selling of articles to be carried from one State to another, may be reached by Congress, under its authority to regulate commerce among the States. The exercise of that authority so as to make trade among the States, in all recognized articles of commerce, absolutely free from unreasonable or illegal restrictions imposed by combinations, is justified by an express grant of power to Congress and would redound to the welfare of the whole country. I am unable to perceive that any such result would imperil the autonomy of the States, especially as that result cannot be attained through the action of any one State.

Undue restrictions or burdens upon the purchasing of goods, in the market for sale, to be transported to other states, cannot be imposed even by a State without violating the freedom of commercial intercourse guaranteed by the Constitution. But if a *State* within whose limits the business of refining sugar is exclusively carried on may not constitutionally impose burdens upon purchases of sugar *to be transported to other States,* how comes it that combinations of corporations or individuals, within the same State, may not be prevented by the national government from putting unlawful restraints upon the purchasing of that article *to be carried from the State in which such purchases are made?* If the national power is competent to repress *State* action in restraint of interstate trade as it may be involved in purchases of refined sugar to be transported from one State to another State, surely it ought to be deemed sufficient to prevent unlawful restraints attempted to be imposed by combinations of corporations or individuals upon those identical purchases; otherwise, illegal combinations of corporations or individuals may—so far as national power and interstate commerce are concerned—do, with impunity, what no State can do. . . .

In committing to Congress the control of commerce with foreign nations and among the several States, the Constitution did not define the means that may be employed to protect the freedom of commercial intercourse and traffic established for the benefit of all the people of the Union. It wisely forbore to impose any limitations upon the exercise of that power except those arising from the general nature of the government, or such as are embodied in the fundamental guarantees of liberty and property. It gives to Congress, in express words, authority to enact all laws necessary and proper for carrying into execution the power to regulate commerce; and whether an

act of Congress, passed to accomplish an object to which
the general government is competent, is within the power
granted, must be determined by the rule announced
through Chief Justice Marshall three-quarters of a century
ago, and which has been repeatedly affirmed by this court.
That rule is: "The sound construction of the Constitution
must allow to the national legislature the discretion with
respect to the means by which the powers it confers are to
be carried into execution, which will enable that body to
perform the high duties assigned to it in the manner most
beneficial to the people. Let the end be legitimate, let it
be within the scope of the Constitution, and all means
which are appropriate, which are plainly adapted to that
end, which are not prohibited, but consistent with the
letter and spirit of the Constitution, are constitutional."
McCulloch v. *Maryland*, 4 Wheat. 316, 421. The end
proposed to be accomplished by the act of 1890 is the
protection of trade and commerce among the States against
unlawful restraints. Who can say that that end is not
legitimate or is not within the scope of the Constitution?
The means employed are the suppression, by legal proceedings, of combinations, conspiracies, and monopolies,
which by their inevitable and admitted tendency, improperly restrain trade and commerce among the States.
Who can say that such means are not appropriate to
attain the end of freeing commercial intercourse among
the States from burdens and exactions imposed upon it by
combinations which, under principles long recognized in
this country as well as at the common law, are illegal and
dangerous to the public welfare? What clause of the
Constitution can be referred to which prohibits the means
thus prescribed in the act of Congress? . . .

We have before us the case of a combination which
absolutely controls, or may, at its discretion, control the
price of all refined sugar in this country. Suppose another
combination, organized for private gain and to control
prices, should obtain possession of all the large flour mills
in the United States; another, of all the grain elevators;
another, of all the oil territory; another, of all the salt-
producing regions; another, of all the cotton mills; and
another, of all the great establishments for slaughtering
animals, and the preparation of meats. What power is

competent to protect the people of the United States against such dangers except a national power—one that is capable of exerting its sovereign authority throughout every part of the territory and over all the people of the nation?

To the general government has been committed the control of commercial intercourse among the States, to the end that it may be free at all times from any restraints except such as Congress may impose or permit for the benefit of the whole country. The common government of all the people is the only one that can adequately deal with a matter which directly and injuriously affects the entire commerce of the country, which concerns equally all the people of the Union, and which, it must be confessed, cannot be adequately controlled by any one State. Its authority should not be so weakened by construction that it cannot reach and eradicate evils that, beyond all question, tend to defeat an object which that government is entitled, by the Constitution, to accomplish. . . .

* PART III *

Agrarian Protest

INTRODUCTION

THE last three decades of the nineteenth century were a period of great trial for those American farmers, especially in the South and West, who raised the cash crops, cotton and wheat, for the international market. In the South, there were, of course, special problems which had been created by the economic disruption of the Civil War and the changed status of Southern farm labor; but Southern farmers also had numerous other grievances in common with those of other sections. What all farmers suffered from was the falling price level. From 1866 to 1897, with only brief interruptions, prices went steadily downward. And while the price the farmer got for his crop in the world market was steadily declining, he had to pay more and more himself for farm machinery and for various products affected by the currently high tariffs. The hazards of nature—drought, hailstorms, grasshopper plagues—gave him no respite, often seemed maleficently intent on increasing the toll they took from his crops. In some sections there were agonizing years when he had almost no crop to sell at any price.

The high cost of shipping and marketing further plagued many farmers, especially those in the newly settled areas far from centers of population. Railroads, grain elevators, and meat packers set their charges more often according to their own capricious finances, speculations in construction, or sheer monopolistic power than by a fair relation to costs, much less by the capacity of the farm industry to pay. Finally, the cost of credit, without which the cash crop farmer especially could not operate, was far beyond his capacity to pay. In the South the credit situation was particularly desperate. The country merchant —or, more often, merchant-planter—made annual advances of food and supplies to share tenants and sharecroppers at interest rates which at the end of the year's work often left the borrower penniless or in debt. Moreover, because the merchant was interested only in the local cash crop— usually cotton—he required his tenants to devote their entire acreage to it, thus cutting them off from whatever help they might have gotten from diversification. In the West, farmers mortgaged their farms at interest rates as high as fifteen percent, either to start their farms or to expand their operations in boom periods, only to be wiped out when prices turned out to be much lower than they had expected, or when a natural disaster ruined their crop.

From time to time, the center of agricultural discontent shifted, as did the remedies upon which farmers pinned their hopes. In the 1870's, the wheat-growers, especially in Illinois, Wisconsin, Iowa, and Minnesota, became very vocal, and organized into farmer's clubs and political parties of considerable strength. This was the heyday of the Grange. Although it was originally organized as a non-political society, the Grange soon took the lead in fighting the railroads, and in proposing other political remedies for agrarian discontents (Document 1). For a time the Grange was able to affect railroad rates through state legislatures, a success for which the Supreme Court's decision in *Munn* v. *Illinois* (1877) (Document 2) helped to lay a legal foundation. The legal issues were not settled with any finality by this case, however. A ringing philosophical dissent on behalf of private property, written by Justice Stephen J. Field (Document 3), influenced later Court decisions which placed severe limits on both state and federal regulation of railroads. Pressure by farmers and other shippers led in 1887 to the passage of the Interstate Commerce Act, but this measure, too, failed to be really effective, partly because of administrative indifference, partly because of legal obstacles posed by an increasingly conservative Court. Railroad regulation did not begin to be really effective until the early twentieth century (see Part V, Documents 7 and 8).

In the first Grange areas, as cities developed, agriculture became more diversified and enjoyed the advantage of producing for a nearby urban market. In some wheat-producing areas, a shift was also made to corn and hogs, which were easier to market; many of the more acute problems were settled, and the center of agrarian discontent moved farther west. As it did so, there was also some change in the direction of protest demands, from railroad regulation to currency reform. The declining price level continued to be the major source of trouble for farmers, and, after six new Western states with strong silver movements were admitted to the Union in 1889–90, a monetary grievance presented itself to them with growing force. When the People's (or Populist) Party was first organized, during the late 1880's and early 1890's, it had a broad and balanced program of reform, including land, credit, and transportation policies. In 1892, when the Populist Platform (Document 4) was presented to the national party convention in Omaha, the railroad plank was still greeted as enthusiastically as the plank on currency. But in a few years, by 1895, enthusiasm for free silver as a cure-all for agrarian ills had overshadowed all other demands. The movement for an enlargement of the currency supply through buying silver for coinage was not new; the major parties had made a concession to it as early as the Bland-Allison Act of 1878. Then the Sherman Silver Purchase Act had been passed in 1890; it required that the Treasury purchase 4,500,000 ounces of silver monthly, which was to be used as the basis for the issuance of legal tender notes. But when the panic of 1893 showed signs of developing into a major depression, orthodox economists pointed out that the alarming decline in the United States gold reserve, which had helped start the panic, was in good part caused by the Sherman Silver Purchase Act. President Cleveland called Congress into special session and asked for emergency repeal of the measure (Document 5). Silver advocates in Congress were outraged over the blow to silver and the contraction of the currency, but after heated debate, Congress repealed the act in October 1893. Cleveland's own party was hopelessly split over the issue, however, and the West and South continued to demand unlimited coinage of silver. The cause of free silver found a tremendously effective spokesman in "Coin" Harvey, whose *Coin's Financial School*, published in 1894 (Document 6), was weak in theory, but strong in its expression of silverite demands and hatred of the gold standard, Wall Street bankers, and, at the end of the chain, the British Empire, which silver men believed to be the power behind gold. Orthodox refutations of "Coin" were published (Document 7); but the cry for free silver, in part financed by silver mine owners, swept the forces of dissent, and dominated the Democratic as well as the Populist party. The Democratic convention of 1896 repudiated Cleveland, and as its presidential candidate chose young William Jennings Bryan of Nebraska, whose Cross of Gold speech (Document 8) had rocked the convention. The Bryan-McKinley campaign of 1896 was one of the most hard-fought in American history; Bryan's energy was heroic, but he could not overcome the hostility against him in the East, nor the fear felt by many people throughout the country of the dangers of free silver. Even in Kansas, then a Populist stronghold, a young editor from Emporia, William Allen White, attracted nationwide attention with a savage editorial (Document 9) attacking the Populists for their lack of both respectability and responsibility. Controversial as some of the Populist and silverite remedies were, however, they were aimed at pressing grievances. Many of their demands, which seemed so outrageous in the 1890's, were at least given serious consideration in the Progressive era (Part V), and some were actually incorporated into the law of the land.

DOCUMENT 1

RESOLUTIONS OF A MEETING OF THE ILLINOIS STATE FARMERS' ASSOCIATION,

APRIL 1873

These resolutions, passed in Springfield at a convention of the Illinois State Farmers' Association, typify the grievances the Granger movement tried to remedy, particularly the farmers' complaints against the railroads and their demand for effective state regulation.

Resolved, By the Farmers of Illinois, in Mass Meeting Assembled, That all chartered monopolies, not regulated and controlled by law, have proved in that respect detrimental to the public prosperity, corrupting in their management, and dangerous to republican institutions.

Resolved, That the railways of the world, except in those countries where they have been held under the strict regulation and supervision of the government, have proved themselves arbitrary, extortionate and as opposed to free institutions and free commerce between states as were the feudal barons of the middle ages.

Resolved, That we hold, declare and resolve, that this despotism, which defies our laws, plunders our shippers, impoverishes our people, and corrupts our government, shall be subdued and made to subserve the public interest at whatever cost. . . .

Resolved, That in view of the present extortions, we look with alarm upon the future of an interest which can combine in the hands of a few men a capital of nearly $250,000,000, and we believe it essential to the prosperity of all classes that this contest continue until these corporations acknowledge the supremacy of law.

Resolved, That we regard it as the undoubted power, and the imperative duty of the legislature, to pass laws fixing reasonable maximum rates for freight and passengers, without classification of roads, and that we urge upon our General Assembly the passage of such laws. . . .

Resolved, That we urge the passage of a bill enforcing the principle that railroads are public highways, and requiring railroads to make connections with all roads whose tracks meet or cross their own, and to receive and transmit cars and trains offered over their roads at reasonable maximum rates, whether offered at such crossings, or at stations along their roads, and empowering the making of connections by municipal corporations for that purpose, and for the public use. . . .

Resolved, That we indorse most fully the action of those who tender legal rates of fare upon the railroads, and refuse to pay more; and that it is the duty of the Legislature to provide by law for the defense by the State of Illinois of suits commenced, or that hereafter may be commenced, by railroad companies against individuals who have in good faith insisted, or hereafter may insist, upon the right to ride on railroads at legal rates.

Resolved, That the presentation of railroad passes to our legislators, whatever may be the spirit and intent with which they are accepted, are demoralizing . . . ; and we look to our legislature, now in session, to rise above personal considerations of pecuniary interest or convenience, and to pass a law making it a misdemeanor for any Senator, or other State or county officers, to accept any railroad pass. . . .

Whereas, The Constitution of 1848, Article X, prohibits the legislature from granting special railroad charters . . . it is extremely doubtful whether any railroad charter granted since April 1, 1848, by the legislature of Illinois, is of any validity, and that the vested rights of railroad monopolies in this State exist only by assumption of the monopolies and the suffering of the people. . . .

Whereas, The Constitution of 1870, Article XI, Section 13, prohibits any railroad company from issuing watered stock . . . and whereas, this article of the Constitution has probably been violated by nearly all the railroad companies in the state; therefore, *Resolved,* that it is the duty of the railroad commissioners to look carefully into this matter, and to commence proceedings in all clear cases . . . against all railroad companies which have disregarded this important provision of the organic law of the State. . . .

Resolved, That we are in favor of the immediate repeal of the protective duties on iron, steel, lumber, and all materials which enter into the construction of railroad cars, steamships, sailing vessels, agricultural implements, etc., and that we urge upon Congress immediate action for this purpose, that cheap railroads and cheap ships are necessary to cheap freights; and that we invite the railroad companies to co-operate with us to that end.

DOCUMENT 2

MUNN v. ILLINOIS
1877

This case involved the right of the Illinois legislature to prescribe maximum charges for the storage of grain. Its implications, however, were far more sweeping, because it directly affected the constitutionality of state railroad regulation as well. The case arose because nine business firms acting together were able to fix the prices of storage and handling in Chicago grain elevators and warehouses, through which the produce of a vast middle-western farming area had to pass on its way to market. The Illinois legislature passed a law regulating warehouse storage charges. When the Illinois law was tested in the Supreme Court, the problem before the Court was to find a legal basis for regulating such property as grain elevators and railroads without setting a precedent for the regulation of all private property. For precedent, Chief Justice Morrison R. Waite went back to Sir Matthew Hale, a seventeenth-century English jurist, who had laid down the principle that property "affected with a public interest" ceases to be an object of private law alone and becomes liable to public regulation. Having applied this doctrine to elevators, Chief Justice Waite in other cases applied it to railroads as well. The Munn decision set a legal foundation for regulation, but its value was whittled down by later decisions which took their cue from Justice Field's dissent (Document 3) in this case.

WAITE, C. J. The question to be determined in this case is whether the general assembly of Illinois can, under the limitations upon the legislative powers of the States imposed by the Constitution of the United States, fix by law the maximum of charges for the storage of grain in warehouses at Chicago and other places in the State having not less than one hundred thousand inhabitants, "in which grain is stored in bulk, and in which the grain of different owners is mixed together, or in which grain is stored in such a manner that the identity of different lots or parcels cannot be accurately preserved."

It is claimed that such a law is repugnant—

1. To that part of sect. 8, art. I, of the Constitution of the United States which confers upon Congress the power "to regulate commerce with foreign nations and among the several States;"

2. To that part of sect. 9 of the same article which provides that "no preference shall be given by any regulation of commerce or revenue to the ports of one State over those of another;" and

3. To that part of amendment 14 which ordains that no State shall "deprive any person of life, liberty, or property, without due process of law, nor deny to any person within its jurisdiction the equal protection of the laws."

We will consider the last of these objections first. . . .

The Constitution contains no definition of the word "deprive," as used in the Fourteenth Amendment. To determine its signification, therefore, it is necessary to ascertain the effect which usage has given it, when employed in the same or a like connection.

While this provision of the amendment is new in the Constitution of the United States, as a limitation upon the powers of the States, it is old as a principle of civilized government. It is found in Magna Charta, and, in substance if not in form, in nearly or quite all the constitutions that have been from time to time adopted by the several States of the Union. By the Fifth Amendment, it was introduced into the Constitution of the United States

as a limitation upon the powers of the national government, and by the Fourteenth, as a guarantee against any
encroachment upon an acknowledged right of citizenship
by the legislatures of the States. . . .

When one becomes a member of society, he eces-
sarily parts with some rights or privileges which, as an
individual not affected by his relations to others, he might
retain. "A body politic," as aptly defined in the preamble
of the Constitution of Massachusetts, "is a social compact
by which the whole people covenants with each citizen,
and each citizen with the whole people, that all shall be
governed by certain laws for the common good." This
does not confer power upon the whole people to control
rights which are purely and exclusively private . . . but
it does authorize the establishment of laws requiring each
citizen to so conduct himself, and so use his own property,
as not unnecessarily to injure another. . . . From this
source came the police powers, which, as was said by Mr.
Chief Justice Taney in the *License Cases* . . . "are
nothing more or less than the powers of government inherent in every sovereignty, . . . that is to say, . . . the
power to govern men and things." Under these powers the
government regulates the conduct of its citizens one towards another, and the manner in which each shall use
his own property, when such regulation becomes necessary
for the public good.

From this it is apparent that, down to the time of the
adoption of the Fourteenth Amendment, it was not supposed that statutes regulating the use, or even the price of
the use, of private property necessarily deprived an
owner of his property without due process of law. Under
some circumstances they may, but not under all. The
amendment does not change the law in this particular:
it simply prevents the States from doing that which will
operate as such a deprivation.

This brings us to inquire as to the principles upon
which this power of regulation rests, in order that we may
determine what is within and what without its operative
effect. Looking, then, to the common law, from whence
came the right which the Constitution protects, we find that
when private property is "affected with a public interest,

it ceases to be *juris privati* only." This was said by Lord Chief Justice Hale more than two hundred years ago, in his treatise *De Portibus Maris* . . . and has been accepted without objection as an essential element in the law of property ever since. Property does become clothed with a public interest when used in a manner to make it of public consequence, and affect the community at large. When, therefore, one devotes his property to a use in which the public has an interest, he, in effect, grants to the public an interest in that use, and must submit to be controlled by the public for the common good, to the extent of the interest he has thus created. He may withdraw his grant by discontinuing the use; but, so long as he maintains the use, he must submit to the control. . . .

From the same source comes the power to regulate the charges of common carriers, which was done in England as long ago as the third year of the reign of William and Mary, and continued until within a comparatively recent period. . . .

Common carriers exercise a sort of public office, and have duties to perform in which the public is interested. . . . Their business is, therefore, "affected with a public interest," within the meaning of the doctrine which Lord Hale has so forcibly stated.

But we need not go further. Enough has already been said to show that, when private property is devoted to a public use, it is subject to public regulation. It remains only to ascertain whether the warehouses of these plaintiffs in error, and the business which is carried on there, come within the operation of this principle. . . .

Neither is it a matter of any moment that no precedent can be found for a statute precisely like this. It is conceded that the business is one of recent origin, that its growth has been rapid, and that it is already of great importance. And it must also be conceded that it is a business in which the whole public has a direct and positive interest. It presents, therefore, a case for the application of a long-known and well-established principle in social science, and this statute simply extends the law so as to meet this new development of commercial progress. There is no attempt to compel these owners to grant the public

an interest in their property, but to decline their obligations, if they use it in this particular manner. . . .

It is insisted, however, that the owner of property is
entitled to a reasonable compensation for its use, even
though it be clothed with a public interest, and that what
is reasonable is a judicial and not a legislative question.

As has already been shown, the practice has been
otherwise. In countries where the common law prevails, it
has been customary from time immemorial for the legislature to declare what shall be a reasonable compensation
under such circumstances, or perhaps more properly
speaking, to fix a maximum beyond which any charge
made would be unreasonable. Undoubtedly in mere private
contracts, relating to matters in which the public has no
interest, what is reasonable must be ascertained judicially.
But this is because the legislature has no control over
such a contract. So, too, in matters which do not affect the
public interest, and as to which legislative control may be
exercised . . . the courts must determine what is reasonable. The controlling fact is the power to regulate at all.
If that exists, the right to establish the maximum of
charge, as one of the means of regulation, is implied. . . .

We know that this is a power which may be abused;
but that is no argument against its existence. For protection against abuses by legislatures the people must resort
to the polls, not to the courts. . . .

We come now to consider the effect upon this
statute of the power of Congress to regulate commerce. . . .

The warehouses of these plaintiffs in error are
situated and their business carried on exclusively within
the limits of the State of Illinois. They are used as instruments by those engaged in State as well as those engaged
in inter-state commerce. . . . Incidentally they may become connected with inter-state commerce, but not necessarily so. Their regulation is a thing of domestic concern
and, certainly, until Congress acts in reference to their
inter-state relations, the State may exercise all the powers
of government over them, even though in so doing it may
indirectly operate upon commerce outside its immediate
jurisdiction. . . .

DOCUMENT 3

STEPHEN J. FIELD, DISSENTING OPINION IN *MUNN* v. *ILLINOIS*, 1877

This dissent became one of the most important in the history of the Supreme Court when it began to influence subsequent decisions governing the regulatory power of the states. Justice Field denounced the decision as "subversive of the rights of private property" and of "the constitutional prohibition that no state shall deprive any person of his property except by due process of law." In later years the Court receded from Chief Justice Waite's position that for protection against legislative abuse of the regulatory power "the people must resort to the polls, not to the courts." In 1890, the Court dealt a vital blow to the doctrine of Munn v. Illinois; in the Minnesota Rate Case (Chicago, Minneapolis and St. Paul Railroad Co. v. Minnesota) it declared unconstitutional a Minnesota law providing that the ruling of a state regulatory commission as to the reasonableness of rates should be final, and that no appeal could be made to the courts. The Court found this provision a violation of due process of law, and said that the question of the reasonableness of a rate "is eminently a question for judicial investigation." In Reagan v. Farmers' Loan and Trust Co. (1894), the Court asserted its right not only to pass on the reasonableness of a rate but, further, to award returns to shippers who it found had paid excessive charges. Finally, in Smyth v. Ames (1898) it declared that courts could not only decide on reasonableness but also on whether the designated rate gave the business firm a fair return on a fair valuation of its investment. Thus by the end of the century, the Court had moved to a position similar to Field's in 1877; and many new developments (Part V, Documents 7 and 8)

*had to take place before railroads could be regulated
effectively by the federal government.*

The question presented, therefore, is one of the greatest
importance,—whether it is within the competency of a
State to fix the compensation which an individual may
receive for the use of his own property in his private
business, and for his services in connection with it.

The declaration of the Constitution [of the state of
Illinois] of 1870, that private buildings used for private
purposes shall be deemed public institutions, does not
make them so. The receipt and storage of grain in a
building erected by private means for that purpose does
not constitute the building a public warehouse. There is
no magic in the language, though used by a constitutional
convention, which can change a private business into a
public one, or alter the character of the building in which
the business is transacted. A tailor's or a shoemaker's
shop would still retain its private character, even though
the assembled wisdom of the State should declare, by
organic act or legislative ordinance, that such a place was
a public workshop, and that the workmen were public
tailors or public shoemakers. One might as well attempt
to change the nature of colors, by giving them a new
designation. The defendants were no more public ware-
housemen, as justly observed by counsel, than the merchant
who sells his merchandise to the public is a public
merchant, or the blacksmith who shoes horses for the
public is a public blacksmith; and it was a strange notion
that by calling them so they would be brought under
legislative control.

The Supreme Court of the State—divided, it is true,
by three to two of its members—has held that this legislation was a legitimate exercise of State authority over
private business; and the Supreme Court of the United
States, two only of its members dissenting, has decided
that there is nothing in the Constitution of the United
States, or its recent amendments, which impugns its
validity. It is, therefore, with diffidence I presume to
question the soundness of the decision.

The validity of the legislation was, among other
grounds, assailed in the State court as being in conflict

with that provision of the State Constitution which declares that no person shall be deprived of life, liberty, or
property without due process of law, and with that
provision of the Fourteenth Amendment of the Federal
Constitution which imposes a similar restriction upon the
action of the State. . . . In this court the legislation was
also assailed on the same ground, our jurisdiction arising
upon the clause of the Fourteenth Amendment, ordain-
ing that no State shall deprive any person of life, liberty,
or property without due process of law. But it would
seem from its opinion that the court holds that property
loses something of its private character when employed in
such a way as to be generally useful. The doctrine
declared is that property "becomes clothed with a public
interest when used in a manner to make it of public consequence, and affect the community at large;" and from
such clothing the right of the legislative is deduced to
control the use of the property, and to determine the
compensation which the owner may receive for it. When
Sir Matthew Hale, and the sages of the law in his day,
spoke of property as affected by a public interest, and
ceasing from that cause to be *juris privati* solely, that is,
ceasing to be held merely in private right, they referred
to property dedicated by the owner to public uses, or to
property the use of which was granted by the government,
or in connection with which special privileges were conferred. Unless the property was thus dedicated, or some
right bestowed by the government was held with the
property, either by specific grant or by prescription of so
long a time as to imply a grant originally, the property
was not affected by any public interest so as to be taken
out of the category of property held in private right. But
it is not in any such sense that the terms "clothing
property with a public interest" are used in this case.
From the nature of the business under consideration—the
storage of grain—which, in any sense in which the words
can be used, is a private business, in which the public are
interested only as they are interested in the storage of
other products of the soil, or in articles of manufacture, it
is clear that the court intended to declare that, whenever
one devotes his property to a business which is useful
to the public,—"affects the community at large,"—the

legislature can regulate the compensation which the owner may receive for its use, and for his own services in connection with it. "When, therefore," says the court, "one devotes his property to a use in which the public has an interest, he, in effect, grants to the public an interest in that use, and must submit to be controlled by the public for the common good, to the exent of the interest he has thus created. He may withdraw his grant by discontinuing the use; but, so long as he maintains the use, he must submit to the control." The building used by the defendants was for the storage of grain: in such storage, says the court, the public has an interest; therefore the defendants, by devoting the building to that storage, have granted the public an interest in that use, and must submit to have their compensation regulated by the legislature.

If this be sound law, if there be no protection, either in the principles upon which our republican government is founded, or in the prohibitions of the Constitution against such invasion of private rights, all property and all business in the State are held at the mercy of a majority of its legislature. The public has no greater interest in the use of buildings for the storage of grain than it has in the use of buildings for the residences of families, nor, indeed, any thing like so great an interest; and, according to the doctrine announced, the legislature may fix the rent of all tenements used for residences, without reference to the cost of their erection. If the owner does not like the rates prescribed, he may cease renting his houses. . . . Indeed, there is hardly an enterprise or business engaging the attention and labor of any considerable portion of the community, in which the public has not an interest in the sense in which that term is used by the court in its opinion; and the doctrine which allows the legislature to interfere with and regulate the charges which the owners of property thus employed shall make for its use, that is, the rates at which all these different kinds of business shall be carried on, has never before been asserted, so far as I am aware, by any judicial tribunal in the United States.

The doctrine of the State court, that no one is deprived of his property, within the meaning of the constitutional inhibition, so long as he retains its title and possession, and the doctrine of this court, that, whenever one's property is used in such a manner as to affect the community at large, it becomes by that fact clothed with a public interest, and ceases to be *juris privati* only, appear to me to destroy, for all useful purposes, the efficacy of the constitutional guarantee. All that is beneficial in property arises from its use, and the fruits of that use; and whatever deprives a person of them deprives him of all that is desirable or valuable in the title and possession. If the constitutional guarantee extends no further than to prevent a deprivation of title and possession, and allows a deprivation of use, and the fruits of that use, it does not merit the encomiums it has received. Unless I have misread the history of the provision now incorporated into all our State constitutions, and by the Fifth and Fourteenth Amendments into our Federal Constitution, and have misunderstood the interpretation it has received, it is not thus limited in its scope, and thus impotent for good. It has a much more extended operation than either court, State, or Federal has given to it. The provision, it is to be observed, places property under the same protection as life and liberty. Except by due process of law, no State can deprive any person of either. The provision has been supposed to secure to every individual the essential conditions for the pursuit of happiness; and for that reason has not been heretofore, and should never be, construed in any narrow or restricted sense.

No State "shall deprive any person of life, liberty, or property without due process of law," says the Fourteenth Amendment to the Constitution. By the term "life," as here used, something more is meant than mere animal existence. The inhibition against its deprivation extends to all those limbs and faculties by which life is enjoyed. The provision equally prohibits the mutilation of the body by the amputation of an arm or leg, or the putting out of an eye, or the destruction of any other organ of the body through which the soul communicates with the outer world. The deprivation not only of life, but of whatever God has given to every one with life, for its growth and enjoyment, is prohibited by the provision in question, if its efficacy be not frittered away by judicial decision.

By the term "liberty," as used in the provision, something more is meant than mere freedom from physical restraint or the bounds of a prison. It means freedom to go where one may choose, and to act in such manner, not inconsistent with the equal rights of others, as his judgment may dictate for the promotion of his happiness; that is, to pursue such callings and avocations as may be most suitable to develop his capacities, and give to them their highest enjoyment.

The same liberal construction which is required for the protection of life and liberty, in all particulars in which life and liberty are of any value, should be applied to the protection of private property. If the legislature of a State under pretence of providing for the public good, or for any other reason, can determine, against the consent of the owner, the uses to which private property shall be devoted, or the prices which the owner shall receive for its uses, it can deprive him of the property as completely as by a special act for its confiscation or destruction. . . .

DOCUMENT 4

POPULIST PARTY PLATFORM,
JULY 4, 1892

This platform, adopted by the People's (Populist) Party at its first national convention in Omaha, was put together largely from statements already made by other conventions of the Farmers' Alliances since 1889. The preamble, composed by the flamboyant Minnesota writer and Populist leader, Ignatius Donnelly, had first been presented by him at the St. Louis convention in February 1892. The platform, an excellent statement of Populist philosophy and aims, was greeted by the Omaha convention with a tremendous demonstration that was likened by a reporter to "the enthusiastic Bastille demonstration in France."

Assembled upon the one hundred and sixteenth anniversary of the Declaration of Independence, the People's Party of

America, in their first national convention, invoking upon their action the blessing of Almighty God, put forth in the name and on behalf of the people of this country, the following preamble and declaration of principles:

The conditions which surround us best justify our co-operation; we meet in the midst of a nation brought to the verge of moral, political, and material ruin. Corruption dominates the ballot-box, the Legislatures, the Congress, and touches even the ermine of the bench. The people are demoralized; most of the States have been compelled to isolate the voters at the polling places to prevent universal intimidation or bribery. The newspapers are largely subsidized or muzzled, public opinion silenced, business prostrated, homes covered with mortgages, labor impoverished, and the land concentrating in the hands of capitalists. The urban workmen are denied the right of organization for self-protection, imported pauperized labor beats down their wages, a hireling standing army, unrecognized by our laws, is established to shoot them down, and they are rapidly degenerating into European conditions. The fruits of the toil of millions are boldly stolen to build up colossal fortunes for a few, unprecedented in the history of mankind; and the possessors of these, in turn, despise the Republic and endanger liberty. From the same prolific womb of governmental injustice we breed the two great classes—tramps and millionaires.

The national power to create money is appropriated to enrich bond-holders; a vast public debt payable in legal-tender currency has been funded into gold-bearing bonds, thereby adding millions to the burdens of the people.

Silver, which has been accepted as coin since the dawn of history, has been demonetized to add to the purchasing power of gold by decreasing the value of all forms of property as well as human labor, and the supply of currency is purposely abridged to fatten usurers, bankrupt enterprise, and enslave industry. A vast conspiracy against mankind has been organized on two continents, and it is rapidly taking possession of the world. If not met and overthrown at once it forebodes terrible social convulsions, the destruction of civilization, or the establishment of an absolute despotism.

We have witnessed for more than a quarter of a century the struggles of the two great political parties for power and plunder, while grievous wrongs have been inflicted upon the suffering people. We charge that the controlling influences dominating both these parties have permitted the existing dreadful conditions to develop without serious effort to prevent or restrain them. Neither do they now promise us any substantial reform. They have agreed together to ignore, in the coming campaign, every issue but one. They propose to drown the outcries of a plundered people with the uproar of a sham battle over the tariff, so that capitalists, corporations, national banks, rings, trusts, watered stock, the demonetization of silver and the oppressions of the usurers may all be lost sight of. They propose to sacrifice our homes, lives, and children on the altar of mammon; to destroy the multitude in order to secure corruption funds from the millionaires.

Assembled on the anniversary of the birthday of the nation, and filled with the spirit of the grand general and chieftain who established our independence, we seek to restore the government of the Republic to the hands of the "plain people," with which class it originated. We assert our purposes to be identical with the purposes of the National Constitution; to form a more perfect union and establish justice, insure domestic tranquillity, provide for the common defence, promote the general welfare, and secure the blessings of liberty for ourselves and our posterity.

We declare that this Republic can only endure as a free government while built upon the love of the people for each other and for the nation; that it cannot be pinned together by bayonets; that the Civil War is over, and that every passion and resentment which grew out of it must die with it, and that we must be in fact, as we are in name, one united brotherhood of free [men].

Our country finds itself confronted by conditions for which there is no precedent in the history of the world; our annual agricultural productions amount to billions of dollars in value, which must, within a few weeks or months, be exchanged for billions of dollars' worth of commodities consumed in their production; the existing currency supply is wholly inadequate to make this exchange; the results are falling prices, the formation of combines and rings, the impoverishment of the producing class. We pledge ourselves that if given power we will labor to correct these evils by wise and reasonable legislation, in accordance with the terms of our platform.

We believe that the powers of government—in other words, of the people—should be expanded (as in the case of the postal service) as rapidly and as far as the good sense of an intelligent people and the teachings of experience shall justify, to the end that oppression, injustice, and poverty shall eventually cease in the land.

While our sympathies as a party of reform are naturally upon the side of every proposition which will tend to make men intelligent, virtuous, and temperate, we nevertheless regard these questions, important as they are, as secondary to the great issues now pressing for solution, and upon which not only our individual prosperity but the very existence of free institutions depend; and we ask all men to first help us to determine whether we are to have a republic to administer before we differ as to the conditions upon which it is to be administered, believing that the forces of reform this day organized will never cease to move forward until every wrong is righted and equal rights and equal privileges securely established for all the men and women of this country. We declare, therefore—

First.—That the union of the labor forces of the United States this day consummated shall be permanent and perpetual; may its spirit enter into all hearts for the salvation of the Republic and the uplifting of mankind.

Second.—Wealth belongs to him who creates it, and every dollar taken from industry without an equivalent is robbery. "If any will not work, neither shall he eat." The interests of rural and civil labor are the same; their enemies are identical.

Third.—We believe that the time has come when the railroad corporations will either own the people or the people must own the railroads; and should the government enter upon the work of owning and managing all railroads, we should favor an amendment to the constitution by which all persons engaged in the government service shall be placed under a civil-service regulation of the most rigid character, so as to prevent the increase of the power of the national administration by the use of such additional government employes.

FINANCE.—We demand a national currency, safe, sound, and flexible issued by the general government only, a full legal tender for all debts, public and private, and that without the use of banking corporations; a just, equitable, and efficient means of distribution direct to the people, at a tax not to exceed 2 per cent, per annum, to be provided as set forth in the sub-treasury plan of the Farmers' Alliance, or a better system; also by payments in discharge of its obligations for public improvements.

1. We demand free and unlimited coinage of silver and gold at the present legal ratio of 16 to 1.
2. We demand that the amount of circulating medium be speedily increased to not less than $50 per capita.
3. We demand a graduated income tax.
4. We believe that the money of the country should be kept as much as possible in the hands of the people, and hence we demand that all State and national revenues shall be limited to the necessary expenses of the government, economically and honestly administered.
5. We demand that postal savings banks be established by the government for the safe deposit of the earnings of the people and to facilitate exchange.

TRANSPORTATION.—Transportation being a means of exchange and a public necessity, the government should own and operate the railroads in the interest of the people. The telegraph and telephone, like the post-office system, being a necessity for the transmission of news, should be owned and operated by the government in the interest of the people.

LAND.—The land, including all the natural sources of wealth, is the heritage of the people, and should not be monopolized for speculative purposes, and alien ownership of land should be prohibited. All land now held by railroads and other corporations in excess of their actual needs, and all lands now owned by aliens should be reclaimed by the government and held for actual settlers only.

Supplementary Resolutions from Platform Committee

Whereas, Other questions have been presented for our consideration, we hereby submit the following, not as a part of the Platform of the People's Party, but as resolutions expressive of the sentiment of this Convention.

1. RESOLVED, That we demand a free ballot and a fair count in all elections, and pledge ourselves to secure it to every legal voter without Federal intervention, through the adoption by the States of the unperverted Australian or secret ballot system.
2. RESOLVED, That the revenue derived from a graduated income tax should be applied to the reduction of the burden of taxation now levied upon the domestic industries of this country.
3. RESOLVED, That we pledge our support to fair and liberal pensions to ex-Union soldiers and sailors.
4. RESOLVED, That we condemn the fallacy of protecting American labor under the present system, which opens our ports to the pauper and criminal classes of the world and crowds out our wage-earners; and we denounce the present ineffective laws against contract labor, and demand the further restriction of undesirable immigration.
5. RESOLVED, That we cordially sympathize with the efforts of organized workingmen to shorten the hours of labor, and demand a rigid enforcement of the existing eight-hour law on Government work, and ask that a penalty clause be added to the said law.
6. RESOLVED, That we regard the maintenance of a large standing army of mercenaries, known as the Pinkerton system, as a menace to our liberties, and we demand its abolition; and we condemn the recent invasion of the Territory of Wyoming by the hired assassins of plutocracy, assisted by Federal officials.
7. RESOLVED, That we commend to the favorable consideration of the people and to the reform press

the legislative system known as the initiative and
referendum.

8. RESOLVED, That we favor a constitutional provision
limiting the office of President and Vice-President
to one term, and providing for the election of
Senators of the United States by a direct vote of
the people.

9. RESOLVED, That we oppose any subsidy or national
aid to any private corporation for any purpose.

10. RESOLVED, That this convention sympathizes with
the Knights of Labor and their righteous contest
with the tyrannical combine of clothing manufacturers of Rochester, and declare it to be the
duty of all who hate tyranny and oppression to
refuse to purchase the goods made by the said
manufacturers, or to patronize any merchants who
sell such goods.

DOCUMENT 5

GROVER CLEVELAND, MESSAGE ON THE
REPEAL OF THE SHERMAN SILVER
PURCHASE ACT,
AUGUST 8, 1893

*Despite the mounting demand for free coinage of
silver, Cleveland firmly believed that the silver purchases under the act of 1890 were in good part
responsible for the panic that was causing distress in
1893. He called Congress into special session during
the summer and sent them this tactfully phrased,
but widely unpopular message, calling for the repeal
of the Sherman Silver Purchase Act. All but the first
two paragraphs were written by Attorney-General
Richard Olney, but Cleveland went through Olney's
draft to soften some of the Attorney-General's offensive references to silver advocates.*

The existence of an alarming and extraordinary business
situation, involving the welfare and prosperity of all our

people, has constrained me to call together in extra session the people's representatives in Congress, to the end that through a wise and patriotic exercise of the legislative duty, with which they solely are charged, present evils may be mitigated and dangers threatening the future may be averted.

Our unfortunate financial plight is not the result of untoward events nor of conditions related to our natural resources, nor is it traceable to any of the afflictions which frequently check national growth and prosperity. With plenteous crops, with abundant promise of remunerative production and manufacture, with unusual invitation to safe investment, and with satisfactory assurance to business enterprise, suddenly financial distrust and fear have sprung up on every side. . . . Values supposed to be fixed are fast becoming conjectural, and loss and failure have invaded every branch of business.

I believe these things are principally chargeable to Congressional legislation touching the purchase and coinage of silver by the General Government.

This legislation is embodied in a statute passed on the 14th day of July, 1890, which was the culmination of much agitation on the subject involved, and which may be considered a truce, after a long struggle, between the advocates of free silver coinage and those intending to be more conservative. . . .

This law provides that in payment for the 4,500,000 ounces of silver bullion which the Secretary of the Treasury is commanded to purchase monthly there shall be issued Treasury notes redeemable on demand in gold or silver coin, at the discretion of the Secretary of the Treasury, and that said notes may be reissued. It is, however, declared in the act to be "the established policy of the United States to maintain the two metals on a parity with each other upon the present legal ratio or such ratio as may be provided by law." This declaration so controls the action of the Secretary of the Treasury as to prevent his exercising the discretion nominally vested in him if by such action the parity between gold and silver may be disturbed. Manifestly a refusal by the Secretary to pay these Treasury notes in gold if demanded would necessarily result in their discredit and depreciation as obliga-

tions payable only in silver, and would destroy the parity
between the two metals by establishing a discrimination in
favor of gold. . . .

The policy necessarily adopted of paying these notes
in gold has not spared the gold reserve of $100,000,000
long ago set aside by the Government for the redemption
of other notes, for this fund has already been subjected to
the payment of new obligations amounting to about
$150,000,000 on account of silver purchases, and has as a
consequence for the first time since its creation been
encroached upon.

We have thus made the depletion of our gold easy
and have tempted other and more appreciative nations to
add it to their stock. . . .

Unless Government bonds are to be constantly
issued and sold to replenish our exhausted gold, only to be
again exhausted, it is apparent that the operation of the
silver-purchase law now in force leads in the direction of
the entire substitution of silver for the gold in the Government Treasury, and that this must be followed by the
payment of all Government obligations in depreciated
silver.

At this stage gold and silver must part company and
the Government must fail in its established policy to
maintain the two metals on a parity with each other.
Given over to the exclusive use of a currency greatly
depreciated according to the standard of the commercial
world, we could no longer claim a place among nations of
the first class, nor could our Government claim a performance of its obligation, so far as such an obligation has
been imposed upon it, to provide for the use of the people
the best and safest money.

If, as many of its friends claim, silver ought to
occupy a larger place in our currency and the currency of
the world through general international coöperation and
agreement, it is obvious that the United States will not be
in a position to gain a hearing in favor of such an arrangement so long as we are willing to continue our attempt
to accomplish the result single-handed. . . .

The people of the United States are entitled to a
sound and stable currency and to money recognized as
such on every exchange and in every market of the world.

Their Government has no right to injure them by financial experiments opposed to the policy and practice of other civilized states, nor is it justified in permitting an exaggerated and unreasonable reliance on our national strength and ability to jeopardize the soundness of the people's money.

This matter rises above the plane of party politics. It vitally concerns every business and calling and enters every household in the land. There is one important aspect of the subject which especially should never be overlooked. At times like the present, when the evils of unsound finance threaten us, the speculator may anticipate a harvest gathered from the misfortune of others, the capitalist may protect himself by hoarding or may even find profit in the fluctuations of values; but the wage earner—the first to be injured by a depreciated currency and the last to receive the benefit of its correction—is practically defenseless. He relies for work upon the ventures of confident and contented capital. This failing him, his condition is without alleviation, for he can neither prey on the misfortunes of others nor hoard his labor. . . .

It is of the utmost importance that such relief as Congress can afford in the existing situation be afforded at once. The maxim "He gives twice who gives quickly" is directly applicable. It may be true that the embarrassments from which the business of the country is suffering arise as much from evils apprehended as from those actually existing. We may hope, too, that calm counsels will prevail, and that neither the capitalists nor the wage earners will give way to unreasoning panic and sacrifice their property or their interests under the influence of exaggerated fears. Nevertheless, every day's delay in removing one of the plain and principal causes of the present state of things enlarges the mischief already done and increases the responsibility of the Government for its existence. Whatever else the people have a right to expect from Congress, they may certainly demand that legislation condemned by the ordeal of three years' disastrous experience shall be removed from the statute books as soon as their representatives can legitimately deal with it.

It was my purpose to summon Congress in special session early in the coming September, that we might enter promptly upon the work of tariff reform, which the true interests of the country clearly demand, which so large a majority of the people, as shown by their suffrages, desire and expect, and to the accomplishment of which every effort of the present Administration is pledged. But while tariff reform has lost nothing of its immediate and permanent importance and must in the near future engage the attention of Congress, it has seemed to me that the financial condition of the country should at once and before all other subjects be considered by your honorable body.

I earnestly recommend the prompt repeal of the provisions of the act passed July 14, 1890, authorizing the purchase of silver bullion, and that other legislative action may put beyond all doubt or mistake the intention and the ability of the Government to fulfill its pecuniary obligations in money universally recognized by all civilized countries.

DOCUMENT 6

W. H. ("COIN") HARVEY, *COIN'S FINANCIAL SCHOOL*, 1894

"Coin" Harvey's pamphlet was a document, which can be compared in effect, if not in intellectual quality, with the greatest propaganda efforts in American history. A Virginian by birth, Harvey had failed repeatedly in ranching, silver prospecting, and editing; but with this little book he found success at last. His "Professor Coin" taught a school at which the prominent business men and bankers of the day were set straight on free silver. Much of the work was an interchange between "Coin" and his unwilling pupils; the passages selected here represent the substance of "Coin's" argument. Cleverly illustrated and written in plain language, the book caught the fancy of the dis-

> *contented, and in editions at 25 cents, 50 cents, and*
> *$1.00 sold at least 300,000 copies within a year. An-*
> *other 125,000 copies were distributed free by silver*
> *mine owners during Bryan's 1896 campaign. Harvey*
> *wrote other tracts for free silver, but none had the*
> *influence of his first effort.*

Hard times are with us; the country is distracted; very few things are marketable at a price above the cost of production; tens of thousands are out of employment; the jails, penitentiaries, workhouses and insane asylums are full; the gold reserve at Washington is sinking; the government is running at a loss with a deficit in every department; a huge debt hangs like an appalling cloud over the country; taxes have assumed the importance of a mortgage, and 50 per cent of the public revenues are likely to go delinquent; hungered and half-starved men are banding into armies marching toward Washington; the cry of distress is heard on every hand; business is paralyzed; commerce is at a standstill; riots and strikes prevail throughout the land; schemes to remedy our ills when put into execution are smashed like boxcars in a railroad wreck, and Wall Street looks in vain for an excuse to account for the failure of prosperity to return since the repeal of the silver purchase act. . . .

Up to 1873 we were on what was known as a bimetallic basis, but what was in fact a silver basis, with gold as a companion metal enjoying the same privileges as silver, except that silver fixed the unit, and the value of gold was regulated by it. This was bimetallism.

Our forefathers showed much wisdom in selecting silver, of the two metals, out of which to make the unit. Much depended on this decision. For the one selected to represent the unit would thereafter be unchangeable in value. That is, the metal in it could never be worth less than a dollar, for it would be the unit of value itself. The demand for silver in the arts or for money by other nations might make the quantity of silver in a silver dollar sell for more than a dollar, but it could never be worth less than a dollar. Less than itself.

In considering which of these two metals they would thus favor by making it the unit, they were led to adopt silver because it was the most reliable. It was the most favored as money by the people. It was scattered among all the people. Men having a design to injure business by making money scarce, could not easily get hold of all the silver and hide it away, as they could gold. This was the principal reason that led them to the conclusion to select silver, the more stable of the two metals, upon which to fix the unit. It was so much handled by the people and preferred by them, that it was called the people's money.

Gold was considered the money of the rich. It was owned, principally by that class of people, and the poor people seldom handled it, and the very poor people seldom ever saw any of it.

The men who produce the property of the world are the men whose happiness should be consulted. The men who handle this property after it is produced have little regard for the interests of the producers. Their selfishness and greed blind them. Their minds are running in a groove and they cannot see the rights of others.

It is proposed by the bimetallists to remonetize silver, and add it to the quantity of money that is to be used for measuring the value of all other property.

In dollars, at a ratio to gold of sixteen to one, there are about the same number of dollars of silver in the world as gold. The report of the director of our mint says there was in the world in 1890, in the form of silver coin and bullion used as money, $3,820,571,346.

A cubic foot of silver weighs 10,474 troy ounces, and using 371¼ grains to each dollar, this would make a cubic foot of cast silver worth $13,544.

You get this by multiplying the 10,474 by 480, the number of grains in an ounce, and dividing the result by 371¼, the number of grains in a dollar. You then want to divide the $3,820,571,346, the silver of the world, by 13,544, the number of dollars in a cubic foot. It gives 282,085 cubic feet of silver in the world.

Can you comprehend what a quantity of silver this is? I will tell you how. It will make a block of silver sixty-six feet wide, sixty-six feet long, and sixty-six feet high. . . .

We are trying to get at what is the main or underlying cause of our present industrial demoralization, and tariff, pro or con will not account for it. Our decline in values has been going on steadily and persistently since the demonetization of silver. During that period we have had different tariff bills, and of late years a very high tariff schedule; and yet it has had no effect in stopping the fall of prices.

You do not enrich the people of the silver states one cent by the remonetization of silver . . . except in common with the people of the state of Illinois, and of the whole United States.

You increase the value of all property by adding to the number of money units in the land. You make it possible for the debtor to pay his debts; business to start anew, and revivify all the industries of the country, which must remain paralyzed so long as silver as well as all other property is measured by a gold standard.

In the midst of plenty we are in want. . . .

Helpless children and the best womanhood and manhood of America appeal to us for release from a bondage that is destructive of life and liberty. All the nations of the Western Hemisphere turn to their great sister republic for assistance in the emancipation of the people of at least one-half of the world. . . .

It is claimed we must adopt for our money the metal England selects, and can have no independent choice in the matter; let us make the test and find out if it is true. It is not American to give up without trying. If it is true, let us attach England to the United States and blot her name out from among the nations of the earth.

A war with England would be the most popular ever waged on the face of the earth. If it is true that she can dictate the money of the world, and thereby create worldwide misery, it would be the most just war ever waged by man. . . .

England is the creditor nation of the globe, and collects hundreds of millions of dollars in interest annually in gold from the rest of the world. We are paying her two hundred millions yearly in interest. She demands it in gold; the contracts call for it in gold. Do you expect her to voluntarily release any part of it? It has a purchasing power twice what a bimetallic currency would have. She knows it.

The men that control the legislation in England are

citizens of that country with fixed incomes. They are interest gatherers to the amount annually of over one thousand millions of dollars. The men over there holding bimetallic conventions, and passing resolutions have not one-fifth the influence with the law-making power that the bimetallists in the United States have with our Congress and President. No; nothing is to be expected from England.

Whenever property interests and humanity have come in conflict, England has ever been the enemy of human liberty. . . .

The money lenders in the United States, who own substantially all our money, have a selfish interest in maintaining the gold standard. They, too, will not yield. They believe that if the gold standard can survive for a few years longer, the people will get used to it—get used to their poverty—and quietly submit.—To that end they organize international bimetallic committees and say "Wait on England, she will be forced to give us bimetallism." Vain hope! Deception on this subject has been practiced long enough upon a patient and outraged people.

With silver remonetized, and gold at a premium, not one-tenth the hardships could result that now afflict us. . . .

In the impending struggle for the mastery of the commerce of the world, the financial combat between England and the United States cannot be avoided if we are to retain our self-respect, and our people their freedom and prosperity.

The gold standard will give England the commerce and wealth of the world. The bimetallic standard will make the United States the most prosperous nation on the globe.

DOCUMENT 7

JAMES LAURENCE LAUGHLIN, ANSWER TO "COIN" HARVEY, 1895

Laughlin, professor of political economy at the University of Chicago, was one of the outstanding econo-

*mists in the country, and one of the most ardent
defenders of the gold standard. More than once he
tried to expose the crudeness of "Coin" Harvey's
economics. In 1895 he held a public debate with
Harvey, from which this passage is taken.*

I would like to discuss, in connection with the principal
topic of the evening, money as a measure of value. Money
is used as a common denominator, to which other things
are referred for comparison. In order to compare goods
with money there is no more need of as many pieces of
money as there are articles to be compared than there is
of having a quart cup for every quart of milk in existence,
or of having a yard stick in a drygoods store for every
yard of cloth on the shelf. The idea that it is necessary
to multiply the measurements of value is absurd; but it
is of the foremost importance that the measure of values
should not be tampered with, and should not be changed
by legislation to the damage of all transactions based upon
it. Right here is the whole secret of the opposition to silver
as money. Silver has lost its stability of value. It is no
better than any ordinary metal for stability. The action
of India in June, 1893, sends it down 20 per cent. The
mere rumor of the Chinese indemnity sends it up 10 per
cent. The greater or less quantity of money there is roam-
ing about in circulation is no reason why any one gets more
of it. Money, like property, is parted with for a consideration. No matter how many more coins there are coming
from the mint under free coinage and going into the
vaults of the banks to the credit of the mine owners who
own the bullion, there are no more coins in the pockets of
Weary Waggles, who is cooling his heels on the sidewalk
outside the bank. The increased number of handsome
horses and carriages on Michigan avenue does not imply
that I can get them if I have not the wealth to purchase
them with. I must produce, work, turn out goods, and
labor. I must get gold or silver or something equivalent
to the value of the goods, and in that way I shall get them
and in no other way. There is no way of getting rich
by short cuts or by legislation or by merely increasing
the means of exchanging goods, when goods themselves
are the principal thing.

Money is the only machine by which goods are exchanged against one another. No matter how valuable, it is not wanted for itself. It is only a means to an end, like a bridge over a river. Do you suppose that the farmers of this country really believe that with each ton of silver taken out of the mines by the silver law-makers in the Senate that there are created bushels of wheat and bushels of corn and barrels of mess pork? The silver belongs to the mine owners. How will it get into our pockets or the pockets of anyone else? Do we insult any one's penetration by supposing that the Congressional silver kings are going coaching about the country distributing their money for nothing? Our farmers are no fools. They know they can get more money only by producing more commodities to be exchanged for it, and for those commodities they want as good money as any other men in the country have got. . . . Now, as to the free coinage of silver at 16 to 1. Let us get to the point of this question at issue. The market ratio is now about 32 or 34—it skips about so much you can't be really certain. It has been 34 to 1; it is somewhere between 32 and 34 now. If that be the market ratio, and in the mint ratio you propose 16 to 1, there is a premium of sixteen ounces of silver profit on withdrawing every ounce of gold in circulation. Consequently free coinage of silver at 16 to 1 means single silver monometallism; 16 to 1 leads to a single silver standard, and in the language of my opponent, we will start with all the South American countries and Mexico as companions. Free coinage of silver then is absolutely certain to drive all our gold out of circulation. The mere hint of it almost did that in the panic of 1893. May 1, 1895, the first of this month, there were $568,000,000 of gold in circulation. Since gold must be inevitably driven out if free coinage of silver is adopted, there will be no increase in the quantity of money. To the people who support free coinage hoping to increase the quantity of money I say it is perfectly evident on the face of it that it will contract the currency by the total amount of $568,000,000. It could not change prices, therefore, by increasing the amount of the medium of the exchange. That is plain.

The only way it would act would be by increasing the price of everything; because goods would be reckoned in a cheaper medium than that of gold. This my friend admitted this evening. If prices would rise, he says, we would have a glow of satisfaction. It is the kind of glow of satisfaction which comes to the inebriate after he has been supplied with drink, after he has been a long while thirsty. For example, take a pair of gloves worth 100 cents in gold; they would exchange after free coinage for about 210 cents in silver. A dozen eggs, now selling at 15 cents, would sell for about 30 cents, and everything we buy would rise in proportion, since the intrinsic value of the pure silver in the dollar is worth but 51 cents.

As free coinage of silver would inevitably result in a rise of prices it would immediately result in the fall of wages. Its first effect would be to diminish the purchasing power of all our wages. The man who gets $500 or $1,000 a year as a fixed rate of wages or salary will find he could buy just half as much as now. Yes, but someone will say, the employer will raise his wages. Now, will he? But the facts on that point are clear and indisputable. It has been one of the undisputed facts of history that, when prices rise, the wages of labor are the last to advance; and when prices fall, the wages of labor are the first to decline. Free coinage of silver would make all the articles of the laborer's consumption cost him 100 per cent more unless he can get a rise in his wages by dint of strikes and quarrels and all the consequent dissatisfaction arising from friction between the employer and employe! He would be able to buy only one-half as many articles of daily consumption as he had before.

In short, a rise of prices necessarily results in a diminution of the enjoyments of the laboring class until they can force the employers, through a long process of agitation, to make an increase in their wages. Are we willing to sacrifice the interests of the laboring classes to the demands of certain owners of silver mines who hope to hoodwink the people with the cry of more money? This would be, clearly enough, distinct and serious damage.

The damage runs in other directions, however. The proposal to adopt a depreciated standard of value is simply an attempt to transfer from the great mass of the community who have been provident, industrious and successful, a portion of their savings and gains into the pockets of those who have been idle, extravagant, or unfortunate. The provision which has been made for old age, for sickness, for death, for widows and orphans, or by insurance, will be depreciated in the same ratio. No invasion of hostile armies, burning and destroying as they advance, could by any possibility equal the desolation and ruin which would thus be forced upon the great mass of the American people.

Such a depreciation, however—as all experience and history has shown—does not fall alike upon the shrewd and the unsophisticated. The shrewd ones, the bankers, etc., will be easily able to take care of themselves; while we plain people will be robbed of our hard-won earnings without any hope of compensation.

Free coinage of silver at 16:1 would injure all those who wish to borrow; because it would frighten lenders and make them unwilling to lend except at high rates of interest. Moreover, since the average term of mortgages, in general, is not over five or six years, present indebtedness of this kind does not run back to 1873. Free coinage is essentially dishonest. . . .

In conclusion, gentlemen, extraordinary as is the proposal for free coinage it is in truth only a huge deceit. It was born in the private offices of the silver kings, nursed at the hands of speculators, clothed in economic error, fed on boodle, exercised in the lobby of Congress, and as sure as there is honesty and truth in the American heart it will die young and be buried in the same ignominious grave wherein lies the now-forgotten infant once famous as the rag baby. Free coinage is greenbackism galvanized into life. That heresy in its old form of a demand for more money has already been laid low. It will not long deceive us in its new form of a demand for more silver, or for silver fiatism. Nor in any other respect is it what it presumes to be. It is not a proposition for bimetallism. It is a wild leap in the dark for silver monometallism. Under the cry for more money are veiled the plans of a daring syndicate of mine owners and speculators, who have hoodwinked the people in certain parts of the country and who, while deluding them with a specious argument for more money, are laughing in their sleeves at a constituency so easily gulled.

DOCUMENT 8

WILLIAM JENNINGS BRYAN, CROSS OF GOLD SPEECH, JULY 8, 1896

No doubt this is the most famous and the most effective speech ever delivered at a national party convention. The Democrats were debating the monetary plank in their platform. When young Bryan's turn came to speak, a newspaperman scribbled a note on an envelope: "This is a great opportunity," to which Bryan wrote in reply: "You will not be disappointed." The speech, embodying many familiar phrases from Bryan's earlier utterances on the money question, was delivered magnificently. "When I finished my speech," Bryan recalled, "I went to my seat in a silence that was really painful. When I neared my seat, somebody near me raised a shout, and the next thing I was picked up—and bedlam broke loose." For an hour the shouting delegates marched about the hall. Even gold standard men were caught up by the excitement. The next day Bryan was chosen to be the Democratic nominee.

I would be presumptuous, indeed, to present myself against the distinguished gentlemen to whom you have listened if this were a mere measuring of abilities; but this is not a contest between persons. The humblest citizen in all the land, when clad in the armor of a righteous cause, is stronger than all the hosts of error. I come to speak to you in defense of a cause as holy as the cause of liberty—the cause of humanity.

When this debate is concluded, a motion will be made to lay upon the table the resolution offered in commendation of the Administration, and also, the resolution offered in condemnation of the Administration. We object to bringing this question down to the level of persons. The individual is but an atom; he is born, he acts, he dies; but principles are eternal; and this has been a contest over a principle.

Never before in the history of this country has there been witnessed such a contest as that through which we have just passed. Never before in the history of American politics has a great issue been fought out as this issue has been, by the voters of a great party. On the fourth of March 1895, a few Democrats, most of them members of Congress, issued an address to the Democrats of the nation, asserting that the money question was the paramount issue of the hour; declaring that a majority of the Democratic party had the right to control the action of the party on this paramount issue; and concluding with the request that the believers in the free coinage of silver in the Democratic party should organize, take charge of, and control the policy of the Democratic party. Three months later, at Memphis, an organization was perfected, and the silver Democrats went forth openly and courageously proclaiming their belief, and declaring that, if successful, they would crystallize into a platform the declaration which they had made. Then began the struggle. With a zeal approaching the zeal which inspired the Crusaders who followed Peter the Hermit, our silver Democrats went forth from victory unto victory until they are now assembled, not to discuss, not to debate, but to enter up the judgement already rendered by the plain people of this country. In this contest brother has been arrayed against brother, father against son. The warmest ties of love, acquaintance, and association have been disregarded; old leaders have been cast aside when they have refused to give expression to the sentiments of those whom they would lead, and new leaders have sprung up to give direction to this cause of truth. Thus has the contest been waged, and we have assembled here under as binding and solemn instructions as were ever imposed upon representatives of the people.

We do not come as individuals. As individuals we might have been glad to compliment the gentleman from New York [Senator Hill], but we know that the people for whom we speak would never be willing to put him in a position where he could thwart the will of the Democratic party. I say it was not a question of persons; it was a question of principle, and it is not with gladness, my friends, that we find ourselves brought into conflict with those who are now arrayed on the other side. . . .

When you [turning to the gold delegates] come before us and tell us that we are about to disturb your business interests, we reply that you have disturbed our business interests by your course.

We say to you that you have made the definition of a business man too limited in its application. The man who is employed for wages is as much a business man as his employer; the attorney in a country town is as much a business man as the corporation counsel in a great metropolis; the merchant at the cross-roads store is as much a business man as the merchant of New York; the farmer who goes forth in the morning and toils all day, who begins in the spring and toils all summer, and who by the application of brain and muscle to the natural resources of the country creates wealth, is as much a business man as the man who goes upon the Board of Trade and bets upon the price of grain; the miners who go down a thousand feet into the earth, or climb two thousand feet upon the cliffs, and bring forth from their hiding places the precious metals to be poured into the channels of trade are as much business men as the few financial magnates who, in a back room, corner the money of the world. We come to speak of this broader class of business men.

Ah, my friends, we say not one word against those who live upon the Atlantic Coast, but the hardy pioneers who have braved all the dangers of the wilderness, who have made the desert to blossom as the rose—the pioneers away out there [pointing to the West] who rear their children near to Nature's heart, where they can mingle their voices with the voices of the birds—out there where they have erected schoolhouses for the education of their young, churches where they praise their Creator, and cemeteries where rest the ashes of their dead—these people, we say, are as deserving of the consideration of our party as any people in this country. It is for these that we speak. We do not come as aggressors. Our war is not a war of conquest; we are fighting in the defense of our homes, our families, and posterity. We have petitioned, and our petitions have been scorned; we have entreated, and our entreaties have been disregarded; we have begged, and they have mocked when our calamity came. We beg no longer; we entreat no more; we petition no more. We defy them!

The gentleman from Wisconsin [Vilas] has said that he fears a Robespierre. My friends, in this land of the free you need not fear that a tyrant will spring up from among the people. What we need is an Andrew Jackson to stand, as Jackson stood, against the encroachments of organized wealth.

They tell us that this platform was made to catch votes. We reply to them that changing conditions make new issues; that the principles upon which Democracy rests are as everlasting as the hills, but that they must be applied to new conditions as they arise. Conditions have arisen, and we are here to meet those conditions. They tell us that the income tax ought not to be brought in here; that it is a new idea. They criticize us for our criticism of the Supreme Court of the United States. My friends, we have not criticized; we have simply called attention to what you already know. If you want criticisms read the dissenting opinions of the court. There you will find criticisms. They say that we passed an unconstitutional law; we deny it. The income tax was not unconstitutional when it was passed; it was not unconstitutional when it went before the Supreme Court for the first time; it did not become unconstitutional until one of the judges changed his mind, and we cannot be expected to know when a judge will change his mind. The income tax is just. It simply intends to put the burdens of government justly upon the backs of the people. I am in favor of an income tax. When I find a man who is not willing to bear his share of the burdens of the government which protects him, I find a man who is unworthy to enjoy the blessings of a government like ours.

They say that we are opposing national bank currency; it is true. If you will read what Thomas Benton said, you will find he said that, in searching history, he could find but one parallel to Andrew Jackson; that was Cicero, who destroyed the conspiracy of Cataline and saved Rome. Benton said that Cicero only did for Rome what Jackson did for us when he destroyed the bank conspiracy and saved America. We say in our platform we believe that the right to coin and issue money is a function of government. We believe it. We believe that it is a part of sovereignty, and can no more with safety be delegated to private individuals than we could afford to delegate to private individuals the power to make penal statutes or levy taxes. Mr. Jefferson, who was once regarded as good Democratic authority, seems to have differed in opinion from the gentleman who has addressed us on the part of the minority. Those who are opposed to this proposition tell us that the issue of paper money is a function of the bank, and that the government ought to go out of the banking business. I stand with Jefferson rather than with them, and tell them, as he did, that the issue of money is a function of government, and that the banks ought to go out of the governing business.

They complain about the plank which declares against life tenure in office. They have tried to strain it to mean that which it does not mean. What we oppose by that plank is the life tenure which is being built up in Washington, and which excludes from participation in official benefits the humbler members of society. . . .

And now, my friends, let me come to the paramount issue. If they ask us why it is that we say more on the money question than we say upon the tariff question, I reply that, if protection has slain its thousands, the gold standard has slain its tens of thousands. If they ask us why we do not embody in our platform all the things that we believe in, we reply that when we have restored the money of the Constitution, all other necessary reform will be possible; but that until this is done, there is no other reform that can be accomplished.

Why is it that within three months such a change has come over the country? Three months ago when it was confidently asserted that those who believed in the gold standard would frame our platform and nominate our candidates, even the advocates of the gold standard did not think that we could elect a President. And they had good reason for their doubt, because there is scarcely a State here today asking for the gold standard which is not in the absolute control of the Republican Party. But note the change. Mr. McKinley was nominated at St. Louis upon a platform which declared for the maintenance of the gold standard until it can be changed into bimetallism by international agreement. Mr. McKinley was the most popular man among the Republicans, and three months ago everybody in the Republican Party prophesied his election. How is it today? Why, the man who was once pleased to think that he looked like Napoleon—that man shudders today when he remembers that he was nominated on the anniversary of the battle of Waterloo.

Not only that, but as he listens, he can hear with ever-increasing distinctness the sound of the waves as they beat upon the lonely shores at St Helena.

Why this change? Ah, my friends, is not the reason for the change evident to any one who will look at the matter? No private character, however pure, no personal popularity, however great, can protect from the avenging wrath of an indignant people a man who will declare that he is in favor of fastening the gold standard upon this country, or who is willing to surrender the right of self-government and place the legislative control of our affairs in the hands of foreign potentates and powers.

We go forth confident that we shall win. Why? Because upon the paramount issue of this campaign there is not a spot of ground upon which the enemy will dare to challenge battle. If they tell us that the gold standard is a good thing, we shall point to their platform and tell them that their platform pledges the party to get rid of the gold standard and substitute bimetallism. If the gold standard is a good thing why try to get rid of it? I call your attention to the fact that some of the very people who are in this Convention today and who tell us that we ought to declare in favor of international bimetallism—thereby declaring that the gold standard is wrong and that the principle of bimetallism is better—these very people four months ago were open and avowed advocates of the gold standard, and were then telling us that we could not legislate two metals together, even with the aid of all the world. If the gold standard is a good thing, we ought to declare in favor of its retention and not in favor of abandoning it; and if the gold standard is a bad thing why should we wait until other nations are willing to help us to let go? Here is the line of battle, and we care not upon which issue they force the fight; we are prepared to meet them on either issue or on both. If they tell us that the gold standard is the standard of civilization, we reply to them that this, the most enlightened of all the nations of the earth, has never declared for a gold standard and that both the great parties this year are declaring against it. If the gold standard is the standard of civilization, why, my friends, should we not have it? If they come to meet us on that issue we can present the history of our nation. More than that; we can tell them that they will search the pages of history in vain to find a single instance where the common people of any land have ever declared themselves in favor of the gold standard. They can find where the holders of fixed investments have declared for a gold standard, but not where the masses have. Mr. Carlisle said in 1878 that this was a struggle between the "idle holders of idle capital" and "the struggling masses, who produce the wealth and pay the taxes of the country," and, my friends, the question we are to decide is: Upon which side will the Democratic party fight; upon the side of "the idle holders of idle capital" or upon the side of "the struggling masses"? That is the question which the party must answer first, and then it must be answered by each individual hereafter. The sympathies of the Democratic party, as shown by the platform, are on the side of the struggling masses who have ever been the foundation of the Democratic party. There are two ideas of government. There are those who believe that if you will only legislate to make the well-to-do prosperous, their prosperity will leak through on those below. The Democratic idea, however, has been that if you legislate to make the masses prosperous, their prosperity will find its way up through every class which rests upon them.

You come to us and tell us that the great cities are in favor of the gold standard; we reply that the great cities rest upon our broad and fertile prairies. Burn down your cities and leave our farms, and your cities will spring up again as if by magic; but destroy our farms and the grass will grow in the streets of every city in the country.

My friends, we declare that this nation is able to legislate for its own people on every question, without waiting for the aid or consent of any other nation on earth; and upon that issue we expect to carry every state in the Union. I shall not slander the inhabitants of the fair state of Massachusetts nor the inhabitants of the state of New York by saying that, when they are confronted with the proposition, they will declare that this nation is not able to attend to its own business. It is the issue of 1776 over again. Our ancestors, when but three millions in number, had the courage to declare their political independence of every other nation; shall we, their descendants, when we have grown to seventy millions, declare that we are less independent than our forefathers?

No, my friends, that will never be the verdict of our people. Therefore, we care not upon what lines the battle is fought. If they say bimetallism is good, but that we cannot have it until other nations help us, we reply, that instead of having a gold standard because England has, we will restore bimetallism, and then let England have bimetallism because the United States has it. If they dare to come out in the open field and defend the gold standard as a good thing, we will fight them to the uttermost. Having behind us the producing masses of this nation and the world, supported by the commercial interests, the laboring interests and the toilers everywhere, we will answer their demand for a gold standard by saying to them: You shall not press down upon the brow of labor this crown of thorns, you shall not crucify mankind upon a cross of gold.

DOCUMENT 9

WILLIAM ALLEN WHITE,
"WHAT'S THE MATTER WITH KANSAS?"
AUGUST 16, 1896

In his later life William Allen White became known as a liberal and was associated with many reform causes. But in 1896, as a young Kansas editor, he was stoutly conservative, and had little but disdain for the Populist movement, although it was a powerful force in his own state. One day that summer, while the Bryan-McKinley campaign was under way and political fever was high, he was stopped by a group of

Populists on the way to his offices in the Emporia
Gazette. *As he remembered it many years later in
his* Autobiography: *"They ganged me—hooting, jeer-
ing, nagging me about some utterances I had
made. . . . Finally I broke through the cordon and
stalked, as well as a fat man who toddles can stalk,
down the street to the office. I . . . sat down to
write for Monday's paper an editorial, and I headed
it 'What's the Matter with Kansas?' . . . and it came
out pure vitriol."*

Today the Kansas Department of Agriculture sent out
a statement which indicates that Kansas has gained
less than two thousand people in the past year. There are
about two hundred and twenty-five thousand families in
the state, and there were about ten thousand babies born in
Kansas, and yet so many people have left the state that the
natural increase is cut down to less than two thousand
net.

This has been going on for eight years.

If there had been a high brick wall around the state
eight years ago, and not a soul had been admitted or permitted to leave, Kansas would be a half million souls better
off than she is today. And yet the nation has increased
in population. In five years ten million people have been
added to the national population, yet instead of gaining
a share of this—say, half a million—Kansas has apparently been a plague spot and, in the very garden of the
world, has lost population by ten-thousands every year.

Not only has she lost population, but she has lost
money. Every moneyed man in the state who could get
out without loss has gone. Every month in every community sees someone who has a little money pack up and
leave the state. This has been going on for eight years.
Money has been drained out all the time. In towns where
ten years ago there were three or four or half a dozen
money-lending concerns, stimulating industry by furnishing capital, there is now none, or one or two that are
looking after the interests and principal already outstanding.

No one brings any money into Kansas any more.
What community knows over one or two men who have

moved in with more than $5,000 in the past three years? And what community cannot count half a score of men in that time who have left, taking all the money they could scrape together?

Yet the nation has grown rich; other states have increased in population and wealth—other neighboring states. Missouri has gained over two million, while Kansas has been losing half a million. Nebraska has gained in wealth and population while Kansas has gone downhill. Colorado has gained every way, while Kansas has lost every way since 1888.

What's the matter with Kansas?

There is no substantial city in the state. Every big town save one has lost in population. Yet Kansas City, Omaha, Lincoln, St. Louis, Denver, Colorado Springs, Sedalia, the cities of the Dakotas, St. Paul and Minneapolis and Des Moines—all cities and towns in the West— have steadily grown.

Take up the Government Blue Book and you will see that Kansas is virtually off the map. Two or three little scrubby consular places in yellow-fever-stricken communities that do not aggregate ten thousand dollars a year is all the recognition that Kansas has. Nebraska draws about one hundred thousand dollars; little old North Dakota draws about fifty thousand dollars; Oklahoma doubles Kansas; Missouri leaves her a thousand miles behind; Colorado is almost seven times greater than Kansas—the whole west is ahead of Kansas.

Take it by any standard you please, Kansas is not in it.

Go east and you hear them laugh at Kansas; go west and they sneer at her; go south and they "cuss" her; go north and they have forgotten her. Go into any crowd of intelligent people gathered anywhere on the globe, and you will find the Kansas man on the defensive. The newspaper columns and magazines once devoted to praise of her, to boastful facts and startling figures concerning her resources, are now filled with cartoons, jibes and Pefferian speeches. Kansas just naturally isn't in it. She has traded places with Arkansas and Timbuctoo.

What's the matter with Kansas?

We all know; yet here we are at it again. We have

an old mossback Jacksonian who snorts and howls because there is a bathtub in the state house; we are running that old jay for Governor. We have another shabby, wild-eyed, rattle-brained fanatic who has said openly in a dozen speeches that "the rights of the user are paramount to the rights of the owner"; we are running him for Chief Justice, so that capital will come tumbling over itself to get into the state. We have raked the old ash heap of failure in the state and found an old human hoop-skirt who has failed as a businessman, who has failed as an editor, who has failed as a preacher, and we are going to run him for Congressman-at-Large. He will help the looks of the Kansas delegation at Washington. Then we have discovered a kid without a law practice and have decided to run him for Attorney General. Then, for fear some hint that the state had become respectable might percolate through the civilized portions of the nation, we have decided to send three or four harpies out lecturing, telling the people that Kansas is raising hell and letting the corn go to weeds.

Oh, this is a state to be proud of! We are a people who can hold up our heads! What we need is not more money, but less capital, fewer white shirts and brains, fewer men with business judgment, and more of those fellows who boast that they are "just ordinary clodhoppers, but they know more in a minute about finance than John Sherman"; we need more men who are "posted," who can bellow about the crime of '73, who hate prosperity, and who think, because a man believes in national honor, he is a tool of Wall Street. We have had a few of them— some hundred fifty thousand—but we need more.

We need several thousand gibbering idiots to scream about the "Great Red Dragon" of Lombard Street. We don't need population, we don't need wealth, we don't need well-dressed men on the streets, we don't need standing in the nation, we don't need cities on the fertile prairies; you bet we don't! What we are after is the money power. Because we have become poorer and ornerier and meaner than a spavined, distempered mule, we, the people of Kansas, propose to kick; we don't care to build up, we wish to tear down.

"There are two ideas of government," said our noble

Bryan at Chicago. "There are those who believe that if you just legislate to make the well-to-do prosperous, this prosperity will leak through on those below. The Democratic idea has been that if you legislate to make the masses prosperous their prosperity will find its way up and through every class which rests upon them."

That's the stuff! Give the prosperous man the dickens! Legislate the thriftless man into ease, whack the stuffings out of the creditors and tell debtors who borrowed the money five years ago when money "per capita" was greater than it is now, that the contraction of currency gives him a right to repudiate.

Whoop it up for the ragged trousers, put the lazy, greasy fizzle, who can't pay his debts, on an altar, and bow down and worship him. Let the state ideal be high. What we need is not the respect of our fellow men, but the chance to get something for nothing.

Oh, yes, Kansas is a great state. Here are people fleeing from it by the score every day, capital going out of the state by the hundreds of dollars; and every industry but farming paralysed, and that crippled, because its products have to go across the ocean before they can find a laboring man at work who can afford to buy them. Let's don't stop this year. Let's drive all the decent, self-respecting men out of the state. Let's keep the old clodhoppers who know it all. Let's encourage the man who is "posted." He can talk, and what we need is not mill hands to eat our meat, nor factory hands to eat our wheat, nor cities to oppress the farmer by consuming his butter and eggs and chickens and produce. What Kansas needs is men who can talk, who have large leisure to argue the currency question while their wives wait at home for that nickel's worth of bluing.

What's the matter with Kansas?

Nothing under the shining sun. She is losing wealth, population and standing. She has got her statesmen, and the money power is afraid of her. Kansas is all right. She has started in to raise hell, as Mrs. Lease advised, and she seems to have an over-production. But that doesn't matter. Kansas never did believe in diversified crops. Kansas is all right. There is absolutely nothing wrong with Kansas. "Every prospect pleases and only man is vile."

✳ PART IV ✳

Imperialism and War

INTRODUCTION

IN 1889, young Henry Cabot Lodge, then a Republican Congressman from Massachusetts, wrote: "Our relations with foreign nations today fill but a slight place in American politics, and excite generally only a languid interest. We have separated ourselves so completely from the affairs of other people that it is difficult to realize how large a place they occupied when the government was founded." The time was not yet ripe for men who, with Lodge, wanted America to take a larger place in world affairs; the people were wholly absorbed in the great industrial and continental expansion that had been going on since the Civil War. Before many more years, however, events at home and abroad challenged American insularity. Public indifference was soon replaced by receptivity to schemes for promoting overseas commercial and territorial interests, even to plans for entering the worldwide scramble of late nineteenth-century imperialism. This appeared to be a sudden change, but in fact Lodge was only one of several men who, beginning in the eighties, had been preaching extra-continental expansion to a widening audience. Perhaps the most popular of these publicists was Josiah Strong, a Congregational clergyman, whose best-selling tract, *Our Country* (Document 1), had been published in 1885. Expansion across the continent had long been accepted as the manifest destiny of the American people. Strong tied this destiny more closely to racism, and pushed it outside the continental limits; he proclaimed that the Anglo-Saxon race, whose true center was the United States, was fore-destined to spread itself over the earth. Another ardent expansionist, Captain Alfred Thayer Mahan, was more interested in techniques than in theories. He bombarded the country with magazine articles demanding that America acquire naval bases, and in 1890 published his persuasive book, *The Influence of Sea Power upon History, 1660–1783*.

Hawaii, which had a native government but a growing number of American settlers, was a natural target for the expansionists. In 1893, Americans there revolted against the native Queen and established a provisional government which applied for annexation. The United States Minister to Hawaii went so far as to work out a treaty to that effect. But Democratic opposition in the Senate blocked the treaty, and Cleveland, as soon as he took office in March 1893, withdrew it. He then ordered an investigation of American activity in the Hawaiian revolution, and even tried to reinstate Queen Liliuokalani. This infuriated the expansionists. Lodge, now a Senator, tried to make Cleveland's caution a national political issue in the Senate, and in an article on "Our Blundering Foreign Policy" (Document 2) which reviewed the whole issue of expansion.

Issues of profit and loss, no matter how inflated with grandiose images of national pride, could not make expansionism a popular cause. When emotion colored the issues, however, Americans responded with enthusiasm. Emotion was amply provided after 1895 by publicity given to the treatment of Cubans by Spain during a new flare-up of chronic Cuban rebellion. Here was an outrage, and it was taking place on America's very doorstep. A sensational press whipped up feeling that America must intervene, not for gain, but in the name of humanity. While this feeling was mounting, the battleship *Maine* was sunk in Havana harbor, and although the responsibility of the Spaniards was never established, the yellow press screamed for war. An exceptionally courageous man might have withstood the popular demand for war, but President McKinley, despite his preference for peace, was no such man. In his war message to Congress on April 11, 1898 (Document 3), he mentioned only in a casual way the fact that Spain seemed to be about to accede to American demands on behalf of Cuba. Congress then resolved in favor of an extreme set of demands upon Spain, to which Spain responded with a declaration of war. The expansionists had never had any intention of confining American activity to Cuba, however. Assistant Secretary of the Navy, Theodore Roosevelt, without authorization, had made sure that Admiral Dewey's Pacific fleet at Hong Kong was ready for offensive action against the Philippines as soon as war broke out.

The nation had been nearly unanimous behind a war to help the oppressed Cubans; but Dewey's startling victory at Manila Bay presented quite another question, over which opinion was sharply divided. If Americans stayed in the Philippines, they were committed to Pacific expansion; on the other hand, if they left, the islands would be fair game for the European imperialist powers. But sentiment for expansion had been gaining ground throughout this period; the depression of the nineties had stimulated sharp internal conflict and, to many, expansion looked like a way to prevent such conflict from recurring, a safety valve for what was considered to be the naturally aggressive and adventurous American temperament (Document 4). There were many, however, who argued that imperial expansion involved a morally inconsistent and politically dangerous abandonment of classic American principles. Organizations like the American Anti-Imperialist League (Document 5) tried to further this point of view, but they had slight political power, and failed to win a majority of the public. Hawaii was at last annexed in July 1898; and despite strong opposition, a peace treaty with Spain, which provided for annexation of the Philippines, was ratified in 1899.

Although the next decade and a half were years of peace, events kept reminding people how much the country now was involved in the affairs of the outside world. John Hay's "Open Door" notes in 1899; Theodore Roosevelt's aggressive interference in Colombia in 1903 to secure the independence of Panama and the Canal Zone; the building of the canal itself; Roosevelt mediation in 1905 in the Russo-Japanese war; the unsuccessful attempts under Taft to finance railroads in Manchuria; the assertion of American hegemony in the Caribbean under Roosevelt, Taft, and Wilson; and, finally, Wilson's active intervention in Mexican affairs in 1913–14—all these made it clear that Americans were not returning to their former isolation. Yet, when war broke out in Europe in 1914, many Americans recoiled from the implications of their position as a world power. President Wilson immediately called for neutrality (Document 6), forcefully stating the ideal of non-involvement; but when he appealed for neutrality in thought as well as in action, he asked for something which few men in the country, least of all in his own administration, could achieve. From the start, long-range considerations of national security and trade, and—for most Americans—of sentiment and sympathy involved the country on the side of the Allies. While it attempted to protect American rights and interests on the high seas from violation by both sides, the Wilson Administration leaned unmistakably toward the Allies. British violations and Allied attitudes toward a possible settlement irritated Wilson; but German use of submarines aroused hostility throughout the entire nation. Wilson's last plea for neutrality was his greatest, the exceptionally eloquent Peace without Victory address (Document 7) of January 22, 1917. But in less than six weeks Germany resumed unrestricted submarine warfare, and Wilson called upon Congress for a declaration of war (Document 8). Resistance to war was far more vocal and effective in 1917 than it was to be in World War II. Not only had there been no attack upon American territory, but the distaste of German-Americans and Irish-Americans for a British alliance provided the nucleus of a strong opposition; in addition, high-minded liberals like Senator George W. Norris (Document 9) spoke for those former Populists or Progressives who, without regard to ethnic prejudices or loyalties, suspected that the country was being drawn into war chiefly by vested interests and for material gain rather than for principles or legitimate national interest.

Wilson himself believed that America should not enter the war to gain selfish national objectives, but to achieve a better world and a stable peace. His statement of American war aims in the Fourteen Points (Document

10) expressed this belief; it also quickened the hopes of liberal-minded Europeans everywhere and held out to war-weary Germans the hope that their capitulation might be followed by a generous and lasting peace. Wilson pinned his own hopes for an enduring peace on a League of Nations—the Fourteenth Point, and to him clearly the most important. Although negotiating the peace brought Wilson to many compromises and many irksome failures, he was finally able in a proud moment to present the Covenant of the League to the nations assembled at Paris in the famous speech of February 14, 1919 (Document 11), in which he proclaimed that "a living thing is born." But after having dealt creditably with difficult and demanding Allies, he came home to be difficult and demanding himself in dealing with the Senate. Resistance to American participation in the League was uncommonly stubborn, usually adroit, and sometimes violently prejudiced (Document 12). In the end the cause of liberal internationalism was defeated, and Wilson himself was a living corpse.

DOCUMENT 1

JOSIAH STRONG, *OUR COUNTRY,*
1885

The Reverend Josiah Strong was Secretary of the Congregational Home Missionary Society when he was asked to revise a manual put out by the Society on social questions. Instead, Strong expanded the material into a persuasive book which soon sold 170,000 copies and was translated into several foreign languages. Strong was a man of intense prejudices, which he did not hesitate to expound in his book, and which extended to immigrants, Catholics, alcohol, tobacco, large cities, and political machines. He preached that in the future the "Anglo-Saxon race," especially the American part of it, would dominate the world. His was one of the first voices, in a time preoccupied by concern with national development and internal settlement, that urged Americans to think of their future international role and to develop their potentialities as an imperial nation.

It is not necessary to argue to those for whom I write that the two great needs of mankind, that all men may be lifted up into the light of the highest Christian civilization, are, first, a pure, spiritual Christianity, and, second, civil liberty. Without controversy, these are the forces which, in the past, have contributed most to the elevation of the human race, and they must continue to be, in the future, the most efficient ministers to its progress. It follows, then, that the Anglo-Saxon, as the great representative of these two ideas, the depositary of these two greatest blessings, sustains peculiar relations to the world's future, is divinely commissioned to be, in a peculiar sense, his brother's keeper. Add to this the fact of his rapidly increasing strength in modern times, and we have well nigh a demonstration of his destiny. . . .

There can be no reasonable doubt that North America is to be the great home of the Anglo-Saxon, the principal seat of his power, the center of his life and influence. Not only does it constitute seven-elevenths of his possessions, but his empire is unsevered, while the remaining four-elevenths are fragmentary and scattered over the earth. . . .

But we are to have not only the larger portion of the Anglo-Saxon race for generations to come, we may reasonably expect to develop the highest type of Anglo-Saxon civilization. If human progress follows a law of development, if

"Time's noblest offspring is the last,"

our civilization should be the noblest; for we are

"The heirs of all the ages in the foremost files of time,"

and not only do we occupy the latitude of power, but *our land is the last to be occupied in that latitude.* There is no other virgin soil in the North Temperate Zone. If the consummation of human progress is not to be looked for here, if there is yet to flower a higher civilization, where is the soil that is to produce it? . . .

Mr. Darwin is not only disposed to see, in the superior vigor of our people, an illustration of his favorite theory of natural selection, but even intimates that the world's history thus far has been simply preparatory for our future, and tributary to it. He says: "There is apparently much truth in the belief that the wonderful progress of the United States, as well as the character of the people, are the results of natural selection; for the more energetic, restless and courageous men from all parts of Europe have emigrated during the last ten or twelve generations to that great country, and have there succeeded best. Looking at the distant future, I do not think that the Rev. Mr. Zincke takes an exaggerated view when he says: 'All other series of events—as that which resulted in the culture of mind in Greece, and that which resulted in the Empire of Rome—only appear to have purpose and value when viewed in connection with, or rather as subsidiary to, the great stream of Anglo-Saxon emigration to the West.' "

There is abundant reason to believe that the Anglo-Saxon race is to be, is, indeed, already becoming, more effective here than in the mother country. . . .

It may be easily shown, and is of no small significance, that the two great ideas of which the Anglo-Saxon is the exponent are having a fuller development in the United States than in Great Britain. There the union of Church and State tends strongly to paralyze some of the members of the body of Christ. Here there is no such influence to destroy spiritual life and power. Here, also, has been evolved the form of government consistent with the largest possible civil liberty. Furthermore, it is significant that the marked characteristics of this race are being here emphasized most. Among the most striking features of the Anglo-Saxon is his money-making power—a power of increasing importance in the widening commerce of the world's future. We have seen, in a preceding chapter, that, although England is by far the richest nation of Europe, we have already outstripped her in the race after wealth, and we have only begun the development of our vast resources.

Again, another marked characteristic of the Anglo-Saxon is what may be called an instinct or genius for

colonizing. His unequaled energy, his indomitable per-
severance, and his personal independence, made him a
pioneer. He excels all others in pushing his way into new
countries. It was those in whom this tendency was
strongest that came to America, and this inherited
tendency has been further developed by the westward
sweep of successive generations across the continent. So
noticeable has this characteristic become that English
visitors remark it. Charles Dickens once said that the
typical American would hesitate to enter heaven unless
assured that he could go further west.

Again, nothing more manifestly distinguishes the
Anglo-Saxon than his intense and persistent energy; and
he is developing in the United States an energy which, in
eager activity and effectiveness, is peculiarly American.
This is due partly to the fact that Americans are much
better fed than Europeans, and partly to the undeveloped
resources of a new country, but more largely to our
climate, which acts as a constant stimulus. Ten years
after the landing of the Pilgrims, the Rev. Francis Higginson, a good observer, wrote: "A sup of New England air
is better than a whole flagon of English ale." Thus early
had the stimulating effect of our climate been noted. Moreover, our social institutions are stimulating. In Europe
the various ranks of society are, like the strata of the
earth, fixed and fossilized. There can be no great change
without a terrible upheaval, a social earthquake. Here
society is like the waters of the sea, mobile; as General
Garfield said, and so signally illustrated in his own experience, that which is at the bottom today may one day
flash on the crest of the highest wave. Every one is free
to become whatever he can make of himself; free to
transform himself from a rail-splitter or a tanner or a
canal-boy, into the nation's President. Our aristocracy,
unlike that of Europe, is open to all comers. Wealth,
position, influence, are prizes offered for energy; and
every farmer's boy, every apprentice and clerk, every
friendless and penniless immigrant, is free to enter the
lists. Thus many causes co-operate to produce here the
most forceful and tremenduous energy in the world.

What is the significance of such facts? These tendencies infold the future; they are the mighty alphabet

with which God writes his prophecies. May we not, by a careful laying together of the letters, spell out something of his meaning? It seems to me that God, with infinite wisdom and skill, is training the Anglo-Saxon race for an hour sure to come in the world's future. Heretofore there has always been in the history of the world a comparatively unoccupied land westward, into which the crowded countries of the East have poured their surplus populations. But the widening waves of migration, which millenniums ago rolled east and west from the valley of the Euphrates, meet today on our Pacific coast. There are no more new worlds. The unoccupied arable lands of the earth are limited, and will soon be taken. The time is coming when the pressure of population on the means of subsistence will be felt here as it is now felt in Europe and Asia. Then will the world enter upon a new stage of its history—*the final competition of races, for which the Anglo-Saxon is being schooled*. Long before the thousand millions are here, the mighty *centrifugal* tendency, inherent in this stock and strengthened in the United States, will assert itself. Then this race of unequaled energy, with all the majesty of numbers and the might of wealth behind it—the representative, let us hope, of the largest liberty, the purest Christianity, the highest civilization—having developed peculiarly aggressive traits calculated to impress its institutions upon mankind, will spread itself over the earth. If I read not amiss, this powerful race will move down upon Mexico, down upon Central and South America, out upon the islands of the sea, over upon Africa and beyond. And can any one doubt that the result of this competition of races will be the "survival of the fittest"?

DOCUMENT 2

HENRY CABOT LODGE, "OUR BLUNDERING FOREIGN POLICY,"

MARCH 1895

Senator Lodge of Massachusetts, along with his friend Theodore Roosevelt, was one of a group of young statesmen who by the 1890's had come to see in overseas expansion a key to the national future. Lodge found "grotesque and miserable" President Cleveland's scrupulous and conservative position on Hawaiian annexation in 1893 and 1894. In March 1895, Lodge attacked Cleveland in a Senate speech and also published his views, excerpted here, in the Forum *magazine. Lodge's main interest was to make partisan capital out of the issue of expansion, but his views represented the feelings of young men in both parties who believed in a more aggressive foreign policy, commercial expansion, the acquisition of outlying naval bases, and America's entrance into the imperialistic race of the major European powers.*

All the great constructive legislation of this country, with hardly an exception, has been the work of the Republican party and its predecessors. The Federalists organized the Government; the Whigs developed our industries and set on foot our great system of internal improvements; the Republicans maintained the Union, abolished slavery, placed the last great Amendments on the Constitution, and established our credit and our tariff. The record of the Democratic party for constructive legislation, on the other hand, despite their many years of power, is singularly barren. But there is one direction where the Democratic party has done a great work. The Republicans under the lead of Charles Sumner added Alaska to our domain, but with this exception all our great acquisitions of territory have been the work of Democrats. To them we owe the Louisiana purchase, Florida, Texas, and the Mexican cession. If the Democratic party has had one cardinal principle beyond all others, it has been that of pushing forward the boundaries of the United States. Under this Administration, governed as it is by free-trade influences, this great principle of the Democratic party during nearly a century of existence has been utterly abandoned. Thomas Jefferson, admitting that he violated the Constitution while he did it, effected the Louisiana purchase, but Mr. Cleveland has labored to overthrow American interests and American control in Hawaii. Andrew Jackson fought for Florida, but Mr. Cleveland is eager to abandon Samoa.

The Democratic party, in its leaders at least, has been successfully Cobdenized, and that is the underlying reason for their policy of retreat. It is the melancholy outcome of the doctrine that there is no higher aim or purpose for men or for nations than to buy and sell, to trade jack-knives and make everything cheap. No one underrates the importance of the tariffs or the still greater importance of a sound currency. But of late years we have been so absorbed in these economic questions that we have grown unmindful of others. We have had something too much of these disciples of the Manchester school, who think the price of calico more important than a nation's honor, the duties on pig iron of more moment than the advance of a race.

It is time to recall what we have been tending to forget; that we have always had and that we have now a foreign policy which is of great importance to our national well-being. The foundation of that policy was Washington's doctrine of neutrality. To him and to Hamilton we owe the principle that it was not the business of the United States to meddle in the affairs of Europe. When this policy was declared, it fell with a shock upon the Americans of that day, for we were still colonists in habits of thought and could not realize that the struggles of Europe did not concern us. Yet the establishment of the neutrality policy was one of the greatest services which Washington and Hamilton rendered to the cause of American nationality. The corollary of Washington's policy was the Monroe doctrine, the work of John Quincy Adams, a much greater man than the President whose name it bears. Washington declared that it was not the business of the United States to meddle in the affairs of Europe, and John Quincy Adams added that Europe must not meddle in the Western hemisphere. As I have seen it solemnly stated recently that the annexation of Hawaii would be a violation of the Monroe doctrine, it is perhaps not out of place to say that the Monroe doctrine has no bearing on the extension of the United States, but simply holds that no European power shall establish itself in the Americas or interfere with American governments.

The neutrality policy and the Monroe doctrine are

the two great principles established at the outset by far-seeing statesmen in regard to the foreign relations of the United States. But it would be a fatal mistake to suppose that our foreign policy stopped there, or that these fundamental principles in any way fettered the march of the American people. Washington withdrew us from the affairs of Europe, but at the same time he pointed out that our true line of advance was to the West. He never for an instant thought that we were to remain stationary and cease to move forward. He saw, with prophetic vision, as did no other man of his time, the true course for the American people. He could not himself enter into the promised land, but he showed it to his people, stretching from the Blue Ridge to the Pacific Ocean. We have followed the teachings of Washington. We have taken the great valley of the Mississippi and pressed on beyond the Sierras. We have a record of conquest, colonization, and territorial expansion unequalled by any people in the nineteenth century. We are not to be curbed now by the doctrines of the Manchester school which have never been observed in England, and which as an importation are even more absurdly out of place here than in their native land. It is not the policy of the United States to enter, as England has done, upon the general acquisition of distant possession in all parts of the world. Our government is not adapted to such a policy, and we have no need of it, for we have an ample field at home; but at the same time it must be remembered that while in the United States themselves we hold the citadel of our power and greatness as a nation, there are outworks essential to the defence of that citadel which must neither be neglected nor abandoned.

There is a very definite policy for American statesmen to pursue in this respect if they would prove themselves worthy inheritors of the principles of Washington and Adams. We desire no extension to the south, for neither the population nor the lands of Central or South America would be desirable additions to the United States. But from the Rio Grande to the Arctic Ocean there should be but one flag and one country. Neither race nor climate forbids this extension, and every consideration of national growth and national welfare demands it. In the interests of our commerce and of our fullest development we should build the Nicaragua canal, and for the protection of that canal and for the sake of our commercial supremacy in the Pacific we should control the Hawaiian Islands and maintain our influence in Samoa. England has studded the West Indies with strong places which are a standing menace to our Atlantic seaboard. We should have among those islands at least one strong naval station, and when the Nicaragua canal is built, the island of Cuba, still sparsely settled and of almost unbounded fertility, will become to us a necessity. Commerce follows the flag, and we should build up a navy strong enough to give protection to Americans in every quarter of the globe and sufficiently powerful to put our coasts beyond the possibility of successful attack.

The tendency of modern times is toward consolidation. It is apparent in capital and labor alike, and it is also true of nations. Small States are of the past and have no future. The modern movement is all toward the concentration of people and territory into great nations and large dominions. The great nations are rapidly absorbing for their future expansion and their present defence all the waste places of the earth. It is a movement which makes for civilization and the advancement of the race. As one of the great nations of the world, the United States must not fall out of the line of march.

DOCUMENT 3

WILLIAM McKINLEY, WAR MESSAGE TO CONGRESS,
APRIL 11, 1898

Although he would have preferred to stay out of the Cuban struggle for independence, McKinley was not strong enough to resist the mounting clamor for war throughout the country. This message, which put the issue of a declaration of war in the hands of Congress, was his capitulation to war sentiment. Shortly before he planned to deliver it, he was informed by the

American Consul-General in Havana that many Americans had not yet been evacuated from Cuba and that their lives would be endangered if the war message came too soon. Pounding his desk before a crowd of congressmen and senators asking for war, he declared: "That message shall not go to Congress as long as there is a single American life in danger in Cuba," and said to his secretary: "Here—put that in the safe till I call for it." When finally presented to Congress, the greater part of the message simply reviewed the background of the Cuban situation. But its last two paragraphs are among the most curious ever to appear in a presidential message. In them, McKinley referred almost casually to the recent announcement by the Spanish government that it would accede to important American demands—a concession that warranted a reopening of negotiations. McKinley has been much criticized by historians for not taking advantage of these last-minute opportunities for a peaceful and satisfactory settlement. Congress passed resolutions recognizing Cuban independence by 42 to 35 in the Senate and 311 to 6 in the House. Spain reacted to these resolutions by declaring war on April 24; an American declaration followed the next day.

Obedient to that precept of the Constitution which commands the President to give from time to time to the Congress information of the state of the Union and to recommend to their consideration such measures as he shall judge necessary and expedient, it becomes my duty to now address your body with regard to the grave crisis that has arisen in the relations of the United States to Spain by reason of the warfare that for more than three years has raged in the neighboring island of Cuba. . . .

The present revolution is but the successor of other similar insurrections which have occurred in Cuba against the dominion of Spain, extending over a period of nearly half a century, each of which during its progress has subjected the United States to great effort and expense in enforcing its neutrality laws, caused enormous losses to

American trade and commerce, caused irritation, annoyance, and disturbance among our citizens, and, by the exercise of cruel, barbarous, and uncivilized practices of warfare, shocked the sensibilities and offended the humane sympathies of our people. . . .

Our trade has suffered, the capital invested by our citizens in Cuba has been largely lost, and the temper and forbearance of our people have been so sorely tried as to beget a perilous unrest among our own citizens, which has inevitably found its expression from time to time in the National Legislature, so that issues wholly external to our own body politic engross attention and stand in the way of that close devotion to domestic advancement that becomes a self-contained commonwealth whose primal maxim has been the avoidance of all foreign entanglements. All this must needs awaken, and has, indeed, aroused, the utmost concern on the part of this Government, as well during my predecessor's term as in my own.

In April, 1896, the evils from which our country suffered through the Cuban war became so onerous that my predecessor made an effort to bring about a peace through the mediation of this Government in any way that might tend to an honorable adjustment of the contest between Spain and her revolted colony, on the basis of some effective scheme of self-government for Cuba under the flag and sovereignty of Spain. It failed through the refusal of the Spanish government then in power to consider any form of mediation or, indeed, any plan of settlement which did not begin with the actual submission of the insurgents to the mother country, and then only on such terms as Spain herself might see fit to grant. The war continued unabated. The resistance of the insurgents was in no wise diminished. . . .

The war in Cuba is of such a nature that, short of subjugation or extermination, a final military victory for either side seems impracticable. The alternative lies in the physical exhaustion of the one or the other party, or perhaps of both—a condition which in effect ended the ten years' war by the truce of Zanjon. The prospect of such a protraction and conclusion of the present strife is a contingency hardly to be contemplated with equanimity by the civilized world, and least of all by the United States, affected and injured as we are, deeply and intimately, by its very existence.

Realizing this, it appeared to be my duty, in a spirit of true friendliness, no less to Spain than to the Cubans, who have so much to lose by the prolongation of the struggle, to seek to bring about an immediate termination of the war. To this end I submitted on the 27th ultimo, as a result of much representation and correspondence, through the United States minister at Madrid, propositions to the Spanish Government looking to an armistice until October 1 for the negotiation of peace with the good offices of the President.

In addition I asked the immediate revocation of the order of reconcentration, so as to permit the people to return to their farms and the needy to be relieved with provisions and supplies from the United States, co-operating with the Spanish authorities, so as to afford full relief.

The reply of the Spanish cabinet was received on the night of the 31st ultimo. It offered, as the means to bring about peace in Cuba, to confide the preparation thereof to the insular parliament, inasmuch as the concurrence of that body would be necessary to reach a final result, it being, however, understood that the powers reserved by the constitution to the central Government are not lessened or diminished. As the Cuban parliament does not meet until the 4th of May next, the Spanish Government would not object for its part to accept at once a suspension of hostilities if asked for by the insurgents from the general in chief, to whom it would pertain in such case to determine the duration and conditions of the armistice. . . .

With this last overture in the direction of immediate peace, and its disappointing reception by Spain, the Executive is brought to the end of his effort. . . .

In my annual message of December last I said:

Of the untried measures there remain only: Recognition of the insurgents as belligerents; recognition of the independence of Cuba; neutral intervention to end the war by imposing a rational compromise between the contestants, and intervention in favor of one or the other party. I speak not of forcible annexation, for that can not be thought of. That, by our code of morality, would be criminal aggression. . . .

I recognize . . . that the issuance of a proclamation of neutrality, by which process the so-called recognition of belligerents is published, could of itself and unattended by other action accomplish nothing toward the one end for which we labor—the instant pacification of Cuba and the cessation of the misery that afflicts the island. . . .

There remain the alternative forms of intervention to end the war, either as an impartial neutral, by imposing a rational compromise between the contestants, or as the active ally of the one party or the other.

As to the first, it is not to be forgotten that during the last few months the relation of the United States has virtually been one of friendly intervention in many ways, each not of itself conclusive, but all tending to the exertion of a potential influence toward an ultimate pacific result, just and honorable to all interests concerned. The spirit of all our acts hitherto has been an earnest, unselfish desire for peace and prosperity in Cuba, untarnished by differences between us and Spain and unstained by the blood of American citizens.

The forcible intervention of the United States as a neutral to stop the war, according to the large dictates of humanity and following many historical precedents where neighboring states have interfered to check the hopeless sacrifices of life by internecine conflicts beyond their borders, is justifiable on rational grounds. It involves, however, hostile constraint upon both the parties to the contest, as well to enforce a truce as to guide the eventual settlement.

The grounds for such intervention may be briefly summarized as follows:

First. In the cause of humanity and to put an end to the barbarities, bloodshed, starvation, and horrible miseries now existing there, and which the parties to the conflict are either unable or unwilling to stop or mitigate. It is no answer to say this is all in another country, belonging to another nation, and is therefore none of our business. It is specially our duty, for it is right at our door.

Second. We owe it to our citizens in Cuba to afford them that protection and indemnity for life and property which no government there can or will afford, and to that end to terminate the conditions that deprive them of legal protection.

Third. The right to intervene may be justified by the very serious injury to the commerce, trade, and business of our people and by the wanton destruction of property and devastation of the island.

Fourth, and which is of the utmost importance. The present condition of affairs in Cuba is a constant menace to our peace and entails upon this Government an enormous expense. With such a conflict waged for years in an island so near us and with which our people have such trade and business relations; when the lives and liberty of our citizens are in constant danger and their property destroyed and themselves ruined; where our trading vessels are liable to seizure and are seized at our very door by war ships of a foreign nation; the expeditions of filibustering that we are powerless to prevent altogether, and the irritating questions and entanglements thus arising—all these and others that I need not mention, with the resulting strained relations, are a constant menace to our peace and compel us to keep on a semi war footing with a nation with which we are at peace.

These elements of danger and disorder already pointed out have been strikingly illustrated by a tragic event which has deeply and justly moved the American people. I have already transmitted to Congress the report of the naval court of inquiry on the destruction of the battle ship *Maine* in the harbor of Havana during the night of the 15th of February. The destruction of that noble vessel has filled the national heart with inexpressible horror. Two hundred and fifty-eight brave sailors and marines and two officers of our Navy, reposing in the fancied security of a friendly harbor, have been hurled to death, grief and want brought to their homes and sorrow to the nation.

The naval court of inquiry, which, it is needless to say, commands the unqualified confidence of the Government, was unanimous in its conclusion that the destruction of the *Maine* was caused by an exterior explosion—that of a submarine mine. It did not assume to place the responsibility. That remains to be fixed.

In any event, the destruction of the *Maine,* by whatever exterior cause, is a patent and impressive proof of a state of things in Cuba that is intolerable. That condition is thus shown to be such that the Spanish Government can not assure safety and security to a vessel of the American Navy in the harbor of Havana on a mission of peace, and rightfully there. . . .

The long trial has proved that the object for which Spain has waged the war can not be attained. The fire of insurrection may flame or may smolder with varying seasons, but it has not been and it is plain that it can not be extinguished by present methods. The only hope of relief and repose from a condition which can no longer be endured is the enforced pacification of Cuba. In the name of humanity, in the name of civilization, in behalf of endangered American interests which give us the right and the duty to speak and to act, the war in Cuba must stop.

In view of these facts and of these considerations I ask the Congress to authorize and empower the President to take measures to secure a full and final termination of hostilities between the Government of Spain and the people of Cuba, and to secure in the island the establishment of a stable government, capable of maintaining order and observing its international obligations, insuring peace and tranquillity and the security of its citizens as well as our own, and to use the military and naval forces of the United States as may be necessary for these purposes.

And in the interest of humanity and to aid in preserving the lives of the starving people of the island I recommend that the distribution of food and supplies be continued and that an appropriation be made out of the public Treasury to supplement the charity of our citizens.

The issue is now with the Congress. It is a solemn responsibility. I have exhausted every effort to relieve the intolerable condition of affairs which is at our doors. Prepared to execute every obligation imposed upon me by the Constitution and the law, I await your action.

Yesterday, and since the preparation of the foregoing message, official information was received by me that the latest decree of the Queen Regent of Spain directs General Blanco, in order to prepare and facilitate peace, to proclaim a suspension of hostilities, the duration and details of which have not yet been communicated to me.

This fact, with every other pertinent consideration, will, I am sure, have your just and careful attention in the solemn deliberations upon which you are about to enter. If this measure attains a successful result, then our aspirations as a Christian, peace-loving people will be realized. If it fails, it will be only another justification for our contemplated action.

DOCUMENT 4

WALTER HINES PAGE, "THE WAR WITH SPAIN AND AFTER,"
JUNE 1898

Shortly after the news of Dewey's victory at Manila reached America, Walter Hines Page, then editor of the Atlantic Monthly, *wrote this editorial on the meaning of that victory in American history. He gave a remarkably articulate account of what the turn toward imperialism and world power meant to one who saw in it a good, indeed a necessary, thing, if only to stiffen morale in American public life.*

The problems that seem likely to follow the war are graver than those that have led up to it; and if it be too late to ask whether we entered into it without sufficient deliberation, it is not too soon to make sure of every step that we now take. The inspiring unanimity of the people in following their leaders proves to be as earnest and strong as it ever was under any form of government; and this popular acquiescence in war puts a new responsibility on those leaders, and may put our institutions and our people themselves to a new test. A change in our national policy may change our very character; and we are now playing with the great forces that may shape the future of the world—almost before we know it.

Yesterday we were going about the prosaic tasks of peace, content with our own problems of administration and finance, a nation to ourselves,—"commercials," as our enemies call us in derision. Today we are face to face with the sort of problems that have grown up in the management of world-empires, and the policies of other nations are of intimate concern to us. Shall we still be content with peaceful industry, or does there yet lurk in us the adventurous spirit of our Anglo-Saxon fore-fathers? And have we come to a time when, no more great enterprises awaiting us at home, we shall be tempted to seek them abroad?

The race from which we are sprung is a race that for a thousand years has done the adventurous and out-door tasks of the world. The English have been explorers, colonizers, conquerors of continents, founders of states. We ourselves, every generation since we came to America, have had great practical enterprises to engage us,—the fighting with Indians, the clearing of forests, the war for independence, the construction of a government, the extension of our territory, the pushing backward of the frontier, the development of an El Dorado (which the Spaniards owned, but never found), the long internal conflict about slavery, a great civil war, the building of railroads, and the compact unification of a continental domain. These have been as great enterprises and as exciting, coming in rapid succession, as any race of men has ever had to engage it,—as great enterprises for the play of the love of adventure in the blood as our kinsmen over the sea have had in the extension and the management of their world-empire. The old outdoor spirit of the Anglo-Saxon has till lately found wider scope in our own history than we are apt to remember.

But now a generation has come to manhood that has had no part in any great adventure. In politics we have had difficult and important tasks, indeed, but they have not been exciting,—the reform of the civil service and of the system of currency, and the improvement of municipal government. These are chiefly administrative. In a sense they are not new nor positive tasks, but the

correction of past errors. In some communities politics
has fallen into the hands of petty brigands, and in others
into those of second-rate men, partly because it has offered
little constructive work to do. Its duties have been
routine, regulative duties; its prizes, only a commonplace
distinction to honest men, and the vulgar spoil of office
to dishonest ones. The decline in the character of our
public life has been a natural result of the lack of large
constructive opportunities. The best equipped men of this
generation have abstained from it, and sought careers by
criticism of the public servants who owe their power to
the practical inactivity of the very men who criticize
them. In literature as well we have well-nigh lost the art
of constructive writing, for we work too much on indoor
problems, and content ourselves with adventures in
criticism. It is noteworthy that the three books which
have found most readers, and had perhaps the widest
influence on the masses of this generation, are books of
Utopian social programmes (mingled with very different
proportions of truth), by whose fantastic philosophy,
thanks to the dullness of times, men have tried seriously
to shape our national conduct,—Progress and Poverty,
Looking Backward, and Coin's Financial School. Apostolic
fervor, romantic dreaming, and blatant misinformation
have each captivated the idle-minded masses, because their
imaginations were not duly exercised in their routine toil.
It has been a time of social reforms, of the "emancipation" of women, of national organizations of children, of
societies for the prevention of minor vices and for the
encouragement of minor virtues, of the study of genealogy,
of the rise of morbid fiction, of journals for "ladies," of
literature for babes, of melodrama on the stage because
we have had melodrama in life also,—of criticism and
reform rather than of thought and action. These things all
denote a lack of adventurous opportunities, an indoor life
such as we have never before had a chance to enjoy; and
there are many indications that a life of quiet may have
become irksome, and may not yet be natural to us. Greater
facts than these denote a period also of peace and such
well-being as men of our race never before enjoyed,—
sanitary improvements, the multiplication and the development of universities, the establishment of hospitals, and

the application of benevolence to the whole circle of
human life,—such a growth of good will as we had come
to think had surely made war impossible.

Is this dream true? Or is it true that with a thousand
years of adventure behind us we are unable to endure
a life of occupations that do not feed the imagination?
After all, it is temperament that tells, and not schemes of
national policy, whether laid down in Farewell Addresses
or in Utopian books. No national character was ever
shaped by formula or by philosophy; for greater forces
than these lie behind it,—the forces of inheritance and of
events. Are we, by virtue of our surroundings and
institutions, become a different people from our ancestors,
or are we yet the same race of Anglo-Saxons, whose restless energy in colonization, in conquest, in trade, in "the
spread of civilization," has carried their speech into
every part of the world, and planted their habits everywhere?

Within a week such a question, which we had hitherto
hardly thought seriously to ask during our whole national
existence, has been put before us by the first foreign war
that we have had since we became firmly established as a
nation. Before we knew the meaning of foreign possessions
in a world ever growing more jealous, we have found ourselves the captors of islands in both great oceans; and
from our home-staying policy of yesterday we are brought
face to face with world-wide forces in Asia as well as in
Europe, which seem to be working, by the opening of
the Orient, for one of the greatest changes in human
history. Until a little while ago our latest war dispatches
came from Appomattox. Now our latest dispatches (when
this is written) come from Manila. The news from Appomattox concerned us only. The news from Manila sets every
statesman and soldier in the world to thinking new
thoughts about us, and to asking new questions. And to
nobody has the change come more unexpectedly than to
ourselves. Has it come without our knowing the meaning
of it? The very swiftness of these events and the ease with
which they have come to pass are matters for more
serious thought than the unjust rule of Spain in Cuba, or
than any tasks that have engaged us since we rose to
commanding physical power.

DOCUMENT 5

PLATFORM OF THE AMERICAN ANTI-IMPERIALIST LEAGUE,
OCTOBER 17, 1899

Annexation of the Philippines and accompanying visions of an imperial destiny were popular in the United States in 1899, but among the many Americans who had misgivings about them, there were some who were convinced that overseas expansion was a fatal departure from long-standing American principles. They formed various anti-imperialist leagues, and many old reformers became leading members. These leagues, joining in a coalition known as the American Anti-Imperialist League, met at Chicago in 1899, and adopted the platform given here.

We hold that the policy known as imperialism is hostile to liberty and tends toward militarism, an evil from which it has been our glory to be free. We regret that it has become necessary in the land of Washington and Lincoln to reaffirm that all men, of whatever race or color, are entitled to life, liberty, and the pursuit of happiness. We maintain that governments derive their just powers from the consent of the governed. We insist that the subjugation of any people is "criminal aggression" and open disloyalty to the distinctive principles of our government.

We earnestly condemn the policy of the present national administration in the Philippines. It seeks to extinguish the spirit of 1776 in those islands. We deplore the sacrifice of our soldiers and sailors, whose bravery deserves admiration even in an unjust war. We denounce the slaughter of the Filipinos as a needless horror. We protest against the extension of American sovereignty by Spanish methods.

We demand the immediate cessation of the war against liberty, begun by Spain and continued by us. We urge that

Congress be promptly convened to announce to the Filipinos our purpose to concede to them the independence for which they have so long fought and which of right is theirs.

The United States have always protested against the doctrine of international law which permits the subjugation of the weak by the strong. A self-governing state cannot accept sovereignty over an unwilling people. The United States cannot act upon the ancient heresy that might makes right.

Imperialists assume that with the destruction of self-government in the Philippines by American hands, all opposition here will cease. This is a grievous error. Much as we abhor the war of "criminal aggression" in the Philippines, greatly as we regret that the blood of the Filipinos is on American hands, we more deeply resent the betrayal of American institutions at home. The real firing line is not in the suburbs of Manila. The foe is of our own household. The attempt of 1861 was to divide the country. That of 1899 is to destroy its fundamental principles and noblest ideals.

Whether the ruthless slaughter of the Filipinos shall end next month or next year is but an incident in a contest that must go on until the declaration of independence and the constitution of the United States are rescued from the hands of their betrayers. Those who dispute about standards of value while the republic is undermined will be listened to as little as those who would wrangle about the small economies of the household while the house is on fire. The training of a great people for a century, the aspiration for liberty of a vast immigration are forces that will hurl aside those who in the delirium of conquest seek to destroy the character of our institutions.

We deny that the obligation of all citizens to support their government in times of grave national peril applies to the present situation. If an administration may with impunity ignore the issues upon which it was chosen, deliberately create a condition of war anywhere on the face of the globe, debauch the civil service for spoils to promote the adventure, organize a truth-suppressing censorship, and demand of all citizens a suspension of judgment and their unanimous support while it chooses to continue the fighting, representative government itself is imperiled.

We propose to contribute to the defeat of any person or party that stands for the forcible subjugation of any people. We shall oppose for re-election all who in the white house or in congress betray American liberty in pursuit of un-American ends. We still hope that both of our great political parties will support and defend the declaration of independence in the closing campaign of the century.

We hold with Abraham Lincoln, that "no man is good enough to govern another man without that other's consent. When the white man governs himself, that is self-government, but when he governs himself and also governs another man, that is more than self-government —that is despotism." "Our reliance is in the love of liberty which God has planted in us. Our defense is in the spirit which prizes liberty as the heritage of all men in all lands. Those who deny freedom to others deserve it not for themselves, and under a just God cannot long retain it."

We cordially invite the co-operation of all men and women who remain loyal to the declaration of independence and the constitution of the United States.

DOCUMENT 6

WOODROW WILSON, APPEAL
FOR NEUTRALITY,

AUGUST 19, 1914

On August 4, 1914, immediately upon the outbreak of war in Europe, Wilson issued a formal proclamation of neutrality, which he followed, fourteen days later, with this message to his countrymen. He urged that American neutrality be not merely a thing of law but of spirit, that Americans be "impartial in thought as well as in action."

My fellow countrymen: I suppose that every thoughtful man in America has asked himself, during these last troubled weeks, what influence the European war may exert upon the United States, and I take the liberty of addressing a few words to you in order to point out that it is entirely within our own choice what its effects upon us will be and to urge very earnestly upon you the sort of speech and conduct which will best safeguard the Nation against distress and disaster.

The effect of the war upon the United States will depend upon what American citizens say and do. Every man who really loves America will act and speak in the true spirit of neutrality, which is the spirit of impartiality and fairness and friendliness to all concerned. The spirit of the Nation in this critical matter will be determined largely by what individuals and society and those gathered in public meetings do and say, upon what newspapers and magazines contain, upon what ministers utter in their pulpits, and men proclaim as their opinions on the street.

The people of the United States are drawn from many nations, and chiefly from the nations now at war. It is natural and inevitable that there should be the utmost variety of sympathy and desire among them with regard to the issues and circumstances of the conflict. Some will wish one nation, others another, to succeed in the momentous struggle. It will be easy to excite passion and difficult to allay it. Those responsible for exciting it will assume a heavy responsibility, responsibility for no less a thing than that the people of the United States, whose love of their country and whose loyalty to its Government should unite them as Americans all, bound in honor and affection to think first of her and her interests, may be divided in camps of hostile opinion, hot against each other, involved in the war itself in impulse and opinion if not in action.

Such divisions amongst us would be fatal to our peace of mind and might seriously stand in the way of the proper performance of our duty as the one great nation at peace, the one people holding itself ready to play a part of impartial mediation and speak the counsels of peace and accommodation, not as a partisan, but as a friend.

I venture, therefore, my fellow countrymen, to speak a solemn word of warning to you against that deepest, most subtle, most essential breach of neutrality which may spring out of partisanship, out of passionately taking sides. The United States must be neutral in fact as well as in name during these days that are to try men's souls. We must be impartial in thought as well as in action, must put a curb upon our sentiments as well as upon every transaction that might be construed as a preference of one party to the struggle before another.

My thought is of America. I am speaking, I feel sure, the earnest wish and purpose of every thoughtful American that this great country of ours, which is, of course, the first in our thoughts and in our hearts, should show herself in this time of peculiar trial a Nation fit beyond others to exhibit the fine poise of undisturbed judgment, the dignity of self-control, the efficiency of dispassionate action; a Nation that neither sits in judgment upon others nor is disturbed in her own counsels and which keeps herself fit and free to do what is honest and disinterested and truly serviceable for the peace of the world.

Shall we not resolve to put upon ourselves the restraints which will bring to our people the happiness and the great and lasting influence for peace we covet for them?

DOCUMENT 7

WOODROW WILSON, PEACE WITHOUT VICTORY ADDRESS,

JANUARY 22, 1917

This prophetic address was delivered to the Senate in a dark hour. Wilson had just attempted to mediate a peace settlement, but had discovered how far apart the belligerents were in their war aims, and how unlikely it was that he could do anything to reconcile them, for the present at least. Here he attempted to state what kind of peace the United States would support, hoping against hope that his speech might

*be taken as a cue for negotiations. It was, however,
extremely unwelcome to the Allies. And Germany—
though Wilson did not then know it—had already
decided to resume the unrestricted submarine warfare
which was the immediate occasion for America's
entrance into the war.*

I have sought this opportunity to address you because I
thought that I owed it to you, as the counsel associated
with me in the final determination of our international
obligations, to disclose to you without reserve the thought
and purpose that have been taking form in my mind in
regard to the duty of our Government in the days to come
when it will be necessary to lay afresh and upon a new
plan the foundations of peace among the nations.

It is inconceivable that the people of the United
States should play no part in that great enterprise. . . .
They cannot in honor withhold the service to which they
are now about to be challenged. They do not wish to
withhold it. But they owe it to themselves and to the
other nations of the world to state the conditions under
which they will feel free to render it.

That service is nothing less than this, to add their authority and their power to the authority and force of other nations
to guarantee peace and justice throughout the world. Such
a settlement cannot now be long postponed. It is right that
before it comes this Government should frankly formulate the conditions upon which it would feel justified in
asking our people to approve its formal and solemn adherence to a League for Peace. I am here to attempt to
state those conditions.

The present war must first be ended; but we owe it to
candor and to a just regard for the opinion of mankind
to say that, so far as our participation in guarantees of
future peace is concerned, it makes a great deal of difference in what way and upon what terms it is ended. The
treaties and agreements which bring it to an end must
embody terms which will create a peace that is worth
guaranteeing and preserving, a peace that will win the approval of mankind, not merely a peace that will serve the
several interests and immediate aims of the nations engaged. . . .

No covenant of co-operative peace that does not include the peoples of the New World can suffice to keep the future safe against war; and yet there is only one sort of peace that the peoples of America could join in guaranteeing. The elements of that peace must be elements that engage the confidence and satisfy the principles of the American governments, elements consistent with their political faith and with the practical convictions which the peoples of America have once for all embraced and undertaken to defend. . . .

It will be absolutely necessary that a force be created as a guarantor of the permanency of the settlement so much greater than the force of any nation now engaged or any alliance hitherto formed or projected that no nation, no probable combination of nations could face or withstand it. If the peace presently to be made is to endure, it must be a peace made secure by the organized major force of mankind.

The terms of the immediate peace agreed upon will determine whether it is a peace for which such a guarantee can be secured. The question upon which the whole future peace and policy of the world depends is this: Is the present war a struggle for a just and secure peace, or only for a new balance of power? If it be only a struggle for a new balance of power, who will guarantee, who can guarantee the stable equilibrium of the new arrangement? Only a tranquil Europe can be a stable Europe. There must be, not a balance of power, but a community of power; not organized rivalries, but an organized common peace.

Fortunately we have received very explicit assurances on this point. . . . I think it will be serviceable if I attempt to set forth what we understand them to be.

They imply, first of all, that it must be a peace without victory. It is not pleasant to say this. I beg that I may be permitted to put my own interpretation upon it and that it may be understood that no other interpretation was in my thought. I am seeking only to face realities and to face them without soft concealments. Victory would mean peace forced upon the loser, a victor's terms imposed upon the vanquished. It would be accepted in humiliation, under duress, at an intolerable sacrifice, and would leave a sting, a resentment, a bitter memory upon which terms of peace would rest, not permanently, but only as upon quicksand. Only a peace between equals can last. Only a peace the very principle of which is equality and a common participation in a common benefit. The right state of mind, the right feeling between nations, is as necessary for a lasting peace as is the just settlement of vexed questions of territory or of racial and national allegiance.

The equality of nations upon which peace must be founded if it is to last must be an equality of rights; the guarantees exchanged must neither recognize nor imply a difference between big nations and small, between those that are powerful and those that are weak. Right must be based upon the common strength, not upon the individual strength, of the nations upon whose concert peace will depend. Equality of territory or of resources there of course cannot be; nor any sort of equality not gained in the ordinary peaceful and legitimate development of the peoples themselves. But no one asks or expects anything more than an equality of rights. Mankind is looking now for freedom of life, not for equipoises of power.

And there is a deeper thing involved than even equality of right among organized nations. No peace can last, or ought to last, which does not recognize and accept the principle that governments derive all their just powers from the consent of the governed, and that no right anywhere exists to hand peoples about from sovereignty to sovereignty as if they were property. . . .

So far as practicable, moreover, every great people now struggling towards a full development of its resources and of its powers should be assured a direct outlet to the great highways of the sea. Where this cannot be done by the cession of territory, it can no doubt be done by the neutralization of direct rights of way under the general guarantee which will assure the peace itself. With a right comity of arrangement no nation need be shut away from free access to the open paths of the world's commerce.

And the paths of the sea must alike in law and in fact be free. The freedom of the seas is the *sine qua non* of peace, equality, and co-operation. . . . It need not be

difficult either to define or to secure the freedom of the
seas if the governments of the world sincerely desire to
come to an agreement concerning it.

It is a problem closely connected with the limitation
of naval armaments and the co-operation of the navies of
the world in keeping the seas at once free and safe. And
the question of limiting naval armaments opens the wider
and perhaps more difficult question of the limitation of
armies and of all programs of military preparation. Difficult and delicate as these questions are, they must be faced
with the utmost candor and decided in a spirit of real
accommodation if peace is to come with healing in its
wings, and come to stay. Peace cannot be had without
concession and sacrifice. There can be no sense of safety
and equality among the nations if great preponderating
armaments are henceforth to continue here and there to
be built up and maintained. . . .

I have spoken upon these great matters without reserve and with the utmost explicitness because it has
seemed to me to be necessary if the world's yearning
desire for peace was anywhere to find free voice and
utterance. Perhaps I am the only person in high authority
amongst all the peoples of the world who is at liberty to
speak and hold nothing back. I am speaking as an individual, and yet I am speaking also, of course, as the
responsible head of a great government, and I feel confident that I have said what the people of the United
States would wish me to say. . . .

I am proposing, as it were, that the nations should
with one accord adopt the doctrine of President Monroe
as the doctrine of the world: that no nation should seek
to extend its polity over any other nation or people, but
that every people should be left free to determine its own
polity, its own way of development, unhindered, unthreat-
ened, unafraid, the little along with the great and powerful.

I am proposing that all nations henceforth avoid entangling alliances which would draw them into competi-
tions of power; catch them in a net of intrigue and selfish
rivalry, and disturb their own affairs with influences in-
truded from without. There is no entangling alliance in a
concert of power. When all unite to act in the same sense
and with the same purpose all act in the common interest

and are free to live their own lives under a common protection.

I am proposing government by the consent of the governed; that freedom of the seas which in international conference after conference representatives of the United States have urged with the eloquence of those who are the convinced disciples of liberty; and that moderation of armaments which makes of armies and navies a power for order merely, not an instrument of aggression or of selfish violence.

These are American principles, American policies. We could stand for no others. And they are also the principles and policies of forward looking men and women everywhere, of every modern nation, of every enlightened community. They are the principles of mankind and must prevail.

DOCUMENT 8

WOODROW WILSON, SPEECH FOR DECLARATION OF WAR AGAINST GERMANY,

APRIL 2, 1917

Wilson summoned all his eloquence for this war message, yet he could not fully quiet his own misgivings about declaring war. The night before he delivered the message, he told Frank Cobb of the New York World *that America's entry into the war would bring "illiberalism" at home. "Once lead this people into war," he said, "and they'll forget there ever was such a thing as tolerance. To fight you must be brutal and ruthless, and the spirit of ruthless brutality will enter into the very fibre of our national life. . . ." He expressed fear that the Constitution would not survive, that free speech and the right of assembly would be destroyed. "If there is any alternative, for God's sake, let's take it," he exclaimed. In the message itself he declared: "It is a fearful thing to lead this great, peaceful people into*

> *war, into the most terrible and disastrous of all wars, civilization itself seeming to be in the balance." The speech was received with great enthusiasm and prolonged applause; but Wilson, returning to the White House, said to his secretary, Joseph Tumulty: "My message today was a message of death for our young men. How strange it seems to applaud that."*

I have called the Congress into extraordinary session because there are serious, very serious, choices of policy to be made, and made immediately, which it was neither right nor constitutionally permissible that I should assume the responsibility of making.

On the third of February last I officially laid before you the extraordinary announcement of the Imperial German Government that on and after the first day of February it was its purpose to put aside all restraints of law or of humanity and use its submarines to sink every vessel that sought to approach either the ports of Great Britain and Ireland or the western coasts of Europe or any of the ports controlled by the enemies of Germany within the Mediterranean. That had seemed to be the object of the German submarine warfare earlier in the war, but since April of last year the Imperial Government had somewhat restrained the commanders of its undersea craft in conformity with its promise then given to us that passenger boats should not be sunk and that due warning would be given to all other vessels which its submarines might seek to destroy, when no resistance was offered or escape attempted, and care taken that their crews were given at least a fair chance to save their lives in their open boats. The precautions taken were meager and haphazard enough, as was proved in distressing instance after instance in the progress of the cruel and unmanly business, but a certain degree of restraint was observed. The new policy has swept every restriction aside. Vessels of every kind, whatever their flag, their character, their cargo, their destination, their errand, have been ruthlessly sent to the bottom without warning and without thought of help or mercy for those on board, the vessels of friendly neutrals along with those of belligerents. Even hospital ships and ships carrying relief to the sorely bereaved and stricken people of Belgium, though the latter were provided with safe conduct through the proscribed areas by the German Government itself and were distinguished by unmistakable marks of identity, have been sunk with the same reckless lack of compassion or of principle.

I was for a little while unable to believe that such things would in fact be done by any government that had hitherto subscribed to the humane practices of civilized nations. International law had its origin in the attempt to set up some law which would be respected and observed upon the seas, where no nation had right of dominion and where lay the free highways of the world. . . . This minimum of right the German Government has swept aside under the plea of retaliation and necessity and because it had no weapons which it could use at sea except these which it is impossible to employ as it is employing them without throwing to the winds all scruples of humanity or of respect for the understandings that were supposed to underlie the intercourse of the world. I am not now thinking of the loss of property involved, immense and serious as that is, but only of the wanton and wholesale destruction of the lives of non-combatants, men, women, and children, engaged in pursuits which have always, even in the darkest periods of modern history, been deemed innocent and legitimate. Property can be paid for; the lives of peaceful and innocent people cannot be. The present German submarine warfare against commerce is a warfare against mankind.

It is a war against all nations. American ships have been sunk, American lives taken, in ways which it has stirred us very deeply to learn of, but the ships and people of other neutral and friendly nations have been sunk and overwhelmed in the waters in the same way. There has been no discrimination. The challenge is to all mankind. Each nation must decide for itself how it will meet it. The choice we make for ourselves must be made with a moderation of counsel and a temperateness of judgment befitting our character and our motives as a nation. We must put excited feeling away. Our motive will not be revenge or the victorious assertion of the physical might of the nation, but only the vindication of right, of human right, of which we are only a single champion.

When I addressed the Congress on the twenty-sixth of February last I thought that it would suffice to assert our neutral rights with arms, our right to use the seas against unlawful interference, our right to keep our people safe against unlawful violence. But armed neutrality, it now appears, is impracticable. Because submarines are in effect outlaws when used as the German submarines have been used against merchant shipping, it is impossible to defend ships against their attacks as the law of nations has assumed that merchantmen would defend themselves against privateers or cruisers, visible craft giving chase upon the open sea. It is common prudence in such circumstances, grim necessity indeed, to endeavor to destroy them before they have shown their own intention. They must be dealt with upon sight, if dealt with at all. The German Government denies the right of neutrals to use arms at all within the areas of the sea which it has proscribed, even in the defense of rights which no modern publicist has ever before questioned their right to defend. The intimation is conveyed that the armed guards which we have placed on our merchant ships will be treated as beyond the pale of law and subject to be dealt with as pirates would be. Armed neutrality is ineffectual enough at best; in such circumstances and in the face of such pretensions it is worse than ineffectual: it is likely only to produce what it was meant to prevent; it is practically certain to draw us into the war without either the rights or the effectiveness of belligerents. There is one choice we cannot make, we are incapable of making: we will not choose the path of submission and suffer the most sacred rights of our Nation and our people to be ignored or violated. The wrongs against which we now array ourselves are no common wrongs; they cut to the very roots of human life.

With a profound sense of the solemn and even tragical character of the step I am taking and of the grave responsibilities which it involves, but in unhesitating obedience to what I deem my constitutional duty, I advise that the Congress declare the recent course of the Imperial German Government to be in fact nothing less than war against the government and people of the United States; that it formally accept the status of belligerent which has thus been thrust upon it; and that it take immediate steps not only to put the country in a more thorough state of defense but also to exert all its power and employ all its resources to bring the Government of the German Empire to terms and end the war.

What this will involve is clear. It will involve the utmost practicable coöperation in counsel and action with the governments now at war with Germany, and, as incident to that, the extension to those governments of the most liberal financial credits, in order that our resources may so far as possible be added to theirs. It will involve the organization and mobilization of all the material resources of the country to supply the materials of war and serve the incidental needs of the Nation in the most abundant and yet the most economical and efficient way possible. It will involve the immediate full equipment of the navy in all respects but particularly in supplying it with the best means of dealing with the enemy's submarines. It will involve the immediate addition to the armed forces of the United States already provided for by law in case of war at least five hundred thousand men, who should, in my opinion, be chosen upon the principle of universal liability to service, and also the authorization of subsequent additional increments of equal force so soon as they may be needed and can be handled in training. It will involve also, of course, the granting of adequate credits to the Government, sustained, I hope, so far as they can equitably be sustained by the present generation, by well conceived taxation. . . .

While we do these things, these deeply momentous things, let us be very clear, and make very clear to all the world what our motives and our objects are. My own thought has not been driven from its habitual and normal course by the unhappy events of the last two months, and I do not believe that the thought of the Nation has been altered or clouded by them. I have exactly the same things in mind now that I had in mind when I addressed the Senate on the twenty-second of January last; the same that I had in mind when I addressed the Congress on the third of February and on the twenty-sixth of February. Our object now, as then, is to vindicate the principles of peace and justice in the life of the world as against selfish and autocratic power and to set up amongst the really free and self-governed peoples of the world such a concert of purpose and of action as will henceforth insure the observance of those principles. Neutrality is no longer feasible or desirable where the peace of the world is involved and the freedom of its peoples, and the menace to that peace and freedom lies in the existence of autocratic governments backed by organized force which is controlled wholly by their will, not by the will of their people. We have seen the last of neutrality in such circumstances. We are at the beginning of an age in which it will be insisted that the same standards of conduct and of responsibility for wrong done shall be observed among nations and their governments that are observed among the individual citizens of civilized states.

We have no quarrel with the German people. We have no feeling towards them but one of sympathy and friendship. It was not upon their impulse that their government acted in entering this war. It was not with their previous knowledge or approval. It was a war determined upon as wars used to be determined upon in the old, unhappy days when peoples were nowhere consulted by their rulers and wars were provoked and waged in the interest of dynasties or of little groups of ambitious men who were accustomed to use their fellow men as pawns and tools. . . .

We are accepting this challenge of hostile purpose because we know that in such a Government, following such methods, we can never have a friend; and that in the presence of its organized power, always lying in wait to accomplish we know not what purpose, there can be no assured security for the democratic Governments of the world. We are now about to accept gauge of battle with this natural foe to liberty and shall, if necessary, spend the whole force of the nation to check and nullify its pretensions and its power. We are glad, now that we see the facts with no veil of false pretense about them, to fight thus for the ultimate peace of the world and for the liberation of its peoples, the German peoples included: for the rights of nations great and small and the privilege of men everywhere to choose their way of life and of obedience. The world must be made safe for democracy. Its peace must be planted upon the tested foundations of political liberty. We have no selfish ends to serve. We desire no conquest, no dominion. We seek no indemnities for ourselves, no material compensation for the sacrifices we shall freely make. We are but one of the champions of the rights of mankind. We shall be satisfied when those rights have been made as secure as the faith and the freedom of nations can make them.

Just because we fight without rancor and without selfish object, seeking nothing for ourselves but what we shall wish to share with all free peoples, we shall, I feel confident, conduct our operations as belligerents without passion and ourselves observe with proud punctilio the principles of right and of fair play we profess to be fighting for.

I have said nothing of the Governments allied with the Imperial Government of Germany because they have not made war upon us or challenged us to defend our right and our honor. The Austro-Hungarian Government has, indeed, avowed its unqualified indorsement and acceptance of the reckless and lawless submarine warfare adopted now without disguise by the Imperial German Government, and it has therefore not been possible for this Government to receive Count Tarnowski, the Ambassador recently accredited to this Government by the Imperial and Royal Government of Austria-Hungary; but that Government has not actually engaged in warfare against citizens of the United States on the seas, and I take the liberty, for the present at least, of postponing a discussion of our relations with the authorities at Vienna. We enter this war only where we are clearly forced into it because there are no other means of defending our rights.

It will be all the easier for us to conduct ourselves as belligerents in a high spirit of right and fairness because we act without animus, not in enmity towards a people or with the desire to bring any injury or disadvantage upon them, but only in armed opposition to an irresponsible government which has thrown aside all considerations of humanity and of right and is running amuck. We are, let me say again, the sincere friends of the German people, and shall desire nothing so much as the early reëstablishment of intimate relations of mutual advantage between us,—however hard it may be for them, for the time being, to believe that this is spoken from our hearts. We have borne with their present Government through all these bitter months because of that friendship,—exercising a patience and forbearance which would otherwise have been impossible. We shall, happily, still have an opportunity to prove that friendship in our daily attitude and actions towards the millions of men and women of German birth and native sympathy who live amongst us and share our life, and we shall be proud to prove it towards all who are in fact loyal to their neighbors and to the Government in the hour of test. They are, most of them, as true and loyal Americans as if they had never known any other fealty or allegiance. They will be prompt to stand with us in rebuking and restraining the few who may be of a different mind and purpose. If there should be disloyalty, it will be dealt with with a firm hand of stern repression; but, if it lifts its head at all, it will lift it only here and there and without countenance except from a lawless and malignant few.

It is a distressing and oppressive duty, Gentlemen of the Congress, which I have performed in thus addressing you. There are, it may be, many months of fiery trial and sacrifice ahead of us. It is a fearful thing to lead this great peaceful people into war, into the most terrible and disastrous of all wars, civilization itself seeming to be in the balance. But the right is more precious than peace, and we shall fight for the things which we have always carried nearest our hearts,—for democracy, for the right of those who submit to authority to have a voice in their own Governments, for the rights and liberties of small nations, for a universal dominion of right by such a concert of free peoples as shall bring peace and safety to all nations and make the world itself at last free. To such a task we can dedicate our lives and our fortunes, everything that we are and everything that we have, with the pride of those who know that the day has come when America is privileged to spend her blood and her might for the principles that gave her birth and happiness and the peace which she has treasured. God helping her, she can do no other.

DOCUMENT 9

GEORGE W. NORRIS, SPEECH AGAINST DECLARATION OF WAR,

APRIL 4, 1917

Senator George W. Norris of Nebraska had had an honorable record of fourteen years in the House and Senate as a liberal Republican when he rose to make this appeal against a declaration of war. It was an indignant speech, voicing the view of many opponents of entry into the war, that the United States would be fighting not for principles but for profits. Many years later Norris remembered that he had felt powerless "to stop the flow of words coming from my heart." Although his position was far from popular in the country at large, Norris was returned to the Senate where his loyal constituents kept him for another quarter of a century.

There are a great many American citizens who feel that we owe it as a duty to humanity to take part in this war. Many instances of cruelty and inhumanity can be found on both sides. Men are often biased in their judgment on account of their sympathy and their interests. To my mind, what we ought to have maintained from the beginning was the strictest neutrality. If we had done this I do not believe we would have been on the verge of war at the present time. We had a right as a nation, if we desired, to cease at any time to be neutral. We had a technical right to respect the English war zone and to disregard the German war zone, but we could not do that and be neutral. I have no quarrel to find with the man who does not desire our country to remain neutral. While many such people are moved by selfish motives and hopes of gain, I have no doubt but that in a great many instances, through what I believe to be a misunderstanding of the real condition, there are many honest, patriotic citizens who think we ought to engage in this war and who are behind the President in his demand that we should declare war against Germany. I think such people err in judgment and to a great extent have been misled as to the real history and the true facts by the almost unanimous demand of the great combination of wealth that has a direct financial interest in our participation in the war. We have loaned many hundreds of millions of dollars to the allies in this controversy. While such action was legal and countenanced by international law, there is no doubt in my mind but the enormous amount of money loaned to the allies in this country has been instrumental in bringing about a public sentiment in favor of our country taking a course that would make every bond worth a hundred cents on the dollar and making the payment of every debt certain and sure. Through this instrumentality and also through the instrumentality of others who have not only made millions out of the war in the manufacture of munitions, etc., and who would expect to make millions more if our country can be drawn into the catastrophe, a large number of the great newspapers and news agencies of the country have been controlled and enlisted in the greatest propaganda that the world has ever known, to manufacture sentiment in favor of war. It is now demanded that the American citizens shall be used as insurance policies to guarantee the safe delivery of munitions of war to belligerent nations. The enormous profits of munition manufacturers, stockbrokers, and bond dealers must be still further increased by our entrance into the war. This has brought us to the present moment, when Congress, urged by the President and backed by the artificial sentiment, is about to declare war and engulf our country in the greatest holocaust that the world has ever known.

In showing the position of the bondholder and the stockbroker I desire to read an extract from a letter written by a member of the New York Stock Exchange to his customers. This writer says:

Regarding the war as inevitable, Wall Street believes that it would be preferable to this uncertainty about the actual date of its commencement. Canada and Japan are at war, and are more prosperous than ever before. The popular view is that stocks would have a quick, clear, sharp reaction immediately upon outbreak of hostilities, and that then they would enjoy an old-fashioned bull market such as followed the outbreak of war with Spain in 1898. The advent of peace would force a readjustment of commodity prices and would probably mean a postponement of new enterprises. As peace negotiations would be long drawn out, the period of waiting and uncertainty for business would be long. If the United States does not go to war it is nevertheless good opinion that the preparedness program will compensate in good measure for the loss of the stimulus of actual war.

Here we have the Wall Street view. Here we have the man representing the class of people who will be made prosperous should we become entangled in the present war, who have already made millions of dollars, and who will make many hundreds of millions more if we get into the war. Here we have the cold-blooded proposition that war brings prosperity to that class of people who are within the viewpoint of this writer. He expresses the view, undoubtedly, of Wall Street, and of thousands of men elsewhere, who see only dollars coming to them through the handling of stocks and bonds that will be necessary in case of war. "Canada and Japan," he says, "are at war, and are more prosperous than ever before."

To whom does the war bring prosperity? Not to the soldier who for the munificent compensation of $16 per month shoulders his musket and goes into the trench, there to shed his blood and to die if necessary; not to the broken-hearted widow who waits for the return of the mangled body of her husband; not to the mother who weeps at the death of her brave boy; not to the little children who shiver with cold; not to the babe who suffers from hunger; nor to the millions of mothers and daughters who carry broken hearts to their graves. War brings no prosperity to the great mass of common and patriotic citizens. It increases the cost of living of those who toil and those who already must strain every effort to keep soul and body together. War brings prosperity to the stock gambler on Wall Street—to those who are already in possession of more wealth than can be realized or enjoyed. Again this writer says that if we can not get war, "it is nevertheless good opinion that the preparedness program will compensate in good measure for the loss of the stimulus of actual war." That is, if we can not get war, let us go as far in that direction as possible. If we can not get war, let us cry for additional ships, additional guns, additional munitions, and everything else that will have a tendency to bring us as near as possible to the verge of war. And if war comes do such men as these shoulder the musket and go into the trenches?

Their object in having war and in preparing for war is to make money. Human suffering and the sacrifice of human life are necessary, but Wall Street considers only the dollars and the cents. The men who do the fighting, the people who make the sacrifices, are the ones who will not be counted in the measure of this great prosperity that he depicts. The stock brokers would not, of course, go to war, because the very object they have in bringing on the war is profit, and therefore they must remain in their Wall Street offices in order to share in that great prosperity which they say war will bring. The volunteer officer, even the drafting officer, will not find them. They will be concealed in their palatial offices on Wall Street, sitting behind mahogany desks, covered up with clipped coupons—coupons soiled with the sweat of honest toil, coupons stained with mothers' tears, coupons dyed in the lifeblood of their fellow men.

We are taking a step today that is fraught with untold danger. We are going into war upon the command of gold. We are going to run the risk of sacrificing millions of our countrymen's lives in order that other countrymen may coin their lifeblood into money. And even if we do not cross the Atlantic and go into the trenches, we are going to pile up a debt that the toiling masses that shall come many generations after us will have to pay. Unborn millions will bend their backs in toil in order to pay for the terrible step we are now about to take. We are about to do the bidding of wealth's terrible mandate. By our act we will make millions of our countrymen suffer, and the consequences of it may well be that millions of our brethren must shed their lifeblood, millions of broken-hearted women must weep, millions of children must suffer with cold, and millions of babes must die from hunger, and all because we want to preserve the commercial right of American citizens to deliver munitions of war to belligerent nations.

DOCUMENT 10

WOODROW WILSON, SPEECH ON THE FOURTEEN POINTS,

JANUARY 8, 1918

Wilson's liberal and generous statement of war aims in this speech to Congress made him the moral leader of the western world. His promise of a decent peace also undermined the will of the Germans to continue the bloody struggle, and when they sued for peace they did so on the basis of the Fourteen Points. Wilson and his intimate adviser, Colonel Edward M. House, formulated the Fourteen Points after House had convinced the President that he must do something to shore up cracking Allied morale and to keep the Russians in the war. The two men worked over the draft carefully, trying to make the phrasing flexible enough so that the Fourteen Points would have authority and value as statements of principle, no matter what the war's outcome—complete victory, a compromise settlement, or even defeat. For this reason they used the verb must *only a few times (see Points 5, 7, and 14), and formulated most of the Points as* shoulds. *One of the* musts *was "a general association of nations."*

It will be our wish and purpose that the processes of peace, when they are begun, shall be absolutely open, and that they shall involve and permit henceforth no secret understandings of any kind. The day of conquest and aggrandizement is gone by; so is also the day of secret covenants entered into in the interest of particular governments and likely at some unlooked-for moment to upset the peace of the world. It is this happy fact, now clear to the view of every public man whose thoughts do not still linger in an age that is dead and gone, which makes it possible for every nation whose purposes are consistent with justice and the peace of the world to avow now or at any other time the objects it has in view.

We entered this war because violations of right had occurred which touched us to the quick and made the life of our own people impossible unless they were corrected and the world secured once for all against their recurrence. What we demand in this war, therefore, is nothing peculiar to ourselves. It is that the world be made fit and safe to live in; and particularly that it be made safe for every peace-loving nation which, like our own, wishes to live its own life, determine its own institutions, be assured of justice and fair dealings by the other peoples of the world, as against force and selfish aggression. All the peoples of the world are in effect partners in this interest, and for our own part we see very clearly that unless justice be done to others it will not be done to us.

The program of the world's peace, therefore, is our program, and that program, the only possible program, as we see it, is this:

I. Open covenants of peace, openly arrived at, after which there shall be no private international understandings of any kind, but diplomacy shall proceed always frankly and in the public view.

II. Absolute freedom of navigation upon the seas, outside territorial waters, alike in peace and in war, except as the seas may be closed in whole or in part by international action for the enforcement of international covenants.

III. The removal, so far as possible, of all economic barriers and the establishment of an equality of trade conditions among all the nations consenting to the peace and associating themselves for its maintenance.

IV. Adequate guarantees given and taken that national armaments will be reduced to the lowest point consistent with domestic safety.

V. A free, open-minded, and absolutely impartial adjustment of all colonial claims, based upon a strict observance of the principle that in determining all such questions of sovereignty the interests of the populations concerned must have equal weight with the equitable claims of the Government whose title is to be determined.

VI. The evacuation of all Russian territory and such a settlement of all questions affecting Russia as will secure the best and freest co-operation of the other nations of the world in obtaining for her an unhampered and un-embarrassed opportunity for the independent determination of her own political development and national policy, and assure her of a sincere welcome into the society of free nations under institutions of her own choosing; and, more than a welcome, assistance also of every kind that she may need and may herself desire. The treatment accorded Russia by her sister nations in the months to come will be the acid test of their goodwill, of their comprehension of her needs as distinguished from their own interests, and of their intelligent and unselfish sympathy.

VII. Belgium, the whole world will agree, must be evacuated and restored, without any attempt to limit the sovereignty which she enjoys in common with all other free nations. No other single act will serve as this will serve to restore confidence among the nations in the laws which they have themselves set and determined for the government of their relations with one another. Without this healing act the whole structure and validity of international law is forever impaired.

VIII. All French territory should be freed and the invaded portions restored, and the wrong done to France by Prussia in 1871 in the matter of Alsace-Lorraine, which has unsettled the peace of the world for nearly fifty years, should be righted, in order that peace may once more be made secure in the interest of all.

IX. A readjustment of the frontiers of Italy should be effected along clearly recognizable lines of nationality.

X. The peoples of Austria-Hungary, whose place among the nations we wish to see safeguarded and assured, should be accorded the freest opportunity of autonomous development.

XI. Rumania, Serbia, and Montenegro should be evacuated; occupied territories restored; Serbia accorded free and secure access to the sea; and the relations of the several Balkan States to one another determined by friendly counsel along historically established lines of allegiance and nationality; and international guarantees of the political and economic independence and territorial integrity of the several Balkan States should be entered into.

XII. The Turkish portions of the present Ottoman Empire should be assured a secure sovereignty, but the other nationalities which are now under Turkish rule should be assured an undoubted security of life and an absolutely unmolested opportunity of autonomous development, and the Dardanelles should be permanently opened as a free passage to the ships and commerce of all nations under international guarantees.

XIII. An idependent Polish State should be erected which should include the territories inhabited by indisputably Polish populations, which should be assured a free and secure access to the sea, and whose political and economic independence and territorial integrity should be guaranteed by international covenant.

XIV. A general association of nations must be formed under specific covenants for the purpose of affording mutual guarantees of political independence and territorial integrity to great and small states alike.

In regard to these essential rectifications of wrong and assertions of right, we feel ourselves to be intimate partners of all the governments and peoples associated together against the imperialists. We cannot be separated in interest or divided in purpose. We stand together until the end.

For such arrangements and covenants we are willing to fight and to continue to fight until they are achieved; but only because we wish the right to prevail and desire a just and stable peace, such as can be secured only by removing the chief provocations to war, which this program does remove. We have no jealousy of German greatness, and there is nothing in this program that impairs it. We grudge her no achievement or distinction of learning or of pacific enterprise such as have made her record very bright and very enviable. We do not wish to injure her or to block in any way her legitimate influence or power. We do not wish to fight her either with arms or with hostile arrangements of trade, if she is willing to associate herself with us and the other peace-loving nations of the world in covenants of justice and law and fair dealing. We wish her only to accept a place of equality among the peoples of the world—the new world in which we now live—instead of a place of mastery.

Neither do we presume to suggest to her any alteration or modification of her institutions. But it is necessary, we must frankly say, and necessary as a preliminary to any intelligent dealings with her on our part, that we should know whom her spokesmen speak for when they speak to us, whether for the Reichstag majority or for the military party and the men whose creed is imperial domination.

We have spoken, now, surely, in terms too concrete to admit of any further doubt or question. An evident principle runs through the whole program I have outlined. It is the principle of justice to all peoples and nationalities, and their right to live on equal terms of liberty and safety with one another, whether they be strong or weak. Unless this principle be made its foundation, no part of the structure of international justice can stand. The people of the United States could act upon no other principle, and to the vindication of this principle they are ready to devote their lives, their honor, and everything that they possess. The moral climax of this, the culminating and final war for human liberty, has come, and they are ready to put their own strength, their own highest purpose, their own integrity and devotion to the test.

DOCUMENT 11

WOODROW WILSON, SPEECH ON THE COVENANT OF THE LEAGUE OF NATIONS,

FEBRUARY 14, 1919

In this speech, Wilson presented to a plenary session of the Peace Conference the Covenant of the League as it had been approved by the fourteen nations represented on the drafting committee. The President,

now at the peak of his influence, began by reading
the proposed Covenant, and then went on in a calm
and confident manner to make these remarks on the
character he hoped the League of Nations would
have. But this moment of triumph was brief; Wilson's
attempt to win the Senate's consent to membership in
the League is one of the most poignant personal
tragedies in the history of the American Presidency.

Now, as to the character of the document, while it has
consumed some time to read this document, I think you
will see at once that it is very simple, and in nothing so
simple as in the structure which it suggests for a league
of nations, a body of delegates, an executive council, and
a permanent secretariat.

When it came to the question of determining the
character of the representation in the body of delegates
we were all aware of a feeling which is current throughout the world.

Inasmuch as I am stating it in the presence of the
official representatives of the various governments here
present, including myself, I may say that there is a
universal feeling that the world can not rest satisfied with
merely official guidance. There has reached us through
many channels the feeling that if the deliberating body
of the league of nations was merely to be a body of
officials representing the various governments, the peoples
of the world would not be sure that some of the mistakes
which preoccupied officials had admittedly made might
not be repeated.

It was impossible to conceive a method or an
assembly so large and various as to be really representative of the great body of the peoples of the world, because,
as I roughly reckon it, we represent as we sit around
this table more than twelve hundred million people.

You can not have a representative assembly of twelve
hundred million people, but if you leave it to each Government to have, if it pleases, one or two or three representatives, though only with a single vote, it may vary its
representation from time to time, not only, but it may
[originate] the choice of its several representatives. . . .

Therefore we thought that this was a proper and a

very prudent concession to the practically universal opinion of plain men everywhere that they wanted the door left open to a variety of representation, instead of being confined to a single official body with which they could or might not find themselves in sympathy.

And you will notice that this body has unlimited rights of discussion. I mean of discussion of anything that falls within the field of international relations—and that it is especially agreed that war or international misunderstandings or anything that may lead to friction or trouble is everybody's business, because it may affect the peace of the world.

And in order to safeguard the popular power so far as we could of this representative body it is provided, you will notice, that when a subject is submitted it is not to arbitration but to discussion by the executive council; it can, upon the initiative of either of the parties to the dispute, be drawn out of the executive council on the larger form of the general body of delegates, because through this instrument we are depending primarily and chiefly upon one great force, and this is the moral force of the public opinion of the world—the pleasing and clarifying and compelling influences of publicity—so that intrigues can no longer have their coverts, so that designs that are sinister can at any time be drawn into the open, so that those things that are destroyed by the light may be promptly destroyed by the overwhelming light of the universal expression of the condemnation of the world.

Armed force is in the background in this program, but it *is* in the background, and if the moral force of the world will not suffice the physical force of the world shall. But that is the last resort, because this is intended as a constitution of peace, not as a league of war.

The simplicity of the document seems to me to be one of its chief virtues, because, speaking for myself, I was unable to see the variety of circumstances with which this league would have to deal. I was unable, therefore, to plan all the machinery that might be necessary to meet the differing and unexpected contingencies. Therefore I should say of this document that it is not a strait-jacket but a vehicle of life.

A living thing is born, and we must see to it what

clothes we put on it. It is not a vehicle of power, but a vehicle in which power may be varied at the discretion of those who exercise it and in accordance with the changing circumstances of the time. And yet, while it is elastic, while it is general in its terms, it is definite in the one thing that we were called upon to make definite.

It is a definite guaranty of peace. It is a definite guaranty by word against aggression. It is a definite guaranty against the things which have just come near bringing the whole structure of civilization into ruin.

Its purposes do not for a moment lie vague. Its purposes are declared, and its powers are unmistakable. It is not in contemplation that this should be merely a league to secure the peace of the world. It is a league which can be used for cooperation in any international matter.

That is the significance of the provision introduced concerning labor. There are many ameliorations of labor conditions which can be effected by conference and discussion. I anticipate that there will be a very great usefulness in the bureau of labor which it is contemplated shall be set up by the league.

Men and women and children who work have been in the background through long ages and sometimes seemed to be forgotten, while governments have had their watchful and suspicious eyes upon the maneuvers of one another, while the thought of statesmen has been about structural action and the larger transactions of commerce and of finance.

Now, if I may believe the picture which I see, there comes into the foreground the great body of the laboring people of the world, the men and women and children upon whom the great burden of sustaining the world must from day to day fall, whether we wish it to do so or not; people who go to bed tired and wake up without the stimulation of lively hope. These people will be drawn into the field of international consultation and help, and will be among the wards of the combined governments of the world. This is, I take leave to say, a very great step in advance in the mere conception of that.

Then, as you will notice, there is an imperative article concerning the publicity of all international agreements. Henceforth no member of the league can call any agreement valid which it has not registered with the secretary general, in whose office, of course, it will be subject to the examination of any body representing a member of the league. And the duty is laid upon the secretary general to earliest possible time. . . .

There has been no greater advance than this, gentlemen. If you look back upon the history of the world you will see how helpless peoples have too often been a prey to powers that had no conscience in the matter. It has been one of the many distressing revelations of recent years that the great power which has just been, happily, defeated put intolerable burdens and injustices upon the helpless people of some of the colonies which it annexed to itself, that its interest was rather their extermination than their development; that the desire was to possess their land for European purposes, and not to enjoy their confidence in order that mankind might be lifted in these places to the next higher level.

Now, the world, expressing its conscience in law, says there is an end of that, that our consciences shall be settled to this thing. States will be picked out which have already shown that they can exercise a conscience in this matter, and under their tutelage the helpless peoples of the world will come into a new light and into a new hope.

DOCUMENT 12

WILLIAM E. BORAH, SPEECH ON THE LEAGUE OF NATIONS,

NOVEMBER 19, 1919

Senator William E. Borah of Idaho was the most vehement of the Senate "irreconcilables," men who would have no part of the League of Nations on any terms or with any reservations. A remarkable orator, frequently compared by his admirers with Daniel Webster, Borah took an early lead in the effort to stir up public opinion against membership in the

*League. At the moment he delivered the speech
excerpted here, the Senate was prepared to vote, and
Borah thought, with many others, that it was about
to accept membership with the Lodge reservations.
His speech therefore was a final appeal, his eloquence
inspired by desperation. ("When I feel myself in
tears," Lodge said of this effort, "I know I am listening
to a great speech.") But the Senate rejected the treaty
with the Lodge reservations late on the same day by
a vote of 55 to 39. Borah acclaimed the result as "the
greatest victory since Appomattox." This speech represents American isolationism near its peak. After World
War II no speech against American membership in
the United Nations could have been given the wide
and respectful attention this impassioned attack on
the League received in 1919.*

When the league shall have been formed, we shall be a
member of what is known as the council of the league.
Our accredited representative will sit in judgment with
the accredited representatives of the other members of
the league to pass upon the concerns not only of our
country but of all Europe and all Asia and the entire
world. Our accredited representatives will be members
of the assembly. They will sit there to represent the
judgment of these 110,000,000 people—more then—just
as we are accredited here to represent our constituencies.
We can not send our representatives to sit in council with
the representatives of the other great nations of the world
with mental reservations as to what we shall do in case
their judgment shall not be satisfactory to us. If we go
to the council or to the assembly with any other purpose
than that of complying in good faith and in absolute
integrity with all upon which the council or the assembly
may pass, we shall soon return to our country with our
self-respect forfeited and the public opinion of the world
condemnatory.

Why need you gentlemen across the aisle worry
about a reservation here or there when we are sitting in
the council and in the assembly and bound by every
obligation in morals, which the President said was supreme
above that of law, to comply with the judgment which

our representative and the other representatives finally
form? Shall we go there, Mr. President, to sit in judgment, and in case that judgment works for peace join with
our allies, but in case it works for war withdraw our co-
operation? How long would we stand as we now stand, a
great Republic commanding the respect and holding the
leadership of the world, if we should adopt any such
course? . . .

We have said, Mr. President, that we would not
send our troops abroad without the consent of Congress.
Pass by now for a moment the legal proposition. If we
create executive functions, the Executive will perform
those functions without the authority of Congress. Pass
that question by and go to the other question. Our
members of the council are there. Our members of the
assembly are there. Article 11 is complete, and it
authorizes the league, a member of which is our representative, to deal with matters of peace and war, and
the league through its council and its assembly deals
with the matter, and our accredited representative joins
with the others in deciding upon a certain course, which
involves a question of sending troops. What will the
Congress of the United States do? What right will it have
left, except the bare technical right to refuse, which as a
moral proposition it will not dare to exercise? Have we
not been told day by day for the last nine months that
the Senate of the United States, a coordinate part of the
treaty-making power, should accept this league as it was
written because the wise men sitting at Versailles had so
written it, and has not every possible influence and every
source of power in public opinion been organized and
directed against the Senate to compel it to do that thing?
How much stronger will be the moral compulsion upon
the Congress of the United States when we ourselves have
indorsed the proposition of sending our accredited representatives there to vote for us?

Ah, but you say that there must be unanimous consent, and that there is vast protection in unanimous consent.

I do not wish to speak disparagingly; but has not
every division and dismemberment of every nation which
has suffered dismemberment taken place by unanimous

consent for the last 300 years? Did not Prussia and Austria and Russia by unanimous consent divide Poland? Did not the United States and Great Britain and Japan and Italy and France divide China and give Shantung to Japan? Was that not a unanimous decision? Close the doors upon the diplomats of Europe, let them sit in secret, give them the material to trade on, and there always will be unanimous consent. . . .

Mr. President, if you have enough territory, if you have enough material, if you have enough subject peoples to trade upon and divide, there will be no difficulty about unanimous consent.

Do our Democratic friends ever expect any man to sit as a member of the council or as a member of the Assembly equal in intellectual power and in standing before the world with that of our representative at Versailles? Do you expect a man to sit in the council who will have made more pledges, and I shall assume made them in sincerity, for self-determination and for the rights of small peoples, than had been made by our accredited representative? And yet, what became of it? The unanimous consent was obtained nevertheless.

But take another view of it. We are sending to the council one man. That one man represents 110,000,000 people.

Here, sitting in the Senate, we have two from every State in the Union, and over in the other House we have Representatives in accordance with population, and the responsibility is spread out in accordance with our obligations to our constituency. But now we are transferring to one man the stupendous power of representing the sentiment and convictions of 110,000,000 people in tremendous questions which may involve the peace or may involve the war of the world. . . .

What is the result of all this? We are in the midst of all of the affairs of Europe. We have entangled ourselves with all European concerns. We have joined in alliance with all the European nations which have thus far joined the league, and all nations which may be admitted to the league. We are sitting there dabbling in their affairs and intermeddling in their concerns. In other words, Mr. President—and this comes to the question which is fundamental with me—we have forfeited and surrendered, once and for all, the great policy of "no entangling alliances" upon which the strength of this Republic has been founded for 150 years.

My friends of reservations, tell me where is the reservation in these articles which protects us against entangling alliances with Europe?

Those who are differing over reservations, tell me what one of them protects the doctrine laid down by the Father of his Country. That fundamental proposition is surrendered, and we are a part of the European turmoils and conflicts from the time we enter this league. . . .

Lloyd-George is reported to have said just a few days before the conference met at Versailles that Great Britain could give up much, and would be willing to sacrifice much, to have America withdraw from that policy. That was one of the great objects of the entire conference at Versailles, so far as the foreign representatives were concerned. Clemenceau and Lloyd-George and others like them were willing to make any reasonable sacrifice which would draw America away from her isolation and into the internal affairs and concerns of Europe. This league of nations, with or without reservations, whatever else it does or does not do, does surrender and sacrifice that policy; and once having surrendered and become a part of the European concerns, where, my friends, are you going to stop?

You have put in here a reservation upon the Monroe doctrine. I think that, in so far as language could protect the Monroe doctrine, it has been protected. But as a practical proposition, as a working proposition, tell me candidly, as men familiar with the history of your country and of other countries, do you think that you can intermeddle in European affairs; and, secondly, never to permit Europe to [interfere in our affairs].

We can not protect the Monroe doctrine unless we protect the basic principle upon which it rests, and that is the Washington policy. I do not care how earnestly you may endeavor to do so, as a practical working proposition your league will come to the United States. . . .

Mr. President, there is another and even a more commanding reason why I shall record my vote against

this treaty. It imperils what I conceive to be the underlying, the very first principles of this Republic. It is in
conflict with the right of our people to govern themselves
free from all restraint, legal or moral, of foreign
powers. . . .

Sir, since the debate opened months ago those of us
who have stood against this proposition have been taunted
many times with being little Americans. Leave us the
word American, keep that in your presumptuous impeachment, and no taunt can disturb us, no gibe discompose
our purposes. Call us little Americans if you will, but
leave us the consolation and the pride which the term
American, however modified, still imparts. . . . We have
sought nothing save the tranquillity of our own people
and the honor and independence of our own Republic.
No foreign flattery, no possible world glory and power
have disturbed our poise or come between us and our
devotion to the traditions which have made us a people
or the policies which have made us a Nation, unselfish and
commanding. If we have erred we have erred out of too
much love for those things which from childhood you
and we together have been taught to revere—yes, to
defend even at the cost of limb and life. If we have erred
it is because we have placed too high an estimate upon
the wisdom of Washington and Jefferson, too exalted an
opinion upon the patriotism of the sainted Lincoln. . . .

Senators, even in an hour so big with expectancy we
should not close our eyes to the fact that democracy is
something more, vastly more, than a mere form of
government by which society is restrained into free and
orderly life. It is a moral entity, a spiritual force, as well.
And these are things which live only and alone in the
atmosphere of liberty. The foundation upon which
democracy rests is faith in the moral instincts of the people. Its ballot boxes, the franchise, its laws, and constitutions are but the outward manifestations of the deeper
and more essential thing—a continuing trust in the moral
purposes of the average man and woman. When this is
lost or forfeited your outward forms, however democratic
in terms, are a mockery. Force may find expression
through institutions democratic in structure equal with
the simple and more direct processes of a single supreme

ruler. These distinguishing virtues of a real republic you
can not commingle with the discordant and destructive
forces of the Old World and still preserve them. You can
not yoke a government whose fundamental maxim is that
of liberty to a government whose first law is that of force
and hope to preserve the former. These things are in
eternal war, and one must ultimately destroy the other.
You may still keep for a time the outward form, you may
still delude yourself, as others have done in the past, with
appearances and symbols, but when you shall have
committed this Republic to a scheme of world control
based upon force, upon the combined military force of
the four great nations of the world, you will have soon
destroyed the atmosphere of freedom, of confidence in
the self-governing capacity of the masses, in which alone
a democracy may thrive. We may become one of the four
dictators of the world, but we shall no longer be master of
our own spirit. And what shall it profit us as a Nation if
we shall go forth to the domination of the earth and
share with others the glory of world control and lose that
fine sense of confidence in the people, the soul of democracy?

Look upon the scene as it is now presented. Behold
the task we are to assume, and then contemplate the
method by which we are to deal with this task. Is the
method such as to address itself to a Government "conceived in liberty and dedicated to the proposition that all
men are created equal"? When this league, this combination, is formed four great powers representing the dominant people will rule one-half of the inhabitants of the
globe as subject peoples—rule by force, and we shall be
a party to the rule of force. There is no other way by
which you can keep people in subjection. You must
either give them independence, recognize their rights as
nations to live their own life and to set up their own form
of government, or you must deny them these things by
force. That is the scheme, the method proposed by the
league. It proposes no other. We will in time become
inured to its inhuman precepts and its soulless methods,
strange as this doctrine now seems to a free people. If
we stay with our contract, we will come in time to
declare with our associates that force—force, the creed of

the Prussian military oligarchy—is after all the true foundation upon which must rest all stable governments. Korea, despoiled and bleeding at every pore; India, sweltering in ignorance and burdened with inhuman taxes after more than one hundred years of dominant rule; Egypt, trapped and robbed of her birthright; Ireland, with 700 years of sacrifice for independence—this is the task, this is the atmosphere, and this is the creed in and under which we are to keep alive our belief in the moral purposes and self-governing capacity of the people, a belief without which the Republic must disintegrate and die. The maxim of liberty will soon give way to the rule of blood and iron. We have been pleading here for our Constitution. Conform this league, it has been said, to the technical terms of our charter, and all will be well. But I declare to you that we must go further and conform to those sentiments and passions for justice and freedom which are essential to the existence of democracy. . . .

Sir, we are told that this treaty means peace. Even so, I would not pay the price. Would you purchase peace at the cost of any part of our independence? We could have had peace in 1776—the price was high, but we could have had it. James Otis, Sam Adams, Hancock, and Warren were surrounded by those who urged peace and British rule. All through that long and trying struggle, particularly when the clouds of adversity lowered upon the cause, there was a cry of peace—let us have peace. We could have had peace in 1860; Lincoln was counseled by men of great influence and accredited wisdom to let our brothers—and, thank Heaven, they are brothers—depart in peace. But the tender, loving Lincoln, bending under the fearful weight of impending civil war, an apostle of peace, refused to pay the price, and a reunited country will praise his name forevermore—bless it because he refused peace at the price of national honor and national integrity. Peace upon any other basis than national independence, peace purchased at the cost of any part of our national integrity, is fit only for slaves, and even when purchased at such a price it is a delusion, for it can not last.

But your treaty does not mean peace—far, very far, from it. If we are to judge the future by the past it means war. Is there any guaranty of peace other than the guaranty which comes of the control of the war-making power by the people? Yet what great rule of democracy does the treaty leave unassailed? The people in whose keeping alone you can safely lodge the power of peace or war nowhere, at no time and in no place, have any voice in this scheme for world peace. Autocracy which has bathed the world in blood for centuries reigns supreme. Democracy is everywhere excluded. This, you say, means peace.

Can you hope for peace when love of country is disregarded in your scheme, when the spirit of nationality is rejected, even scoffed at? Yet what law of that moving and mysterious force does your treaty not deny? With a ruthlessness unparalleled your treaty in a dozen instances runs counter to the divine law of nationality. Peoples who speak the same language, kneel at the same ancestral tombs, moved by the same traditions, animated by a common hope, are torn asunder, broken in pieces, divided, and parceled out to antagonistic nations. And this you call justice. This, you cry, means peace. Peoples who have dreamed of independence, struggled and been patient, sacrificed and been hopeful, peoples who were told that through this peace conference they should realize the aspirations of centuries, have again had their hopes dashed to earth. One of the most striking and commanding figures in this war, soldier and statesmen, turned away from the peace table at Versailles declaring to the world, "The promise of the new life, the victory of the great humane ideals for which the peoples have shed their blood and their treasure without stint, the fulfillment of their aspirations toward a new international order and a fairer and better world, are not written into the treaty." No; your treaty means injustice. It means slavery. It means war. And to all this you ask this Republic to become a party. You ask it to abandon the creed under which it has grown to power and accept the creed of autocracy, the creed of repression and force.

∗ PART V ∗

Progressivism

INTRODUCTION

MANY advocates of reform were convinced, after the defeat of William Jennings Bryan in 1896, that the mind and heart of America were hopelessly smug and conservative. Yet only a half-dozen years later the nation, in an orgy of self-criticism, launched a drive for reform that did not end until the beginning of war in 1914. Reformers became the political leaders of the country—men like Theodore Roosevelt, Bryan, Woodrow Wilson, and the elder LaFollette. Political thought was dominated by men with a critical cast of mind—Herbert Croly, Walter Lippmann, Walter Weyl, J. Allen Smith, John Dewey, Thorstein Veblen, and Charles A. Beard. The country wanted to understand itself, and was willing not only to endure but to applaud the large doses of criticism served up by the new kind of journalists known as the muckrakers —Ida M. Tarbell, Lincoln Steffens, David Graham Phillips, Upton Sinclair, and others.

The muckrakers attacked abuses in both business and politics, and while much of what they wrote was sensational and evanescent, some of their work still stands as valuable analysis of American problems. Perhaps the best book to come out of the muckraking impulse was Lincoln Steffens's *The Shame of the Cities* (1904) (Document 1), first written as a series of articles for *McClure's* magazine. Single cities had been examined before— Chicago in 1894 by W. T. Stead in his remarkable

If Christ Came to Chicago, New York in the Lexow investigation of 1895. But what Steffens did was to attack the structure of urban life throughout the country, to show that it was riddled with "bossism" and corruption, and that this corruption was not fitful or accidental, but a built-in, constant consequence of the American way of doing things—a consequence, above all, of public apathy. No politician was able to answer Steffens at the level of theory, but American municipalities had been run by the boss system for so long that, on the level of practical politics, it was possible to defend "bossism" as an integral part of the functioning of the American city. A Tammany leader, George Washington Plunkitt (Document 2), genially offered such a defense, not only of the machine but even of "honest graft"; he argued that politics could not be managed by amateurs, and that what was called graft was simply the politician's way of taking advantage of opportunity, and that it was really no worse than the businessman's ways of doing the same thing. One of the most thoughtful of contemporary journalists, young Walter Lippmann (Document 3), agreed with Plunkitt not in defending "honest graft" but in finding it the natural consequence of a social ethos which approved of acquisitiveness in almost every field of activity, but expected self-denial from politicians.

The Progressive spirit fought battles not only of words but of deeds. It sought, for instance, to improve the hazardous lives of those who suffered most from industrialism. In state after state laws were passed affecting the way in which people lived and worked, attempting to improve tenements and sweatshops, to cut down long hours, and to make working conditions safer. Frequently reformers and lawmakers were frustrated by the courts, where judges with nineteenth-century ideas passed judgment on twentieth-century laws. One of the most famous instances of such judicial behavior occurred in the case of *Lochner* v. *New York* (1905) (Document 4) in which the Court struck down a New York law limiting hours of work in bakeries. Yet the biting dissent of Justice Holmes (Document 5) aroused much attention, and in good time had greater influence than the majority decision. Progress toward legislative control of industrial abuses was slowly made. One of the most notable victories was in the case of *Muller* v. *Oregon* (1908) (Document 6); the efforts of Louis D. Brandeis, the attorney for the state, to show that long hours of work were seriously harmful to the health of women won a decision upholding an Oregon law limiting the hours of women's work. Later decisions allowed the states to pass similar laws for men.

While the states were trying to establish social reforms through law, the federal government was rapidly developing and extending its powers in an effort to solve long-existing problems of railroad control, tariff reduction, anti-trust, and currency and banking reform. One of the hardest fought and most intricate issues was that of railroad regulation. Earlier efforts to regulate railroads, under the Interstate Commerce Act of 1887, had been rendered ineffective by a combination of executive sabotage and indifference, and judicial opposition. Now Progressivism brought a new determination to the fight. The Elkins Act of 1903 put new limits on the rebate practice, and also made it a misdemeanor for railroads to deviate from published rates. The Hepburn Act of 1906 gave the Interstate Commerce Commission the power to fix just and reasonable maximum rates and to prescribe uniform methods of accounting for railroads. With this act, truly effective regulation of railroad rates began. Orders of the Commission were made binding upon carriers, until they could appeal to the courts against the Commission's decision. This put the burden of proof in the courts upon the railroads rather than the Commission. So vital a provision was of course resisted strenuously by railroad spokesmen (Document 7) during the debate which preceded the passage of this act, but Representative William P. Hepburn and his associates (Document 8) had not only persuasive arguments but also the backing of President Theodore Roosevelt. After the act was passed, the Commission soon showed that it would be as effective as its advocates had hoped. Almost twice as many formal complaints were filed with the Commission within the next two years as had been filed in all the years between 1887 and 1906. By 1911 the Commission had cut in half over 190,000 of the rates prevailing in 1906.

By the end of the first decade of the twentieth century, a number of reforms in state government—corrupt practices acts, the initiative, referendum, and recall—as well as the impending direct election of United States Senators, led many Progressives to conclude that they would soon completely succeed in regaining the power to govern for the people from machines and bosses. This optimism was voiced by William Allen White, among others; his book, *The Old Order Changeth* (Document 9), published in 1910, was a representative statement of Progressive faith. Conservatives like Elihu Root (Document 10) warned that the pace of progress should not be pushed too fast, and that in a complex society direct popular rule, as opposed to representative government, was impossible; but their arguments ran against a powerful current of hope for the reinvigoration of democracy.

Pervasive as Progressivism was, it was not a fully articulated dogma which would have made all Progressives think alike on all subjects. The most important question on which they differed was the value of consolidation in business and the right method of dealing with it. Theodore Roosevelt both during his presidency and afterward when he was seeking reelection in 1912 under the banner of the Progressive party (Document 11) held that business consolidation was part of the evolution of modern economic society; that it could be regulated, policed, subjected to publicity, and made serviceable to society, but could not be broken up. The "trust" question became the main issue between the two leading candidates, Roosevelt and Wilson, in the campaign of 1912. Wilson believed (Document 12) in regulated competition as fervently as Roosevelt believed in regulated monopoly. As long as business remained big and powerful, Wilson argued, it would be able to dominate any government that proposed to regulate it as Roosevelt did. Wilson's arguments appealed particularly to those who looked wistfully back to an older order of business competition on a smaller scale. The fears of anti-trust men of this school seemed to be justified by the report of the Pujo Committee (Document 13), released only a week before Wilson took office; it showed how immense the concentration of control in American industry now was, and that it had

come about through the activities of a few large investment banking firms. Wilson's brilliantly written First
Inaugural Address (Document 14), with its demand "to
cleanse, to reconsider, to restore, to correct the evil without impairing the good, to purify and humanize every
process of our common life," was in many ways the
climactic statement of the reform spirit. It presaged an
extraordinarily productive administration, the consummation of a dozen years of Progressive agitation.

DOCUMENT 1

LINCOLN STEFFENS,
THE SHAME OF THE CITIES,
1904

*One day in the fall of 1902, during Lincoln Steffens's
first years as an editor at McClure's, the publisher,
S.S. McClure, told him: "You don't know how to
edit a magazine." Steffens angrily asked where he was
to learn, and McClure replied: "Not here. You can't
learn to edit a magazine here in this office. . . . Get
out of here, travel, go—somewhere. . . . Buy a railroad ticket, get on a train, and there, where it lands
you, there you will learn to edit a magazine." Steffens
did just that, and was soon launched upon the remarkable series of muckraking articles which were later
collected in* The Shame of the Cities. *This selection is
from Steffens's Introduction in which he tried to point
up the moral significance of what he had found.*

This is not a book. It is a collection of articles reprinted
from *McClure's Magazine.* Done as journalism, they are
journalism still, and no further pretensions are set up for
them in their new dress. . . . They were written with a
purpose, they were published serially with a purpose, and
they are reprinted now together to further that same
purpose, which was and is—to sound for the civic pride
of an apparently shameless citizenship.

There must be such a thing, we reasoned. All our

big boasting could not be empty vanity, nor our pious pretensions hollow sham. American achievements in science, art, and business mean sound abilities at bottom, and our hypocrisy a race sense of fundamental ethics. Even in government we have given proofs of potential greatness, and our political failures are not complete; they are simply ridiculous. But they are ours. Not alone the triumphs and the statesmen, the defeats and the grafters also represent us, and just as truly. Why not see it so and say it?

Because, I heard, the American people won't "stand for" it. You may blame the politicians, or, indeed, any one class, but not all classes, not the people. Or you may put it on the ignorant foreign immigrant, or any one nationality, but not on all nationalities, not on the American people. But no one class is at fault, nor any one breed, nor any particular interest or group of interests. The misgovernment of the American people is misgovernment by the American people.

When I set out on my travels, an honest New Yorker told me honestly that I would find that the Irish, the Catholic Irish, were at the bottom of it all everywhere. The first city I went to was St. Louis, a German city. The next was Minneapolis, a Scandinavian city, with a leadership of New Englanders. Then came Pittsburg, Scotch Presbyterian, and that was what my New York friend was. "Ah, but they are all foreign populations," I heard. The next city was Philadelphia, the purest American community of all, and the most hopeless. And after that came Chicago and New York, both mongrel-bred, but the one a triumph of reform, the other the best example of good government that I had seen. The "foreign element" excuse is one of the hypocritical lies that save us from the clear sight of ourselves.

Another such conceit of our egotism is that which deplores our politics and lauds our business. This is the wail of the typical American citizen. Now, the typical American citizen is the business man. The typical business man is a bad citizen; he is busy. If he is a "big business man" and very busy, he does not neglect, he is busy with politics, oh, very busy and very businesslike. I found him buying boodlers in St. Louis, defending grafters in Minneapolis, originating corruption in Pittsburg, sharing with bosses in Philadelphia, deploring reform in Chicago, and beating good government with corruption funds in New York. He is a self-righteous fraud, this big business man. He is the chief source of corruption, and it were a boon if he would neglect politics. But he is not the business man that neglects politics; that worthy is the good citizen, the typical business man. He too is busy, he is the one that has no use and therefore no time for politics. When his neglect has permitted bad government to go so far that he can be stirred to action, he is unhappy, and he looks around for a cure that shall be quick, so that he may hurry back to the shop. Naturally, too, when he talks politics, he talks shop. His patent remedy is quack; it is business.

"Give us a business man," he says ("like me," he means). "Let him introduce business methods into politics and government; then I shall be left alone to attend to my business."

There is hardly an office from United States Senator down to Alderman in any part of the country to which the business man has not been elected; yet politics remains corrupt, government pretty bad, and the selfish citizen has to hold himself in readiness like the old volunteer firemen to rush forth at any hour, in any weather, to prevent the fire; and he goes out sometimes and he puts out the fire (after the damage is done) and he goes back to the shop sighing for the business man in politics. The business man has failed in politics as he has in citizenship. Why?

Because politics is business. That's what's the matter with it. That's what's the matter with everything,—art, literature, religion, journalism, law, medicine,—they're all business, and all—as you see them. Make politics a sport, as they do in England, or a profession, as they do in Germany, and we'll have—well, something else than we have now,—if we want it, which is another question. But don't try to reform politics with the banker, the lawyer, and the dry-goods merchant, for these are business men and there are two great hindrances to their achievement of reform: one is that they are different from, but no better than, the politicians; the other is that politics is not "their line." There are exceptions both ways. Many

politicians have gone out into business and done well
(Tammany ex-mayors, and nearly all the old bosses of
Philadelphia are prominent financiers in their cities), and
business men have gone into politics and done well (Mark
Hanna, for example). They haven't reformed their
adopted trades, however, though they have sometimes
sharpened them most pointedly. The politician is a business man with a specialty. When a business man of some
other line learns the business of politics, he is a politician,
and there is not much reform left in him. Consider the
United States Senate, and believe me.

The commercial spirit is the spirit of profit, not patriotism; of credit, not honor; of individual gain, not national
prosperity; of trade and dickering, not principle. "My
business is sacred," says the business man in his heart.
"Whatever prospers my business, is good; it must be.
Whatever hinders it, is wrong; it must be. A bribe is bad,
that is, it is a bad thing to take; but it is not so bad to
give one, not if it is necessary to my business." "Business
is business" is not a political sentiment, but our politician has caught it. He takes essentially the same view
of the bribe, only he saves his self-respect by piling all his
contempt upon the bribe-giver, and he has the great advantage of candor. "It is wrong, maybe," he says, "but if a
rich merchant can afford to do business with me for the
sake of a convenience or to increase his already great
wealth, I can afford, for the sake of a living, to meet him
half way. I make no pretensions to virtue, not even on
Sunday." And as for giving bad government or good, how
about the merchant who gives bad goods or good goods,
according to the demand?

But there is hope, not alone despair, in the commer-
cialism of our politics. If our political leaders are to be
always a lot of political merchants, they will supply any
demand we may create. All we have to do is to establish
a steady demand for good government. The boss has us
split up into parties. To him parties are nothing but means
to his corrupt ends. He "bolts" his party, but we must
not; the bribe-giver changes his party, from one election
to another, from one county to another, from one city
to another, but the honest voter must not. Why? Because
if the honest voter cared no more for his party than the

politician and the grafter, then the honest vote would
govern, and that would be bad—for graft. It is idiotic,
this devotion to a machine that is used to take our sovereignty from us. If we would leave parties to the politicians, and would vote not for the party, not even for
men, but for the city, and the State, and the nation, we
should rule parties, and cities, and States, and nation.
If we would vote in mass on the more promising ticket,
or, if the two are equally bad, would throw out the party
that is in, and wait till the next election and then throw
out the other party that is in—then, I say, the commercial
politician would feel a demand for good government and
he would supply it. That process would take a generation
or more to complete, for the politicians now really do not
know what good government is. But it has taken as long
to develop bad government, and the politicians know
what that is. If it would not "go," they would offer something else, and, if the demand were steady, they, being so
commercial, would "deliver the goods."

But do the people want good government? Tammany
says they don't. Are the people honest? Are the people
better than Tammany? Are they better than the merchant
and the politician? Isn't our corrupt government, after all,
representative?

President Roosevelt has been sneered at for going
about the country preaching, as a cure for our American
evils, good conduct in the individual, simple honesty,
courage, and efficiency. "Platitudes!" the sophisticated
say. Platitudes? If my observations have been true, the
literal adoption of Mr. Roosevelt's reform scheme would
result in a revolution, more radical and terrible to existing
institutions, from the Congress to the Church, from the
bank to the ward organization, than socialism or even than
anarchy. Why, that would change all of us—not alone our
neighbors, not alone the grafters, but you and me.

No, the contemned methods of our despised politics
are the master methods of our braggart business, and the
corruption that shocks us in public affairs we practice ourselves in our private concerns. There is no essential difference between the pull that gets your wife into society
or a favorable review for your book, and that which gets
a heeler into office, a thief out of jail, and a rich man's

son on the board of directors of a corporation; none between the corruption of a labor union, a bank, and a
political machine; none between a dummy director of a
trust and the caucus-bound member of a legislature; none
between a labor boss like Sam Parks, a boss of banks like
John D. Rockefeller, a boss of railroads like J. P. Morgan,
and a political boss like Matthew S. Quay. The boss is
not a political, he is an American institution, the product
of a freed people that have not the spirit to be free.

And it's all a moral weakness; a weakness right where
we think we are strongest. Oh, we are good—on Sunday,
and we are "fearfully patriotic" on the Fourth of July.
But the bribe we pay to the janitor to prefer our interests
to the landlord's, is the little brother of the bribe passed
to the alderman to sell a city street, and the father of the
air-brake stock assigned to the president of a railroad to
have this life-saving invention adopted on his road. And
as for graft, railroad passes, saloon and bawdy-house
blackmail, and watered stock, all these belong to the same
family. We are pathetically proud of our democratic
institutions and our republican form of government, of our
grand Constitution and our just laws. We are a free and
sovereign people, we govern ourselves and the government is ours. But that is the point. We are responsible, not
our leaders, since we follow them. We *let* them divert our
loyalty from the United States to some "party"; we *let*
them boss the party and turn our municipal democracies
into autocracies and our republican nation into a plutocracy. We cheat our govenment and we let our leaders
loot it, and we let them wheedle and bribe our sovereignty
from us. True, they pass for us strict laws, but we are
content to let them pass also bad laws, giving away
public property in exchange; and our good, and often impossible, laws we allow to be used for oppression and
blackmail. And what can we say? We break our own laws
and rob our own government, the lady at the custom-
house, the lyncher with his rope, and the captain of industry with his bribe and his rebate. The spirit of graft
and of lawlessness is the American spirit. . . .

The people are not innocent. That is the only "news"
in all the journalism of these articles, and no doubt that
was not new to many observers. It was to me. When I

set out to describe the corrupt systems of certain typical
cities, I meant to show simply how the people were de-
ceived and betrayed. But in the very first study—St.
Louis—the startling truth lay bare that corruption was
not merely political; it was financial, commercial, social;
the ramifications of boodle were so complex, various, and
far-reaching, that one mind could hardly grasp them, and
not even Joseph W. Folk, the tireless prosecutor, could
follow them all. . . . The first St. Louis article was called
"Tweed Days in St. Louis," and though the "better citizen"
received attention the Tweeds were the center of interest.
In "The Shame of Minneapolis," the truth was put into
the title; It was the Shame of Minneapolis, not of the
Ames administration, not of the Tweeds, but of the city
and its citizens. And yet Minneapolis was not nearly so
bad as St. Louis; police graft is never so universal as
boodle. It is more shocking, but it is so filthy that it cannot involve so large a part of society. So I returned to St.
Louis, and I went over the whole ground again, with the
people in mind, not alone the caught and convicted
boodlers. And this time the true meaning of "Tweed days
in St. Louis" was made plain. The article was called "The
Shamelessness of St. Louis," and that was the burden of
the story. In Pittsburg also the people was the subject,
and though the civic spirit there was better, the extent
of the corruption throughout the social organization of the
community was indicated. But it was not till I got to
Philadelphia that the possibilities of popular corruption
were worked out to the limit of humiliating confession.
That was the place for such a study. There is nothing
like it in the country, except possibly, in Cincinnati. Philadelphia certainly is not merely corrupt, but corrupted, and
this was made clear. Philadelphia was charged up to—the
American citizen.

It was impossible in the space of a magazine article
to cover in any one city all the phases of municipal government, so I chose cities that typified most strikingly some
particular phase or phases. Thus as St. Louis exemplified
boodle; Minneapolis, police graft; Pittsburg, a political
and industrial machine; and Philadelphia, general civic
corruption; so Chicago was an illustration of reform, and
New York of good government. All these things occur in

most of these places. There are, and long have been, reformers in St. Louis, and there is to-day police graft
there. Minneapolis has had boodling and council reform,
and boodling is breaking out there again. Pittsburg has
general corruption, and Philadelphia a very perfect political machine. Chicago has police graft and a low order
of administrative and general corruption which permeates
business, labor, and society generally. As for New York,
the metropolis might exemplify almost anything that occurs anywhere in American cities, but no city has had
for many years such a good administration as was that of
Mayor Seth Low. . . .

They are not such bad fellows, these practical politicians. I wish I could tell more about them: how they
have helped me; how candidly and unselfishly they have
assisted me to facts and an understanding of the facts,
which, as I warned them, as they knew well, were to be
used against them. If I could—and I will some day—
I should show that one of the surest hopes we have is
the politician himself. Ask him for good politics; punish
him when he gives bad, and reward him when he gives
good; make politics pay. Now, he says, you don't know
and you don't care, and that you must be flattered and
fooled—and there, I say, he is wrong. I did not flatter
anybody; I told the truth as near as I could get it, and
instead of resentment there was encouragement. After
"The Shame of Minneapolis," and "The Shamelessness of
St. Louis," not only did citizens of these cities approve,
but citizens of other cities, individuals, groups, and organizations, sent in invitations, hundreds of them, "to come
and show us up; we're worse than they are."

We Americans may have failed. We may be mercenary
and selfish. Democracy with us may be impossible and
corruption inevitable, but these articles, if they have proved
nothing else, have demonstrated beyond doubt that we
can stand the truth; that there is pride in the character
of American citizenship; and that this pride may be a
power in the land. So this little volume, a record of shame
and yet of self-respect, a disgraceful confession, yet a
declaration of honor, is dedicated, in all good faith, to the
accused—to all the citizens of all the cities in the United
States.

DOCUMENT 2

GEORGE WASHINGTON PLUNKITT, HONEST GRAFT,

1905

Plunkitt of Tammany Hall was a skillful and candid Tammany sachem; his observations on politics, taken down by the reporter William L. Riordon and first published as newspaper interviews, still make reward- ing reading. Plunkitt's defense of "honest graft" and his disdainful account of reformers were humorously put, but they were in fact a serious statement of the attitude of political leaders of his type. Plunkitt be- came a millionaire, largely through "honest graft."

Everybody is talkin' these days about Tammany men growin' rich on graft, but nobody thinks of drawin' the distinction between honest graft and dishonest graft. There's all the difference in the world between the two. Yes, many of our men have grown rich in politics. I have myself. I've made a big fortune out of the game, and I'm gettin' richer every day, but I've not gone in for dishonest graft—blackmailin' gamblers, saloon-keepers, dis- orderly people, etc.—and neither has any of the men who have made big fortunes in politics.

There's an honest graft, and I'm an example of how it works. I might sum up the whole thing by sayin': "I seen my opportunities and I took 'em."

Just let me explain by examples. My party's in power in the city, and it's goin' to undertake a lot of public im- provements. Well, I'm tipped off, say, that they're going to lay out a new park at a certain place.

I see my opportunity and I take it. I go to that place and I buy up all the land I can in the neighborhood. Then the board of this or that makes its plan public, and there is a rush to get my land, which nobody cared particular for before.

Ain't it perfectly honest to charge a good price and

make a profit on my investment and foresight? Of course,
it is. Well, that's honest graft.

Or, supposin' it's a new bridge they're goin' to build.
I get tipped off and I buy as much property as I can that
has to be taken for approaches. I sell at my own price later
on and drop some more money in the bank.

Wouldn't you? It's just like lookin' ahead in Wall
Street or in the coffee or cotton market. It's honest graft,
and I'm lookin' for it every day in the year. I will tell
you frankly that I've got a good lot of it, too.

I'll tell you of one case. They were goin' to fix up a
big park, no matter where. I got on to it, and went lookin'
about for land in that neighborhood.

I could get nothin' at a bargain but a big piece of
swamp, but I took it fast enough and held on to it. What
turned out was just what I counted on. They couldn't
make the park complete without Plunkitt's swamp, and
they had to pay a good price for it. Anything dishonest
in that?

Up in the watershed I made some money, too. I
bought up several bits of land there some years ago and
made a pretty good guess that they would be bought up
for water purposes later by the city.

Somehow, I always guessed about right, and shouldn'
I enjoy the profit of my foresight? It was rather amusin'
when the condemnation commissioners came along and
found piece after piece of the land in the name of George
Plunkitt of the Fifteenth Assembly District, New York
City. They wondered how I knew just what to buy. The
answer is—I seen my opportunity and I took it. I haven't
confined myself to land; anything that pays is in my
line. . . .

I've told you how I got rich by honest graft. Now,
let me tell you that most politicians who are accused of
robbin' the city get rich the same way.

They didn't steal a dollar from the city treasury. They
just seen their opportunities and took them. That is why,
when a reform administration comes in and spends a half
million dollars in tryin' to find the public robberies they
talked about in the campaign, they don't find them.

The books are always all right. The money in the
city treasury is all right. Everything is all right. All they

can show is that the Tammany heads of departments looked after their friends, within the law, and gave them what opportunities they could to make honest graft. Now, let me tell you that's never goin' to hurt Tammany with the people. Every good man looks after his friends, and any man who doesn't isn't likely to be popular. If I have a good thing to hand out in private life, I give it to a friend. Why shouldn't I do the same in public life?

Another kind of honest graft. Tammany has raised a good many salaries. There was an awful howl by the reformers, but don't you know that Tammany gains ten votes for every one it lost by salary raisin'?

The Wall Street banker thinks it shameful to raise a department clerk's salary from $1500 to $1800 a year, but every man who draws a salary himself says: "That's all right. I wish it was me." And he feels very much like votin' the Tammany ticket on election day, just out of sympathy. . . .

The fact is that a reformer can't last in politics. He can make a show for a while, but he always comes down like a rocket. Politics is as much a regular business as the grocery or the dry-goods or the drug business. You've got to be trained up to it or you're sure to fall. Suppose a man who knew nothing about the grocery trade suddenly went into the business and tried to conduct it according to his own ideas. Wouldn't he make a mess of it? He might make a splurge for a while, as long as his money lasted, but his store would soon be empty. It's just the same with a reformer. He hasn't been brought up in the difficult business of politics and he makes a mess of it every time.

I've been studyin' the political game for forty-five years, and I don't know it all yet. I'm learnin' somethin' all the time. How, then, can you expect what they call "business men" to turn into politics all at once and make a success of it? It is just as if I went up to Columbia University and started to teach Greek. They usually last about as long in politics as I would last at Columbia.

You can't begin too early in politics if you want to succeed at the game. I began several years before I could vote, and so did every successful leader in Tammany Hall. When I was twelve years old I made myself useful around the district headquarters and did work at all the polls on election day. Later on, I hustled about gettin' out voters who had jags on or who were too lazy to come to the polls. There's a hundred ways that boys can help, and they get an experience that's the first real step in statesmanship. Show me a boy that hustles for the organization on election day, and I'll show you a comin' statesman.

That's the a, b, c of politics. It ain't easy work to get up to y and z. You have to give nearly all your time and attention to it. Of course, you may have some business or occupation on the side, but the great business of your life must be politics if you want to succeed in it. A few years ago Tammany tried to mix politics and business in equal quantities, by havin' two leaders for each district, a politician and a business man. They wouldn't mix. They were like oil and water. The politician looked after the politics of his district; the business man looked after his grocery store or his milk route, and whenever he appeared at an executive meeting, it was only to make trouble. The whole scheme turned out to be a farce and was abandoned mighty quick.

Do you understand now, why it is that a reformer goes down and out in the first or second round, while a politician answers to the gong every time? It is because the one has gone into the fight without trainin', while the other trains all the time and knows every fine point of the game.

DOCUMENT 3

WALTER LIPPMANN, "THE THEMES OF MUCKRAKING,"

1914

The young journalist Walter Lippmann was one of the most astute observers of Progressivism, and his book, Drift and Mastery, *was one of the most impressive contemporary assessments of American political life. In the first chapter, he made these comments upon the significance of the muckraking movement.*

There is in American to-day a distinct prejudice in favor of those who make the accusations. Thus if you announced that John D. Rockefeller was going to vote the Republican ticket it would be regarded at once as a triumph for the Democrats. Something has happened to our notions of success: no political party these days enjoys publishing the names of its campaign contributors, if those names belong to the pillars of society. The mere statement that George W. Perkins is an active Progressive has put the whole party somewhat on the defensive. . . .

You have only to write an article about some piece of corruption in order to find yourself the target of innumerable correspondents, urging you to publish their wrongs. The sense of conspiracy and secret scheming which transpire is almost uncanny. "Big Business," and its ruthless tentacles, have become the material for the feverish fantasy of illiterate thousands thrown out of kilter by the rack and strain of modern life. It is possible to work yourself into a state where the world seems a conspiracy and your daily going is beset with an alert and tingling sense of labyrinthine evil. Everything askew—all the frictions of life are readily ascribed to a deliberate evil intelligence, and men like Morgan and Rockefeller take on attributes of omnipotence, that ten minutes of cold sanity would reduce to a barbarous myth. I know a socialist who seriously believes that the study of eugenics is a Wall Street scheme for sterilizing working-class leaders. And the cartoons which pictured Morgan sitting arrogantly in a chariot drawn by the American people in a harness of ticker tape,—these are not so much caricatures as pictures of what no end of fairly sane people believe. Not once but twenty times have I been told confidentially of a nation-wide scheme by financiers to suppress every radical and progressive periodical. But even though the most intelligent muckrakers have always insisted that the picture was absurd, it remains to this day a very widespread belief. I remember how often Lincoln Steffens used to deplore the frightened literalness with which some of his articles were taken. One day in the country he and I were walking the railroad track. The ties, of course, are not well spaced for an ordinary stride, and I complained about it. "You see," said Mr. Steffens with mock obviousness, "Morgan controls the New Haven and he prefers to make the people ride."

Now it is not very illuminating to say that this smear of suspicion has been worked up by the muckrakers. If business and politics really served American need, you could never induce people to believe so many accusations against them. It is said, also, that the muckrakers played for circulation, as if that proved their insincerity. But the mere fact that muckraking was what people wanted to hear is in many ways the most important revelation of the whole campaign.

There is no other way of explaining the quick approval which the muckrakers won. They weren't voices crying in a wilderness, or lonely prophets who were stoned. They demanded a hearing; it was granted. They asked for belief; they were believed. They cried that something should be done and there was every appearance of action. There must have been real causes for dissatisfaction, or the land notorious for its worship of success would not have turned so savagely upon those who had achieved it. A happy husband will endure almost anything, but an unhappy one is capable of flying into a rage if his carpet-slippers are not in the right place. For America, the willingness to believe the worst was a strange development in the face of its traditional optimism, a sign perhaps that the honeymoon was over. For muckraking flared up at about the time when land was no longer freely available and large scale industry had begun to throw vast questions across the horizon. It came when success had ceased to be easily possible for everyone.

The muckrakers spoke to a public willing to recognize as corrupt an incredibly varied assortment of conventional acts. That is why there is nothing mysterious or romantic about the business of exposure,—no putting on of false hair, breaking into letter-files at midnight, hypnotizing financiers, or listening at keyholes. The stories of graft, written and unwritten, are literally innumerable. Often muckraking consists merely in dressing up a public document with rhetoric and pictures, translating a court record into journalese, or writing the complaints of a minority stockholder, a dislodged politician, or a boss gone "soft." No journalist need suffer from a want of material. . . .

These charges and counter-charges arose because the world has been altered radically, not because Americans fell in love with honesty. If we condemn what we once honored, if we brand as criminal the conventional acts of twenty years ago, it's because we have developed new necessities and new expectations.

They are the clue to the clouds of accusation which hang over American life. You cannot go very far by reiterating that public officials are corrupt, that business men break the law. The unbribed official and the law-abiding business man are not ideals that will hold the imagination very long. And that is why the earlier kind of muckraking exhausted itself. There came a time when the search for not-dishonest men ceased to be interesting. We all know now what tepid failures were those first opponents of corruption, the men whose only claim to distinction was that they had done no legal wrong. For without a vivid sense of what politics and business might be, you cannot wage a very fruitful campaign.

Now if you study the chief themes of muckraking I think it is possible to see the outlines of what America has come to expect.

The first wave of exposure insisted upon the dishonesty of politicians. Close upon it came widespread attack upon big business men, who were charged with bribing officials and ruining their competitors. Soon another theme appeared: big business men were accused of grafting upon the big corporations which they controlled. We are entering upon another period now: not alone big business, but all business and farming too, are being criticized for inefficiency, for poor product, and for exploitation of employees.

This classification is, of course, a very rough one. It would be easy enough to dispute it, for the details are endlessly complicated and the exceptions may appear very large to some people. But I think, nevertheless, that this classification does no essential violence to the facts. It doesn't matter for my purposes that some communities are still in what I call the first period, while others are in the third. For a nation like ours doesn't advance at the same rate everywhere. All I mean to suggest is that popular muckraking in the last decade has shifted its interest in something like this order: First, to the corruption of aldermen and mayors and public servants by the boss acting for a commercial interest, and to the business methods of those who built up the trusts. Then, muckraking turned, and began to talk about the milking of railroads by banks, and of one corporation by another. This period laid great emphasis on the "interlocking directorate." Now, muckraking is fastening upon the waste in management, upon working conditions as in the Steel Mills or at Lawrence, or upon the quality of service rendered by the larger corporations. These have been the big themes.

Why should they have been? Why, to begin with, should politicians have been attacked so fiercely? Some people would say flatly: because politicians were dishonest. Yet that is an utterly unfounded generalization. The morals of politicians cannot by any stretch of the imagination be described as exceptionally bad. Politicians were on the make. To be sure. But who in this sunny land isn't? They gave their relatives and friends pleasant positions. What father doesn't do that for his son if he can, and with every feeling of righteousness? They helped their friends, they were loyal to those who had helped them: who will say that in private life these are not admirable virtues? And what were the typical grafts in politics—the grafts for which we tried to send politicians to jail? The city contracts for work, and the public official is in league with the contractor; but railroads also contract for work, and corporation officials are at least as frequently as politicians, financially interested in the wrong side of the deal. The city buys real estate, and the city official manages to buy it from himself or his friends. But railroad directors have been known to sell their property to the road they govern.

We can see, I think, what people meant by the word graft. They did not mean robbery. It is rather confused rhetoric to call a grafter a thief. His crime is not that he filches money from the safe but that he betrays a trust. The grafter is a man whose loyalty is divided and whose motives are mixed. A lawyer who takes a fee from both sides in some case; a public official who serves a private interest; a railroad director who is also a director in the supply company; a policeman in league with outlawed

vice: those are the relationships which the American people denounce as "corrupt." The attempt to serve at the
same time two antagonistic interests is what constitutes
"corruption."

The crime is serious in proportion to the degree of
loyalty that we expect. A President of the United States
who showed himself too friendly to some private interest
would be denounced, though he may not have made one
cent out of the friendship. But where we have not yet
come to expect much loyalty we do very little muckraking.
So if you inquired into the ethics of the buyer in almost
any manufacturing house, you would find him doing things
daily that would land the purchasing agent of a city in
jail. Who regards it as especially corrupt if the selling
firm "treats" the buyer, gives him or her a "present," perhaps a commission, or at least a "good time"? American
life is saturated with the very relationship which in
politics we call corrupt. The demand for a rake-off
penetrates to the kitchen where a sophisticated cook
expects a commission from the butcher, and tampers with
the meat if it is refused; you can find it in the garage
where the chauffeur has an understanding about the
purchase of supplies; it extends to the golf caddie who
regards a "lost" ball as his property and proceeds to sell
it to the next man for half the original cost,—it extends
to the man who buys that ball; and it ramifies into the
professions when doctors receive commissions from spe-
cialists for sending patients to them; it saturates the work-
a-day world with tips and fees and "putting you on to a
good thing" and "letting you in on the ground floor." But
in the politician it is mercilessly condemned.

That is because we expect more of the politician. We
say in effect that no public servant must allow himself to
follow the economic habits of his countrymen. The
corrupt politician is he who brings into public service the
traditions of a private career. Perhaps that is a cynical
reflection. I do not know how to alter it. When I hear
politicians talk "reform," I know they are advocating
something which most drummers on the road would
regard as the scruples of a prig, and I know that when
business men in a smoking-room are frank, they are taking

for granted acts which in a politician we should call criminal.

For the average American will condemn in an alderman what in his partner he would consider reason for opening a bottle of champagne. In literal truth the politician is attacked for displaying the morality of his constituents. You might if you didn't understand the current revolution, consider that hypocrisy. It isn't: it is one of the hopeful signs of the age. For it means that unconsciously men regard some of the interests of life as too important for the intrusion of commercial ethics.

DOCUMENT 4

LOCHNER v. NEW YORK,
1905

The New York legislature had passed a law providing that no bakery could employ anyone to work more than 60 hours a week or more than 10 hours a day. Lochner had been convicted for a violation, and the case was brought to the Supreme Court. Speaking for a five to four majority, Justice Rufus W. Peckham handed down a decision invalidating the New York law on the strength of a rigidly conservative interpretation of liberty of contract. He ruled that the act exceeded the police power of the state—i.e., the power to protect health and welfare—and that it interfered with the freedom of contract protected by the Fourteenth Amendment.

PECKHAM, J. . . .
The State . . . has power to prevent the individual from making certain kinds of contracts, and in regard to them the Federal Constitution offers no protection. If the contract be one which the State, in the legitimate exercise of its police power, has the right to prohibit, it is not prevented from prohibiting it by the Fourteenth Amendment. . . .

This court has recognized the existence and upheld the exercise of the police powers of the States in many cases which might fairly be considered as border ones, and it has, in the course of its determination of questions regarding the asserted invalidity of such statutes, on the ground of their violation of the rights secured by the Federal Constitution, been guided by rules of a very liberal nature, the application of which has resulted, in numerous instances, in upholding the validity of state statutes thus assailed. . . .

It must, of course, be conceded that there is a limit to the valid exercise of the police power by the State. There is no dispute concerning this general proposition. Otherwise the Fourteenth Amendment would have no efficacy and the legislatures of the States would have unbounded power, and it would be enough to say that any piece of legislation was enacted to conserve the morals, the health or the safety of the people; such legislation would be valid, no matter how absolutely without foundation the claim might be. The claim of the police power would be a mere pretext—become another and delusive name for the supreme sovereignty of the State to be exercised free from constitutional restraint. This is not contended for. In every case that comes before this court, therefore, where legislation of this character is concerned and where the protection of the Federal Constitution is sought, the question necessarily arises: Is this a fair, reasonable and appropriate exercise of the police power of the State, or is it an unreasonable, unnecessary, and arbitrary interference with the right of the individual to his personal liberty or to enter into those contracts in relation to labor which may seem to him appropriate or necessary for the support of himself and his family? Of course the liberty of contract relating to labor includes both parties to it. The one has as much right to purchase as the other to sell labor. . . .

The question whether this act is valid as a labor law, pure and simple, may be dismissed in a few words. There is no reasonable ground for interfering with the liberty of person or the right of free contract, by determining the hours of labor, in the occupation of a baker. There is no contention that bakers as a class are not equal in intelligence and capacity to men in other trades or manual occupations, or that they are not able to assert their rights and care for themselves without the protecting arm of the State, interfering with their independence of judgment and of action. They are in no sense wards of the State. Viewed in the light of a purely labor law, with no reference whatever to the question of health, we think that a law like the one before us involves neither the safety, the morals, nor the welfare, of the public, and that the interest of the public is not in the slightest degree affected by such an act. The law must be upheld, if at all, as a law pertaining to the health of the individual engaged in the occupation of a baker. It does not affect any other portion of the public than those who are engaged in that occupation. Clean and wholesome bread does not depend upon whether the baker works but ten hours per day or only sixty hours a week. The limitation of the hours of labor does not come within the police power on that ground.

It is a question of which of two powers or rights shall prevail—the power of the State to legislate or the right of the individual to liberty of person and freedom of contract. The mere assertion that the subject relates, though but in a remote degree to the public health, does not necessarily render the enactment valid. The act must have a more direct relation, as a means to an end, and the end itself must be appropriate and legitimate, before an act can be held to be valid which interferes with the general right of an individual to be free in his person and in his power to contract in relation to his own labor. . . .

We think the limit of the police power has been reached and passed in this case. There is, in our judgment, no reasonable foundation for holding this to be necessary or appropriate as a health law to safeguard the public health or the health of the individuals who are following the trade of a baker. If this statute be valid, and if, therefore, a proper case is made out in which to deny the right of an individual, *sui juris,* as employer or employee, to make contracts for the labor of the latter under the protection of the provisions of the Federal Constitution, there would seem to be no length to which legislation of this nature might not go. . . .

The act is not, within any fair meaning of the term, a health law, but is an illegal interference with the rights of individuals, both employers and employees, to make contracts regarding labor upon such terms as they may think best, or which they may agree upon with the other parties to such contracts. Statutes of the nature of that under review, limiting the hours in which grown and intelligent men may labor to earn their living, are mere meddlesome interferences with the rights of the individual, and they are not saved from condemnation by the claim that they are passed in the exercise of the police power and upon the subject of the health of the individual whose rights are interfered with, unless there be some fair ground, reasonable in and of itself, to say that there is material danger to the public health, or to the health of the employees, if the hours of labor are not curtailed. . . .

It is impossible for us to shut our eyes to the fact that many of the laws of this character, while passed under what is claimed to be the police power for the purpose of protecting the public health or welfare, are, in reality, passed from other motives. We are justified in saying so when, from the character of the law and the subject upon which it legislates, it is apparent that the public health or welfare bears but the most remote relation to the law. The purpose of a statute must be determined from the natural and legal effect of the language employed; and whether it is or is not repugnant to the Constitution of the United States must be determined from the natural effect of such statutes when put into operation, and not from their proclaimed purpose. . . . The court looks beyond the mere letter of the law in such cases.

It is manifest to us that the limitation of the hours of labor as provided for in this section of the statute . . . has no such direct relation to and no such substantial effect upon the health of the employee, as to justify us in regarding the section as really a health law. It seems to us that the real object and purpose were simply to regulate the hours of labor between the master and his employees . . . in a private business, not dangerous in any degree to morals or in any real and substantial degree, to the health of the employees. Under such circumstances the freedom of master and employee to contract with each other in relation to their employment, and in defining the same, cannot be prohibited or interfered with, without violating the Federal Constitution.

DOCUMENT 5

OLIVER WENDELL HOLMES, DISSENTING OPINION IN *LOCHNER* v. *NEW YORK*, 1905

The four minority justices in this case wrote two dissents. Justice Harlan, with the concurrence of Justices White and Day, did not quarrel with the fundamental conceptions of the majority decision, but argued that long hours of work in bakeshops are in fact injurious to health, and also maintained that the statute was not palpably inconsistent with the Constitution. Holmes's lone dissent, which had a more fundamental quarrel with the majority, is remembered as one of his most famous opinions. It argues powerfully for judicial restraint, and urges judges to set aside their own prejudices when deciding on the validity of laws. ("The accident of our finding certain opinions natural and familiar or novel and even shocking ought not to conclude our judgment upon the question whether statutes embodying them conflict with the Constitution of the United States.") Holmes's argument had a profound effect on subsequent American jurisprudence.

This case is decided upon an economic theory which a large part of the country does not entertain. If it were a question whether I agreed with that theory, I should desire to study it further and long before making up my mind. But I do not conceive that to be my duty, because

I strongly believe that my agreement or disagreement has nothing to do with the right of a majority to embody their opinions in law. It is settled by various decisions of this court that state constitutions and state laws may regulate life in many ways which we as legislators might think as injudicious or if you like as tyrannical as this, and which equally with this interfere with the liberty to contract. Sunday laws and usury laws are ancient examples. A more modern one is the prohibition of lotteries. The liberty of the citizen to do as he likes so long as he does not interfere with the liberty of others to do the same, which has been a shibboleth for some well-known writers, is interfered with by school laws, by the Post Office, by every state or municipal institution which takes his money for purposes thought desirable, whether he likes it or not. The Fourteenth Amendment does not enact Mr. Herbert Spencer's Social Statics. . . . United States and state statutes and decisions cutting down the liberty to contract by way of combination are familiar to this court. . . . Some of these laws embody convictions or prejudices which judges are likely to share. Some may not. But a constitution is not intended to embody a particular economic theory, whether of paternalism and the organic relation of the citizen to the State or of *laissez faire.* It is made for people of fundamentally differing views, and the accident of our finding certain opinions natural and familiar or novel and even shocking ought not to conclude our judgement upon the question whether statutes embodying them conflict with the Constitution of the United States.

General propositions do not decide concrete cases. The decision will depend on a judgement or intuition more subtle than any articulate major premise. But I think that the proposition just stated, if it is accepted, will carry us far toward the end. Every opinion tends to become a law. I think that the word liberty in the Fourteenth Amendment is perverted when it is held to prevent the natural outcome of a dominant opinion, unless it can be said that a rational and fair man necessarily would admit that the statute proposed would infringe fundamental principles as they have been understood by the traditions of our people and our law. It does not need research to show that no such sweeping condemnation can be passed upon the statute before us. A reasonable man might think it a proper measure on the score of health. Men whom I certainly could not pronounce unreasonable would uphold it as a first instalment of a general regulation of the hours of work. Whether in the latter aspect it would be open to the charge of inequality I think it unnecessary to discuss.

DOCUMENT 6

MULLER v. OREGON,
1908

In this case the Court showed far greater respect for social legislation than in Lochner v. New York (Documents 4 and 5). Oregon had imposed a maximum of 10 hours a day for women in factories and laundries. Louis D. Brandeis, arguing for the constitutionality of the law, presented an impressive, revolutionary brief in which the legal argument itself was dwarfed by a mass of testimony from a variety of sources directed to the facts and not the law. Brandeis was trying to establish beyond doubt that long hours of work were in fact harmful to the health and morals of women; and the reference of Justice David J. Brewer to his "very copious collection of these matters" pays tribute to Brandeis's brief. The scope of this decision was limited, for it applied specifically to women, and Lochner v. New York was not overruled. But it gave hope to the proponents of social legislation and evidence to the country that the Court was not as rigid as it had seemed three years before when it decided the Lochner case. Nine years later in Bunting v. Oregon (1917) the Court went still further and sustained a law that required (with some qualifications for overtime pay) that no person, of either sex, should be employed in a factory or mill for more than 10 hours a day.

BREWER, J. . . . The single question is the constitutionality of the statute under which the defendant was convicted so far as affects the work of a female in a
laundry. . . .

It is the law of Oregon that women, whether married
or single, have equal contractual and personal rights with
men. . . .

It thus appears that, putting to one side the elective
franchise, in the matter of personal and contractual rights
they stand on the same plane as the other sex. Their rights
in these respects can no more be infringed than the equal
rights of their brothers. We held in Lochner v. New York,
198 U.S. 45, that a law providing that no laborer shall
be required or permitted to work in a bakery more than
sixty hours in a week or ten hours in a day was not as
to men a legitimate exercise of the police power of the
State, but an unreasonable, unnecessary and arbitrary
interference with the right and liberty of the individual
to contract in relation to his labor, and as such was in
conflict with, and void under, the Federal Constitution.
That decision is invoked by plaintiff in error as decisive
of the question before us. But this assumes that the
difference between the sexes does not justify a different
rule respecting a restriction of the hours of labor.

It may not be amiss, in the present case, before
examining the constitutional question, to notice the course
of legislation as well as expressions of opinion from other
than judicial sources. In the brief filed by Mr. Louis D.
Brandeis, for the defendant in error is a very copious
collection of all these matters. . . .

The legislation and opinions referred to [in Brandeis's
brief] . . . may not be, technically speaking, authorities,
and in them is little or no discussion of the constitutional
question presented to us for determination, yet they are
significant of a widespread belief that woman's physical
structure, and the functions she performs in consequence
thereof, justify special legislation restricting or qualifying
the conditions under which she should be permitted to
toil. Constitutional questions, it is true, are not settled by
even a consensus of present public opinion, for it is
the peculiar value of a written constitution that it places
in unchanging form limitations upon legislative action,

and thus gives a permanence and stability to popular government which otherwise would be lacking. At the same time, when a question of fact is debated and debatable, and the extent to which a special constitutional limitation goes is affected by the truth in respect to that fact, a widespread and long-continued belief concerning it is worthy of consideration. We take judicial cognizance of all matters of general knowledge. . . .

That woman's physical structure and the performance of maternal functions place her at a disadvantage in the struggle for subsistence is obvious. This is especially true when the burdens of motherhood are upon her. Even when they are not, by abundant testimony of the medical fraternity continuance for a long time on her feet at work, repeating this from day to day, tends to injurious effects upon the body, and as healthy mothers are essential to vigorous offspring, the physical well-being of woman becomes an object of public interest and care in order to preserve the strength and vigor of the race. . . .

Differentiated by these matters from the other sex, she is properly placed in a class by herself, and legislation designed for her protection may be sustained, even when like legislation is not necessary for men and could not be sustained. It is impossible to close one's eyes to the fact that she still looks to her brother and depends upon him. Even though all restrictions on political, personal and contractual rights were taken away, and she stood, so far as statutes are concerned, upon an absolutely equal plane with him, it would still be true that she is so constituted that she will rest upon and look to him for protection; that her physical structure and a proper discharge of her maternal functions—having in view not merely her own health, but the well-being of the race —justify legislation to protect her from the greed as well as the passion of man. The limitations which this statute places upon her contractual powers, upon her right to agree with her employer as to the time she shall labor, are not imposed solely for her benefit, but also largely for the benefit of all. Many words cannot make this plainer. The two sexes differ in structure of body, in the functions to be performed by each, in the amount of physical strength, in the capacity for long-continued labor, particularly when done standing, the influence of vigorous health upon the future well-being of the race, the self-reliance which enables one to assert full rights, and in the capacity to maintain the struggle for subsistence. This difference justifies a difference in legislation and upholds that which is designed to compensate for some of the burdens which rest upon her. . . .

For these reasons, and without questioning in any respect the decision in *Lochner* v. *New York,* we are of the opinion that it cannot be adjudged that the act in question is in conflict with the federal Constitution, so far as it respects the work of a female in a laundry. . . .

DOCUMENT 7

DAVID WILCOX, TESTIMONY ON RAILROAD REFORM,

JANUARY 21, 1905

During 1905, the House Committee on Interstate and Foreign Commerce held hearings on various bills to amend the Interstate Commerce Act. One of the more formidable witnesses to appear was David Wilcox, President of the Delaware and Hudson Railroad Company. Wilcox did not profess opposition to regulation of the railroads as such, but his remarks to the committee, represented here, show a characteristic anxiety among railroad men that advances in regulation might be seriously detrimental to the earning power of the companies. He also attempted to persuade the committee that existing rates were reasonable.

When I applied to the chairman of this committee for a hearing, I did not apply on behalf of the Delaware and Hudson Company, but on behalf of its employees and security holders and on behalf of those who are dependent upon them. My constituency, I may say, is perhaps 100,000; probably that. What has been the cause of the prosperity of this property and upon what depend its

100,000 people? Upon nothing else in the world but the income of the property. Without the income the property is of no value. Without the income there would be no incentive to operate it; and therefore, necessarily, any proposition which tends to place in the hands of the Government, however ably administered, the question as to whether or not this substantial mass of property shall earn anything, which tends to qualify or limit its earning capacity, affects not the company, for these companies, gentlemen, are of very little real importance. They are artificial persons. They are the means by which the property of the owners is held together and is made productive. That is all there is of it.

If the American people so wish, the corporations may die. But what is to become of the people who are interested in them? What is to become of this enormous mass of property, upon which rests the prosperity not merely of the class whom I have named, but also of those who sell supplies to them, and of the communities through which they pass, and of the communities which will be built up by their extension? It seems to me that that is the serious question, What effect is what you may do here going to have upon the future welfare, productiveness, and value of the greatest single industrial interest of the country? It is a great responsibility, gentlemen. I do not come here as an extremist. If you can devise anything which will be to the benefit of the country as a whole, who will welcome it more than those who are interested in the railroad property? . . .

Now, gentlemen, great as I feel my own responsibility with reference to the company with which I am connected, I realize that the responsibility of this committee is very, very much more serious. It may pass an act which shall put it in the power of those who, however well intentioned they are—and I do not wish to join the super-heated gentlemen who sometimes want to have the Interstate Commerce Commission abolished because they are not doing anything, and I will say that they are not railroad men, that I ever heard of—yet, having the power, may do great harm. I do not share in that feeling toward the Commission. But, as I say, gentlemen, you may pass an act that will so compromise the

value of the property, and the prosperity of the communities of the country, that it will bring widespread
disaster. On the other hand, you may pass an act which
will fail of operation. Some people say that the present
act has not accomplished what was hoped, although I do
not agree with that exactly. But you may do the same
thing, not intentionally but unintentionally, and the act
which you may pass may become a gold brick in legislation. And there are those two great possibilities. You may
pass an act which will so compromise the value of the
greatest mass of accumulated resources of the country
that its efficiency will in a measure cease, or at any rate
become less, or you may pass an act which will fail of
accomplishing the desired results, and this agitation may
go on, stimulated and kept on foot in the methods which
you gentlemen know so well, apparently ad infinitum.

What I say, gentlemen, is that it is a very, very
serious moment when an Anglo-Saxon government undertakes the charge of people's money and says how much
they shall earn by the exercise of their constitutional rights
of liberty and property. And it should be recognized that
possibly we are at the parting of the ways, and that if
this be done it will go on until those constitutional
guaranties have but little value, and the only profession
worth exercising in the country will be that of holding
office in some administrative board. . . .

I will just venture to say this, gentlemen, that when
I took office as president of this company, which was
less than two years ago, I had been practicing law then
for thirty years, and I suppose that I am still a good deal
more of a lawyer than a railroad man. I believe most of
the committee are lawyers, and therefore we may sympathize with each other. When I took up the office various
gentlemen who had been engaged in the railroad service
for a great many years, whom I met, said: "Now, we have
one piece of advice to offer you, and only one." I said:
"That is very kind. I should be glad to have more, but I
should be obliged for the one. What is that?" They said:
"Go slow." And, gentlemen, I have found that the most
valuable piece of advice that I could possibly have had.
So I want to say to the committee, not merely as a railroad man or as a lawyer, but as an American citizen,

that inasmuch as this matter has been forced upon the committee by an agitation which has been largely based, as I conceive, upon misapprehension, and if I had the time I think I could demonstrate that to the committee— I want to urge the committee with the utmost earnestness which is in my power to go slowly about this thing, because a step once taken can not be retraced, and unless it is the right step, as I said a while ago, it may lead to great disaster or it may lead to cruel and exasperating disappointment. Do not do anything until you are sure that you are going to do something effective. That is what the railroad owners of the country would say to you. Do not be in a hurry and do not pass statutes because you think people want something done. Be sure that you are doing something for the good of the country as a whole, not merely for the good of the special regions which are particularly exasperated.

And I will say here we know very little of these conditions in the East—almost nothing. Do not do something merely for the sake of doing something. This is too serious a question for that sort of treatment. If you do anything, if in your ripe judgment, in your wisdom, you conclude that it is desirable to do something, do something which will have value, not something with which your names will be associated either as a failure or as a disaster.

I said that I was not one of those who believe in abolishing the Interstate Commerce Commission. Of course the great benefit of that Commission has been the settlement of claims without controversy. In that manner it has settled over 90 per cent of the claims which have come before it. That is the business way of carrying on business, for the parties to settle. I do not know of any business, gentlemen, which is carried on successfully by third parties who have no interest in the ultimate result, and no business which is carried on by lawsuit. Business by lawsuit would be a thing to be abhorred, a thing which would be impossible. That is where the Interstate Commerce Commission has been useful. . . .

I suppose that the committee, by the discussions

that have been had, has been fully advised of the fact
that upon the record there is no question of the reasonableness of rates per se. Upon a brief which I shall have
the pleasure of filing that matter is fully argued out. It
admits of no question. Even as those advances from 1899
until 1903, regarding which the Commission reported
last year to the Senate—even as to them the Commission
itself says that it does not claim that they were unreasonable. In an article in the North American Review,
which was written by one of the most productive of the
Commissioners last June, the same statement was repeated, that he did not claim that they were unreasonable,
but simply that the Government ought to have the
right to fix them. That is simply and baldly that the
Government should fix future rates. There is nobody
complaining; there is no case and there has never been
a case, as I have no doubt that the committee has been
informed over and over again, of unreasonable rates
which has been sustained; but the position of the Com-
missioner who wrote this article was that, as a matter of
right, the Government should always intervene in these
circumstances.

Now, that advance in rates amounted to what?
Thirty-nine thousandths of a cent per ton per mile. And
it is interesting to notice that in the report for 1902, in
commenting upon the relation of rates between 1898 and
1902, the Commission uses the expression that the rates
were about the same. Now, the difference between those
two years consisted of a difference of forty-one thousandths of a cent, and the Commission said that the
rates were about the same, and the Commission said that
the increase in gross earnings was due to the increased
volume of traffic. When they came to comparing the
rates of 1899 and those of 1903, the difference was thirty-
nine thousandths of a cent, two thousandths of a cent less
than they had been between 1898 and 1902, when the
Commission said they were about the same. Nevertheless,
this difference of thirty-nine thousandths of a cent was
described as having made enormous additions to the
expenses of railway transportation, although a difference
of forty-one thousandths of a cent, taking the two previous

corresponding years for purposes of comparison, was described as leaving the rates about the same. . . .

The efforts of the traffic officials of the road to meet the necessities of the shippers and to enable their manufacturers and shippers to ship to farther markets all the time are what have led, more, in my belief, than anything else, to the downward course of rates, which has been practically continuous. When you consider the increase in the cost of materials in the past few years, it is not too much to say that that has been a continuous course. The traffic official is constantly endeavoring to enable his own patrons to reach farther markets. Now, there can not be any question that that encourages competition, enables the consumer to have the benefit of constantly increasing sources of supply, and yet, naturally, when the dealers in the farther markets find that a new element of competition has entered they claim that they are prejudiced, and that the first market is receiving an undue preference.

DOCUMENT 8

WILLIAM P. HEPBURN, SPEECH ON RAILROAD REFORM,

FEBRUARY 7, 1906

During the debates in the House on the Hepburn bill, Representative Hepburn of Iowa spoke at length in defense of the measure to which his name was attached. In the brief selection here, he points to the way in which railroads have prospered under governmental regulation, explains the difficulties of private action on rates under existing laws, and argues the reasonableness of the procedures he proposed to introduce for arriving at maximum rates.

Mr. Chairman, I remember twenty years ago, about this time, when the first act—the [Interstate Commerce] act of 1887—was being discussed in this House. I remember

with what zeal that measure was attacked as destructive
to the great interests of the country, revolutionary in
character, full of socialism. It was a measure that was to
introduce then, as now, European methods in place of
American, and was in the direction of an experiment that
would be fatal to the great commercial institutions of the
country, and it was amidst denunciations of that character, prophecies of that doleful nature, that the legislation
was had and that the bill became law. What one of
those prophecies in the fullness of time do we now
recognize as facts? Not one.

Then, Mr. Chairman, the railway mileage of the
United States was 137,000 miles, now 220,000; then the
gross earnings of the railways were $931,000,000, now
$2,100,000,000; then the cost per ton per mile was 1.17,
now 0.74; then the dividend on stocks was only 1.81 per
cent, now 3.03 per cent; then the gross earnings per mile
were $6,861, now $9,301; then in 1887, 61,000,000,000
of tons of freight were carried 1 mile. In 1893,
171,000,000,000 of tons of freight were carried 1 mile.
. . . Under this legislation the facts show that this great
industry has prospered beyond compare. Nowhere else
in all the world is there such a state of prosperity, notwithstanding the fact of this governmental supervision
and notwithstanding the dolorous fears of the gentlemen who indulged in jeremiads twenty years ago. . . .

Mr. Chairman, this is a great question. Any proposition of law that involves an interest so great as the railway
interests of the United States ought to be regarded with
solicitude by those who are charged with responsibility in
that behalf.

One-twelfth of all the wealth in the United States is
involved in greater or less degree in this bill. The earnings
of the railways are so colossal that two billions and one
hundred millions mark the amount of this great interest
in one year. Our whole wealth production is but ten
times more than that. Think how colossal this is. But the
aggregate of investments, the aggregate of annual earnings, does not mark fairly the importance of this subject
to the American people. Think how dependent we are for
our prosperity, for the comforts of life even, upon the

common carriers of the land. Think of the infinitude of the transactions between the carriers and those they serve —millions and millions of transactions. . . .

I was about saying that the courts had proved inadequate because of these reasons: The subject of the controversy in all of the cases that I can conceive is an involved one to the plaintiff; the knowledge and information that would enable the plaintiff to maintain his action for an overcharge are not in his possession. He could not give that expert testimony as to all the elements that would enter into the composition of a just and reasonable charge or an overcharge, while a knowledge of all these facts are in the hands of his adversary, and therefore he could not recover.

That is one of the difficulties, not with the courts, but because of the peculiarities of the subject of controversy. The courts have not been adequate and therefore some other means had to be substituted. With what abhorrence would we look upon a proposition, if gentlemen should make it, with reference to controversies other than of this class that were certain to rise and be numerous in the community, providing that one of the parties alone should determine the rightfulness of the controversy; and yet that is what is involved in all of these multitudes of possible disputes between carrier and shipper. It is the carrier that fixes the rate. He imposes upon the other party the necessity of accepting his rate. There is no escape from it. He may pay the charge and then the common law, says the gentleman from Maine (Mr. Littlefield), gives him a remedy and allows him to recover for the overcharge. Ah, how barren is that remedy, and while it is a known fact that the cases where such suits might be instituted are counted by millions, none is ever brought because of the expense, because of the delay, because of the inability to secure the proof whereby a judgment is within the limits of possibility. Therefore it is futile to talk about the courts as they are constituted furnishing that remedy that ought to be somewhere existent. Now, what do we do by this bill? The gentlemen who oppose it have discussed it as though it conferred upon the railway commission the power to establish schedule and rates. They have, I think, sometimes purposely set up this bogy for the purpose of combating it. No one has proposed that. The jurisdiction of the Commission is limited, as is its power limited, by this law. They can not at pleasure establish a rate. Before their jurisdiction attaches it must be ascertained that a wrong has been done, an overcharge has been made, a wrong in an extravagant, unreasonable rate, because the law to-day and the common law provide that the carriers' charge shall be just and reasonable. That is the limit to which he is permitted to go in fixing his tariff of schedules.

Now, under the operation of this bill, if it should become a law, it is necessary for some one to allege a violation of the statute—that a crime, in other words, has been done—because the overcharge is a crime, as well as being prohibited, and remedies furnished civilly by the courts. He has committed a crime. What then? Investigation follows, and if it is ascertained that the carrier is in violation of the law, then the jurisdiction of the Commission attaches, and it is permitted to do what? Fix a rate? Oh, no; oh, no. It is permitted to establish a just, reasonable, and fairly remunerative rate that shall be the maximum rate that the carrier shall charge. That is all. Can you think of any legislative effort in the direction of control more conservative than this? First, the carrier must be in the wrong—the carrier must be a criminal. His criminality must be ascertained. When it is ascertained by a dispassionate Commission then a rate within limitations, fair and certain and well defined, may be established as the maximum that the carrier may charge, leaving the feature of flexibility still remaining in the rate, and permitting the carrier to charge that lower sum that the exigencies of business or the activities of competition may make it prudent and wise for him to adopt.

DOCUMENT 9

WILLIAM ALLEN WHITE, *THE OLD ORDER CHANGETH,*
1910

This passage from White's book breathes Progressive optimism, and the confidence that devices intended to put government back in the hands of the people would indeed work.

But the secret ballot, the direct primary, and the purged party—which are now fairly well assured in American politics—do not set the metes and bounds of progress toward self-government in this country. They are fundamental reforms, it is true, and they are the steps that are necessary before there may be any real forward movement. For it will be seen that each one of these movements is a leveling process, a tendency to make money, capital, property, wealth, or financial distinction count for nothing save as an indirect influence in the ballot box. Each of these innovations, the secret ballot, the primary, and the reformed party, is a step toward democracy—a step toward the Declaration of Independence and away from the Constitution, which so feared majority rule that the majority was hedged about with checks and balances at every possible point. In the early days of the Republic the people annulled the Constitution by getting a direct vote on the President, and thus obtained the executive branch of the government. Now they are capturing the legislative branch through the primary, which to-day puts over half the United States senators under the direct vote of the people. When one stops to think that in Oregon, Washington, Nevada, Idaho, California, North Dakota, South Dakota, Nebraska, Kansas, Oklahoma, Texas, Louisiana, Arkansas, Missouri, Iowa, Wisconsin, Ohio, Alabama, Mississippi, Florida, Georgia, Tennessee, South Carolina, Virginia, New Jersey, and Kentucky, United States senators at the next election will go directly to the people for nominations, and not to the railroads and the public service corporations of their respective states, in short, not to capital as they did ten years ago, one realizes how revolutionary are the changes that are coming into our system. The democracy that was gathering strength in the days of Hanna is beginning to move in the nation.

Indeed, the growth of fundamental democracy in this country is astonishing. Thirty years ago the secret ballot was regarded as a passing craze by professional politicians. Twenty years ago it was a vital issue in nearly every American state. To-day the secret ballot is universal in American politics. Ten years ago the direct primary was the subject of an academic discussion in the University of Michigan by a young man named La Follette of Wisconsin. Now it is in active operation in over two-thirds of our American states, and over half of the American people use the direct primary as a weapon of self-government. Five years ago the recall was a piece of freak legislation in Oregon. To-day more American citizens are living under laws giving them the power of recall than were living under the secret ballot when Garfield came to the White House, and many times more people have the power to recall certain public officers to-day than had the advantages of the direct primary form of party nominations when Theodore Roosevelt came to Washington. The referendum is only five years behind the primary. Prophecy with these facts before one becomes something more than a rash guess.

The democracy has the executive and the legislative branches of the state and federal government under its direct control; for in the nomination of a majority of the members of the House and of the Senate the personification of property is unimportant. By making the party a legalized state institution, by paying for the party primaries with state taxes, by requiring candidates at primaries to file their expense accounts and a list of their contributors (as is done in some states), by limiting the amount to be spent (as is done in certain states), and by guaranteeing a secret vote and a fair count, the state has broken the power of money in politics. Capital is not eliminated from politics, but it is hampered and circumscribed, and is not the dominant force that it was ten years ago. Then the political machine was financed by capital invested in public service corporations and was continually trying to avoid the responsibility of its public partnership. Then the political machine quietly sold special privileges to public service corporations. Now the political machine is in a fair way to be reduced to mere political scrap iron by the rise of the people. To-day in states having the primary under the state control the corporation candidate for any public office is handicapped. The men elected to the United States Senate from states having the Northern type of primary generally have been free men, free from machine and corporation taint. Under the primary system any clean, quick-witted man in these states can defeat the corporation senatorial candidate at the primary if the people desire to defeat him. . . .

However, just now the people are finding a way around the legislative veto of the state courts. And this they are doing more generally than may be realized by many people. The voters are taking two methods of circumventing the legislative veto of the courts: first, by amending their state constitutions, or making new constitutions; and, second, by direct legislation, or the modification of it known as the initiative and referendum. State courts are elective, and therefore are afraid of majorities. They cannot declare constitutional amendments unconstitutional, and they handle laws adopted by a direct vote of the people with great care. Hence the prevalence of the constitutional amendment in American states, and the growth of the initiative and referendum from Maine to California. . . .

For the veto power of the American courts over legislation—under the assumed right to declare legislation "unconstitutional"—is one of the most ruthless checks upon democracy permitted by any civilized people. European kings and courts do not have such reactionary power; yet in the end it seems to make for righteousness. Because under that power in America people have developed a patience and a conscience and a patriotic self-abnegation which fits them to progress in the light of the vision within them. So the initiative and referendum—a most outlandish phrase—which is coming into state governments and city governments all over the country will be the instrument of a self-restrained people. It will not be the weapon of a mob.

DOCUMENT 10

ELIHU ROOT, EXPERIMENTS IN GOVERNMENT,

1913

Elihu Root was a Republican Senator from New York when he delivered the lecture from which this selection is taken. He was trying to warn that the pace of political change cannot be too hurried, and to suggest that caution should constrain current efforts to bring about direct popular rule.

When proposals are made to change these institutions there are certain general considerations which should be observed.

The first consideration is that free government is impossible except through prescribed and established governmental institutions, which work out the ends of government through many separate human agents, each doing his part in obedience to law. Popular will cannot execute itself directly except through a mob. Popular will cannot get itself executed through an irresponsible executive, for that is simple autocracy. An executive limited only by the direct expression of popular will cannot be held to responsibility against his will, because, having possession of all the powers of government, he can prevent any true, free, and general expression adverse to himself, and unless he yields voluntarily he can be overturned only by a revolution. . . .

We should, therefore, reject every proposal which involves the idea that the people can rule merely by voting, or merely by voting and having one man or group of men to execute their will.

A second consideration is that in estimating the value of any system of governmental institutions due regard must be had to the true functions of government and to the limitations imposed by nature upon what it is possible for government to accomplish. We all know of course that we cannot abolish all the evils in this world by statute or by the enforcement of statutes, nor can we prevent the inexorable law of nature which decrees that suffering shall follow vice, and all the evil passions and folly of mankind. Law cannot give to depravity the rewards of virtue, to indolence the rewards of industry, to indifference the rewards of ambition, or to ignorance the rewards of learning. The utmost that government can do is measurably to protect men, not against the wrong they do themselves but against wrong done by others, and to promote the long, slow process of educating mind and character to a better knowledge and nobler standards of life and conduct. We know all this, but when we see how much misery there is in the world and instinctively cry out against it, and when we see some things that government may do to mitigate it, we are apt to forget how little after all it is possible for any government to do, and to hold the particular government of the time and place to a standard of responsibility which no government can possibly meet. The chief motive power which has moved mankind along the course of development which we call the progress of civilization has been the sum total of intelligent selfishness in a vast number of individuals, each working for his own support, his own gain, his own betterment. . . .

A third consideration is that it is not merely useless but injurious for government to attempt too much. It is manifest that to enable it to deal with the new conditions I have described we must invest government with authority to interfere with the individual conduct of the citizen to a degree hitherto unknown in this country. When government undertakes to give the individual citizen protection by regulating the conduct of others towards him in the field where formerly he protected himself by his freedom of contract, it is limiting the liberty of the citizen whose conduct is regulated and taking a step in the direction of paternal government. While the new conditions of industrial life make it plainly necessary that many such steps shall be taken, they should be taken only so far as they are necessary and are effective. Interference with individual liberty by government should be jealously watched and restrained, because the habit of undue interference destroys that independence of character without which in its citizens no free government can endure.

We should not forget that while institutions receive their form from national character they have a powerful reflex influence upon that character. Just so far as a nation allows its institutions to be moulded by its weaknesses of character rather than by its strength it creates an influence to increase weakness at the expense of strength.

The habit of undue interference by government in private affairs breeds the habit of undue reliance upon government in private affairs at the expense of individual initiative, energy, enterprise, courage, independent manhood.

The strength of self-government and the motive power of progress must be found in the characters of the individual citizens who make up a nation. Weaken individual character among a people by comfortable reliance upon paternal government and a nation soon becomes incapable of free self-government and fit only to be governed: the higher and nobler qualities of national life that make for ideals and effort and achievement become atrophied and the nation is decadent.

A fourth consideration is that in the nature of things all government must be imperfect because men are imperfect. Every system has its shortcomings and inconveniences; and these are seen and felt as they exist in the system under which we live, while the shortcomings and inconveniences of other systems are forgotten or ignored.

It is not unusual to see governmental methods reformed and after a time, long enough to forget the evils that caused the change, to have a new movement for a reform which consists in changing back to substantially the same old methods that were cast out by the first reform.

DOCUMENT 11

THEODORE ROOSEVELT, ACCEPTANCE SPEECH,

AUGUST 6, 1912

Theodore Roosevelt had never believed that big business could or should be broken up by the Sherman Act method. Instead he thought the Sherman Act should be retained only as an occasional basis for controlling big businesses that misbehaved. His thesis that regulating monopoly was more feasible than restoring competition, here expressed in his Acceptance Address, or "Confession of Faith," as it was called, to the Progressive party convention of 1912, disappointed some members of his party; but it represented the former President's considered views.

Again and again while I was President, from 1902 to 1908, I pointed out that under the anti-trust law alone it was neither possible to put a stop to business abuses nor possible to secure the highest efficiency in the service rendered by business to the general public. The anti-trust law must be kept on our statute books, and, as hereafter shown, must be rendered more effective in the cases where it is applied. But to treat the anti-trust law as an adequate, or as by itself a wise, measure of relief and betterment is a sign not of progress, but of toryism and reaction. It has been of benefit so far as it has implied the recognition of a real and great evil, and the at least sporadic application of the principle that all men alike must obey the law. But as a sole remedy, universally applicable, it has in actual practice completely broken down; as now applied it works more mischief than benefit. It represents the waste of effort—always damaging to a community—which arises from the attempt to meet new conditions by the application of outworn remedies instead of fearlessly and in common-sense fashion facing the new conditions and devising the new remedies which alone can work effectively for good.

The anti-trust law, if interpreted as the Baltimore platform demands it shall be interpreted, would apply to every agency by which not merely industrial but agricultural business is carried on in this country; under such an interpretation it ought in theory to be applied universally, in which case practically all industries would stop; as a matter of fact, it is utterly out of the question to enforce it universally, and, when enforced sporadically, it causes continual unrest, puts the country at a disadvantage with its trade competitors in international commerce, hopelessly puzzles honest business men and honest farmers as to what their rights are, and yet, as has just been shown in the cases of the Standard Oil and the Tobacco Trusts, it is no real check on the great trusts at which it was in theory aimed, and, indeed, operates to their benefit. Moreover, if we are to compete with other nations in the markets of the world as well as to develop our own material civilization at home, we must utilize those forms of industrial organization that are indispensable to the highest industrial productivity and efficiency.

An important volume entitled "Concentration and Control" has just been issued by President Charles R. Van Hise of the University of Wisconsin. The University of Wisconsin has been more influential than any other agency in making Wisconsin what it has become, a laboratory for wise social and industrial experiment in the betterment of conditions. President Van Hise is one of those thoroughgoing but sane and intelligent radicals from whom much of leadership is to be expected in such a matter. The sub-title of his book shows that his endeavor is to turn the attention of his countrymen toward practically solving the trust problem of the United States.

In his preface he states that his aim is to suggest a way to gain the economic advantages of the concentration of industry and at the same time to guard the interests of the public and to assist in the rule of enlightenment, reason, fair play, mutual consideration, and toleration. In sum, he shows that unrestrained competition as an economic principle has become too destructive to be

permitted to exist, and that the small men must be
allowed to co-operate under penalty of succumbing before
their big competitors; and yet such co-operation, vitally
necessary to the small man, is criminal under the present
law. He says:

"With the alternative before the business men of co-
operation or failure, we may be sure that they will co-
operate. Since the law is violated by practically every
group of men engaged in trade from one end of the
country to the other, they do not feel that in combining
they are doing a moral wrong. The selection of the individual or corporation for prosecution depends upon the
arbitrary choice of the Attorney General, perhaps somewhat influenced by the odium which attaches to some of
the violators of the law. They all take their chance, hoping
that the blow will fall elsewhere. With general violation
and sporadic enforcement of an impracticable law, we
cannot hope that our people will gain respect for it.

"In conclusion, there is presented as the solution of
the difficulties of the present industrial situation, concentration, co-operation, and control. Through concentration
we may have the economic advantages coming from
magnitude of operations. Through co-operation we may
limit the wastes of the competitive system. Through control by commission we may secure freedom for fair
competition, elimination of unfair practices, conservation
of our natural resources, fair wages, good social conditions, and reasonable prices.

"Concentration and co-operation in industry in order
to secure efficiency are a world-wide movement. The
United States cannot resist it. If we isolate ourselves and
insist upon the subdivision of industry below the highest
economic efficiency, and do not allow co-operation, we
shall be defeated in the world's markets. We cannot
adopt an economic system less efficient than our great
competitors, Germany, England, France, and Austria.
Either we must modify our present obsolete laws regarding concentration and co-operation so as to conform
with the world movement, or else fall behind in the
race for the world's markets. Concentration and co-operation are conditions imperatively essential for industrial
advance; but if we allow concentration and co-operation

there must be control in order to protect the people, and adequate control is only possible through the administrative commission. Hence concentration, co-operation, and control are the keywords for a scientific solution of the mighty industrial problem which now confronts this Nation." . . .

We Progressives stand for the rights of the people. When these rights can best be secured by insistence upon States' rights, then we are for States' rights; when they can best be secured by insistence upon National rights, then we are for National rights. Inter-State commerce can be effectively controlled only by the Nation. The States cannot control it under the Constitution, and to amend the Constitution by giving them control of it would amount to a dissolution of the Government. The worst of the big trusts have always endeavored to keep alive the feeling in favor of having the States themselves, and not the Nation, attempt to do this work, because they know that in the long run such effort would be ineffective. There is no surer way to prevent all successful effort to deal with the trusts than to insist that they be dealt with by the States rather than by the Nation, or to create a conflict between the States and the Nation on the subject. The well-meaning ignorant man who advances such a proposition does as much damage as if he were hired by the trusts themselves, for he is playing the game of every big crooked corporation in the country. The only effective way in which to regulate the trusts is through the exercise of the collective power of our people as a whole through the Governmental agencies established by the Constitution for this very purpose.

Grave injustice is done by the Congress when it fails to give the National Government complete power in this matter; and still graver injustice by the Federal courts when they endeavor in any way to pare down the right of the people collectively to act in this matter as they deem wise; such conduct does itself tend to cause the creation of a twilight zone in which neither the Nation nor the States have power. Fortunately, the Federal courts have more and more of recent years tended to adopt the true doctrine, which is that all these matters are to be settled by the people themselves, and that the conscience of the people, and not the preferences of any servants of the people, is to be the standard in deciding what action shall be taken by the people. As Lincoln phrased it: "The [question] of National power and State rights as a principle is no other than the principle of generality and locality. Whatever concerns the whole should be confided to the whole—to the General Government; while whatever concerns only the State should be left exclusively to the State."

It is utterly hopeless to attempt to control the trusts merely by the anti-trust law, or by any law the same in principle, no matter what the modifications may be in detail. In the first place, these great corporations cannot possibly be controlled merely by a succession of lawsuits. The administrative branch of the Government must exercise such control. The preposterous failure of the Commerce Court has shown that only damage comes from the effort to substitute judicial for administrative control of great corporations. In the next place, a loosely drawn law which promises to do everything would reduce business to complete ruin if it were not also so drawn as to accomplish almost nothing. . . .

Contrast what has actually been accomplished under the inter-State commerce law with what has actually been accomplished under the anti-trust law. The first has, on the whole, worked in a highly efficient manner and achieved real and great results; and it promises to achieve even greater results, (although I firmly believe that if the power of the Commissioners grows greater it will be necessary to make them and their superior, the President, even more completely responsible to the people for their acts). The second has occasionally done good, has usually accomplished nothing, but generally left the worst conditions wholly unchanged, and has been responsible for a considerable amount of downright and positive evil.

What is needed is the application to all industrial concerns and all co-operating interests engaged in inter-State commerce in which there is either monopoly or control of the market of the principles on which we have gone in regulating transportation concerns engaged in such commerce. The anti-trust law should be kept on the statute books and strengthened so as to make it genuinely and thoroughly effective against every big concern tending to monopoly or guilty of anti-social practices.

At the same time, a National industrial commission should be created which should have complete power to regulate and control all the great industrial concerns engaged in inter-State business—which practically means all of them in this country. This commission should exercise over these industrial concerns like powers to those exercised over the railways by the Inter-State Commerce Commission, and over the National banks by the Controller of the Currency, and additional powers if found necessary. The establishment of such a commission would enable us to punish the individual rather than merely the corporation, just as we now do with banks, where the aim of the Government is not to close the bank but to bring to justice personally any bank official who has gone wrong.

This commission should deal with all the abuses of the trusts—all the abuses such as those developed by the Government suit against the Standard Oil and Tobacco Trusts—as the Inter-State Commerce Commission now deals with rebates. It should have complete power to make the capitalization absolutely honest and put a stop to all stock watering. Such supervision over the issuance of corporate securities would put a stop to exploitation of the people by dishonest capitalists desiring to declare dividends on watered securities, and would open this kind of industrial property to ownership by the people at large. It should have free access to the books of each corporation and power to find out exactly how it treats its employes, its rivals, and the general public. It should have power to compel the unsparing publicity of all the acts of any corporation which goes wrong.

The regulation should be primarily under the administrative branch of the Government and not by lawsuit. It should prohibit and effectually punish monopoly achieved through wrong, and also actual wrongs done by industrial corporations which are not monopolies, such as the artificial raising of prices, the artificial restriction on productivity, the elimination of competition by unfair or predatory practices, and the like; leaving industrial organizations free within the limits of fair and honest dealing to promote through the inherent efficiency of organization the power of the United States as a competitive Nation among Nations, and the greater abundance at home that will come to our people from that power wisely exercised.

DOCUMENT 12

WOODROW WILSON, *THE NEW FREEDOM,*
1913

Few men could express as eloquently as Wilson the anxieties of the common man in America about monopoly in business and the shrinkage in business opportunities. The passages chosen here are from some of his campaign speeches of 1912, which were selected and arranged by William Bayard Hale and published the following year as The New Freedom.

A trust is formed in this way: a few gentlemen "promote" it—that is to say, they get it up, being given enormous fees for their kindness, which fees are loaded on to the undertaking in the form of securities of one kind or another. The argument of the promoters is, not that every one who comes into the combination can carry on his business more efficiently than he did before; the argument is: we will assign to you as your share in the pool twice, three times, four times, or five times what you could have sold your business for to an individual competitor who would have to run it on an economic and competitive basis. We can afford to buy it at such a figure because we are shutting out competition. We can afford to make the stock of the combination half a dozen times what it naturally would be and pay dividends on it, because there will be nobody to dispute the prices we shall fix.

Talk of that as sound business? Talk of that as inevitable? It is based upon nothing except power. It is not based upon efficiency. It is no wonder that the big trusts are not prospering in proportion to such competitors as they still have in such parts of their business as competitors have access to; they are prospering freely only in those fields to which competition has no access. Read the statistics of the Steel Trust, if you don't believe it. Read the statistics of any trust. They are constantly nervous about competition, and they are constantly buying up new competitors in order to narrow the field. The United States Steel Corporation is gaining in its supremacy in the American market only with regard to the cruder manufactures of iron and steel, but wherever, as in the field of more advanced manufactures of iron and steel, it has important competitors, its portion of the product is not increasing but is decreasing, and its competitors, where they have a foothold, are often more efficient than it is.

Why? Why, with unlimited capital and innumerable mines and plants everywhere in the United States, can't they beat the other fellows in the market? Partly because they are carrying too much. Partly because they are unwieldy. Their organization is imperfect. They bought up inefficient plants along with efficient, and they have got to carry what they have paid for, even if they have to shut some of the plants up in order to make any interest on their investments; or, rather, not interest on their investments, because that is an incorrect word,—on their alleged capitalization. Here we have a lot of giants staggering along under an almost intolerable weight of artificial burdens, which they have put on their own backs, and constantly looking about lest some little pigmy with a round stone in a sling may come out and slay them.

For my part, I want the pigmy to have a chance to come out. And I foresee a time when the pigmies will be so much more athletic, so much more astute, so much more active, than the giants, that it will be a case of Jack the giant-killer. Just let some of the youngsters I know have a chance and they'll give these gentlemen points. Lend them a little money. They can't get any now. See to it that when they have got a local market they can't be squeezed out of it. . . . For I'll undertake to put a water-logged giant out of business any time, if you will give me a fair field and as much credit as I am entitled to, and let the law do what from time immemorial law has been expected to do,—see fair play. . . .

I take my stand absolutely, where every progressive

ought to take his stand, on the proposition that private monopoly is indefensible and intolerable. And there I will fight my battle. And I know how to fight it. Everybody who has even read the newspapers knows the means by which these men built up their power and created these monopolies. Any decently equipped lawyer can suggest to you statutes by which the whole business can be stopped. What these gentlemen do not want is this: they do not want to be compelled to meet all comers on equal terms. I am perfectly willing that they should beat any competitor by fair means; but I know the foul means they have adopted, and I know that they can be stopped by law. If they think that coming into the market upon the basis of mere efficiency, upon the mere basis of knowing how to manufacture goods better than anybody else and to sell them cheaper than anybody else, they can carry the immense amount of water that they have put into their enterprises in order to buy up rivals, then they are perfectly welcome to try it. But there must be no squeezing out of the beginner, no crippling his credit; no discrimination against retailers who buy from a rival; no threats against concerns who sell supplies to a rival; no holding back of raw material from him; no secret arrangements against him. All the fair competition you choose, but no unfair competition of any kind. And then when unfair competition is eliminated, let us see these gentlemen carry their tanks of water on their backs. All that I ask and all I shall fight for is that they shall come into the field against merit and brains everywhere. If they can beat other American brains, then they have got the best brains.

But if you want to know how far brains go, as things now are, suppose you try to match your better wares against these gentlemen, and see them undersell you before your market is any bigger than the locality and make it absolutely impossible for you to get a fast foothold. If you want to know how brains count, originate some invention which will improve the kind of machinery they are using, and then see if you can borrow enough money to manufacture it. You may be offered something for your patent by the corporation,—which will perhaps lock it up in a safe and go on using the old machinery; but you will not be allowed to manufacture. I know men who have tried it, and they could not get the money, because the great money lenders of this country are in the arrangement with the great manufacturers of this country, and they do not propose to see their control of the market interfered with by outsiders. And who are outsiders? Why, all the rest of the people of the United States are outsiders.

They are rapidly making us outsiders with respect even of the things that come from the bosom of the earth, and which belong to us in a peculiar sense. Certain monopolies in this country have gained almost complete control of the raw material, chiefly in the mines, out of which the great body of manufactures are carried on, and they now discriminate, when they will, in the sale of that raw material between those who are rivals of the monopoly and those who submit to the monopoly. We must soon come to the point where we shall say to the men who own these essentials of industry that they have got to part with these essentials by sale to all citizens of the United States with the same readiness and upon the same terms. Or else we shall tie up the resources of this country under private control in such fashion as will make our independent development absolutely impossible.

There is another injustice that monopoly engages in. The trust that deals in the cruder products which are to be transformed into the more elaborate manufactures often will not sell these crude products except upon the terms of monopoly—that is to say, the people that deal with them must buy exclusively from them. And so again you have the lines of development tied up and the connections of development knotted and fastened so that you cannot wrench them apart.

Again, the manufacturing monopolies are so interlaced in their personal relationships with the great shipping interests of this country, and with the great railroads, that they can often largely determine the rates of shipment. . . .

And when you reflect that the twenty-four men who control the United States Steel Corporation, for example, are either presidents or vice-presidents or directors in 55 per cent. of the railways of the United States, reckoning by the valuation of those railroads and the amount of their stock and bonds, you know just how close the whole thing is knitted together in our industrial system, and how great the temptation is. These twenty-four gentlemen administer that corporation as if it belonged to them. The amazing thing to me is that the people of the United States have not seen that the administration of a great business like that is not a private affair; it is a public affair. . . .

The big trusts, the big combinations, are the most wasteful, the most uneconomical, and, after they pass a certain size, the most inefficient, way of conducting the industries of this country.

A notable example is the way in which Mr. Carnegie was bought out of the steel business. Mr. Carnegie could build better mills and make better steel rails and make them cheaper than anybody else connected with what afterward became the United States Steel Corporation. They didn't dare leave him outside. He had so much more brains in finding out the best processes; he had so much more shrewdness in surrounding himself with the most successful assistants; he knew so well when a young man who came into his employ was fit for promotion and was ripe to put at the head of some branch of his business and was sure to make good, that he could undersell every mother's son of them in the market for steel rails. And they bought him out at a price that amounted to three or four times,—I believe actually five times,—the estimated value of his properties and of his business, because they couldn't beat him in competition. And then in what they charged afterward for their product,—the product of his mills included,—they made us pay the interest on the four or five times the difference.

That is the difference between a big business and a trust. A trust is an arrangement to get rid of competition, and a big business is a business that has survived competition by conquering in the field of intelligence and economy. A trust does not bring efficiency to the aid of business; it *buys efficiency out of business*. I am for big business, and I am against the trusts. Any man who can survive by his brains, any man who can put the others out of the business by making the thing cheaper to the consumer at the same time that he is increasing its intrinsic value and quality, I take off my hat to, and I say:

"You are the man who can build up the United States, and I wish there were more of you." . . .

Shall we try to get the grip of monopoly away from our lives, or shall we not? Shall we withhold our hand and say monopoly is inevitable, that all that we can do is to regulate it? Shall we say that all that we can do is to put government in competition with monopoly and try its strength against it? Shall we admit that the creature of our own hands is stronger than we are? We have been dreading all along the time when the combined power of high finance would be greater than the power of the government. Have we come to a time when the President of the United States or any man who wishes to be the President must doff his cap in the presence of this high finance, and say, "You are our inevitable master, but we will see how we can make the best of it?"

We are at the parting of the ways. We have, not one or two or three, but many, established and formidable monopolies in the United States. We have, not one or two, but many, fields of endeavor into which it is difficult, if not impossible, for the independent man to enter. We have restricted credit, we have restricted opportunity, we have controlled development, and we have come to be one of the worst ruled, one of the most completely controlled and dominated, governments in the civilized world—no longer a government by free opinion, no longer a government by conviction and the vote of the majority, but a government by the opinion and the duress of small groups of dominant men.

If the government is to tell big business men how to run their business, then don't you see that big business men have to get closer to the government even than they are now? Don't you see that they must capture the government, in order not to be restrained too much by it? Must capture the government? They have already captured it. Are you going to invite those inside to stay inside? They don't have to get there. They are there. Are you going to own your own premises, or are you not? That is your choice. Are you going to say: "You didn't get into the house the right way, but you are in there, God bless you; we will stand out here in the cold and you can hand us out something once in a while"?

At the least, under the plan I am opposing, there will be an avowed partnership between the government and the trusts. I take it that the firm will be ostensibly controlled by the senior member. For I take it that the government of the United States is at least the senior member, though the younger member has all along been running the business. But when all the momentum, when all the energy, when a great deal of the genius, as so often happens in partnerships the world over, is with the junior partner, I don't think that the superintendence of the senior partner is going to amount to very much. And I don't believe that benevolence can be read into the hearts of the trusts by the superintendence and suggestions of the federal government; because the government has never within my recollection had its suggestions accepted by the trusts. On the contrary, the suggestions of the trusts have been accepted by the government.

There is no hope to be seen for the people of the United States until the partnership is dissolved. And the business of the party now entrusted with power is going to be to dissolve it.

DOCUMENT 13

REPORT OF THE PUJO COMMITTEE,
FEBRUARY 28, 1913

Many observers felt that the fears of the Progressives about the domination of the country by the "money trust" were justified by the revelations of the Pujo Committee. This subcommittee of the House Committee on Banking and Currency had been authorized by the House in February 1912 to inquire into the concentration of financial resources and financial power in the country. Under the chairmanship of Arsène Pujo of Louisiana, it took much testimony from leading bankers and businessmen, and found in its report, represented in part here, that concentration in finance was increasing. The appearance of this report

*just on the eve of Wilson's assumption of office gave
strength to his demands for reform.*

That in recent years concentration of control of the
banking resources and consequently of credit by the group
to which we will refer has grown apace in the city of New
York is defended by some witnesses and regretted by
others, but acknowledged by all to be a fact. . . .

This increased concentration of control of money and
credit has been effected principally as follows:

First, through consolidations of competitive or potentially competitive banks and trust companies, which
consolidations in turn have recently been brought under
sympathetic management.

Second, through the same powerful interests becoming large stockholders in potentially competitive banks and
trust companies. This is the simplest way of acquiring
control, but since it requires the largest investment of
capital, it is the least used, although the recent investments in that direction for that apparent purpose amount
to tens of millions of dollars in present market values.

Third, through the confederation of potentially competitive banks and trust companies by means of the
system of interlocking directorates.

Fourth, through the influence which the more powerful banking houses, banks, and trust companies have
secured in the management of insurance companies, railroads, producing and trading corporations, and public
utility corporations, by means of stockholdings, voting
trusts, fiscal agency contracts, or representation upon their
boards of directors, or through supplying the money requirements of railway, industrial, and public utilities corporations and thereby being enabled to participate in the
determination of their financial and business policies.

Fifth, through partnership or joint account arrangements between a few of the leading banking houses, banks,
and trust companies in the purchase of security issues of
the great interstate corporations, accompanied by understandings of recent growth—sometimes called "banking
ethics"—which have had the effect of effectually destroying competition between such banking houses, banks, and

trust companies in the struggle for business or in the purchase and sale of large issues of such securities.

It is a fair deduction from the testimony that the most active agents in forwarding and bringing about the concentration of control of money and credit through one or another of the processes above described have been and are—

J. P. Morgan & Co.
First National Bank of New York
National City Bank of New York
Lee, Higginson & Co., of Boston and New York
Kidder, Peabody & Co., of Boston and New York
Kuhn, Loeb & Co. . . .

Summary of Directorships Held by These Members of the Group. . . . shows the combined directorships in the more important enterprises held by Morgan & Co., the First National Bank, the National City Bank and the Bankers and Guaranty Trust Cos., which latter two, as previously shown, are absolutely controlled by Morgan & Co. through voting trusts. It appears there that firm members or directors of these institutions together hold:

One hundred and eighteen directorships in 34 banks and trust companies having total resources of $2,679,000,-000 and total deposits of $1,983,000,000.

Thirty directorships in 10 insurance companies having total assets of $2,293,000,000.

One hundred and five directorships in 32 transportation systems having a total capitalization of $11,784,000,-000 and a total mileage (excluding express companies and steamship lines) of 150,200.

Sixty-three directorships in 24 producing and trading corporations having a total capitalization of $3,339,000,-000.

Twenty-five directorships in 12 public utility corporations having a total capitalization of $2,150,000,000.

In all, 341 directorships in 112 corporations having aggregate resources or capitalization of $22,245,000,000.

The members of the firm of J. P. Morgan & Co. hold 72 directorships in 47 of the greater corporations; George F. Baker, chairman of the board, F. L. Hine, president, and George F. Baker, jr., and C. D. Norton, vice-presidents,

of the First National Bank of New York, hold 46 directorships in 37 of the greater corporations; and James Still-
man, chairman of the board, Frank A. Vanderlip, president,
and Samuel McRoberts, J. T. Talbert, W. A. Simonson,
vice-presidents, of the National City Bank of New York,
hold 32 directorships in 26 of the greater corporations;
making in all for these members of the group 150 directorships in 110 of the greater corporations. . . .

DOCUMENT 14

WOODROW WILSON, FIRST
INAUGURAL ADDRESS,

MARCH 4, 1913

*Wilson's First Inaugural is usually considered one of
the finest of presidential inaugural addresses, and also
one of the most articulate expressions of the aspirations and concerns of the Progressive mind.*

There has been a change of government. It began two
years ago, when the House of Representatives became
Democratic by a decisive majority. It has now been completed. The Senate about to assemble will also be Democratic. The offices of President and Vice-President have
been put into the hands of Democrats. What does the
change mean? That is the question that is uppermost in
our minds to-day. That is the question I am going to try
to answer, in order, if I may, to interpret the occasion.

It means much more than the mere success of a
party. The success of a party means little except when
the Nation is using that party for a large and definite purpose. No one can mistake the purpose for which the
Nation now seeks to use the Democratic Party. It seeks to
use it to interpret a change in its own plans and point of
view. Some old things with which we had grown familiar,
and which had begun to creep into the very habit of our
thought and of our lives, have altered their aspect as we
have latterly looked critically upon them, with fresh,
awakened eyes; have dropped their disguises and shown

themselves alien and sinister. Some new things, as we look frankly upon them, willing to comprehend their real character, have come to assume the aspect of things long believed in and familiar, stuff of our own convictions. We have been refreshed by a new insight into our own life.

We see that in many things that life is very great. It is incomparably great in its material aspects, in its body of wealth, in the diversity and sweep of its energy, in the industries which have been conceived and built up by the genius of individual men and the limitless enterprise of groups of men. It is great, also, very great, in its moral force. Nowhere else in the world have noble men and women exhibited in more striking forms the beauty and the energy of sympathy and helpfulness and counsel in their efforts to rectify wrong, alleviate suffering, and set the weak in the way of strength and hope. We have built up, moreover, a great system of government, which has stood through a long age as in many respects a model for those who seek to set liberty upon foundations that will endure against fortuitous change, against storm and accident. Our life contains every great thing, and contains it in rich abundance.

But the evil has come with the good, and much fine gold has been corroded. With riches has come inexcusable waste. We have squandered a great part of what we might have used, and have not stopped to conserve the exceeding bounty of nature, without which our genius for enterprise would have been worthless and impotent, scorning to be careful, shamefully prodigal as well as admirably efficient. We have been proud of our industrial achievements, but we have not hitherto stopped thoughtfully enough to count the human cost, the cost of lives snuffed out, of energies overtaxed and broken, the fearful physical and spiritual cost to the men and women and children upon whom the dead weight and burden of it all has fallen pitilessly the years through. The groans and agony of it all had not yet reached our ears, the solemn, moving undertone of our life, coming up out of the mines and factories and out of every home where the struggle had its intimate and familiar seat. With the great Government went many deep secret things which we too long delayed to look into and scrutinize with candid, fearless eyes. The great Government we loved has too often been made use of for private and selfish purposes, and those who used it had forgotten the people.

At last a vision has been vouchsafed us of our life as a whole. We see the bad with the good, the debased and decadent with the sound and vital. With this vision we approach new affairs. Our duty is to cleanse, to reconsider, to restore, to correct the evil without impairing the good, to purify and humanize every process of our common life without weakening or sentimentalizing it. There has been something crude and heartless and unfeeling in our haste to succeed and be great. Our thought has been "Let every man look out for himself, let every generation look out for itself," while we reared giant machinery which made it impossible that any but those who stood at the levers of control should have a chance to look out for themselves. We had not forgotten our morals. We remembered well enough that we had set up a policy which was meant to serve the humblest as well as the most powerful, with an eye single to the standards of justice and fair play, and remembered it with pride. But we were very heedless and in a hurry to be great.

We have come now to the sober second thought. The scales of heedlessness have fallen from our eyes. We have made up our minds to square every process of our national life again with the standards we so proudly set up at the beginning and have always carried at our hearts. Our work is a work of restoration.

We have itemized with some degree of particularity the things that ought to be altered and here are some of the chief items: A tariff which cuts us off from our proper part in the commerce of the world, violates the just principles of taxation, and makes the Government a facile instrument in the hands of private interest; a banking and currency system based upon the necessity of the Government to sell its bonds fifty years ago and perfectly adapted to concentrating cash and restricting credits; an industrial system which, take it on all its sides, financial as well as administrative, holds capital in leading strings, restricts the liberties and limits the opportunities of labor, and exploits without renewing or conserving the natural resources of the country; a body of agricultural activities never yet given the efficiency of great business undertakings or served as it should be through the instrumentality of science taken directly to the farm, or afforded the facilities of credit best suited to its practical needs; watercourses undeveloped, waste places unreclaimed, forests untended, fast disappearing without plan or prospect of renewal, unregarded waste heaps at every mine. We have studied as perhaps no other nation has the most effective means of production, but we have not studied cost or economy as we should either as organizers of industry, as statesmen, or as individuals.

Nor have we studied and perfected the means by which government may be put at the service of humanity, in safeguarding the health of the Nation, the health of its men and its women and its children, as well as their rights in the struggle for existence. This is no sentimental duty. The firm basis of government is justice, not pity. These are matters of justice. There can be no equality or opportunity, the first essential of justice in the body politic, if men and women and children be not shielded in their lives, their very vitality, from the consequences of great industrial and social processes which they can not alter, control, or singly cope with. Society must see to it that it does not itself crush or weaken or damage its own constituent parts. The first duty of law is to keep sound the society it serves. Sanitary laws, pure food laws, and laws determining conditions of labor which individuals are powerless to determine for themselves are intimate parts of the very business of justice and legal efficiency.

These are some of the things we ought to do, and not leave the others undone, the old-fashioned, never-to-be-neglected, fundamental safeguarding of property and of individual right. This is the high enterprise of the new day: To lift everything that concerns our life as a Nation to the light that shines from the hearthfire of every man's conscience and vision of the right. It is inconceivable that we should do this as partisans; it is inconceivable we should do it in ignorance of the facts as they are or in blind haste. We shall restore, not destroy. We shall deal with our economic system as it is and as it may be modified, not as it might be if we had a clean sheet of paper to write upon; and step by step we shall make it what it should be, in the spirit of those who question their own wisdom and seek counsel and knowledge, not shallow self-satisfaction or the excitement of excursions whither they can not tell. Justice, and only justice, shall always be our motto.

And yet it will be no cool process of mere science. The Nation has been deeply stirred, stirred by a solemn passion, stirred by the knowledge of wrong, of ideals lost, of government too often debauched and made an instrument of evil. The feelings with which we face this new age of right and opportunity sweep across our heartstrings like some air out of God's own presence, where justice and mercy are reconciled and the judge and the brother are one. We know our task to be no mere task of politics but a task which shall search us through and through, whether we be able to understand our time and the need of our people, whether we be indeed their spokesmen and interpreters, whether we have the pure heart to comprehend and the rectified will to choose our high course of action.

This is not a day of triumph; it is a day of dedication. Here muster, not the forces of party, but the forces of humanity. Men's hearts wait upon us; men's lives hang in the balance; men's hopes call upon us to say what we will do. Who shall live up to the great trust? Who dares fail to try? I summon all honest men, all patriotic, all forward-looking men, to my side. God helping me, I will not fail them, if they will but counsel and sustain me!

✱ PART VI ✱

Prosperity and Depression

✱ ✱ ✱ ✱ ✱ ✱ ✱

THE twenty years between wars, from 1919 to 1939, were years of violent ups and downs—in the business cycle, in politics, and in the public mood. In the immediate post-war years there was a sharp reaction against Progressive idealism, made worse by the exaggerated fears of radicalism that had been excited by the success of the Bolshevik revolution in Russia. After 1920 the country quickly recovered from a short post-war depression; but, as Woodrow Wilson had sadly foreseen, recovery from the war-born shock to national confidence was difficult and slow. A new wave of political feeling, sometimes surprisingly reactionary, swept the country. The Supreme Court decision in *Hammer* v. *Dagenhart* (1918), which struck down a child labor law (Documents 1 and 2), is perhaps an extreme example of this mood. Several other important Court decisions of the 1920's undermined the legal position of organized labor and of social legislation. Like the country at large, the Court also tended to lose faith in the value of traditional guarantees to freedom of thought. In the *Abrams* case of 1919 (Document 3) it employed a somewhat tortured construction of the Espionage Act of 1918 to uphold a questionable conviction. Justice Oliver Wendell Holmes protested in an eloquent dissent (Document 4) which later became a rallying cry for spokesmen of freedom.

Perhaps the ugliest manifestation of the post-war reaction was the resurgence of a kind of acute ethnic intolerance which had been relatively muted for a quarter of a century. The Ku Klux Klan reappeared just after the war, reviving a name that had been famous during Reconstruction but had long since become devoid of importance. Now the new Klan, which gained a wide following even outside the South and notably within the Democratic party, began to exercise important political influence, besides making life miserable for many Catholics, Negroes, and Jews. The Klan, as one of its leaders explained (Document 5), had its touching side; it was a manifestation of the discomfort of certain long-established, once-dominant ethnic groups who found their rural or small-town, often puritanical, social values and their public position challenged by the prosperous polyglot urban areas. Actually, the Klan was a radical, activist expression of this feeling, so widely shared that in 1921 and 1924 it was to lead to successive acts of Congress ending the historic American policy of liberal immigration. A movement to repudiate the Klan made a shambles of the Democratic national convention in 1924. But the violence and corruption with which the Klan wielded its power soon brought it into disrepute among liberals and conservatives alike. In Kansas, where the Klan was very powerful, William Allen White (Document 6) fought it as stubbornly as he had once fought the Populists (Part III, Document 9).

Though confused, divided, and somewhat demoralized, Progressivism was not altogether dead in the 1920's. Some intellectuals and socialists kept an unshaken faith in reform. Their discontents were shared by the farming community which did not benefit from the returning prosperity, by the Railroad Brotherhoods and some other organized labor groups, and by those Americans who had never reconciled themselves to the country's entrance into the war. These groups united to back the candidacy of Senator Robert M. La Follette for President on a new Progressive Party ticket in 1924. La Follette's platform (Document 7) documents the grievances and objectives of those who still looked at national policies from the point of view of Progressive ideals. La Follette waged a courageous campaign without a national organization and on pathetically inadequate funds; his defeat was not a measure of his personal capacities but of the decline of Progressivism. He carried only his own state of Wisconsin, re-

ceiving sixteen percent of the national vote; the impec-
cably conservative Coolidge overwhelmed not only La
Follette but the compromise Democratic candidate, John
W. Davis. Clearly, this was a victory for optimism, for the
conviction that American individualism was unsurpassed
as a way for getting the best out of human energy and
that the American "system" was finally about to triumph
altogether over poverty. The classic expression of this
conservative optimism is Herbert Hoover's famous speech
on "the American system of rugged individualism" (Document 8) given during the 1928 campaign. That year,
Hoover's faith in American business was not challenged
in any fundamental way by his somewhat more liberal
opponent, Alfred E. Smith. Not until the crash, and until
long months of anguished waiting for business to right
itself brought only further suffering and frustration, did
another political leader oppose Hoover's convictions with
an equally formidable statement. During the 1932 campaign, at the Commonwealth Club in San Francisco,
Franklin D. Roosevelt delivered a speech (Document 9)
setting forth a view of American history which completely differed from that of rugged individualism. Roosevelt's analysis was in fact based less upon his own views
than upon those of certain intellectuals both inside and
outside the Brain Trust. He argued that the motives
and ideas behind the great age of nineteenth-century industrial expansion had now outlived their usefulness. What
America needed now were administrative and distributive
rather than exploitative skills. Confidence in the sufficiency
of rugged individualism must be replaced by "an economic
constitutional order . . . a more permanently safe order
of things." In his self-assured First Inaugural address
(Document 10), Roosevelt promised "direct, vigorous
action" to deal with the depression, and went on—to the
alarm of men like Hoover—to say that if ordinary techniques failed, he would not hesitate to "ask the Congress
for the one remaining instrument to meet the crisis—broad
Executive power to wage a war against the emergency,
as great as the power that would be given to me if we
were in fact invaded by a foreign foe."

Roosevelt's first term began in a frenzy of legislative
action. Within a few years Congress passed major laws

on banking, securities regulation, currency, production and price codes for industry, control of agricultural production, public works, unemployment relief, reforestation, public power, social security, and taxation. Some of these measures, of course, were temporary, but the sum pointed to the new kind of administrative economics Roosevelt had first announced in his Commonwealth Club speech. Many Republicans, and even some Democrats, found Roosevelt's New Deal abhorrent. They were genuinely frightened by the increasing apparatus of economic control, and the accompanying heavy expenditure, expansion of governmental power, and appeal to the working class. The New Deal, for them, was not an arguable way of attacking social ills but a startling abandonment of American traditions. The Republicans' campaign of 1936 was based on this feeling; their platform declared: "America is in peril. We invite all Americans, irrespective of party, to join us in the defense of American institutions." It went on to repudiate, as later Republican platforms did not, the entire New Deal, from first to last. In this campaign, the mild Republican candidate, Alfred M. Landon of Kansas, was over-shadowed by the outspoken ex-President Hoover. Hoover declared that the New Deal was not merely a set of ill-conceived laws, but a "challenge to liberty" (Document 11). It is doubtful, however, that a less unbending stand would have helped the Republicans to withstand Roosevelt's popularity; he was re-elected by one of the most decisive votes in the history of presidential elections.

Despite their domination of Congress, however, the New Dealers were not able to have everything their way. Although they controlled the legislature, the Supreme Court's opposition was formidable. During Roosevelt's first administration, the Court threw out New Deal legislation in case after case. Among these measures were a railroad retirement plan, the Bituminous Coal Act which was meant to rescue a declining industry, a municipal bankruptcy act, and legislation to protect farm mortgages. The Court's unanimous decision against the National Recovery Act, which embodied the administration's basic program for industry, received a great deal of publicity, but was not as damaging as it first appeared, because the

Act was not working out well. Far more serious was the
Court's six to three decision in *U.S.* v. *Butler et al.*
(1936) (Document 12), which invalidated the Agricultural Adjustment Act of 1933, the administration's major
effort to raise farm prices. In this case Justice Stone
dissented (Document 13); he said, and many liberals and
legal scholars agreed with him, that the Court had here
overreached its powers. New ways to regulate agriculture
without running afoul of the Court were later found by
Congress, but concern about the Court grew throughout the
country. Roosevelt accused it of belonging to the "horse
and buggy age," and after his tremendous victory in 1936,
risked a daring assault upon it. In his reform proposal of
1937 (Document 14) he asked that he be empowered to
add as many as six new justices, on the plainly disingenu-
ous ground that the advanced age of several of the
justices made the Court inefficient. This was a mistake.
Although some Democrats went along with him, many
were offended and, despite their liberal record on economic
issues, joined the Republican opposition. The press, bench,
and bar and, gradually, public opinion, opposed the plan;
on June 7, 1937, when it was clear that the proposal had
no chance, the Senate Judiciary Committee reported
stingingly against it (Document 15). But while this debate
had been going on, the Court's decisions had become more
liberal, and many recent laws had been upheld. The New
Dealers could console themselves with the thought that
their agitation may have influenced the Court's attitudes.
In the following year, Roosevelt failed in an attempt to
defeat Democrats who had obstructed some New Deal
legislation; clearly, the high point of New Deal power
had passed, and the period of reform legislation was almost
over. But by this time, domestic issues were elbowed
aside by pressing issues of foreign policy (Part VII).

DOCUMENT 1

HAMMER v. DAGENHART,
1918

*This decision blocked the development of social legis-
lation for many years. State-by-state regulation of
child labor was irregular and ineffective—especially
in those states which were trying to lure employers
with a cheap labor supply. In 1916, therefore, Congress took over; it passed an act prohibiting interstate or foreign shipment of commodities produced in
factories employing children under 14, and in mines
employing children under 16. Dagenhart, who had
two sons working in a North Carolina cotton mill,
challenged the constitutionality of the act. The issue
before the Court was whether the power of Congress
to regulate commerce embraced the power to prohibit
commerce in articles produced under conditions of
which Congress disapproved. Justice William R. Day,
in deciding that it did not, spoke for a Court that was
divided five to four (see Document 2). The decision
remained intensely controversial for many years.*

DAY, J. . . .
It is insisted that adjudged cases in this court establish the
doctrine that the power to regulate given to Congress
incidentally includes the authority to prohibit the movement of ordinary commodities, and therefore that the
subject is not open for discussion. The cases demonstrate
the contrary. They rest upon the character of the particular
subjects dealt with and the fact that the scope of governmental authority, state or national, possessed over them, is
such that the authority to prohibit is, as to them, but the
exertion of the power to regulate. [Cites various cases.]
    In each of these instances the use of interstate trans-
portation was necessary to the accomplishment of harmful
results. In other words, although the power over inter-

state transportation was to regulate, that could only be accomplished by prohibiting the use of the facilities of interstate commerce to effect the evil intended.

This element is wanting in the present case. The thing intended to be accomplished by this statute is the denial of the facilities of interstate commerce to those manufacturers in the States who employ children within the prohibited ages. The act in its effect does not regulate transportation among the States, but aims to standardize the ages at which children may be employed in mining and manufacturing within the States. The goods shipped are of themselves harmless. The act permits them to be freely shipped after thirty days from the time of their removal from the factory. When offered for shipment, and before transportation begins, the labor of their production is over, and the mere fact that they were intended for interstate commerce transportation does not make their production subject to federal control under the commerce power.

Commerce "consists of intercourse and traffic . . . and includes the transportation of persons and property, as well as the purchase, sale and exchange of commodities." The making of goods and the mining of coal are not commerce, nor does the fact that these things are to be afterwards shipped, or used in interstate commerce, make their production a part thereof.

Over interstate transportation, or its incidents, the regulatory power of Congress is ample, but the production of articles intended for interstate commerce is a matter of local regulation. . . . If it were otherwise, all manufacture intended for interstate shipment would be brought under federal control to the practical exclusion of the authority of the states, a result certainly not contemplated by the framers of the Constitution when they vested in Congress the authority to regulate commerce among the states. . . .

The grant of power to Congress over the subject of interstate commerce was to enable it to regulate such commerce, and not to give it authority to control the States in their exercise of the police power over local trade and manufacture.

The grant of authority over a purely federal matter

was not intended to destroy the local power always existing and carefully reserved to the States in the Tenth Amendment to the Constitution. . . .

That there should be limitations upon the right to employ children in mines and factories in the interest of their own and the public welfare, all will admit. That such employment is generally deemed to require regulation is shown by the fact that the brief of counsel states that every state in the Union has a law upon the subject, limiting the right to thus employ children. In North Carolina, the State wherein is located the factory in which the employment was had in the present case, no child under twelve years of age is permitted to work.

It may be desirable that such laws be uniform, but our federal government is one of enumerated powers. . . .

To sustain this statute would not be, in our judgment, a recognition of the lawful exertion of congressional authority over interstate commerce, but would sanction an invasion by the federal power of the control of a matter purely local in its character, and over which no authority has been delegated to Congress in conferring the power to regulate commerce among the states. . . .

In our view the necessary effect of this act is, by means of a prohibition against the movement in interstate commerce of ordinary commercial commodities, to regulate the hours of labor of children in factories and mines within the States, a purely state authority. Thus the act in a twofold sense is repugnant to the Constitution. It not only transcends the authority delegated to Congress over commerce, but also exerts a power as to a purely local matter to which the federal authority does not extend. The far-reaching result of upholding the act cannot be more plainly indicated than by pointing out that if Congress can thus regulate matters intrusted to local authority by prohibition of the movement of commodities in interstate commerce, all freedom of commerce will be at an end, and the power of the states over local matters may be eliminated, and thus our system of government be practically destroyed.

For these reasons we hold that this law exceeds the constitutional authority of Congress.

DOCUMENT 2

OLIVER WENDELL HOLMES, DISSENTING OPINION IN *HAMMER* v. *DAGENHART*,
1918

The tone of this dissent, with which Justices Mc-Kenna, Brandeis, and Clarke concurred, indicates the outrage Holmes felt at the Court's excessively sweeping assertion of its power in this case. The minority justices felt that this case was the same in principle as those where the prohibition by Congress of the interstate movement of lottery tickets had been upheld; and those in which bans on the interstate movement of women for immoral purposes, of liquor, and of adulterated food and drugs had similarly been sustained. They were aware that this decision not only crippled efforts to eliminate child labor but created a legal no-man's-land. The states could not legally exclude products made in other states, for that usurped a power belonging to Congress; and yet Congress could not forbid the interstate shipment of goods made by child labor, for that usurped a power belonging to the states. Almost a quarter century later, in United States v. Darby (1941), *the Court vindicated Holmes and his fellow dissenters, by explicitly overruling* Hammer v. Dagenhart *in a case involving the constitutionality of the Fair Labor Standards Act of 1938. In the* Darby *case the Court, speaking through Justice Harlan Fiske Stone, declared: "Hammer v. Dagenhart has not been followed. . . . Hammer v. Dagenhart was a departure from the principles which have prevailed in the interpretation of the commerce clause both before and since the decision and . . . such vitality, as a precedent, as it then had has long since been exhausted. It should be and now is overruled."*

The single question in this case is whether Congress has power to prohibit the shipment in interstate or foreign commerce of any product of a cotton mill [made by child labor under certain specified conditions]. . . . The objection urged against the power is that the States have exclusive control over their methods of production and that Congress cannot meddle with them, and taking the proposition in the sense of direct intermeddling I agree to it and suppose that no one denies it. But if an act is within the powers specifically conferred upon Congress, it seems to me that it is not made any less constitutional because of the indirect effects that it may have, however obvious it may be that it will have those effects, and that we are not at liberty upon such grounds to hold it void.

The first step in any argument is to make plain what no one is likely to dispute—that the statute in question is within the power expressly given to Congress if considered only as to its immediate effects and that if invalid it is so only upon some collateral ground. The statute confines itself to prohibiting the carriage of certain goods in interstate or foreign commerce. Congress is given power to regulate such commerce in unqualified terms. It would not be argued today that the power to regulate does not include the power to prohibit. Regulation means the prohibition of something, and when interstate commerce is the matter to be regulated I cannot doubt that the regulations may prohibit any part of such commerce that Congress sees fit to forbid. At all events it is established by the *Lottery Case* [Champion v. Ames, 1903] and others that have followed it that a law is not beyond the regulative power of Congress merely because it prohibits certain transportation out and out. . . . So I repeat that this statute in its immediate operation is clearly within the Congress's constitutional power.

The question then is narrowed to whether the exercise of its otherwise constitutional power by Congress can be pronounced unconstitutional because of its possible reaction upon the conduct of the States in a matter upon which I have admitted that they are free from direct control. I should have thought that that matter had been disposed of so fully as to leave no room for doubt. I should have thought that the most conspicuous decisions of this Court had made it clear that the power to regulate commerce and other constitutional powers could not be cut down or qualified by the fact that it might interfere with the carrying out of the domestic policy of any State. . . . [Cites examples in previous decisions]

The notion that prohibition is any less prohibition when applied to things now thought evil I do not understand. But if there is any matter upon which civilized countries have agreed—far more unanimously than they have with regard to intoxicants and some other matters over which this country is now emotionally aroused—it is the evil of premature and excessive child labor. I should have thought that if we were to introduce our own moral conceptions where in my opinion they do not belong, this was preëminently a case for upholding the exercise of all its powers by the United States.

But I had thought that the propriety of the exercise of a power admitted to exist in some cases was for the consideration of Congress alone and that this Court always had disavowed the right to intrude its judgment upon questions of policy or morals. It is not for this Court to pronounce when prohibition is necessary to regulation if it ever may be necessary—to say that it is permissible as against strong drink but not as against the product of ruined lives.

The act does not meddle with anything belonging to the States. They may regulate their internal affairs and their domestic commerce as they like. But when they seek to send their products across the state line they are no longer within their rights. If there were no Constitution and no Congress their power to cross the line would depend upon their neighbors. Under the Constitution such commerce belongs not to the States but to Congress to regulate. It may carry out its views of public policy whatever indirect effect they may have upon the activities of the States. Instead of being encountered by a prohibitive tariff at her boundaries the State encounters the public policy of the United States which it is for Congress to express. The public policy of the United States is shaped with a view to the benefit of the nation as a whole. . . .

DOCUMENT 3

ABRAMS v. U.S.,
1919

This case involved the Espionage Act of 1918. Abrams and four other plaintiffs had been convicted for distributing leaflets attacking the United States and her Allies for intervening against the Bolsheviks in Russia. Conviction was upheld for reasons stated here by Justice John H. Clarke. The differences of opinion within the Court were clearly stated by both sides—the majority's here and the minority's in the famous Holmes dissent (Document 4).

CLARKE, J.: On a single indictment, containing four counts, the five plaintiffs . . . were convicted of conspiring to violate provisions of the [Espionage] Act . . . of May 16, 1918. . . .

Each of the first three counts charged the defendants with conspiring, when the United States was at war with the Imperial Government of Germany, to unlawfully utter, print, write and publish: In the first count, "disloyal, scurrilous and abusive language about the form of Government of the United States"; in the second count, language "intended to bring the form of Government of the United States into contempt, scorn, contumely and disrepute"; and in the third count, language "intended to incite, provoke and encourage resistance to the United States in said war." The charge in the fourth count was that the defendants conspired "when the United States was at war with the Imperial German Government, . . . unlawfully and wilfully, by utterance, writing, printing and publication, to urge, incite and advocate curtailment of production of things and products, to wit, ordinance and ammunition, necessary and essential to the prosecution of the war." The offenses were charged in the language of the act of Congress.

It was charged in each count of the indictment that

it was part of the conspiracy that the defendants would attempt to accomplish their unlawful purpose by printing, writing and distributing in the City of New York many copies of a leaflet or circular, printed in the English language, and of another printed in the Yiddish language, copies of which, properly identified, were attached to the indictment.

All of the five defendants were born in Russia. They were intelligent, had considerable schooling, and at the time they were arrested they had lived in the United States terms varying from five to ten years, but none of them had applied for naturalization. Four of them testified as witnesses in their own behalf and of these, three frankly avowed that they were "rebels," "revolutionists," "anarchists," that they did not believe in government in any form, and they declared that they had no interest whatsoever in the Government of the United States. The fourth defendant testified that he was a "socialist" and believed in "a proper kind of government, not capitalistic," but in his classification the Government of the United States was "capitalistic."

It was admitted on the trial that the defendants had united to print and distribute the described circulars and that five thousand of them had been printed and distributed about the 22nd day of August, 1918. The group had a meeting place in New York City, in rooms rented by defendant Abrams, under an assumed name, and there the subject of printing the circulars was discussed about two weeks before the defendants were arrested. The defendant Abrams, although not a printer, on July 27, 1918, purchased the printing outfit with which the circulars were printed and installed it in a basement room where the work was done at night. The circulars were distributed some by throwing them from a window of a building where one of the defendants was employed and others secretly, in New York City.

The defendants pleaded "not guilty," and the case of the Government consisted in showing the facts we have stated, and in introducing in evidence copies of the two printed circulars attached to the indictment, a sheet entitled "Revolutionists Unite for Action," written by the defendant Lipman, and found on him when he was arrested, and another paper, found at the headquarters of the group, and for which Abrams assumed responsibility.

Thus the conspiracy and the doing of the overt acts charged were largely admitted and were fully established.

On the record thus described it is argued, somewhat faintly, that the acts charged against the defendants were not unlawful because within the protection of that freedom of speech and of the press which is guaranteed by the First Amendment to the Constitution of the United States, and that the entire Espionage Act is unconstitutional because in conflict with that Amendment. . . .

The first of the two articles attached to the indictment is conspicuously headed, "The Hypocrisy of the United States and her Allies." After denouncing President Wilson as a hypocrite and a coward because troops were sent into Russia, it proceeds to assail our Government in general . . .

It will not do to say, as is now argued, that the only intent of these defendants was to prevent injury to the Russian cause. Men must be held to have intended, and to be accountable for, the effects which their acts were likely to produce. Even if their primary purpose and intent was to aid the cause of the Russian Revolution, the plan of action which they adopted necessarily involved, before it could be realized, defeat of the war program of the United States, for the obvious effect of this appeal, if it should become effective, as they hoped it might, would be to persuade persons of character such as those whom they regarded themselves as addressing, not to aid government loans and not to work in ammunition factories, where their work would produce "bullets, bayonets, cannon" and other munitions of war, the use of which would cause the "murder" of Germans and Russians. . . .

That the interpretation we have put upon these articles, circulated in the greatest port of our land, from which great numbers of soldiers were at that time taking ship daily, and in which great quantities of war supplies of every kind were at the time being manufactured for transportation overseas, is not only the fair interpretation of them, but that it is the meaning which their authors consciously intended should be conveyed by them to others is further shown by the additional writings found in the meeting place of the defendant group and on the person of one of them. . . .

These excerpts sufficiently show, that while the immediate occasion for this particular outbreak of lawlessness, on the part of the defendant alien anarchists, may have been resentment caused by our Government sending troops into Russia as a strategic operation against the Germans on the eastern battle front, yet the plain purpose of their propaganda was to excite, at the supreme crisis of the war, disaffection, sedition, riots, and, as they hoped, revolution, in this country for the purpose of embarrassing and if possible defeating the military plans of the Government in Europe. A technical distinction may perhaps be taken between disloyal and abusive language applied to the *form* of our government or language intended to bring the *form* of our government into contempt and disrepute, and language of like character and intended to produce like results directed against the President and Congress, the agencies through which that form of government must function in time of war. But it is not necessary to a decision of this case to consider whether such distinction is vital or merely formal, for the language of these circulars was obviously intended to provoke and to encourage resistance to the United States in the war, as the third count runs, and, the defendants, in terms, plainly urged and advocated a resort to a general strike of workers in ammunition factories for the purpose of curtailing the production of ordnance and munitions necessary and essential to the prosecution of the war as is charged in the fourth count. Thus it is clear not only that some evidence but that much persuasive evidence was before the jury tending to prove that the defendants were guilty as charged in both the third and fourth counts of the indictment. . . .

DOCUMENT 4

OLIVER WENDELL HOLMES, DISSENTING OPINION IN *ABRAMS* v. *U.S.,*
1919

*This opinion, in which Justice Louis D. Brandeis con-
curred, was perhaps the greatest written by the great
dissenter; it has become famous for its plea for "free
trade in ideas," and for its assertion that "the best test
of truth is the power of the thought to get itself accepted in the competition of the market." "I hope that
we have heard the last, or nearly the last, of the Espionage Act cases," wrote Holmes at the time to his
English friend Sir Frederick Pollock. "Some of our
subordinate Judges seem to me to have been hysteri-
cal during the war." Holmes's view that the expression
of opinions should be left free "unless they so imminently threaten immediate interference with the
lawful and pressing purposes of the law that an immediate check is required to save the country" (elsewhere referred to as the "clear and present danger"
test) has been subject to much subsequent judicial
qualification, and has not always been followed. The
Court departed notably from the principle in a major
case involving Communists after World War II, the
Dennis case of 1951.*

No argument seems to me necessary to show that these
pronunciamentos [made by the defendants in two leaflets]
in no way attack the form of government of the United
States, or that they do not support either of the first two
counts. What little I have to say about the third count may
be postponed until I have considered the fourth. With
regard to that it seems too plain to be denied that the
suggestion to workers in the ammunition factories that
they are producing bullets to murder their dearest, and
the further advocacy of a general strike, both in the
second leaflet, do urge curtailment of production of things

necessary to the prosecution of the war within the meaning of the Act of May 16, 1918. . . . But to make the conduct criminal that statute requires that it should be "with intent by such curtailment to cripple or hinder the United States in the prosecution of the war." It seems to me that no such intent is proved.

I am aware of course that the word intent as vaguely used in ordinary legal discussion means no more than knowledge at the time of the act that the consequences said to be intended will ensue. Even less than that will satisfy the general principle of civil and criminal liability. A man may have to pay damages, may be sent to prison, at common law might be hanged, if at the time of his act he knew facts from which common experience showed that the consequences would follow, whether he individually could foresee them or not. But, when words are used exactly, a deed is not done with intent to produce a consequence unless that consequence is the aim of the deed. It may be obvious, and obvious to the actor, that the consequence will follow, and he may be liable for it even if he regrets it, but he does not do the act with intent to produce it unless the aim to produce it is the proximate motive of the specific act, although there may be some deeper motive behind. . . .

I do not see how anyone can find the intent required by the statute in any of the defendants' words. The second leaflet is the only one that affords even a foundation for the charge, and there, without invoking the hatred of German militarism expressed in the former one, it is evident from the beginning to the end that the only object of the paper is to help Russia and stop American intervention there against the popular government—not to impede the United States in the war that it was carrying on. To say that two phrases taken literally might import a suggestion of conduct that would have interference with the war as an indirect and probably undesired effect seems to me by no means enough to show an attempt to produce that effect. . . .

In this case sentences of twenty years imprisonment have been imposed for the publishing of two leaflets that I believe the defendants had as much right to publish as the Government has to publish the Constitution of the

United States now vainly invoked by them. Even if I am
technically wrong and enough can be squeezed from these
poor and puny anonymities to turn the color of legal
litmus paper; I will add, even if what I think the necessary
intent were shown; the most nominal punishment seems
to me all that possibly could be inflicted, unless the
defendants are to be made to suffer not for what the
indictment alleges but for the creed that they avow—a
creed that I believe to be the creed of ignorance and
immaturity when honestly held, as I see no reason to doubt
that it was held here, but which, although made the subject
of examination at the trial, no one has a right even to
consider in dealing with the charges before the Court.

Persecution for the expression of opinions seems to
me perfectly logical. If you have no doubt of your premises
or your power and want a certain result with all your
heart you naturally express your wishes in law and sweep
away all opposition. To allow opposition by speech seems
to indicate that you think the speech impotent, as when a
man says that he has squared the circle, or that you do not
care whole-heartedly for the result, or that you doubt
either your power or your premises. But when men have
realized that time has upset many fighting faiths, they
may come to believe even more than they believe the very
foundations of their own conduct that the ultimate good
desired is better reached by free trade in ideas—that the
best test of truth is the power of the thought to get itself
accepted in the competition of the market, and that truth
is the only ground upon which their wishes safely can be
carried out. That at any rate is the theory of our Constitution. It is an experiment, as all life is an experiment.
Every year if not every day we have to wager our salvation upon some prophecy based upon imperfect knowledge. While that experiment is part of our system I think
that we should be eternally vigilant against attempts to
check the expression of opinions that we loathe and
believe to be fraught with death, unless they so imminently
threaten immediate interference with the lawful and pressing purposes of the law that an immediate check is
required to save the country. I wholly disagree with the
argument of the Government that the First Amendment
left the common law as to seditious libel in force. History

seems to me against the notion. I had conceived that the United States through many years had shown its repentance for the Sedition Act of 1798, by repaying fines that it imposed. Only the emergency that makes it immediately dangerous to leave the correction of evil counsels to time warrants making any exception to the sweeping command, "Congress shall make no law . . . abridging the freedom of speech." Of course I am speaking only of expressions of opinion and exhortations, which were all that were uttered here, but I regret that I cannot put into more impressive words my belief that in their conviction upon this indictment the defendants were deprived of their rights under the Constitution of the United States.

DOCUMENT 5

HIRAM W. EVANS, "THE KLAN'S FIGHT FOR AMERICANISM," 1926

In the article from which this passage is taken, the Imperial Wizard of the Ku Klux Klan explained in moderate and sometimes poignant language the plight of the unsuccessful and unsophisticated men who had joined this movement that was so frequently immoderate, violent, and corrupt.

The Klan, therefore, has now come to speak for the great mass of Americans of the old pioneer stock. We believe that it does fairly and faithfully represent them, and our proof lies in their support. To understand the Klan, then, it is necessary to understand the character and present mind of the mass of old-stock Americans. The mass, it must be remembered, as distinguished from the intellectually mongrelized "Liberals."

These are, in the first place, a blend of various peoples of the so-called Nordic race, the race which, with all its faults, has given the world almost the whole of modern civilization. The Klan does not try to represent any people but these.

There is no need to recount the virtues of the American pioneers; but it is too often forgotten that in the pioneer period a selective process of intense rigor went on. From the first only hardy, adventurous and strong men and women dared the pioneer dangers; from among these all but the best died swiftly, so that the new Nordic blend which became the American race was bred up to a point probably the highest in history. This remarkable race character, along with the new-won continent and the new-created nation, made the inheritance of the old-stock Americans the richest ever given to a generation of men.

In spite of it, however, these Nordic Americans for the last generation have found themselves increasingly uncomfortable, and finally deeply distressed. There appeared first confusion in thought and opinion, a groping and hesitancy about national affairs and private life alike, in sharp contrast to the clear, straightforward purposes of our earlier years. There was futility in religion, too, which was in many ways even more distressing. Presently we began to find that we were dealing with strange ideas; policies that always sounded well, but somehow always made us still more uncomfortable.

Finally came the moral breakdown that has been going on for two decades. One by one all our traditional moral standards went by the boards, or were so disregarded that they ceased to be binding. The sacredness of our Sabbath, of our homes, of chastity, and finally even of our right to teach our own children in our own schools fundamental facts and truths were torn away from us. Those who maintained the old standards did so only in the face of constant ridicule.

Along with this went economic distress. The assurance for the future of our children dwindled. We found our great cities and the control of much of our industry and commerce taken over by strangers, who stacked the cards of success and prosperity against us. Shortly they came to dominate our government. The *bloc* system by which this was done is now familiar to all. Every kind of inhabitant except the Americans gathered in groups which operated as units in politics, under orders of corrupt, self-seeking and un-American leaders, who both by purchase and threat enforced their demands on politicians. Thus it came about that the interests of Americans were always the last to be considered by either national or city governments, and that the native Americans were constantly discriminated against, in business, in legislation and in administrative government.

So the Nordic American today is a stranger in large parts of the land his fathers gave him. Moreover, he is a most unwelcome stranger, one much spit upon, and one to whom even the right to have his own opinions and to work for his own interests is now denied with jeers and revilings. "We must Americanize the Americans," a distinguished immigrant said recently. Can anything more clearly show the state to which the real American has fallen in this country which was once his own?

Our falling birth rate, the result of all this, is proof of our distress. We no longer feel that we can be fair to children we bring into the world, unless we can make sure from the start that they shall have capital or education or both, so that they need never compete with those who now fill the lower rungs of the ladder of success. We dare no longer risk letting our youth "make its own way" in the conditions under which we live. So even our unborn children are being crowded out of their birthright!

All this has been true for years, but it was the World War that gave us our first hint of the real cause of our troubles, and began to crystallize our ideas. The war revealed that millions whom we had allowed to share our heritage and prosperity, and whom we had assumed had become part of us, were in fact not wholly so. They had other loyalties: each was willing—anxious!—to sacrifice the interests of the country that had given him shelter to the interests of the one he was supposed to have cast off; each in fact did use the freedom and political power we had given him against ourselves whenever he could see any profit for his older loyalty.

This, of course, was chiefly in international affairs, and the excitement caused by the discovery of disloyalty subsided rapidly after the war ended. But it was not forgotten by the Nordic Americans. They had been awakened and alarmed; they began to suspect that the hyphenism which had been shown was only a part of what existed; their quiet was not that of renewed sleep, but of strong men waiting very watchfully. And presently they began to form decisions about all those aliens who were Americans for profit only.

They decided that even the crossing of salt-water did not dim a single spot on a leopard; that an alien usually remains an alien no matter what is done to him, what veneer of education he gets, what oaths he takes, nor what public attitudes he adopts. They decided that the melting pot was a ghastly failure, and remembered that the very name was coined by a member of one of the races—the Jews—which most determinedly refuses to melt. They decided that in every way, as well as in politics, the alien in the vast majority of cases is un-alterably fixed in his instincts, character, thought and interests by centuries of racial selection and development, that he thinks first for his own people, works only with and for them, cares entirely for their interests, considers himself always one of them, and never an American. They decided that in character, instincts, thought, and purposes—in his whole soul—an alien remains fixedly alien to America and all it means.

They saw, too, that the alien was tearing down the American standard of living, especially in the lower walks. It became clear that while the American can out-work the alien, the alien can so far under-live the American as to force him out of all competitive labor. So they came to realize that the Nordic can easily survive and rule and increase if he holds for himself the advantages won by strength and daring of his ancestors in times of stress and peril, but that if he surrenders those advantages to the peoples who could not share the stress, he will soon be driven below the level at which he can exist by their low standards, low living and fast breeding. And they saw that the low standard aliens of Eastern and Southern Europe were doing just that thing to us.

They learned, though more slowly, that alien ideas are just as dangerous to us as the aliens themselves, no matter how plausible such ideas may sound. With most of the plain people this conclusion is based simply on the fact that the alien ideas do not work well for them. Others went deeper and came to understand that the differences in racial background, in breeding, instinct, character and emotional point of view are more important than logic. So ideas which may be perfectly healthy for an alien may also be poisonous for Americans.

Finally they learned the great secret of the propagandists; that success in corrupting public opinion depends on putting out the subversive ideas without revealing their source. They came to suspect that "prejudice" against foreign ideas is really a protective device of nature against mental food that may be indigestible. They saw, finally, that the alien leaders in America act on this theory, and that there is a steady flood of alien ideas being spread over the country, always carefully disguised as American.

As they learned all this the Nordic Americans have been gradually arousing themselves to defend their homes and their own kind of civilization. They have not known just how to go about it; the idealist philanthropy and good-natured generosity which led to the philosophy of the melting pot have died hard. Resistance to the peaceful invasion of the immigrant is no such simple matter as snatching up weapons and defending frontiers, nor has it much spectacular emotionalism to draw men to the colors.

The old-stock Americans are learning, however. They have begun to arm themselves for this new type of warfare. Most important, they have broken away from the fetters of the false ideals and philanthropy which put aliens ahead of their own children and their own race.

To do this they have had to reject completely—and perhaps for the moment the rejection is a bit too complete —the whole body of "Liberal" ideas which they had followed with such simple, unquestioning faith. The first and immediate cause of the break with Liberalism was that it had provided no defense against the alien invasion, but instead had excused it—even defended it against Americanism. Liberalism is today charged in the mind of most Americans with nothing less than national, racial and spiritual treason. . . .

We are a movement of the plain people, very weak in the matter of culture, intellectual support, and trained leadership. We are demanding, and we expect to win, a return of power into the hands of the everyday, not highly cultured, not overly intellectualized, but entirely unspoiled and not de-Americanized, average citizen of the old stock. Our members and leaders are all of this class—the opposition of the intellectuals and liberals who held the leadership, betrayed Americanism, and from whom we expect to wrest control, is almost automatic.

This is undoubtedly a weakness. It lays us open to the charge of being "hicks" and "rubes" and "drivers of second hand Fords." We admit it. Far worse, it makes it hard for us to state our case and advocate our crusade in the most effective way, for most of us lack skill in language. Worst of all, the need of trained leaders constantly hampers our progress and leads to serious blunders and internal troubles. If the Klan ever should fail it would be from this cause. All this we on the inside know far better than our critics, and regret more. Our leadership is improving, but for many years the Klan will be seeking better leaders, and the leaders praying for greater wisdom.

Serious as this is, and strange though our attitude may seem to the intellectuals, it does not worry us greatly. Every popular movement has suffered from just this handicap, yet the popular movements have been the mainsprings of progress, and have usually had to win against the "best people" of their time. Moreover, we can depend on getting this intellectual backing shortly. It is notable that when the plain people begin to win with one of their movements, such as the Klan, the very intellectuals who have scoffed and fought most bitterly presently begin to dig up sound—at least well-sounding! —logic in support of the success. The movement, so far as can be judged, is neither hurt nor helped by this process. . . .

Our critics have accused us of being merely a "protest movement," of being frightened; they say we fear alien competition, are in a panic because we cannot hold our own against the foreigners. That is partly true. We are a protest movement—protesting against being robbed. We are afraid of competition with peoples who would destroy our standard of living. We are suffering in many ways, we have been betrayed by our trusted leaders, we are half beaten already. But we are not frightened nor in a panic. We have merely awakened to the fact that we must fight for our own. We are going to fight—and win!

The Klan does not believe that the fact that it is emotional and instinctive, rather than coldly intellectual, is a weakness. All action comes from emotion, rather than from ratiocination. Our emotions and the instincts on which they are based have been bred into us for thousands of years; far longer than reason has had a place in the human brain. They are the many-times distilled product of experience; they still operate much more surely and promptly than reason can. For centuries those who obeyed them have lived and carried on the race; those in whom they were weak, or who failed to obey, have died. They are the foundations of our American civilization, even more than our great historic documents; they can be trusted where the fine-haired reasoning of the denatured intellectuals cannot. . . .

DOCUMENT 6

WILLIAM ALLEN WHITE, LETTER ON THE KU KLUX KLAN,
SEPTEMBER 17, 1921

A number of distinguished Americans criticized the Klan during the days of its power. Among these was White, who fought the organization in one of its main strongholds, Kansas. This letter to Herbert Bayard Swope of the New York World *expresses White's disdain for the Klan and his feeling about the danger it represented. The reference to "suckers with $10 each to squander" was a jibe at the crassness of Klan agitation, which gave organizers a substantial cut of each membership fee.*

An organizer of the Ku-Klux Klan was in Emporia the other day, and the men whom he invited to join his band at ten dollars per join turned him down. Under the leadership of Dr. J. B. Brickell and following their own judgment after hearing his story, the Emporians told him that they had no time for him. The proposition seems to be:

Anti foreigners
Anti Catholics
Anti Negroes.

There are, of course, bad foreigners and good ones, good Catholics and bad ones, and all kinds of Negroes. To make a case against a birthplace, a religion, or a race is wickedly un-American and cowardly. The whole trouble with the Ku-Klux Klan is that it is based upon such deep foolishness that it is bound to be a menace to good government in any community. Any man fool enough to be Imperial Wizard would have power without responsibility and both without any sense. That is social dynamite.

American institutions, our courts, our legislators, our executive officers are strong enough to keep the peace and promote justice and good will in the community. If they are not, then the thing to do is to change these institutions and do it quickly, but always legally. For a self-constituted body of moral idiots, who would substitute the findings of the Ku-Klux Klan for the processes of law to try to better conditions, would be a most un-American outrage which every good citizen should resent.

It is to the everlasting credit of Emporia that the organizer found no suckers with $10 each to squander here. Whatever Emporia may be otherwise, it believes in law and order, and absolute freedom under the constitution for every man, no matter what birth or creed or race, to speak and meet and talk and act as a free law-abiding citizen. The picayunish cowardice of a man who would substitute Klan rule and mob law for what our American fathers have died to establish and maintain should prove what a cheap screw outfit the Klan is.

DOCUMENT 7

PROGRESSIVE PARTY PLATFORM,
1924

The Progressive Party convention of 1924 nominated Senator Robert M. La Follette of Wisconsin by acclamation, and adopted unanimously and without argument the platform upon which he wished to stand. Clear and outspoken as it was on most of the issues of the day, it neglected to make any declaration on two prickly issues: prohibition and the Ku Klux Klan. La Follette personally declared himself "unalterably opposed to the evident purposes of the secret organization known as the Ku Klux Klan." He was more evasive on prohibition, though he announced that so long as the Volstead Act remained law "it should be enforced for rich and poor alike, without hypocrisy or favoritism."

The great issue before the American people today is the control of government and industry by private monopoly.

For a generation the people have struggled patiently, in the face of repeated betrayals by successive administrations, to free themselves from this intolerable power which has been undermining representative government.

Through control of government, monopoly has steadily extended its absolute dominion to every basic industry.

In violation of law, monopoly has crushed competition, stifled private initiative and independent enterprise, and without fear of punishment now exacts extortionate profits upon every necessity of life consumed by the public.

The equality of opportunity proclaimed by the Declaration of Independence and asserted and defended by Jefferson and Lincoln as the heritage of every American citizen has been displaced by special privilege for the few, wrested from the government of the many.

Fundamental Rights In Danger

That tyrannical power which the American people denied to a king, they will no longer endure from the monopoly system. The people know they cannot yield to any group the control of the economic life of the nation and preserve their political liberties. They know monopoly has its representatives in the halls of Congress, on the Federal bench, and in the executive departments; that these servile agents barter away the nation's natural resources, nullify acts of Congress by judicial veto and administrative favor, invade the people's rights by unlawful arrests and unconstitutional searches and seizures, direct our foreign policy in the interests of predatory wealth, and make wars and conscript the sons of the common people to fight them.

The usurpation in recent years by the federal courts of the power to nullify laws duly enacted by the legislative branch of the government is a plain violation of the Constitution. . . .

Distress Of American Farmers

The present condition of American agriculture constitutes an emergency of the gravest character. The Department of Commerce report shows that during 1923 there was a steady and marked increase in dividends paid by the great industrial corporations. The same is true of the steam and electric railways and practically all other large corporations. On the other hand, the Secretary of Agriculture reports that in the fifteen principal wheat growing states more than 108,000 farmers since 1920 have lost their farms through foreclosure or bankruptcy; that more than 122,000 have surrendered their property without legal proceedings, and that nearly 375,000 have retained possession of their property only through the leniency of their creditors, making a total of more than 600,000 or 26 per cent of all farmers who have virtually been bankrupted since 1920 in these fifteen states alone.

Almost unlimited prosperity for the great corporations and ruin and bankruptcy for agriculture is the direct and logical result of the policies and legislation which deflated the farmer while extending almost unlimited credit to the great corporations; which protected with exorbitant tariffs the industrial magnates, but depressed the prices of the farmers' products by financial juggling while greatly increasing the cost of what he must buy: which guaranteed excessive freight rates to the railroads and put a premium on wasteful management while saddling an unwarranted burden on to the backs of the American farmer; which permitted gambling in the products of the farm by grain speculators to the great detriment of the farmer and to the great profit of the grain gambler.

A Covenant With The People

Awakened by the dangers which menace their freedom and prosperity the American people still retain the right and courage to exercise their sovereign control over their government. In order to destroy the economic and political power of monopoly, which has come between the people and their government, we pledge ourselves to the following principles and policies:

The House Cleaning

1. We pledge a complete housecleaning in the Department of Justice, the Department of the Interior, and the other executive departments. We demand that the power of the Federal Government be used to crush private monopoly, not to foster it.

Natural Resources

2. We pledge recovery of the navy's oil reserves and all other parts of the public domain which have been fraudulently or illegally leased, or otherwise wrongfully transferred, to the control of private interests; vigorous prosecution of all public officials, private citizens and corporations that participated in these transactions; complete revision of the water-power act, the general leasing act, and all other legislation relating to the public domain. We favor public ownership of the nation's water power and the creation and development of a national super-water-power system, including Muscle Shoals, to supply at actual cost light and power for the people and nitrate for the farmers, and strict public control and permanent conservation of all the nation's resources, including coal,

iron and other ores, oil and timber lands, in the interest of the people.

Railroads

3. We favor repeal of the Esch-Cummins railroad law and the fixing of railroad rates upon the basis of actual, prudent investment and cost of service. . . . We declare for public ownership of railroads with definite safeguards against bureaucratic control as the only final solution of the transportation problem.

Tax Reduction

4. We favor reduction of Federal taxes upon individual incomes and legitimate business, limiting tax exactions strictly to the requirements of the government administered with rigid economy, particularly by the curtailment of the eight hundred million dollars now annually expended for the army and navy in preparation for future wars; by the recovery of the hundreds of millions of dollars stolen from the Treasury through fraudulent war contracts and the corrupt leasing of the public resources; and by diligent action to collect the accumulated interest upon the eleven billion dollars owing us by foreign governments.

We denounce the Mellon tax plan as a device to relieve multimillionaires at the expense of other tax payers, and favor a taxation policy providing for immediate reductions upon moderate incomes, large increases in the inheritance tax rates upon large estates to prevent the indefinite accumulation by inheritance of great fortunes in a few hands; taxes upon excess profits to penalize profiteering, and complete publicity, under proper safeguards, of all Federal tax returns.

The Courts

5. We favor submitting to the people, for their considerate judgment, a constitutional amendment providing that Congress may by enacting a statute make it effective over a judicial veto.

We favor such amendment to the constitution as may be necessary to provide for the election of all Federal Judges, without party designation, for fixed terms not exceeding ten years, by direct vote of the people.

The Farmers

6. We favor drastic reduction of the exorbitant duties on manufactures provided in the Fordney-Mc-Cumber tariff legislation, the prohibiting of gambling by speculators and profiteers in agricultural products; the reconstruction of the Federal Reserve and Federal Farm Loan Systems, so as to eliminate control by usurers, speculators and international financiers, and to make the credit of the nation available upon fair terms to all and without discrimination to business men, farmers and home-builders. We advocate the calling of a special session of Congress to pass legislation for the relief of American agriculture. We favor such further legislation as may be needful or helpful in promoting and protecting co-opera-tive enterprises. We demand that the Interstate Commerce Commission proceed forthwith to reduce by an approximation to pre-war levels the present freight rates on agricultural products, including live stock, and upon the materials required upon American farms for agricultural purposes.

Labor

7. We favor abolition of the use of injunctions in labor disputes and declare for complete protection of the right of farmers and industrial workers to organize, bargain collectively through representatives of their own choosing, and conduct without hindrance co-operative enterprises.

We favor prompt ratification of the Child Labor amendment, and subsequent enactment of a Federal law to protect children in industry. . . .

Peace On Earth

12. We denounce the mercenary system of foreign policy under recent administrations in the interests of financial imperialists, oil monopolists and international bankers, which has at times degraded our State Department from its high service as a strong and kindly intermediary of defenseless governments to a trading outpost for those interests and concession-seekers engaged in the exploitations of weaker nations, as contrary to the will

of the American people, destructive of domestic development and provocative of war. We favor an active foreign policy to bring about a revision of the Versailles treaty in accordance with the terms of the armistice, and to promote firm treaty agreements with all nations to outlaw wars, abolish conscription, drastically reduce land, air and naval armaments, and guarantee public referendum on peace and war.

DOCUMENT 8

HERBERT HOOVER, RUGGED INDIVIDUALISM SPEECH,

OCTOBER 22, 1928

This speech, given in New York near the close of the 1928 campaign, is a classic statement of the optimism, the faith in economic individualism, and the opposition to the expansion of governmental functions that was central to Hoover's philosophy. Many years later, explaining the background of the speech, Hoover recalled: "I was determined that the Republican party should draw the issue of the American system, as opposed to all forms of collectivism."

After the war, when the Republican Party assumed administration of the country, we were faced with the problem of determination of the very nature of our national life. During 150 years we have builded up a form of self-government and a social system which is peculiarly our own. It differs essentially from all others in the world. It is the American system. It is just as definite and positive a political and social system as has ever been developed on earth. It is founded upon a particular conception of self-government in which decentralized local responsibility is the very base. Further than this, it is founded upon the conception that only through ordered liberty, freedom and equal opportunity to the individual will his initiative and enterprise spur on the march of

progress. And in our insistence upon equality of opportunity has our system advanced beyond all the world.

During the war we necessarily turned to the Government to solve every difficult economic problem. The
Government having absorbed every energy of our people
for war, there was no other solution. For the preservation
of the State the Federal Government became a centralized
despotism which undertook unprecedented responsibilities,
assumed autocratic powers, and took over the business
of citizens. To a large degree we regimented our whole
people temporarily into a socialistic state. However
justified in time of war if continued in peace time it
would destroy not only our American system but with
it our progress and freedom as well.

When the war closed, the most vital of all issues
both in our own country and throughout the world was
whether Governments should continue their wartime
ownership and operation of many instrumentalities of
production and distribution. We were challenged with a
peace-time choice between the American system of rugged
individualism and a European philosophy of diametrically
opposed doctrines—doctrines of paternalism and state
socialism. The acceptance of these ideas would have
meant the destruction of self-government through cen-
tralization of government. It would have meant the undermining of the individual initiative and enterprise
through which our people have grown to unparalleled
greatness.

The Republican Party from the beginning resolutely
turned its face away from these ideas and these war
practices. . . . When the Republican Party came into full
power it went at once resolutely back to our fundamental
conception of the State and the rights and responsibilities
of the individual. Thereby it restored confidence and hope
in the American people, it freed and stimulated enterprise, it restored the Government to its position as an
umpire instead of a player in the economic game. For
these reasons the American people have gone forward in
progress while the rest of the world has halted, and some
countries have even gone backwards. If anyone will
study the causes of retarded recuperation in Europe, he

will find much of it due to the stifling of private initiative on one hand, and overloading of the Government with business on the other.

There has been revived in this campaign, however, a series of proposals which, if adopted, would be a long step toward the abandonment of our American system and a surrender to the destructive operation of governmental conduct of commercial business. Because the country is faced with difficulty and doubt over certain national problems—that is, prohibition, farm relief and electrical power —our opponents propose that we must thrust government a long way into the businesses which give rise to these problems. In effect, they abandon the tenets of their own party and turn to State socialism as a solution for the difficulties presented by all three. It is proposed that we shall change from prohibition to the State purchase and sale of liquor. If their agricultural relief program means anything, it means that the Government shall directly or indirectly buy and sell and fix prices of agricultural products. And we are to go into the hydro-electric-power business. In other words, we are confronted with a huge program of government in business.

There is, therefore, submitted to the American people a question of fundamental principle. That is: shall we depart from the principles of our American political and economic system, upon which we have advanced beyond all the rest of the world, in order to adopt methods based on principles destructive of its very foundations? And I wish to emphasize the seriousness of these proposals. I wish to make my position clear; for this goes to the very roots of American life and progress.

I should like to state to you the effect that this projection of government in business would have upon our system of self-government and our economic system. That effect would reach to the daily life of every man and woman. It would impair the very basis of liberty and freedom not only for those left outside the fold of expanded bureaucracy but for those embraced within it.

Let us first see the effect upon self-government. When the Federal Government undertakes to go into commercial business it must at once set up the organization and administration of that business, and it immediately finds itself in a labyrinth, every alley of which leads to the destruction of self-government.

Commercial business requires a concentration of responsibility. Self-government requires decentralization and many checks and balances to safeguard liberty. Our Government to succeed in business would need become in effect a despotism. There at once begins the destruction of self-government. . . .

It is a false liberalism that interprets itself into the Government operation of commercial business. Every step of bureaucratizing of the business of our country poisons the very roots of liberalism—that is, political equality, free speech, free assembly, free press, and equality of opportunity. It is the road not to more liberty, but to less liberty. Liberalism should be found not striving to spread bureaucracy but striving to set bounds to it. True liberalism seeks all legitimate freedom, first in the confident belief that without such freedom the pursuit of all other blessings and benefits is vain. That belief is the foundation of all American progress, political as well as economic.

Liberalism is a force truly of the spirit, a force proceeding from the deep realization that economic freedom cannot be sacrificed if political freedom is to be preserved. Even if Governmental conduct of business could give us more efficiency instead of less efficiency, the fundamental objection to it would remain unaltered and unabated. It would destroy political equality. It would increase rather than decrease abuse and corruption. It would stifle initiative and invention. It would undermine the development of leadership. It would cramp and cripple the mental and spiritual energies of our people. It would extinguish equality and opportunity. It would dry up the spirit of liberty and progress. For these reasons primarily it must be resisted. For a hundred and fifty years liberalism has found its true spirit in the American system, not in the European systems.

I do not wish to be misunderstood in this statement. I am defining a general policy. It does not mean that our Government is to part with one iota of its national resources without complete protection to the public interest. . . .

Nor do I wish to be misinterpreted as believing that

the United States is free-for-all and devil-take-the-hind-most. The very essence of equality of opportunity and of American individualism is that there shall be no domination by any group or combination in this Republic, whether it be business or political. On the contrary, it demands economic justice as well as political and social justice. It is no system of laissez faire.

I feel deeply on this subject because during the war I had some practical experience with governmental operation and control. I have witnessed not only at home but abroad the many failures of Government in business. I have seen its tyrannies, its injustices, its destructions of self-government, its undermining of the very instincts which carry our people forward to progress. I have witnessed the lack of advance, the lowered standards of living, the depressed spirits of people working under such a system. My objection is based not upon theory or upon a failure to recognize wrong or abuse, but I know the adoption of such methods would strike at the very roots of American life and would destroy the very basis of American progress.

Our people have the right to know whether we can continue to solve our great problems without abandonment of our American system. I know we can. . . .

And what have been the results of our American system? Our country has become the land of opportunity to those born without inheritance, not merely because of the wealth of its resources and industry, but because of this freedom of initiative and enterprise. Russia has natural resources equal to ours. Her people are equally industrious, but she has not had the blessings of 150 years of our form of government and of our social system.

By adherence to the principles of decentralized self-government, ordered liberty, equal opportunity and free-dom to the individual, our American experiment in human welfare has yielded a degree of well-being un-paralleled in all the world. It has come nearer to the abolition of poverty, to the abolition of fear of want, than humanity has ever reached before. Progress of the past seven years is the proof of it. This alone furnishes the answer to our opponents who ask us to introduce destructive elements into the system by which this has been accomplished. . . .

I have endeavored to present to you that the greatness of America has grown out of a political and social system and a method of control of economic forces distinctly its own—our American system—which has carried this great experiment in human welfare further than ever before in all history. We are nearer today to the ideal of the abolition of poverty and fear from the lives of men and women than ever before in any land. And I again repeat that the departure from our American system by injecting principles destructive to it which our opponents propose will jeopardize the very liberty and freedom of our people, will destroy equality of opportunity, not alone to ourselves but to our children.

DOCUMENT 9

FRANKLIN D. ROOSEVELT, COMMONWEALTH CLUB SPEECH,

SEPTEMBER 23, 1932

Most of Franklin D. Roosevelt's speeches in the 1932 campaign dealt either with specific issues or with the central charge that the depression had been fostered by Republican policies. But in this speech, delivered in San Francisco, he presented a general view of the American past and future which was directly at odds with the views of Hoover and the business individualists (Document 8). Roosevelt argued, as many intellectuals were also arguing, that the United States had come to a turning point at which a new kind of governmental policy was necessary. The speech was considered the most momentous of the campaign, because it was the one indication Roosevelt gave of the drastic innovations he would make. Ironically, it did not express Roosevelt's own views at the time, but those of some of his advisors. In his illuminating book, The Democratic Roosevelt, *Rexford Guy Tugwell, a mem-*

ber of Roosevelt's Brain Trust, has this to say concern-
ing the Commonwealth Club Speech: "For once he
[Roosevelt] was caught without even a moment for
revision. He never saw that speech until he opened
it on the lectern. . . . It was written by Adolf
Berle with some assistance from me, although it was
not altogether congenial, so far as I was concerned;
nor, as I thought, was it an accurate representation of
Franklin's attitude. He was much more an optimist
than he appeared to be in that speech." The passage
selected here follows some opening remarks on the
earlier phases of the American political tradition.

So began, in American political life, the new day, the
day of the individual against the system, the day in which
individualism was made the great watchword of American
life.

The happiest of economic conditions made that day
long and splendid. On the western frontier land was
substantially free. No one who did not shirk the task of
earning a living was entirely without opportunity to do
so. Depressions could, and did, come and go; but they
could not alter the fundamental fact that most of the
people lived partly by selling their labor and partly by
extracting their livelihood from the soil, so that starvation
and dislocation were practically impossible.

At the very worst there was always the possibility
of climbing into a covered wagon and moving West,
where the untilled prairies afforded a haven for men to
whom the East did not provide a place.

So great were our natural resources that we could
offer this relief not only to our own people but to the
distressed of all the world. We could invite immigration
from Europe and welcome it with open arms.

Traditionally, when a depression came a new section
of land was opened in the West. And even our temporary
misfortune served our manifest destiny.

It was in the middle of the nineteenth century that
a new force was released and a new dream created. The
force was what is called the industrial revolution, the advance of steam and machinery and the rise of the fore-
runners of the modern industrial plant.

The dream was the dream of an economic machine, able to raise the standard of living for everyone; to bring luxury within the reach of the humblest; to annihilate distance by steam power and later by electricity, and to release everyone from the drudgery of the heaviest manual toil.

It was to be expected that this would necessarily affect government. Heretofore, government had merely been called upon to produce conditions within which people could live happily, labor peacefully and rest secure. Now it was called upon to aid in the consummation of this new dream.

There was, however, a shadow over this dream. To be made real it required use of the talents of men of tremendous will and tremendous ambition, since by no other force could the problems of financing and engineering and new developments be brought to a consummation.

So manifest were the advantages of the machine age, however, that the United States fearlessly, cheerfully and, I think, rightly accepted the bitter with the sweet.

It was thought that no price was too high to pay for the advantages which we could draw from a finished industrial system.

The history of the last half century is accordingly in large measure a history of a group of financial titans, whose methods were not scrutinized with too much care and who were honored in proportion as they produced the results, irrespective of the means they used.

The financiers who pushed the railroads to the Pacific were always ruthless, often wasteful and frequently corrupt, but they did build railroads and we have them today.

It has been estimated that the American investor paid for the American railway system more than three times over in the process, but despite this fact the net advantage was to the United States.

As long as we had free land, as long as population was growing by leaps and bounds, as long as our industrial plants were insufficient to supply our own needs, society chose to give the ambitious man free play and unlimited reward, provided only that he produced the economic plant so much desired.

During this period of expansion there was equal opportunity for all, and the business of government was not to interfere but to assist in the development of industry.

This was done at the request of business men themselves. The tariff was originally imposed for the purpose of "fostering our infant industry," a phrase I think the older among you will remember as a political issue not so long ago.

The railroads were subsidized, sometimes by grants of money, oftener by grants of land. Some of the most valuable oil lands in the United States were granted to assist the financing of the railroad which pushed through the Southwest.

A nascent merchant marine was assisted by grants of money or by mail subsidies, so that our steam shipping might ply the seven seas.

Some of my friends tell me that they do not want the government in business. With this I agree, but I wonder whether they realize the implications of the past.

For while it has been American doctrine that the government must not go into business in competition with private enterprises, still it has been traditional, particularly in Republican administrations, for business urgently to ask the government to put at private disposal all kinds of government assistance.

The same man who tells you that he does not want to see the government interfere in business—and he means it and has plenty of good reasons for saying so—is the first to go to Washington and ask the government for a prohibitory tariff on his product.

When things get just bad enough—as they did two years ago—he will go with equal speed to the United States Government and ask for a loan. And the Reconstruction Finance Corporation is the outcome of it.

Each group has sought protection from the government for its own special interests without realizing that the function of government must be to favor no small group at the expense of its duty to protect the rights of personal freedom and of private property of all its citizens.

In retrospect we can now see that the turn of the tide came with the turn of the century. We were reaching our last frontier; there was no more free land and our industrial combinations had become great uncontrolled and irresponsible units of power within the State.

Clear-sighted men saw with fear the danger that opportunity would no longer be equal; that the growing corporation, like the feudal baron of old, might threaten the economic freedom of individuals to earn a living. In that hour our antitrust laws were born.

The cry was raised against the great corporations. Theodore Roosevelt, the first great Republican Progressive, fought a Presidential campaign on the issue of "trust busting" and talked freely about malefactors of great wealth. If the government had a policy it was rather to turn the clock back, to destroy the large combinations and to return to the time when every man owned his individual small business.

This was impossible. Theodore Roosevelt, abandoning the idea of "trust busting," was forced to work out a difference between "good" and "bad" trusts.

The Supreme Court set forth the famous "rule of reason" by which it seems to have meant that a concentration of industrial power was permissible if the method by which it got its power, and the use it made of that power, was reasonable.

Woodrow Wilson, elected in 1912, saw the situation more clearly. Where Jefferson had feared the encroachment of political power on the lives of individuals, Wilson knew that the new power was financial. He saw, in the highly centralized economic system, the despot of the twentieth century, on whom great masses of individuals relied for their safety and their livelihood, and whose irresponsibility and greed (if it were not controlled) would reduce them to starvation and penury.

The concentration of financial power had not proceeded so far in 1912 as it has today, but it had grown far enough for Mr. Wilson to realize fully its implications. . . .

A glance at the situation today only too clearly indicates that equality of opportunity as we have known it no longer exists. Our industrial plant is built. The problem just now is whether, under existing conditions, it is not overbuilt.

Our last frontier has long since been reached, and

there is practically no more free land. More than half of our people do not live on the farms or on lands and cannot derive a living by cultivating their own property.

There is no safety valve in the form of a Western prairie to which those thrown out of work by the Eastern economic machines can go for a new start. We are not able to invite the immigration from Europe to share our endless plenty. We are now providing a drab living for our own people.

Our system of constantly rising tariffs has at last reacted against us to the point of closing our Canadian frontier on the north, our European markets on the east, many of our Latin-American markets to the south and a goodly proportion of our Pacific markets on the west through the retaliatory tariffs of those countries.

It has forced many of our great industrial institutions, who exported their surplus production to such countries, to establish plants in such countries, within the tariff walls.

This has resulted in the reduction of the operation of their American plants and opportunity for employment.

Just as freedom to farm has ceased, so also the opportunity in business has narrowed. It still is true that men can start small enterprises, trusting to native shrewdness and ability to keep abreast of competitors; but area after area has been pre-empted altogether by the great corporations, and even in the fields which still have no great concerns the small man starts under a handicap.

The unfeeling statistics of the past three decades show that the independent business man is running a losing race. Perhaps he is forced to the wall; perhaps he cannot command credit; perhaps he is "squeezed out," in Mr. Wilson's words, by highly organized corporate competitors, as your corner grocery man can tell you.

Recently a careful study was made of the concentration of business in the United States.

It showed that our economic life was dominated by some 600-odd corporations who controlled two-thirds of American industry. Ten million small business men divided the other third.

More striking still, it appeared that if the process of

concentration goes on at the same rate, at the end of another century we shall have all American industry controlled by a dozen corporations and run by perhaps a hundred men.

Put plainly, we are steering a steady course toward economic oligarchy, if we are not there already.

Clearly, all this calls for a re-appraisal of values.

A mere builder of more industrial plants, a creator of more railroad systems, an organizer of more corporations, is as likely to be a danger as a help.

The day of the great promoter or the financial titan, to whom we granted anything if only he would build or develop, is over. Our task now is not discovery or exploitation of natural resources or necessarily producing more goods.

It is the soberer, less dramatic business of administering resources and plants already in hand, of seeking to re-establish foreign markets for our surplus production, of meeting the problem of under-consumption, of adjusting production to consumption, of distributing wealth and products more equitably, of adapting existing economic organizations to the service of the people.

The day of enlightened administration has come.

Just as in older times the central government was first a haven of refuge and then a threat, so now in a closer economic system the central and ambitious financial unit is no longer a servant of national desire but a danger. I would draw the parallel one step further. We did not think because national government had become a threat in the eighteenth century that therefore we should abandon the principle of national government.

Nor today should we abandon the principle of strong economic units called corporations merely because their power is susceptible of easy abuse.

In other times we dealt with the problem of an unduly ambitious central government by modifying it gradually into a constitutional democratic government. So today we are modifying and controlling our economic units.

As I see it, the task of government in its relation to business is to assist the development of an economic declaration of rights, an economic constitutional order. This is the common task of statesman and business man. It is the minimum requirement of a more permanently safe order of things. . . .

Every man has a right to life, and this means that he has also a right to make a comfortable living. He may by sloth or crime decline to exercise that right, but it may not be denied him.

We have no actual famine or dearth; our industrial and agricultural mechanism can produce enough and to spare.

Our government formal and informal, political and economic, owes to every one an avenue to possess himself of a portion of that plenty sufficient for his needs through his own work.

Every man has a right to his own property, which means a right to be assured, to the fullest extent attainable, in the safety of his savings. By no other means can men carry the burdens of those parts of life which in the nature of things afford no chance of labor—childhood, sickness, old age.

In all thought of property, this right is paramount; all other property rights must yield to it.

If, in accord with this principle, we must restrict the operations of the speculator, the manipulator, even the financier, I believe we must accept the restriction as needful not to hamper individualism but to protect it. . . .

The government should assume the function of economic regulation only as a last resort, to be tried only when private initiative, inspired by high responsibility, with such assistance and balance as government can give, has finally failed.

As yet there has been no final failure, because there has been no attempt; and I decline to assume that this nation is unable to meet the situation.

The final term of the high contract was for liberty and the pursuit of happiness.

We have learned a great deal of both in the past century. We know that individual liberty and individual happiness mean nothing unless both are ordered in the sense that one man's meat is not another man's poison.

We know that the old "rights of personal competency"

—the right to read, to think, to speak, to choose and live a mode of life,—must be respected at all hazards.

We know that liberty to do anything which deprives others of those elemental rights is outside the protection of any compact, and that government in this regard is the maintenance of a balance within which every individual may have a place if he will take it, in which every individual may find safety if he wishes it, in which every individual may attain such power as his ability permits, consistent with his assuming the accompanying responsibility. . . .

Faith in America, faith in our tradition of personal responsibility, faith in our institutions, faith in ourselves demands that we recognize the new terms of the old social contact.

We shall fulfill them, as we fulfilled the obligation of the apparent utopia which Jefferson imagined for us in 1776 and which Jefferson, Roosevelt and Wilson sought to bring to realization.

We must do so, lest a rising tide of misery, engendered by our common failure, engulf us all.

But failure is not an American habit, and in the strength of great hope we must all shoulder our common load.

DOCUMENT 10

FRANKLIN D. ROOSEVELT, FIRST INAUGURAL ADDRESS,

MARCH 4, 1933

During the hectic campaign of 1932, most of Roosevelt's speeches had been drafted by his staff; he himself merely retouched them. But this speech is really his own—the first draft was written in his own hand. The moment at which he gave it was one of immense anxiety for the nation, and Roosevelt was very conscious of the national need for reassurance. Later Roosevelt wrote: "I sought principally . . . to ban-

*ish, so far as possible, the fear of the present and of
the future which held the American people and the
American spirit in its grasp." In this he succeeded
admirably. The most quoted line in his speech, "the
only thing we have to fear is fear itself," was probably inspired by a lucky chance. Shortly before the
day of his inauguration, Roosevelt happened to be
reading a volume of Henry David Thoreau, and it is
more than likely that he fixed upon a sentence which
read: "Nothing is so much to be feared as fear."*

This is a day of national consecration, and I am certain
that my fellow-Americans expect that on my induction
into the Presidency I will address them with a candor and
a decision which the present situation of our nation impels.

This is pre-eminently the time to speak the truth, the
whole truth, frankly and boldly. Nor need we shrink from
honestly facing conditions in our country today. This
great nation will endure as it has endured, will revive and
will prosper.

So first of all let me assert my firm belief that the
only thing we have to fear is fear itself—nameless, unreasoning, unjustified terror which paralyzes needed efforts
to convert retreat into advance.

In every dark hour of our national life a leadership
of frankness and vigor has met with that understanding and
support of the people themselves which is essential to victory. I am convinced that you will again give that support
to leadership in these critical days.

In such a spirit on my part and on yours we face
our common difficulties. They concern, thank God, only
material things. Values have shrunken to fantastic levels;
taxes have risen; our ability to pay has fallen; government
of all kinds is faced by serious curtailment of income;
the means of exchange are frozen in the currents of trade;
the withered leaves of industrial enterprise lie on every
side; farmers find no market for their produce; the savings
of many years in thousands of families are gone.

More important, a host of unemployed citizens face
the grim problem of existence, and an equally great number toil with little return. Only a foolish optimist can
deny the dark realities of the moment.

Yet our distress comes from no failure of substance. We are stricken by no plague of locusts. Compared with the perils which our forefathers conquered because they believed and were not afraid, we have still much to be thankful for. Nature still offers her bounty and human efforts have multiplied it. Plenty is at our doorstep, but a generous use of it languishes in the very sight of the supply.

Primarily, this is because the rulers of the exchange of mankind's goods have failed through their own stubbornness and their own incompetence, have admitted their failure and abdicated. Practices of the unscrupulous money changers stand indicted in the court of public opinion, rejected by the hearts and minds of men.

True, they have tried, but their efforts have been cast in the pattern of an outworn tradition. Faced by failure of credit, they have proposed only the lending of more money.

Stripped of the lure of profit by which to indure our people to follow their false leadership, they have resorted to exhortations, pleading tearfully for restored confidence. They know only the rules of a generation of self-seekers.

They have no vision, and when there is no vision the people perish.

The money changers have fled from their high seats in the temple of our civilization. We may now restore that temple to the ancient truths.

The measure of the restoration lies in the extent to which we apply social values more noble than mere monetary profit.

Happiness lies not in the mere possession of money; it lies in the joy of achievement, in the thrill of creative effort.

The joy and moral stimulation of work no longer must be forgotten in the mad chase of evanescent profits. These dark days will be worth all they cost us if they teach us that our true destiny is not to be ministered unto but to minister to ourselves and to our fellow men.

Recognition of the falsity of material wealth as the standard of success goes hand in hand with the abandonment of the false belief that public office and high political position are to be valued only by the standards of pride of place and personal profit; and there must be an end to a conduct in banking and in business which too often has given to a sacred trust the likeness of callous and selfish wrongdoing.

Small wonder that confidence languishes, for it thrives only on honesty, on honor, on the sacredness of obligations, on faithful protection, on unselfish performance; without them it cannot live.

Restoration calls, however, not for changes in ethics alone. This nation asks for action, and action now.

Our greatest primary task is to put people to work. This is no unsolvable problem if we face it wisely and courageously.

It can be accomplished in part by direct recruiting by the government itself, treating the task as we would treat the emergency of a war, but at the same time, through this employment, accomplishing greatly needed projects to stimulate and reorganize the use of our natural resources.

Hand in hand with this, we must frankly recognize the overbalance of population in our industrial centers and, by engaging on a national scale in a redistribution, endeavor to provide a better use of the land for those best fitted for the land.

The task can be helped by definite efforts to raise the values of agricultural products and with this the power to purchase the output of our cities.

It can be helped by preventing realistically the tragedy of the growing loss, through foreclosure, of our small homes and our farms.

It can be helped by insistence that the Federal, State and local governments act forthwith on the demand that their cost be drastically reduced.

It can be helped by the unifying of relief activities which today are often scattered, uneconomical and unequal. It can be helped by national planning for and supervision of all forms of transportation and of communications and other utilities which have a definitely public character.

There are many ways in which it can be helped, but it can never be helped merely by talking about it. We must act, and act quickly.

Finally, in our progress toward a resumption of work we require two safeguards against a return of the evils of the old order; there must be a strict supervision of all banking and credits and investments; there must be an end to speculation with other people's money, and there must be provision for an adequate but sound currency.

These are the lines of attack. I shall presently urge upon a new Congress in special session detailed measures for their fulfillment, and I shall seek the immediate assistance of the several States.

Through this program of action we address ourselves to putting our own national house in order and making income balance outgo.

Our international trade relations, though vastly important, are, in point of time and necessity, secondary to the establishment of a sound national economy.

I favor as a practical policy the putting of first things first. I shall spare no effort to restore world trade by international economic readjustment, but the emergency at home cannot wait on that accomplishment.

The basic thought that guides these specific means of national recovery is not narrowly nationalistic.

It is the insistence, as a first consideration upon the interdependence of the various elements in and parts of the United States—a recognition of the old and permanently important manifestation of the American spirit of the pioneer.

It is the way to recovery. It is the immediate way. It is the strongest assurance that the recovery will endure.

In the field of world policy I would dedicate this nation to the policy of the good neighbor—the neighbor who resolutely respects himself, and, because he does so, respects the rights of others—the neighbor who respects his obligations and respects the sanctity of his agreements in and with a world of neighbors.

If I read the temper of our people correctly, we now realize as we have never realized before, our interdependence on each other; that we cannot merely take, but we must give as well; that if we are to go forward we must move as a trained and loyal army willing to sacrifice for the good of a common discipline, because, without such discipline, no progress is made, no leadership becomes effective.

We are, I know, ready and willing to submit our lives and property to such discipline because it makes possible a leadership which aims at a larger good.

This I propose to offer, pledging that the larger purposes will bind upon us all as a sacred obligation with a unity of duty hitherto evoked only in time of armed strife.

With this pledge taken, I assume unhesitatingly the leadership of this great army of our people, dedicated to a disciplined attack upon our common problems.

Action in this image and to this end is feasible under the form of government which we have inherited from our ancestors.

Our Constitution is so simple and practical that it is possible always to meet extraordinary needs by changes in emphasis and arrangement without loss of essential form.

That is why our constitutional system has proved itself the most superbly enduring political mechanism the modern world has produced. It has met every stress of vast expansion of territory, of foreign wars, of bitter internal strife, of world relations.

It is to be hoped that the normal balance of executive and legislative authority may be wholly adequate to meet the unprecedented task before us. But it may be that an unprecedented demand and need for undelayed action may call for temporary departure from that normal balance of public procedure.

I am prepared under my constitutional duty to recommend the measures that a stricken nation in the midst of a stricken world may require.

These measures, or such other measures as the Congress may build out of its experience and wisdom, I shall seek, within my constitutional authority, to bring to speedy adoption.

But in the event that the Congress shall fail to take one of these two courses, and in the event that the national emergency is still critical, I shall not evade the clear course of duty that will then confront me.

I shall ask the Congress for the one remaining instrument to meet the crisis—broad executive power to wage a war against the emergency as great as the power that would be given to me if we were in fact invaded by a foreign foe.

For the trust reposed in me I will return the courage and the devotion that befit the time. I can do no less.

We face the arduous days that lie before us in the warm courage of national unity; with the clear consciousness of seeking old and precious moral values; with the clean satisfaction that comes from the stern performance of duty by old and young alike.

We aim at the assurance of a rounded and permanent national life.

We do not distrust the future of essential democracy. The people of the United States have not failed. In their need they have registered a mandate that they want direct, vigorous action.

They have asked for discipline and direction under leadership. They have made me the present instrument of their wishes. In the spirit of the gift I take it.

In this dedication of a nation we humbly ask the blessing of God. May He protect each and every one of us! May He guide me in the days to come!

DOCUMENT 11

HERBERT HOOVER, THIS CHALLENGE
TO LIBERTY,

OCTOBER 30, 1936

Here Hoover returns to the attack. The speech excerpted here, one of the bitterest of a bitter campaign, reflects the views of many Republicans who feared that the New Deal was destroying American traditions.

Through four years of experience this New Deal attack upon free institutions has emerged as the transcendent issue in America.

All the men who are seeking for mastery in the world today are using the same weapons. They sing the same songs. They all promise the joys of Elysium without effort.

But their philosophy is founded on the coercion and compulsory organization of men. True liberal government is founded on the emancipation of men. This is the issue upon which men are imprisoned and dying in Europe right now. . . .

Freedom does not die from frontal attack. It dies because men in power no longer believe in a system based upon liberty. . . .

I gave the warning against this philosophy of government four years ago from a heart heavy with anxiety for the future of our country. It was born from many years' experience of the forces moving in the world which would weaken the vitality of American freedom. It grew in four years of battle as President to uphold the banner of free men.

And that warning was based on sure ground from my knowledge of the ideas that Mr. Roosevelt and his bosom colleagues had covertly embraced despite the Democratic platform.

Those ideas were not new. Most of them had been urged upon me.

During my four years powerful groups thundered at the White House with these same ideas. Some were honest, some promising votes, most of them threatening reprisals, and all of them yelling "reactionary" at us.

I rejected the notion of great trade monopolies and price-fixing through codes. That could only stifle the little business man by regimenting him under the big brother. That idea was born of certain American Big Business and grew up to be the NRA.

I rejected the schemes of "economic planning" to regiment and coerce the farmer. That was born of a Roman despot 1,400 years ago and grew up into the AAA.

I refused national plans to put the government into business in competition with its citizens. That was born of Karl Marx.

I vetoed the idea of recovery through stupendous spending to prime the pump. That was born of a British professor.

I threw out attempts to centralize relief in Washington for politics and social experimentation. I defeated other plans to invade States' rights, to centralize power in Washington. Those ideas were born of American radicals.

I stopped attempts at currency inflation and repudiation of government obligation. That was robbery of insurance policy holders, savings bank depositors and wage-earners. That was born of the early Brain Trusters.

I rejected all these things because they would not only delay recovery but because I knew that in the end they would shackle free men.

Rejecting these ideas we Republicans had erected agencies of government which did start our country to prosperity without the loss of a single atom of American freedom. . . .

Our people did not recognize the gravity of the issue when I stated it four years ago. That is no wonder, for the day Mr. Roosevelt was elected recovery was in progress, the Constitution was untrampled, the integrity of the government and the institutions of freedom were intact.

It was not until after the election that the people began to awake. Then the realization of intended tinkering with the currency drove bank depositors into the panic that greeted Mr. Roosevelt's inauguration.

Recovery was set back for two years, and hysteria was used as the bridge to reach the goal of personal government.

I am proud to have carried the banner of free men to the last hour of the term my countrymen entrusted it to me. It matters nothing in the history of a race what happens to those who in their time have carried the banner of free men. What matters is that the battle shall go on.

The people know now the aims of this New Deal philosophy of government.

We propose instead leadership and authority in government within the moral and economic framework of the American System.

We propose to hold to the Constitutional safeguards of free men.

We propose to relieve men from fear, coercion and spite that are inevitable in personal government.

We propose to demobilize and decentralize all this spending upon which vast personal power is being built.

We propose to amend the tax laws so as not to defeat free men and free enterprise.

We propose to turn the whole direction of this country toward liberty, not away from it.

The New Dealers say that all this that we propose is a worn-out system; that this machine age requires new measures for which we must sacrifice some part of the freedom of men. Men have lost their way with a confused idea that governments should run machines.

Man-made machines cannot be of more worth than men themselves. Free men made these machines. Only free spirits can master them to their proper use.

The relation of our government with all these questions is complicated and difficult. They rise into the very highest ranges of economics, statesmanship and morals.

And do not mistake. Free government is the most difficult of all government. But it is everlastingly true that the plain people will make fewer mistakes than any group of men no matter how powerful. But free government implies vigilant thinking and courageous living and self-reliance in a people.

Let me say to you that any measure which breaks our dikes of freedom will flood the land with misery.

DOCUMENT 12

U.S. v. BUTLER ET AL.,
1936

The Agricultural Adjustment Act of 1933 attempted to raise and stabilize the prices paid to farmers by making agreements with them to reduce production. For cooperating with the program farmers were to be paid with funds raised by taxing the processors of agricultural products. Butler, a processor, challenged the tax in the courts. In a six to three decision, the Court held the processing tax unconstitutional because it was levied to support an unconstitutional object, that of regulating agricultural production. Speaking through Justice Owen J. Roberts, the Court expressed

*grave concern over possible future abuses of such
powers. The fundamental goal of controlling agriculture was later achieved by Congress through the commerce power. But this decision was among the most
important of those which, at the time, led supporters
of the administration to conclude that no broad and
effective attack upon the depression could be made
while the personnel of the Court remained unchanged.*

ROBERTS, J. . . . The tax can only be sustained by ignor-
ing the avowed purpose and operation of the act, and holding it a measure merely laying on excise upon processors
to raise revenue for the support of government. Beyond
cavil the sole object of the legislation is to restore the purchasing power of agricultural products to a parity with
that prevailing in an earlier day; to take money from the
processor and bestow it upon farmers who will reduce their
acreage for the accomplishment of the proposed end, and,
meanwhile to aid these farmers during the period required
to bring the prices of their crops to the desired level.

The tax plays an indispensable part in the plan of
regulation. As stated by the Agricultural Adjustment Ad-
ministrator, it is "the heart of the law"; a means of "accomplishing one or both of two things intended to help
farmers attain parity prices and purchasing power." . . .

It is inaccurate and misleading to speak of the exaction
from processors prescribed by the challenged act as a tax,
or to say that as a tax it is subject to no infirmity. A tax,
in the general understanding of the term, and as used in
the Constitution, signifies an exaction for the support of
the Government. The word has never been thought to con-
note the expropriation of money from one group for the
benefit of another. We may concede that the latter sort of
imposition is constitutional when imposed to effectuate
regulation of a matter in which both groups are interested
and in respect of which there is a power of legislative
regulation. But manifestly no justification for it can be
found unless as an integral part of such regulation. . . .

We conclude that the act is one regulating agricultural
production; that the tax is a mere incident of such regulation and that the respondents have standing to challenge
the legality of the exaction. . . .

The Government asserts that even if the respondents may question the propriety of the appropriation embodied in the statute their attack must fail because Article I, Section 8 of the Constitution authorizes the contemplated expenditure of the funds raised by the tax. This contention presents the great and the controlling question in the case. . . .

There should be no misunderstanding as to the function of this court in such a case. It is sometimes said that the court assumes a power to overrule or control the action of the people's representatives. This is a misconception. The Constitution is the supreme law of the land ordained and established by the people. All legislation must conform to the principles it lays down. When an act of Congress is appropriately challenged in the courts as not conforming to the constitutional mandate the judicial branch of the Government has only one duty,—to lay the article of the Constitution which is invoked beside the statute which is challenged and to decide whether the latter squares with the former. All the court does, or can do, is to announce its considered judgment upon the question. The only power it has, if such it may be called, is the power of judgment. This court neither approves nor condemns any legislative policy. Its delicate and difficult office is to ascertain and declare whether the legislation is in accordance with, or in contravention of, the provisions of the Constitution; and, having done that, its duty ends. . . .

Article I, Section 8, of the Constitution vest sundry powers in the Congress. But two of its clauses have any bearing upon the validity of the statute under review.

The third clause endows the Congress with power "to regulate Commerce . . . among the several States." Despite a reference in its first section to a burden upon, and an obstruction of the normal currents of commerce, the act under review does not purport to regulate transactions in interstate or foreign commerce. Its stated purpose is the control of agricultural production, a purely local activity in an effort to raise the prices paid the farmer. Indeed, the Government does not attempt to uphold the validity of the act on the basis of the commerce clause, which, for the purpose of the present case, may be put aside as irrelevant.

The clause thought to authorize the legislation,—the first,—confers upon the Congress power "to lay and collect Taxes, Duties, Imposts and Excises, to pay the Debts and provide for the common Defence and general Welfare of the United States." . . .

The Government asserts that warrant is found in this clause for the adoption of the Agricultural Adjustment Act. The argument is that Congress may appropriate and authorize the spending of moneys for the "general welfare"; that the phrase should be liberally construed to cover anything conducive to national welfare; that decision as to what will promote such welfare rests with Congress alone, and the courts may not review its determination; and finally that the appropriation under attack was in fact for the general welfare of the United States. . . .

Since the foundation of the nation sharp differences of opinion have persisted as to the true interpretation of the phrase. Madison asserted it amounted to no more than a reference to the other powers enumerated in the subsequent clauses of the same section; that, as the United States is a government of limited and enumerated powers, the grant of power to tax and spend for the general national welfare must be confined to the enumerated legislative fields committed to the Congress. In this view the phrase is mere tautology, for taxation and appropriation are or may be necessary incidents of the exercise of any of the enumerated legislative powers. Hamilton, on the other hand, maintained the clause confers a power separate and distinct from those later enumerated, is not restricted in meaning by the grant of them, and Congress consequently has a substantive power to tax and to appropriate, limited only by the requirement that it shall be exercised to provide for the general welfare of the United States. Each contention has had the support of those whose views are entitled to weight. This court has noticed the question, but has never found it necessary to decide which is the true construction. Mr. Justice Story, in his Commentaries, espouses the Hamiltonian position. . . . While, therefore, the power to tax is not unlimited, its confines are set in the clause which confers it, and not in those of section 8 which bestow and define the legislative powers of the Congress. It results that the power of Congress to authorize expenditure of public moneys for public purposes is not limited by the direct grants of legislative power found in the Constitution.

But the adoption of the broader construction leaves the power to spend subject to limitations. . . .

That the qualifying phrase must be given effect all advocates of broad construction admit. Hamilton, in his well known Report on Manufactures, states that the purpose must be "general, and not local." . . .

We are not now required to ascertain the scope of the phrase "general welfare of the United States" or to determine whether an appropriation in aid of agriculture falls within it. Wholly apart from that question, another principle embedded in our Constitution prohibits the enforcement of the Agricultural Adjustment Act. The act invades the reserved rights of the states. It is a statutory plan to regulate and control agricultural production, a matter beyond the powers delegated to the federal government. The tax, the appropriation of the funds raised, and the direction for their disbursement, are but parts of the plan. They are but means to an unconstitutional end. . . .

The power of taxation, which is expressly granted, may, of course, be adopted as a means to carry into operation another power also expressly granted. But resort to the taxing power to effectuate an end which is not legitimate, not within the scope of the Constitution, is obviously inadmissible. . . .

If the taxing power may not be used as the instrument to enforce a regulation of matters of state concern with respect to which the Congress has no authority to interfere, may it, as in the present case, be employed to raise the money necessary to purchase a compliance which the Congress is powerless to command? The Government asserts that whatever might be said against the validity of the plan, if compulsory, it is constitutionally sound because the end is accomplished by voluntary cooperation. There are two sufficient answers to the contention. The regulation is not in fact voluntary. The farmer, of course, may refuse to comply, but the price of such refusal is the loss of benefits. The amount offered is intended to be sufficient to exert pressure on him to agree to the proposed regulation. The power to confer or withhold unlimited benefits is the power to coerce or destroy. If the cotton grower elects not to accept the benefits, he will receive less for his crops; those who receive payments will be able to undersell him. The result may well be financial ruin. The coercive purpose and intent of the statute is not obscured by the fact that it has not been perfectly successful. . . . The Department of Agriculture has properly described the plan as one to keep a non-coöperating minority in line. This is coercion by economic pressure. The asserted power of choice is illusory. . . .

But if the plan were one for purely voluntary coöperation it would stand no better so far as federal power is concerned. At best it is a scheme for purchasing with federal funds submission to federal regulation of a subject reserved to the states. . . .

Congress has no power to enforce its commands on the farmer to the ends sought by the Agricultural Adjustment Act. It must follow that it may not indirectly accomplish those ends by taxing and spending to purchase compliance. The Constitution and the entire plan of our government negative any such use of the power to tax and to spend as the act undertakes to authorize. It does not help to declare that local conditions throughout the nation have created a situation of national concern; for this is but to say that whenever there is a widespread similarity of local conditions, Congress may ignore constitutional limitations upon its own powers and usurp those reserved to the states. If, in lieu of compulsory regulation of subjects within the states' reserved jurisdiction, which is prohibited, the Congress could invoke the taxing and spending power as a means to accomplish the same end, clause 1 of Section 8 of Article I would become the instrument for total subversion of the governmental powers reserved to the individual states.

If the act before us is a proper exercise of the federal taxing power, evidently the regulation of all industry throughout the United States may be accomplished by similar exercises of the same power. It would be possible to exact money from one branch of an industry and pay it to another branch in every field of activity which lies within the province of the states. The mere threat of such a procedure might well induce the surrender of rights and

the compliance with federal regulation as the price of continuance in business. . . .

DOCUMENT 13

HARLAN FISKE STONE, DISSENTING OPINION IN *U.S.* v. *BUTLER ET AL.*, 1936

This dissent, written with the concurrence of Justices Brandeis and Cardozo, accused the majority of "a tortured construction of the Constitution," and sharply reminded them that "Courts are not the only agency of government that must be assumed to have capacity to govern." Liberal critics of the majority decision found much ammunition in Stone's dissent. Professor Howard Lee McBain said in a newspaper article: "Never before has a dissenting minority gone quite so far toward calling into question the motives of the majority and clearly implying that they have abused their prerogative." At this, Stone was impelled to write to his former colleague: "I do not question the motives of my brethren. . . . I do question a method of thinking which is perhaps the greatest stumbling block to the right administration of judicial review of legislation. . . . Such an approach to constitutional construction tends to increase the dead areas in the Constitution, the lacunæ in which no power exists, either state or national, to deal with the problems of government."

The present stress of widely held and strongly expressed differences of opinion of the wisdom of the Agricultural Adjustment Act makes it important, in the interest of clear thinking and sound result, to emphasize at the outset certain propositions which should have controlling influence in determining the validity of the Act. They are:

1. The power of courts to declare a statute unconstitutional is subject to two guiding principles of decision which ought never to be absent from judicial consciousness.

One is that courts are concerned only with the power to enact statutes, not with their wisdom. The other is that while unconstitutional exercise of power by the executive and legislative branches of the government is subject to judicial restraint, the only check upon our own exercise of power is our own sense of self-restraint. For the removal of unwise laws from the statute books appeal lies not to the courts but to the ballot and to the processes of democratic government.

2. The constitutional power of Congress to levy an excise tax upon the processing of agricultural products is not questioned. The present levy is held invalid, not for any want of power in Congress to lay such a tax to defray public expenditures, including those for the general welfare, but because the use to which its proceeds are put is disapproved.

3. As the present depressed state of agriculture is nation wide in its extent and effects, there is no basis for saying that the expenditure of public money in aid of farmers is not within the specifically granted power of Congress to levy taxes to "provide for the . . . general welfare." The opinion of the Court does not declare otherwise. . . .

It is with these preliminary and hardly controverted matters in mind that we should direct our attention to the pivot on which the decision of the Court is made to turn. It is that a levy unquestionably within the taxing power of Congress may be treated as invalid because it is a step in a plan to regulate agricultural production and is thus a forbidden infringement of state power. The levy is not any the less an exercise of taxing power because it is intended to defray an expenditure for the general welfare rather than for some other support of government. Nor is the levy and collection of the tax pointed to as effecting the regulation. While all federal taxes inevitably have some influence on the internal economy of the states, it is not contended that the levy of a processing tax upon manufacturers using agricultural products as raw material has any perceptible regulatory effect upon either their production or manufacture. . . .

Of the assertion that the payments to farmers are coercive, it is enough to say that no such contention is pressed by the taxpayer, and no such consequences were to be anticipated or appear to have resulted from the administration of the Act. The suggestion of coercion finds no support in the record or in any data showing the actual operation of the Act. Threat of loss, not hope of gain, is the essence of economic coercion. . . . The presumption of constitutionality of a statute is not to be overturned by an assertion of its coercive effect which rests on nothing more substantial than groundless speculation.

It is upon the contention that state power is infringed by purchased regulation of agricultural production that chief reliance is placed. It is insisted that, while the Constitution gives to Congress, in specific and unambiguous terms, the power to tax and spend, the power is subject to limitations which do not find their origin in any express provision of the Constitution and to which other expressly delegated powers are not subject. . . .

It makes no difference that there is a promise to do an act which the condition is calculated to induce. Condition and promise are alike valid since both are in furtherance of the national purpose for which the money is appropriated.

. . . "Let the end be legitimate," said the great Chief Justice, "let it be within the scope of the Constitution, and all means which are appropriate, which are plainly adapted to that end, which are not prohibited, but consist with the letter and spirit of the Constitution, are constitutional." *McCulloch* v. *Maryland*. This cardinal guide to constitutional exposition must now be rephrased so far as the spending power of the federal government is concerned. Let the expenditure be to promote the general welfare, still, if it is needful in order to insure its use for the intended purpose to influence any action which Congress cannot command because within the sphere of state government, the expenditure is unconstitutional. And taxes otherwise lawfully levied are likewise unconstitutional if they are appropriated to the expenditure whose incident is condemned. . . .

Such a limitation is contradictory and destructive of the power to appropriate for the public welfare, and is incapable of practical application. The spending power of Congress is in addition to the legislative power and not subordinate to it. This independent grant of the power of the purse, and its very nature, involving in its exercise the duty to insure expenditure within the granted power, presuppose freedom of selection among divers ends and aims, and the capacity to impose such conditions as will render the choice effective. It is a contradiction in terms to say that there is power to spend for the national welfare, while rejecting any power to impose conditions reasonably adapted to the attainment of the end which alone would justify the expenditure.

The limitation now sanctioned must lead to absurd consequences. The government may give seeds to farmers, but may not condition the gift upon their being planted in places where they are most needed or even planted at all. The government may give money to the unemployed, but may not ask that those who get it shall give labor in return, or even use it to support their families. It may give money to sufferers from earthquake, fire, tornado, pestilence or flood, but may not impose conditions—health precautions designed to prevent the spread of disease, or induce the movement of population to safer or more sanitary areas. All that, because it is purchased regulation infringing state powers, must be left for the states, who are unable or unwilling to supply the necessary relief. The government may spend its money for vocational rehabilitation, but it may not, with the consent of all concerned, supervise the process which it undertakes to aid. It may spend its money for the suppression of the boll weevil, but may not compensate the farmers for suspending the growth of cotton in the infected areas. It may aid state reforestation and forest fire prevention agencies, but may not be permitted to supervise their conduct. It may support rural schools, but may not condition its grant by the requirement that certain standards be maintained. It may appropriate moneys to be expended by the Reconstruction Finance Corporation "to aid in financing agriculture, commerce and industry," and to facilitate "the exportation of agricultural and other products." Do all its activities collapse because, in order to effect the permissible purpose, in myriad ways the money is paid out upon terms and conditions which influence action of the recipients within the states, which Congress cannot command? The answer would seem plain. If the expenditure is for a national public purpose, that purpose will not be thwarted because payment is on condition which will advance that purpose. The action which Congress induces by payments of money to promote the general welfare, but which it does not command or coerce, is but an incident to a specifically granted power, but a permissible means to a legitimate end. . . .

That the governmental power of the purse is a great one is not now for the first time announced. . . .

The suggestion that it must now be curtailed by judicial fiat because it may be abused by unwise use hardly rises to the dignity of argument. So may judicial power be abused. . . .

A tortured construction of the Constitution is not to be justified by recourse to extreme examples of reckless congressional spending which might occur if courts could not prevent expenditures which, even if they could be thought to effect any national purpose, would be possible only by action of a legislature lost to all sense of public responsibility. Such suppositions are addressed to the mind accustomed to believe that it is the business of courts to sit in judgment on the wisdom of legislative action. Courts are not the only agency of government that must be assumed to have capacity to govern. Congress and the courts both unhappily may falter or be mistaken in the performance of their constitutional duty. But interpretation of our great charter of government which proceeds on any assumption that the responsibility for the preservation of our institutions is the exclusive concern of any one of the three branches of government, or that it alone can save them from destruction is far more likely, in the long run, "to obliterate the constituent members" of "an indestructible union of indestructible states" than the frank recognition that language, even of a constitution, may mean what it says: that the power to tax and spend includes the power to relieve a nationwide economic maladjustment by conditional gifts of money.

DOCUMENT 14

FRANKLIN D. ROOSEVELT, RADIO ADDRESS ON SUPREME COURT REFORM,

MARCH 9, 1937

This address, the first of Roosevelt's radio appeals made during his second term, defends the Supreme Court Reform proposal at length. Roosevelt's argument was that in the past fifty years "the balance of power between the three great branches of the Federal Government has been tipped out of balance by the courts in direct contradiction of the high purposes of the framers of the Constitution." In preparing this address Roosevelt was helped by a group of close associates: Thomas Corcoran, Benjamin Cohen, Donald Richberg, and Samuel Rosenman.

I want to talk with you very simply about the need for present action in this crisis—the need to meet the unanswered challenge of one-third of a nation ill-nourished, ill-clad, ill-housed.

Last Thursday I described the American form of government as a three-horse team provided by the Constitution to the American people so that their field might be plowed. The three horses are, of course, the three branches of government—the Congress, the Executive and the Courts. Two of the horses are pulling in unison today, the third is not. Those who have intimated that the President of the United States is trying to drive that team overlook the simple fact that the President, as Chief Executive, is, himself, one of the three horses.

It is the American people themselves who are in the driver's seat.

It is the American people themselves who want the furrow plowed.

It is the American people themselves who expect the third horse to pull in unison with the other two.

I hope that you have reread the Constitution of the

United States. Like the Bible, it ought to be read again
and again. . . .

Since the rise of the modern movement for social
and economic progress through legislation, the court has
more and more often and more and more boldly asserted
a power to veto laws passed by the Congress and State
Legislatures in complete disregard of this original limitation.

In the last four years the sound rule of giving statutes
the benefit of all reasonable doubt has been cast aside. The
court has been acting not as a judicial body but as a policy-
making body.

When the Congress has sought to stabilize national
agriculture, to improve the conditions of labor, to safeguard business against unfair competition, to protect our
national resources, and in many other ways to serve our
clearly national needs, the majority of the court has been
assuming the power to pass on the wisdom of these acts
of the Congress—and to approve or disapprove the public
policy written into these laws.

That is not only my accusation. It is the accusation
of most distinguished justices of the present Supreme
Court. I have not the time to quote to you all the language used by dissenting justices in many of these cases.
But in the case holding the Railroad Retirement Act unconstitutional, for instance, Chief Justice Hughes said in
a dissenting opinion that the majority opinion was a "departure from sound principles" and placed "an unwarranted
limitation upon the commerce clause." And three other
justices agreed with him.

In the case holding the AAA unconstitutional Justice
Stone said of the majority opinion that it was a "tortured
construction of the Constitution." And two other justices
agreed with him.

In the case holding the New York Minimum Wage
Law unconstitutional Justice Stone said that the majority
were actually reading into the Constitution their own
"personal economic predilections" and that if the legislative power is not left free to choose the methods of solving
the problems of poverty, subsistence and health of large
numbers in the community, then "government is to be

rendered impotent." And two other justices agreed with him.

In the face of these dissenting opinions, there is no basis for the claim made by some members of the court that something in the Constitution has compelled them regretfully to thwart the will of the people.

In the face of such dissenting opinions, it is perfectly clear, that as Chief Justice Hughes has said: "We are under a Constitution but the Constitution is what the judges say it is."

The court in addition to the proper use of its judicial functions has improperly set itself up as a third house of the Congress—a super-legislature, as one of the justices has called it—reading into the Constitution words and implications which are not there, and which were never intended to be there.

We have, therefore, reached the point as a nation where we must take action to save the Constitution from the court and the court from itself. We must find a way to take an appeal from the Supreme Court to the Constitution itself. We want a Supreme Court which will do justice under the Constitution—not over it. In our courts we want a government of laws and not of men.

I want—as all Americans want—an independent judiciary as proposed by the framers of the Constitution. That means a Supreme Court that will enforce the Constitution as written—that will refuse to amend the Constitution by the arbitrary exercise of judicial power—amendment by judicial say-so. It does not mean a judiciary so independent that it can deny the existence of facts universally recognized.

How then could we proceed to perform the mandate given us? It was said in last year's Democratic platform "If these problems cannot be effectively solved within the Constitution, we shall seek such clarifying amendment as will assure the power to enact those laws, adequately to regulate commerce, protect public health and safety and safeguard economic security." In other words, we said we would seek an amendment only if every other possible means by legislation were to fail.

When I commenced to review the situation with the

problem squarely before me, I came by a process of elimination to the conclusion that short of amendments the only method which was clearly constitutional, and would at the same time carry out other much-needed reforms, was to infuse new blood into all our courts. We must have men worthy and equipped to carry out impartial justice. But, at the same time, we must have judges who will bring to the courts a present-day sense of the Constitution—judges who will retain in the courts the judicial functions of a court and reject the legislative powers which the courts have today assumed. . . .

[Roosevelt here summarized his proposal]

Those opposing this plan have sought to arouse prejudice and fear by crying that I am seeking to "pack" the Supreme Court and that a baneful precedent will be established.

What do they mean by the words "packing the Court"?

Let me answer this question with a bluntness that will end all honest misunderstanding of my purposes.

If by that phrase, "packing the court," it is charged that I wish to place on the bench spineless puppets who would disregard the law and would decide specific cases as I wished them to be decided, I make this answer—that no President fit for his office would appoint, and no Senate of honorable men fit for their office would confirm, that kind of appointees to the Supreme Court.

But, if by that phrase the charge is made that I would appoint and the Senate would confirm justices worthy to sit beside present members of the court who understand those modern conditions that I will appoint justices who will not undertake to override the judgment of the Congress on legislative policy—that I will appoint justices who will act as justices and not as legislators—if the appointment of such justices can be called "packing the courts," then I say that I and with me the vast majority of the American people favor doing just that thing—now.

Is it a dangerous precedent for the Congress to change the number of the justices? The Congress has always had, and will have, that power. The number of justices has been changed several times before—in the administrations of

John Adams and Thomas Jefferson, both signers of the Declaration of Independence—Andrew Jackson, Abraham Lincoln, and Ulysses S. Grant.

I suggest only the addition of justices to the bench in accordance with a clearly defined principle relating to a clearly defined age limit. Fundamentally, if in the future, America cannot trust the Congress it elects to refrain from abuse of our constitutional usages, democracy will have failed far beyond the importance to it of any kind of precedent concerning the judiciary. . . .

Like all lawyers, like all Americans, I regret the necessity of this controversy. But the welfare of the United States, and indeed of the Constitution itself, is what we all must think about first. Our difficulty with the Court today rises not from the court as an institution but from human beings within it. But we cannot yield our constitutional destiny to the personal judgment of a few men who, being fearful of the future, would deny us the necessary means of dealing with the present.

This plan of mine is no attack on the court; it seeks to restore the court to its rightful and historic place in our system of constitutional government and to have it resume its high task of building anew on the Constitution "a system of living law." . . .

During the past half century the balance of power between the three great branches of the Federal Government has been tipped out of balance by the courts in direct contradiction of the high purposes of the framers of the Constitution. It is my purpose to restore that balance. You who know me will accept my solemn assurance that in a world in which democracy is under attack I seek to make American democracy succeed.

DOCUMENT 15

REPORT OF THE SENATE JUDICIARY COMMITTEE ON SUPREME COURT REFORM,
JUNE 7, 1937

This adverse report, one of the great defeats the New Deal suffered, illustrates the difficulty of interfering with so august a body as the Supreme Court. It led to the tabling of the President's proposal, and the passage of a law embodying only minor changes in the lower courts.

The committee recommends that the measure be rejected for the following primary reasons:

I. The bill does not accomplish any one of the objectives for which it was originally offered.

II. It applies force to the judiciary and in its initial and ultimate effect would undermine the independence of the courts.

III. It violates all precedents in the history of our Government and would in itself be a dangerous precedent for the future.

IV. The theory of the bill is in direct violation of the spirit of the American Constitution and its employment would permit alteration of the Constitution without the people's consent or approval; it undermines the protection our constitutional system gives to minorities and is subversive of the rights of individuals.

V. It tends to centralize the Federal district judiciary by the power of assigning judges from one district to another at will.

VI. It tends to expand political control over the judicial department by adding to the powers of the legislative and executive departments respecting the judiciary. . . .

Let us, for the purpose of the argument, grant that the Court has been wrong, wrong not only in that it has rendered mistaken opinions but wrong in the far more serious sense that it has substituted its will for the congressional will in the matter of legislation. May we nevertheless safely punish the Court?

Today it may be the Court which is charged with forgetting its constitutional duties. Tomorrow it may be the Congress. The next day it may be the Executive. If we yield to temptation now to lay the lash upon the Court, we are only teaching others how to apply it to ourselves and to the people when the occasion seems to warrant. Manifestly, if we may force the hand of the Court to secure our interpretation of the Constitution, then some succeeding Congress may repeat the process to secure another and a different interpretation and one which may not sound so pleasant in our ears as that for which we now contend.

There is a remedy for usurpation or other judicial wrongdoing. If this bill be supported by the toilers of this country upon the ground that they want a Court which will sustain legislation limiting hours and providing minimum wages, they must remember that the procedure employed in the bill could be used in another administration to lengthen hours and to decrease wages. If farmers want agricultural relief and favor this bill upon the ground that it gives them a Court which will sustain legislation in their favor, they must remember that the procedure employed might some day be used to deprive them of every vestige of a farm relief.

When members of the Court usurp legislative powers or attempt to exercise political power, they lay themselves open to the charge of having lapsed from that "good behavior" which determines the period of their official life. But, if you say, the process of impeachment is difficult and uncertain, the answer is, the people made it so when they framed the Constitution. It is not for us, the servants of the people, the instruments of the Constitution, to find a more easy way to do that which our masters made difficult.

But, if the fault of the judges is not so grievous as to warrant impeachment, if their offense is merely that they have grown old, and we feel, therefore, that there should be a "constant infusion of new blood," then obviously the way to achieve that result is by constitutional amendment fixing definite terms for the members of the judiciary or making mandatory their retirement at a given age. Such a provision would indeed provide for the constant infusion of new blood, not only now but at all times in the future. The plan before us is but a temporary expedient which operates once and then never again, leaving the Court as permanently expanded to become once more a court of old men, gradually year by year falling behind the times. . . .

Shall we now, after 150 years of loyalty to the constitutional ideal of an untrammeled judiciary, duty bound to protect the constitutional rights of the humblest citizen even against the Government itself, create the vicious precedent which must necessarily undermine our system? The only argument for the increase which survives analysis is that Congress should enlarge the Court so as to make the policies of this administration effective.

We are told that a reactionary oligarchy defies the will of the majority, that this is a bill to "unpack" the Court and give effect to the desires of the majority; that is to say, a bill to increase the number of Justices for the express purpose of neutralizing the views of some of the present members. In justification we are told, but without authority, by those who would rationalize this program, that Congress was given the power to determine the size of the Court so that the legislative branch would be able to impose its will upon the judiciary. This amounts to nothing more than the declaration that when the Court stands in the way of a legislative enactment, the Congress may reverse the ruling by enlarging the Court. When such a principle is adopted, our constitutional system is overthrown!

This, then, is the dangerous precedent we are asked to establish. When proponents of the bill assert, as they have done, that Congress in the past has altered the number of Justices upon the Supreme Court and that this is reason enough for our doing it now, they show how important precedents are and prove that we should now refrain from any action that would seem to establish one which could be followed hereafter whenever a Congress and an executive should become dissatisfied with the decision of the Supreme Court.

This is the first time in the history of our country that

a proposal to alter the decisions of the court by enlarging its personnel has been so boldly made. Let us meet it. Let us now set a salutary precedent that will never be violated. Let us, of the Seventy-fifth Congress, in words that will never be disregarded by any succeeding Congress, declare that we would rather have an independent Court, a fearless Court, a Court that will dare to announce its honest opinions in what it believes to be the defense of the liberties of the people, than a Court that, out of fear or sense of obligation to the appointing power, or factional passion, approves any measure we may enact. We are not the judges of the judges. We are not above the Constitution.

Even if every charge brought against the so-called "reactionary" members of this Court be true, it is far better that we await orderly but inevitable change of personnel than that we impatiently overwhelm them with new members. Exhibiting this restraint, thus demonstrating our faith in the American system, we shall set an example that will protect the independent American judiciary from attack as long as this Government stands. . . .

True it is, that courts like Congresses, should take account of the advancing strides of civilization. True it is that the law, being a progressive science, must be pronounced progressively and liberally; but the milestones of liberal progress are made to be noted and counted with caution rather than merely to be encountered and passed. Progress is not a mad mob march; rather, it is a steady, invincible stride. . . .

If, under the "hydraulic pressure" of our present need for economic justice, we destroy the system under which our people have progressed to a higher degree of justice and prosperity than that ever enjoyed by any other people in all the history of the human race, then we shall destroy not only all opportunity for further advance but everything we have thus far achieved. . . .

Inconvenience and even delay in the enactment of legislation is not a heavy price to pay for our system. Constitutional democracy moves forward with certainty rather than with speed. The safety and the permanence of the progressive march of our civilization are far more important to us and to those who are to come after us than the enactment now of any particular law. The Constitution of the United States provides ample opportunity for the expression of popular will to bring about such reforms and changes as the people may deem essential to their present and future welfare. It is the people's charter of the powers granted those who govern them. . . .

SUMMARY

We recommend the rejection of this bill as a needless, futile, and utterly dangerous abandonment of constitutional principle.

It was presented to the Congress in a most intricate form and for reasons that obscured its real purpose.

It would not banish age from the bench nor abolish divided decisions.

It would not affect the power of any court to hold laws unconstitutional nor withdraw from any judge the authority to issue injunctions.

It would not reduce the expense of litigation nor speed the decision of cases.

It is a proposal without precedent and without justification.

It would subjugate the courts to the will of Congress and the President and thereby destroy the independence of the judiciary, the only certain shield of individual rights.

It contains the germ of a system of centralized administration of law that would enable an executive so minded to send his judges into every judicial district in the land to sit in judgment on controversies between the Government and the citizen.

It points the way to the evasion of the Constitution and establishes the method whereby the people may be deprived of their right to pass upon all amendments of the fundamental law.

It stands now before the country, acknowledged by its proponents as a plan to force judicial interpretation of the Constitution, a proposal that violates every sacred tradition of American democracy.

Under the form of the Constitution it seeks to do that which is unconstitutional.

Its ultimate operation would be to make this Government one of men rather than one of law, and its practical operation would be to make the Constitution what the executive or legislative branches of the Government choose to say it is—an interpretation to be changed with each change of administration.

It is a measure which should be so emphatically rejected that its parallel will never again be presented to the free representatives of the free people of America.

[Names omitted.]

PART VII

World War II and the Post-War World

INTRODUCTION

FROM 1933 to 1937 American foreign policy seemed to be dominated by a desire to withdraw from the affairs of the world. Secretary of State Cordell Hull did negotiate a large number of trade agreements lowering tariff barriers; but the effect of these was offset by severely nationalist American currency policies. Moreover, the Neutrality Acts of 1935 and 1937 were plainly an attempt by Congress to set up legal devices calculated to keep the United States from involvement in any European struggle for power. Fascism in Italy and Germany and military despotism in Japan were on the march. In October 1935, Premier Mussolini attacked and soon conquered Ethiopia. In 1936 a Fascist rebellion broke out against the Republican government of Spain; both Mussolini and Hitler sent planes, supplies, and technicians to the aid of the Fascists, and Mussolini sent troops as well. When the Soviet Union also sent supplies, technicians, and political agents it became clear that Spain had become a battleground of the worldwide struggle for power. Then, in July 1937, fighting broke out again between China and Japan, and Japanese troops went pouring into North China.

In October 1937, President Roosevelt delivered a

speech (Document 1) at Chicago in which he posed the issues that the American people were to debate, in one form or another, for the next four years. Although ninety percent of the people of the world wanted peace, Roosevelt declared, the remaining ten percent did not. "War," he continued, "is a contagion," and like an epidemic it must be contained by quarantining the aggressor nations. What he hoped to do was to use American power to give force to a program of collective security. He closed by saying: "America actively engages in the search for peace."

When World War II broke out in 1939, Americans were preponderantly sympathetic with the cause of the Allies, and many feared that a Fascist victory would gravely threaten American security. Most Americans still wanted to stop short of outright participation. However, in the summer of 1940, after German armies had crushed France, the administration began to move as rapidly as public opinion would allow toward greater solidarity with the British Commonwealth. In September 1940, Roosevelt exchanged fifty over-age American destroyers for eight naval sites at various points in the Western Hemisphere from Newfoundland to British Guiana. Shortly after his decisive defeat of Wendell Willkie in the 1940 presidential election, he proposed a lend-lease system of economic aid to the British (Document 2), under which they were to be loaned American arms, which would be returned or replaced after the war was over. In a memorable speech of January 6, 1941 (Document 3) he spoke of the United States as the "arsenal" of democracy, and declared that American policy in the world crisis was governed by the search for "four essential human freedoms": freedom of speech and expression throughout the world, freedom of worship, freedom from want, and freedom from fear. Lend-lease aroused intense resistance among isolationists in Congress (Document 4) and in the country at large; but both the House and Senate passed the Lend-Lease Act in March 1941 by very substantial majorities. Heated resistance to further involvement on the side of the Allies, organized under the America First Committee (Document 5), continued throughout 1941, while Roosevelt, in a series of dramatic moves, edged closer to open involvement. In May he

proclaimed an unlimited national emergency; in June he
asked Germany and Italy to close their American con-
sulates; in July he announced an agreement with the
Icelandic government under which the United States was
taking over from Britain the defense of Iceland. In
August he met Prime Minister Winston Churchill dramatically on a British battleship off Newfoundland, and
the two leaders drew up an eight-point Atlantic Charter
(Document 6) expressing their common concern for
"the final destruction of the Nazi tyranny" and their goals
for the post-war world. By this time the United States
was openly allied with Britain, without engaging in actual
warfare, and In June 1941, when Hitler invaded Russia
in a mad gamble for an invincible continental empire,
the emerging coalition had acquired a formidable third
ally. But America did not actually declare war until
Japan attacked American installations at Pearl Harbor and
elsewhere in the Pacific (Document 7).

The alliance between the Soviets and the two great
Western powers was not based upon broad common goals
or mutual understanding but simply upon the existence
of a common foe. So long as the enemy was formidable,
differences could be subordinated. But even before the
war was over, profound antagonisms could no longer be
ignored; and after 1945 American foreign policy concentrated upon working out a means to stem Soviet power
and Communist influence in various parts of the world.
When Communists threatened Greece and Turkey, and
the British government proved no longer able to play its
former strong role in the eastern Mediterranean, the
United States met this challenge with the Truman Doctrine, in March 1947 (Document 8), which called for
military and economic assistance to those countries. A
more positive program of assistance to the general economic rehabilitation of Europe became known as the
Marshall Plan, after Secretary of State George C. Marshall
proposed it in an arresting speech at Harvard in June
1947 (Document 9). A theoretical basis for American
policy vis-a-vis Russia was worked out by the distinguished
State Department adviser on Soviet Affairs, George
F. Kennan, and first published anonymously in *Foreign
Affairs* (Document 10). The central concept in Kennan's

widely discussed essay was "containment"—the idea that the United States must build its own strength and meet Soviet pressure wherever it developed. "The Soviet pressure against the free institutions of the Western world," wrote Kennan, "is something that can be contained by the adroit and vigilant application of counter-force at a series of constantly shifting geographical and political points, corresponding to the shifts and maneuvers of Soviet policy, but which cannot be charmed or talked out of existence." The focal point, of course, was western Europe, where both the governments and the people stood for Western ideals. The attempt to coordinate western Europe for common defense, in the North Atlantic Treaty Organization (NATO) was presented with wisdom and understanding by President Truman and by Secretary of State Dean Acheson (Document 11). They enlisted the aid of a number of internationalist Republicans, but were met with intense resistance by a small minority in Congress, led by Senator Robert A. Taft (Document 12), who felt that the North Atlantic pact was an invitation to war.

The outbreak of the war in Korea posed the issue of containment in a more urgent form. President Truman's promptness in leading the United Nations to meet the open military threat of Communist expansion there won widespread endorsement within the United States. The method of conducting the war, however, soon led to another heated debate. General Douglas MacArthur argued that because the Chinese were helping North Korea, America should blockade the Chinese coast, bombard the Chinese mainland from planes and ships, and launch an invasion of China by the Nationalist forces of Chiang Kai Shek on Formosa. The Joint Chiefs of Staff, unwilling to risk spreading the war, resisted this proposal. When MacArthur insisted on going over the heads of his military and ·civilian superiors to Congress and the American public, to appeal for an attempt at all-out victory instead of limited war, President Truman removed him from his command for insubordination. MacArthur's return led to an investigation of the conduct of the war (Documents 13 and 14) in which the administration strategy of fighting a limited war for limited objectives and avoiding the risk of a third world war was thoroughly debated, and justified. MacArthur's popularity soon faded.

Nonetheless, for a number of reasons, perhaps the most important of which was discontent over the Korean war, the strength of the Democratic party was waning, and in 1952 Dwight D. Eisenhower overwhelmed Adlai Stevenson at the polls. Much had been said about the policy of containment as being too negative; and some Republicans had spoken hopefully of a policy of "liberation" which would commit the United States to taking the offensive in an effort to free dominated peoples from the grip of Soviet power. How "liberation" could be made meaningful without resorting to war was something its advocates had difficulty in explaining. President Eisenhower's designated Secretary of State, John Foster Dulles, reassured Senators shortly before taking office by explaining that "liberation does not mean a war of liberation" (Document 15). Increasingly, the prospect of the complete destruction of the human race in a war waged with nuclear weapons made any sort of aggressive action less thinkable to sober men (Document 16). The predictable horror of future war exerted a restraining influence on the diplomacy of the United States and on the thinking of political leaders throughout the world. In a 1954 press conference (Document 17) Eisenhower endorsed the idea of "peaceful co-existence" and remarked: "We have got to find ways of living together"—a theme which he continued to develop in the major statements of his second term.

DOCUMENT 1

FRANKLIN D. ROOSEVELT, QUARANTINE THE AGGRESSORS SPEECH,

OCTOBER 5, 1937

This speech was delivered at Chicago three months after Japan had attacked China. In it Roosevelt first indicated what was to be the aim of his foreign policy for the next three years: to put the strength of the

United States into some collective effort to check aggression.

The political situation in the world, which of late has
been growing progressively worse, is such as to cause
grave concern and anxiety to all the peoples and nations
who wish to live in peace and amity with their neighbors.

Some nine years ago the hopes of mankind for a
continuing era of international peace were raised to great
heights when more than sixty nations solemnly pledged
themselves not to resort to arms in furtherance of their
national aims and policies. The high aspirations expressed
in the Briand-Kellogg Peace Pact and the hopes for peace
thus raised have of late given way to a haunting fear of
calamity.

The present reign of terror and international lawlessness began a few years ago. It began through unjustified interference in the internal affairs of other nations
or the invasion of alien territory in violation of treaties,
and has now reached a stage where the very foundations
of civilization are seriously threatened.

The landmarks and traditions which have marked
the progress of civilization toward a condition of law,
order and justice are being wiped away.

Without a declaration of war and without warning
or justification of any kind, civilians, including women
and children, are being ruthlessly murdered with bombs
from the air.

In times of so-called peace, ships are being attacked
and sunk by submarines without cause or notice. Nations
are fomenting and taking sides in civil warfare in nations
that have never done them any harm. Nations claiming
freedom for themselves deny it to others.

Innocent peoples, innocent nations are being cruelly
sacrificed to a greed for power and supremacy which is
devoid of all sense of justice and humane consideration.

To paraphrase a recent author: "Perhaps we foresee
a time when men, exultant in the technique of homicide,
will range so hotly over the world that every precious
thing will be in danger, every book and picture and
harmony, every treasure garnered through two millenniums,

the small, the delicate, the defenseless—all will be lost or wrecked or utterly destroyed."

If those things come to pass in other parts of the world, let no one imagine that America will escape, that it may expect mercy, that this Western Hemisphere will not be attacked and that it will continue tranquilly and peacefully to carry on the ethics and the arts of civilization.

If those days come, "there will be no safety by arms, no help from authority, no answer in science. The storm will rage till every flower of culture is trampled and all human beings are leveled in a vast chaos."

If those days are not to come to pass—if we are to have a world in which we can breathe freely and live in amity without fear—then the peace-loving nations must make a concerned effort to uphold laws and principles on which alone peace can rest secure.

The peace-loving nations must make a concerted effort in opposition to those violations of treaties and those ignorings of humane instincts which today are creating a state of international anarchy and instability from which there is no escape through mere isolation or neutrality.

Those who cherish their freedom and recognize and respect the equal right of their neighbors to be free and live in peace must work together for the triumph of law and moral principles in order that peace, justice and confidence may prevail throughout the world.

There must be a return to a belief in the pledged word, in the value of a signed treaty. There must be recognition of the fact that national morality is as vital as private morality. . . .

There is a solidarity, an interdependence about the modern world, both technically and morally, which makes it impossible for any nation completely to isolate itself from economic and political upheavals in the rest of the world, especially when such upheavals appear to be spreading and not declining.

There can be no stability or peace either within nations or between nations except under laws and moral standards adhered to by all. International anarchy destroys every foundation for peace. It jeopardizes either the immediate or the future security of every nation, large or small.

It is, therefore, a matter of vital interest and concern to the people of the United States that the sanctity of international treaties and the maintenance of international morality be restored.

The overwhelming majority of all the peoples and nations of the world today want to live in peace.

They seek the removal of barriers against trade.

They want to exert themselves in industry, in agriculture and in business, that they may increase their wealth through the production of wealth-producing goods rather than striving to produce military planes and bombs and machine guns and cannon for the destruction of human lives and useful property.

In those nations of the world which seem to be piling armament on armament for purposes of aggression, and those other nations which fear acts of aggression against them and their security, a very high proportion of their national income is being spent directly for armaments. It runs from 30 to as high as 50 per cent.

The proportion that we in the United States spend is far less—11 or 12 per cent.

How happy we are that the circumstances of the moment permit us to put our money into bridges and boulevards, dams and reforestation, the conservation of our soil and many other kinds of useful works, rather than into huge standing armies and vast supplies of implements of war.

I am compelled and you are compelled, to look ahead. The peace, the freedom and the security of 90 per cent of the population of the world is being jeopardized by the remaining 10 per cent who are threatening a breakdown of all international order and law.

Surely the 90 per cent who want to live in peace under law and in accordance with moral standards that have received almost universal acceptance through the centuries, can and must find some way to make their will prevail. . . .

It is true that the moral consciousness of the world must recognize the importance of removing injustices and well-founded grievances; but at the same time it must be aroused to the cardinal necessity of honoring sanctity of treaties, of respecting the rights and liberties of others and of putting an end to acts of international aggression.

It seems to be unfortunately true that the epidemic of world lawlessness is spreading.

When an epidemic of physical disease starts to spread, the community approves and joins in a quarantine of the patients in order to protect the health of the community against the spread of the disease.

It is my determination to pursue a policy of peace and to adopt every practicable measure to avoid involvement in war.

It ought to be inconceivable that in this modern era, and in the face of experience, any nation could be so foolish and ruthless as to run the risk of plunging the whole world into war by invading and violating, in contravention of solemn treaties, the territory of other nations that have done them no real harm and which are too weak to protect themselves adequately. Yet the peace of the world and the welfare and security of every nation is today being threatened by that very thing.

No nation which refuses to exercise forbearance and to respect the freedom and rights of others can long remain strong and retain the confidence and respect of other nations. No nation ever loses its dignity or its good standing by conciliating its differences, and by exercising great patience with, and consideration for, the rights of other nations.

War is a contagion, whether it be declared or undeclared. It can engulf states and peoples remote from the original scene of hostilities. We are determined to keep out of war, yet we cannot insure ourselves against the disastrous effects of war and the dangers of involvement. We are adopting such measures as will minimize our risk of involvement, but we cannot have complete protection in a world of disorder in which confidence and security have broken down.

If civilization is to survive, the principles of the Prince of Peace must be restored. Shattered trust between nations must be revived.

Most important of all, the will for peace on the part

of peace-loving nations must express itself to the end that nations that may be tempted to violate their agreements and the rights of others will desist from such a cause. There must be positive endeavors to preserve peace.

America hates war. America hopes for peace. Therefore, America actively engages in the search for peace.

DOCUMENT 2

FRANKLIN D. ROOSEVELT, PRESS CONFERENCE ON LEND-LEASE,
DECEMBER 17, 1940

The remarks reported here were made at a press conference when Roosevelt was trying to build up public sentiment for aid to the Allies. This conference preceded that famous fireside chat on national security during which the President urged that the United States become "the arsenal of democracy." Robert E. Sherwood has commented on Roosevelt's "garden hose" analogy in this statement: "I believe it may accurately be said that with that neighborly analogy, Roosevelt won the fight for lend-lease."

In the present world situation, there was no doubt in the minds of an overwhelming number of Americans that the best immediate defense of the United States is the success of Great Britain in defending herself. Quite aside from our historic and current interest in the survival of democracy, therefore, it is important from the selfish viewpoint of American defense that we should do everything to help the British Empire defend itself.

He had read a great deal of nonsense about finances in the past few days by people who could think only in traditional terms. No major war was ever won or lost through lack of money. . . .

Now in speeches and stories, the same attitude is being expressed in this war. This is wrong. It is not merely a matter of doing things in the traditional way. Additional production facilities—factories, ship-building ways, munitions plants, etc.—are most important to the United States.

Talking selfishly, from the viewpoint of American defense, orders from Great Britain are a tremendous asset because they automatically create additional facilities. There are several ways of encouraging this. Narrow-minded men assumed that the only way was to repeal certain statutes like the Neutrality Act and the Johnson Act (prohibiting loans to nations whose war debts are in default) and then lend money either through private banks or the government.

That is the banal type of mind. There is another, also somewhat banal, that suggests outright cash gifts (although we might come to it). . . . It was not at all certain that this was necessary, or that Britain, which had her amour propre would accept a gift from the American taxpayers. One had to place one's self in the other man's shoes.

There are other ways and these are now being explored. This exploration has been proceeding for three or four weeks. The essential thing is to increase our production facilities and the flow of supplies to Great Britain. The following is put up as one of several plans that might be devised.

It is possible for the United States to take over British orders, and because they are essentially the same kind of munitions we use ourselves, turn them into American orders. We have enough money to do it. Thereafter, such portion of them as military events would determine to be right and proper would be allowed to go to the other side. The materials could either be leased or sold subject to mortgage to the people on the other side of the ocean.

This is in line with the idea that the best possible defense of Great Britain is the best defense of the United States. The materials would be more useful in Great Britain than if kept in storage here. What the President was trying to do was eliminate the silly-fool dollar sign, and that was something brand-new. . . .

Suppose the house of the President's neighbor catches fire and he has a length of garden hose, 400 or 500 feet. If he can take the hose and connect it to the neighbor's hydrant, he may be able to put out the fire. He does not say his hose cost $15; pay me $15. He doesn't want $15, but his hose back when the fire is over. The neighbor gives back the hose and pays him for the use of it. If it gets smashed in the fire, the President says he was glad to lend it. The neighbor says he will replace the part destroyed. If the President has got back his hose, he has done a pretty good job.

The broad thought in this connection is that if we take over not all but a large part of future British war orders when they come off the production line and come to an arrangement for their use by the British and get repaid in kind when the war is over, that would be satisfactory. We would leave out the dollar mark in the transaction, whether it dealt with guns, planes or merchant ships, substituting a gentleman's agreement to pay in kind.

DOCUMENT 3

FRANKLIN D. ROOSEVELT, FOUR FREEDOMS SPEECH,
JANUARY 6, 1941

Though it was not yet clear to what extent America would ultimately become involved in the war, this speech was, in effect, a statement of war aims on the part of the United States. By this time details of lend-lease had been worked out, and it was also in this speech that the President called for its enactment.

I address you, the members of this new Congress, at a moment unprecedented in the history of the union. I use the word "unprecedented" because at no previous time has American security been as seriously threatened from without as it is today. . . .

I suppose that every realist knows that the democratic way of life is at this moment being directly assailed in every part of the world—assailed either by arms or by secret spreading of poisonous propaganda by those who seek to destroy unity and promote discord in nations that are still at peace.

During sixteen months this assault has blotted out the whole pattern of democratic life in an appalling number of independent nations, great and small. And the assailants are still on the march, threatening other nations, great and small.

Therefore, as your President, performing my constitutional duty to "give to the Congress information of the state of the union," I find it unhappily necessary to report that the future and the safety of our country and of our democracy are overwhelmingly involved in events far beyond our borders.

Armed defense of democratic existence is now being gallantly waged in four continents. If that defense fails, all the population and all the resources of Europe and Asia, Africa and Australia will be dominated by the conquerors. And let us remember that the total of those populations and their resources greatly exceeds the sum total of the population and resources of the whole of the Western Hemisphere—yes, many times over. . . .

No realistic American can expect from a dictator's peace international generosity, or return of true independence, or world disarmament, or freedom of expression, or freedom of religion—or even good business. Such a peace would bring no security for us or for our neighbors. . . .

I have recently pointed out how quickly the tempo of modern warfare could bring into our very midst the physical attack which we must eventually expect if the dictator nations win this war.

There is much loose talk of our immunity from immediate and direct invasion from across the seas. Obviously, as long as the British Navy retains its power, no such danger exists. Even if there were no British Navy it is not probable that any enemy would be stupid enough to attack us by landing troops in the United States from across thousands of miles of ocean, until it had acquired strategic bases from which to operate.

But we learn much from the lessons of the past years in Europe—particularly the lesson of Norway, whose essential seaports were captured by treachery and surprise built up over a series of years.

The first phase of the invasion of this hemisphere would not be the landing of regular troops. The necessary strategic points would be occupied by secret agents and their dupes—and great numbers of them are already here and in Latin America.

As long as the aggressor nations maintain the offensive they, not we, will choose the time and the place and the method of their attack.

And that is why the future of all the American Republics is today in serious danger. That is why this annual message to the Congress is unique in our history. That is why every member of the executive branch of the government and every member of the Congress face great responsibility—great accountability.

The need of the moment is that our actions and our policy should be devoted primarily—almost exclusively —to meeting this foreign peril. For all our domestic problems are now a part of the great emergency. . . .

Our national policy is this:

First, by an impressive expression of the public will and without regard to partisanship, we are committed to all-inclusive national defense.

Second, by an impressive expression of the public will and without regard to partisanship, we are committed to full support of all those resolute people everywhere who are resisting aggression and are thereby keeping war away from our hemisphere. By this support we express our determination that the democratic cause shall prevail, and we strengthen the defense and the security of our own nation.

Third, by an impressive expression of the public will and without regard to partisanship, we are committed to the proposition that principles of morality and considerations for our own security will never permit us to acquiesce in a peace dictated by aggressors and sponsored by appeasers. We know that enduring peace cannot be bought at the cost of other people's freedom.

In the recent national election there was no substantial difference between the two great parties in respect to that national policy. No issue was fought out on this line before the American electorate. And today it is abundantly evident that American citizens everywhere are demanding and supporting speedy and complete action in recognition of obvious danger.

Therefore, the immediate need is a swift and driving increase in our armament production. . . .

Our most useful and immediate role is to act as an arsenal for them as well as for ourselves. They do not need man power, but they do need billions of dollars worth of the weapons of defense. . . .

Let us say to the democracies: "We Americans are vitally concerned in your defense of freedom. We are putting forth our energies, our resources and our organizing powers to give you the strength to regain and maintain a free world. We shall send you in ever-increasing numbers, ships, planes, tanks, guns. That is our purpose and our pledge."

In fulfillment of this purpose we will not be intimidated by the threats of dictators that they will regard as a breach of international law and as an act of war our aid to the democracies which dare to resist their aggression. Such aid is not an act of war, even if a dictator should unilaterally proclaim it to so be.

And when the dictators—if the dictators—are ready to make war upon us, they will not wait for an act of war on our part.

They did not wait for Norway or Belgium or the Netherlands to commit an act of war. Their only interest is in a new one-way international law which lacks mutuality in its observance and therefore, becomes an instrument of oppression. The happiness of future generations of Americans may well depend on how effective and how immediate we can make our aid felt. No one can tell the exact character of the emergency situations that we may be called upon to meet. The nation's hands must not be tied when the nation's life is in danger.

Yes, and we must prepare, all of us prepare, to make the sacrifices that the emergency—almost as serious as war itself—demands. Whatever stands in the way of speed and efficiency in defense preparations must give way to the national need. . . .

As men do not live by bread alone, they do not fight

by armaments alone. Those who man our defenses and those behind them who build our defenses must have the stamina and the courage which come from an unshakable belief in the manner of life which they are defending. The mighty action that we are calling for cannot be based on a disregard of all the things worth fighting for.

The nation takes great satisfaction and much strength from the things which have been done to make its people conscious of their individual stake in the preservation of democratic life in America. Those things have toughened the fibre of our people, have renewed their faith and strengthened their devotion to the institutions we make ready to protect.

Certainly this is no time for any of us to stop thinking about the social and economic problems which are the root cause of the social revolution which is today a supreme factor in the world. For there is nothing mysterious about the foundations of a healthy and strong democracy.

The basic things expected by our people of their political and economic systems are simple. They are:

Equality of opportunity for youth and for others.

Jobs for those who can work.

Security for those who need it.

The ending of special privilege for the few.

The preservation of civil liberties for all.

The enjoyment of the fruits of scientific progress in a wider and constantly rising standard of living.

These are the simple, the basic things that must never be lost sight of in the turmoil and unbelievable complexity of our modern world. The inner and abiding strength of our economic and political systems is dependent upon the degree to which they fulfill these expectations. . . .

I have called for personal sacrifice, and I am assured of the willingness of almost all Americans to respond to that call. . . .

In the future days which we seek to make secure, we look forward to a world founded upon four essential humaɪ freedoms.

The first is freedom of speech and expression—everywhere in the world.

The second is freedom of every person to worship God in his own way—everywhere in the world.

The third is freedom from want—which, translated into world terms, means economic understandings which will secure to every nation a healthy peacetime life for its inhabitants—everywhere in the world.

The fourth is freedom from fear, which, translated into world terms, means a world-wide reduction of armaments to such a point and in such a thorough manner that no nation will be in a position to commit an act of physical aggression against any neighbor—anywhere in the world.

That is no vision of a distant millennium. It is a definite basis for a kind of world attainable in our own time and generation. That kind of world is the very antithesis of the so-called "new order" of tyranny which the dictators seek to create with the crash of a bomb.

To that new order we oppose the greater conception—the moral order. A good society is able to face schemes of world domination and foreign revolutions alike without fear.

Since the beginning of our American history we have been engaged in change, in a perpetual, peaceful revolution, a revolution which goes on steadily, quietly, adjusting itself to changing conditions without the concentration camp or the quick-lime in the ditch. The world order which we seek is the co-operation of free countries, working together in a friendly, civilized society.

This nation has placed its destiny in the hands, heads and hearts of its millions of free men and women, and its faith in freedom under the guidance of God. Freedom means the supremacy of human rights everywhere. Our support goes to those who struggle to gain those rights and keep them. Our strength is in our unity of purpose.

To that high concept there can be no end save victory.

DOCUMENT 4

BURTON K. WHEELER, SPEECH ON LEND-LEASE,

JANUARY 12, 1941

The speech by Senator Wheeler of Montana was one of the most unrestrained in a passionate debate. The Senator's remark about plowing under "every fourth American boy" stung Roosevelt, who called it "the rottenest thing that has been said in public life in my generation."

The lend-lease policy, translated into legislative form, stunned a Congress and a nation wholly sympathetic to the cause of Great Britain. . . . It warranted my worst fears for the future of America, and it definitely stamps the President as war-minded.

The lend-lease-give program is the New Deal's triple A foreign policy; it will plow under every fourth American boy.

Never before have the American people been asked or compelled to give so bounteously and so completely of their tax dollars to any foreign nation. Never before has the Congress of the United States been asked by any President to violate international law. Never before has this Nation resorted to duplicity in the conduct of its foreign affairs. Never before has the United States given to one man the power to strip this Nation of its defenses. Never before has a Congress coldly and flatly been asked to abdicate.

If the American people want a dictatorship—if they want a totalitarian form of government and if they want war—this bill should be steam-rollered through Congress, as is the wont of President Roosevelt.

Approval of this legislation means war, open and complete warfare. I, therefore, ask the American people before they supinely accept it, Was the last World War worth while?

If it were, then we should lend and lease war materials. If it were, then we should lend and lease American boys. President Roosevelt has said we would be repaid by England. We will be. We will be repaid, just as England repaid her war debts of the first World War—repaid those dollars wrung from the sweat of labor and the toil of farmers with cries of "Uncle Shylock." Our boys will be returned—returned in caskets, maybe; returned with bodies maimed; returned with minds warped and twisted by sights of horrors and the scream and shriek of high-powered shells.

Considered on its merits and stripped of its emotional appeal to our sympathies, the lend-lease-give bill is both ruinous and ridiculous. . . .

It gives to one man—responsible to no one—the power to denude our shores of every warship. It gives to one individual the dictatorial power to strip the American Army of our every tank, cannon, rifle, or antiaircraft gun. No one would deny that the lend-lease-give bill contains provisions that would enable one man to render the United States defenseless, but they will tell you, "The President would never do it." To this I say, "Why does he ask the power if he does not intend to use it?" Why not, I say, place some check on American donations to a foreign nation? . . .

I say in the kind of language used by the President—shame on those who ask the powers—and shame on those who would grant them.

DOCUMENT 5

CHARLES A. LINDBERGH, SPEECH ON AMERICA AND THE WAR,
APRIL 23, 1941

Colonel Charles A. Lindbergh, Jr., a national hero since his solo flight to Paris in 1927, was the son of a Minnesota Congressman with a fervently isolationist record during World War I. The younger Lindbergh became a leading member of the isolationist

America First Committee. In the same month during which this speech was given, President Roosevelt called him a "copperhead," and he resigned his commission in the army. In this radio address he stated why he felt the United States must stay out of the war.

There are many viewpoints from which the issues of this war can be argued. Some are primarily idealistic. Some are primarily practical. One should, I believe, strive for a balance of both. But, since the issues that can be covered in a single address are limited, tonight I shall discuss the war from a viewpoint which is primarily practical. It is not that I believe ideals are unimportant, even among the realities of war; but if a nation is to survive in a hostile world, its ideals must be backed by the hard logic of military practicability. If the outcome of war depended upon ideals alone, this would be a different world than it is today.

I know I will be severely criticized by the interventionists in America when I say we should not enter a war unless we have a reasonable chance of winning. That, they will claim, is far too materialistic a standpoint. They will advance again the same arguments that were used to persuade France to declare war against Germany in 1939. But I do not believe that our American ideals, and our way of life, will gain through an unsuccessful war. And I know that the United States is not prepared to wage war in Europe successfully at this time. We are no better prepared today than France was when the interventionists in Europe persuaded her to attack the Siegfried Line.

I have said before, and I will say again, that I believe it will be a tragedy to the entire world if the British Empire collapses. That is one of the main reasons why I opposed this war before it was declared, and why I have constantly advocated a negotiated peace. I did not feel that England and France had a reasonable chance of winning. France has now been defeated: and, despite the propaganda and confusion of recent months, it is now obvious that England is losing the war. I believe this is realized even by the British Government. But they have one last desperate plan remaining. They hope that they may be able to persuade us to send another American Expeditionary Force to Europe and to share with England militarily, as well as financially, the fiasco of this war.

I do not blame England for this hope, or for asking for our assistance. But we now know that she declared a war under circumstances which led to the defeat of every nation that sided with her from Poland to Greece. We know that in the desperation of war England promised to all these nations armed assistance that she could not send. We know that she misinformed them, as she has misinformed us, concerning her state of preparation, her military strength, and the progress of the war.

In time of war, truth is always replaced by propaganda. I do not believe we should be too quick to criticize the actions of a belligerent nation. There is always the question whether we, ourselves, would do better under similar circumstances. But we in this country have a right to think of the welfare of America first, just as the people in England thought first of their own country when they encouraged the smaller nations of Europe to fight against hopeless odds. When England asks us to enter this war, she is considering her own future, and that of her empire. In making our reply, I believe we should consider the future of the United States and that of the Western Hemisphere.

It is not only our right, but it is our obligation as American citizens to look at this war objectively and to weigh our chances for success if we should enter it. I have attempted to do this, especially from the standpoint of aviation; and I have been forced to the conclusion that we cannot win this war for England, regardless of how much assistance we extend.

I ask you to look at the map of Europe today and see if you can suggest any way in which we could win this war if we entered it. Suppose we had a large army in America, trained and equipped. Where would we send it to fight? The campaigns of the war show only too clearly how difficult it is to force a landing, or to maintain an army, on a hostile coast.

Suppose we took our Navy from the Pacific, and used it to convoy British shipping. That would not win the war for England. It would, at best, permit her to exist under the constant bombing of the German air fleet. Suppose we had an air force that we could send to Europe. Where could it operate? Some of our squadrons might be based in the British Isles; but it is physically impossible to base enough aircraft in the British Isles alone to equal in strength the aircraft that can be based on the Continent of Europe.

I have asked these questions on the supposition that we had in existence an Army and an air force large enough and well enough equipped to send to Europe; and that we would dare to remove our Navy from the Pacific. Even on this basis, I do not see how we could invade the Continent of Europe successfully as long as all of that Continent and most of Asia is under Axis domination. But the fact is that none of these suppositions are correct. We have only a one-ocean Navy. Our Army is still untrained and inadequately equipped for foreign war. Our air force is deplorably lacking in modern fighting planes because most of them have already been sent to Europe.

When these facts are cited, the interventionists shout that we are defeatists, that we are undermining the principles of democracy, and that we are giving comfort to Germany by talking about our military weakness. But everything I mention here has been published in our newspapers, and in the reports of congressional hearings in Washington. Our military position is well known to the governments of Europe and Asia. Why, then, should it not be brought to the attention of our own people?

I say it is the interventionist in America, as it was in England and in France, who gives comfort to the enemy. I say it is they who are undermining the principles of democracy when they demand that we take a course to which more than 80 per cent of our citizens are opposed. I charge them with being the real defeatists, for their policy has led to the defeat of every country that followed their advice since the war began. There is no better way to give comfort to an enemy than to divide the people of a nation over the issue of foreign war. There is no shorter road to defeat than by entering a war with inadequate preparation. Every nation that has adopted the interventionist policy of depending on some one else for its own defense has met with nothing but defeat and failure.

When history is written, the responsibility for the downfall of the democracies of Europe will rest squarely upon the shoulders of the interventionists who led their nations into war uninformed and unprepared. With their shouts of defeatism, and their disdain of reality, they have already sent countless thousands of young men to death in Europe. From the campaign of Poland to that of Greece, their prophecies have been false and their policies have failed. Yet these are the people who are calling us defeatists in America today. And they have led this country, too, to the verge of war.

There are many such interventionists in America, but there are more people among us of a different type. That is why you and I are assembled here tonight. There is a policy open to this nation that will lead to success—a policy that leaves us free to follow our own way of life, and to develop our own civilization. It is not a new and untried idea. It was advocated by Washington. It was incorporated in the Monroe Doctrine. Under its guidance, the United States has become the greatest nation in all the world.

It is based upon the belief that the security of a nation lies in the strength and character of its own people. It recommends the maintenance of armed forces sufficient to defend this hemisphere from attack by any combination of foreign powers. It demands faith in an independent American destiny. This is the policy of the America First Committee today. It is a policy not of isolation, but of independence; not of defeat, but of courage. It is a policy that led this nation to success during the most trying years of our history, and it is a policy that will lead us to success again.

We have weakened ourselves for many months, and still worse, we have divided our own people by this dabbling in Europe's wars. While we should have been concentrating on American defense we have been forced to argue over foreign quarrels. We must turn our eyes and our faith back to our own country before it is too late. And when we do this, a different vista opens before us. Practically every difficulty we would face in invading Europe becomes an asset to us in defending America. Our enemy, and not we, would then have the problem of transporting millions of troops across the ocean and landing them on a hostile shore. They, and not we, would have to furnish the convoys to transport guns and trucks and munitions and fuel across three thousand miles of water. Our battle-ships and our submarines would then be fighting close to their home bases. We would then do the bombing from the air and the torpedoing at sea. And if any part of an enemy convoy should ever pass our navy and our air force, they would still be faced with the guns of our coast artillery and behind them the divisions of our Army.

The United States is better situated from a military standpoint than any other nation in the world. Even in our present condition of unpreparedness no foreign power is in a position to invade us today. If we concentrate on our own defenses and build the strength that this nation should maintain, no foreign army will ever attempt to land on American shores.

War is not inevitable for this country. Such a claim is defeatism in the true sense. No one can make us fight abroad unless we ourselves are willing to do so. No one will attempt to fight us here if we arm ourselves as a great nation should be armed. Over a hundred million people in this nation are opposed to entering the war. If the principles of democracy mean anything at all, that is reason enough for us to stay out. If we are forced into a war against the wishes of an overwhelming majority of our people, we will have proved democracy such a failure at home that there will be little use fighting for it abroad.

The time has come when those of us who believe in an independent American destiny must band together and organize for strength. We have been led toward war by a minority of our people. This minority has power. It has influence. It has a loud voice. But it does not represent the American people. During the last several years I have traveled over this country from one end to the other. I have talked to many hundreds of men and women, and I have letters from tens of thousands more, who feel the same way as you and I.

Most of these people have no influence or power. Most of them have no means of expressing their convictions, except by their vote which has always been against this war. They are the citizens who have had to work too hard at their daily jobs to organize political meetings. Hitherto, they have relied upon their vote to express their feelings; but now they find that it is hardly remembered except in the oratory of a political campaign. These people—the majority of hardworking American citizens, are with us. They are the true strength of our country. And they are beginning to realize, as you and I, that there are times when we must sacrifice our normal interests in life in order to insure the safety and the welfare of our nation.

Such a time has come. Such a crisis is here. That is why the America First Committee has been formed—to give voice to the people who have no newspaper, or newsreel, or radio station at their command to give voice to the people who must do the paying, and the fighting, and the dying if this country enters the war. . . .

DOCUMENT 6

THE ATLANTIC CHARTER,
AUGUST 14, 1941

At the Atlantic Conference Roosevelt and Churchill announced their war aims in this statement, which had been drafted in preliminary form for Roosevelt by Under Secretary Sumner Welles, Churchill had hoped that the President would agree to say that the two powers aspired to keep peace "by effective international organization"; but Roosevelt, mindful of Wilson's fate, struck out these words. For Roosevelt's and Churchill's original drafts, and a full account of the writing of the final statement, see the first chapter of Sumner Welles's book, Where Are We Heading? *(1946).*

The President of the United States of America and the Prime Minister, Mr. Churchill, representing His Majesty's Government in the United Kingdom, being met together, deem it right to make known certain common principles in the national policies of their respective countries on which they base their hopes for a better future for the world.

FIRST, their countries seek no aggrandizement, territorial or other;

· SECOND, they desire to see no territorial changes that do not accord with the freely expressed wishes of the peoples concerned;

THIRD, they respect the right of all peoples to choose the form of government under which they will live; and they wish to see sovereign rights and self-government restored to those who have been forcibly deprived of them;

FOURTH, they will endeavor, with due respect for their existing obligations, to further the enjoyment by all States, great or small, victor or vanquished, of access, on equal terms, to the trade and to the raw materials of the world which are needed for their economic prosperity;

FIFTH, they desire to bring about the fullest collaboration between all nations in the economic field with the object of securing, for all, improved labor standards, economic adjustment and social security;

SIXTH, after the final destruction of the Nazi tyranny, they hope to see established a peace which will afford to all nations the means of dwelling in safety within their own boundaries, and which will afford assurance that all the men in all the lands may live out their lives in freedom from fear and want;

SEVENTH, such a peace should enable all men to traverse the high seas and oceans without hindrance;

EIGHTH, they believe that all of the nations of the world, for realistic as well as spiritual reasons, must come to the abandonment of the use of force. Since no future peace can be maintained if land, sea or air armaments continue to be employed by nations which threaten, or may threaten, aggression outside of their frontiers, they believe, pending the establishment of a wider and permanent system of general security, that the disarmament of such nations is essential. They will likewise aid and encourage all other practicable measures which will lighter for peace-loving peoples the crushing burden of armaments.

FRANKLIN D. ROOSEVELT
WINSTON S. CHURCHILL

DOCUMENT 7

FRANKLIN D. ROOSEVELT, WAR MESSAGE TO CONGRESS,
DECEMBER 8, 1941

The morning after the Japanese attack on Pearl Harbor, Roosevelt delivered this speech before a joint session of Congress. Except for the second last sentence, which was suggested by Harry Hopkins, Roosevelt wrote this effective speech himself. The vote for war was unanimous in the Senate; in the House one vote was recorded in opposition.

Yesterday, December 7, 1941—a date which will live in infamy—the United States of America was suddenly and deliberately attacked by naval and air forces of the empire of Japan.

The United States was at peace with that nation and, at the solicitation of Japan, was still in conversation with its government and its emperor looking toward the maintenance of peace in the Pacific.

Indeed, one hour after Japanese air squadrons had commenced bombing in the American Island of Oahu the Japanese Ambassador to the United States and his colleague delivered to our Secretary of State a formal reply to a recent American message. And, while this reply stated that it seemed useless to continue the existing diplomatic negotiations, it contained no threat or hint of war or of armed attack.

It will be recorded that the distance of Hawaii from Japan makes it obvious that the attack was deliberately planned many days or even weeks ago. During the intervening time the Japanese Government has deliberately sought to deceive the United States by false statements and expressions of hope for continued peace.

The attack yesterday on the Hawaiian Islands has caused severe damage to American naval and military forces. I regret to tell you that very many American lives have been lost. In addition American ships have been reported torpedoed on the high seas between San Francisco and Honolulu.

Yesterday the Japanese Government also launched an attack against Malaya.

Last night Japanese forces attacked Hong Kong.

Last night Japanese forces attacked Guam.

Last night Japanese forces attacked the Philippine Islands.

Last night the Japanese attacked Wake Island.

And this morning the Japanese attacked Midway Island.

Japan has therefore undertaken a surprise offensive extending throughout the Pacific area. The facts of yesterday and today speak for themselves. The people of the United States have already formed their opinions and well understand the implications to the very life and safety of our nation.

As Commander in Chief of the Army and Navy I have directed that all measures be taken for our defense.

Always will our whole nation remember the character of the onslaught against us.

No matter how long it may take us to overcome this premeditated invasion, the American people, in their righteous might, will win through to absolute victory.

I believe that I interpret the will of the Congress and of the people when I assert that we will not only defend ourselves to the uttermost but will make it very certain that this form of treachery shall never again endanger us.

Hostilities exist. There is no blinking at the fact that our people, our territory and our interests are in grave danger.

With confidence in our armed forces, with the unbounding determination of our people, we will gain the inevitable triumph. So help us God.

I ask that the Congress declare that since the unprovoked and dastardly attack by Japan on Sunday, Dec.

7, 1941, a state of war has existed between the United States and the Japanese Empire.

DOCUMENT 8

THE TRUMAN DOCTRINE,
MARCH 12, 1947

*"I . . . wished to state, for all the world to know,"
Truman later recalled concerning the origin of this
address delivered to Congress, "what the position of
the United States was in the face of the new totalitarian challenge. . . . This was, I believe, the turning point in America's foreign policy, which now declared that wherever aggression, direct or indirect,
threatened the peace, the security of the United States
was involved." As Truman first formulated it, the Truman doctrine gave a somewhat belligerent and negative
expression to the idea of containment of Soviet power.
A more positive expression of American policy was
supplied, with Truman's encouragement, a few
months later in the Marshall Plan (Document 9).*

The gravity of the situation which confronts the world today necessitates my appearance before a joint session of the Congress. The foreign policy and the national security of this country are involved.

One aspect of the present situation, which I wish to present to you at this time for your consideration and decision, concerns Greece and Turkey.

The United States has received from the Greek Government an urgent appeal for financial and economic assistance. Preliminary reports from the American Economic Mission now in Greece and reports from the American Ambassador in Greece corroborate the statement of the Greek Government that assistance is imperative if Greece is to survive as a free nation.

I do not believe that the American people and the Congress wish to turn a deaf ear to the appeal of the Greek Government. . . .

The very existence of the Greek state is today

threatened by the terrorist activities of several thousand armed men, led by Communists, who defy the Government's authority at a number of points, particularly along the northern boundaries. A commission appointed by the United Nations Security Council is at present investigating disturbed conditions in Northern Greece and alleged border violations along the frontier between Greece on the one hand and Albania, Bulgaria and Yugoslavia on the other.

Meanwhile, the Greek Government is unable to cope with the situation. The Greek Army is small and poorly equipped. It needs supplies and equipment if it is to restore the authority to the Government throughout Greek territory.

Greece must have assistance if it is to become a self-supporting and self-respecting democracy. The United States must supply this assistance. We have already extended to Greece certain types of relief and economic aid but these are inadequate. There is no other country to which democratic Greece can turn. No other nation is willing and able to provide the necessary support for a democratic Greek Government.

The British Government, which has been helping Greece, can give no further financial or economic aid after March 31. Great Britain finds itself under the necessity of reducing or liquidating its commitments in several parts of the world, including Greece.

We have considered how the United Nations might assist in this crisis. But the situation is an urgent one requiring immediate action, and the United Nations and its related organizations are not in a position to extend help of the kind that is required. . . .

Greece's neighbor, Turkey, also deserves our attention. The future of Turkey as an independent and economically sound state is clearly no less important to the freedom-loving peoples of the world than the future of Greece. The circumstances in which Turkey finds itself today are considerably different from those of Greece. Turkey has been spared the disasters that have beset Greece. And during the war, the United States and Great Britain furnished Turkey with material aid.

Nevertheless, Turkey now needs our support.

Since the war Turkey has sought financial assistance from Great Britain and the United States for the purpose of effecting that modernization necessary for the maintenance of its national integrity.

That integrity is essential to the preservation of order in the Middle East.

The British Government has informed us that, owing to its own difficulties, it can no longer extend financial or economic aid to Turkey. As in the case of Greece, if Turkey is to have the assistance it needs, the United States must supply it. We are the only country able to provide that help

I am fully aware of the broad implications involved if the United States extends assistance to Greece and Turkey, and I shall discuss these implications with you at this time.

One of the primary objectives of the foreign policy of the United States is the creation of conditions in which we and other nations will be able to work out a way of life free from coercion. This was a fundamental issue in the war with Germany and Japan. Our victory was won over countries which sought to impose their will, and their way of life, upon other nations. . . .

The peoples of a number of countries of the world have recently had totalitarian regimes forced upon them against their will. The Government of the United States has made frequent protests against coercion and intimidation, in violation of the Yalta Agreement, in Poland, Rumania, and Bulgaria. I must also state that in a number of other countries there have been similar developments.

At the present moment in world history nearly every nation must choose between alternative ways of life. The choice is too often not a free one.

One way of life is based upon the will of the majority, and is distinguished by free institutions, representative government, free elections, guarantees of individual liberty, freedom of speech and religion, and freedom from political oppression.

The second way of life is based upon the will of a minority forcibly imposed upon the majority. It relies upon terror and oppression, a controlled press and radio, fixed elections, and the suppression of personal freedoms.

I believe that it must be the policy of the United States to support free peoples who are resisting attempted subjugation by armed minorities or by outside pressures.

I believe that we must assist free peoples to work out their own destinies in their own way.

I believe that our help should be primarily through economic and financial aid, which is essential to economic stability and orderly political processes.

The world is not static and the status quo is not sacred. But we cannot allow changes in the status quo in violation of the Charter of the United Nations by such methods as coercion, or by such subterfuges as political infiltration. In helping free and independent nations to maintain their freedom, the United States will be giving effect to the principles of the Charter of the United Nations.

It is necessary only to glance at a map to realize that the survival and integrity of the Greek nation are of grave importance in a much wider situation. If Greece should fall under the control of an armed minority, the effect upon its neighbor, Turkey, would be immediate and serious. Confusion and disorder might well spread throughout the entire Middle East.

Moreover, the disappearance of Greece as an independent state would have a profound effect upon those countries in Europe whose peoples are struggling against great difficulties to maintain their freedoms and their independence while they repair the damages of war.

It would be an unspeakable tragedy if these countries, which have struggled so long against overwhelming odds, should lose that victory for which they sacrificed so much. Collapse of free institutions and loss of independence would be disastrous not only for them but for the world. Discouragement and possibly failure would quickly be the lot of neighboring peoples striving to maintain their freedom and independence.

Should we fail to aid Greece and Turkey in this fateful hour, the effect will be far reaching to the West as well as to the East. We must take immediate and resolute action.

I therefore ask the Congress to provide authority for assistance to Greece and Turkey in the amount of $400,000,000 for the period ending June 30, 1948. . . .

In addition to funds, I ask the Congress to authorize the detail of American civilian and military personnel to Greece and Turkey, at the request of those countries, to assist in the tasks of reconstruction, and for the purpose of supervising the use of such financial and material assistance as may be furnished. I recommend that authority also be provided for the instruction and training of selected Greek and Turkish personnel.

Finally, I ask that the Congress provide authority which will permit the speediest and most effective use, in terms of needed commodities, supplies, and equipment, of such funds as may be authorized. . . .

This is a serious course upon which we embark.

I would not recommend it except that the alternative is much more serious.

The United States contributed $341,000,000,000 toward winning World War II. This is an investment in world freedom and world peace.

The assistance that I am recommending for Greece and Turkey amounts to little more than one-tenth of 1 percent of this investment. It is only common sense that we should safeguard this investment and make sure that it was not in vain.

The seeds of totalitarian regimes are nurtured by misery and want. They spread and grow in the evil soil of poverty and strife. They reach their full growth when the hope of a people for a better life has died.

We must keep that hope alive.

The free peoples of the world look to us for support in maintaining their freedoms.

If we falter in our leadership, we may endanger the peace of the world—and we shall surely endanger the welfare of our own Nation.

Great responsibilities have been placed upon us by the swift movement of events.

I am confident that the Congress will face these responsibilities squarely.

DOCUMENT 9

GEORGE C. MARSHALL, THE MARSHALL PLAN,
JUNE 5, 1947

The idea of a planned program for aid to Europe was originated chiefly by Dean Acheson, while he was Under Secretary of State. Actually the plan itself also was first presented to the public by Acheson, in a speech at Cleveland, Mississippi, on May 8, 1947 It had been intended that President Truman should give this speech, but he was unable to appear, and Acheson substituted for him. The Mississippi speech was carefully formulated, submitted to all departments of the government to which the subject matter pertained, and reviewed by the President. This first announcement aroused much interest in Europe, but because it was given by the Under Secretary rather than the President, it got relatively little attention at home. One month later, Secretary of State Marshall presented the plan again, this time in a commencement address at Harvard University; this second speech was widely publicized, and became the standard statement of the idea of American aid.

I need not tell you gentlemen that the world situation is very serious. That must be apparent to all intelligent people. I think one difficulty is that the problem is one of such enormous complexity that the very mass of facts presented to the public by press and radio make it exceedingly difficult for the man in the street to reach a clear appraisement of the situation. Furthermore, the people of this country are distant from the troubled areas of the earth and it is hard for them to comprehend the plight and consequent reactions of the long-suffering peoples, and the effect of those reactions on their governments in connection with our efforts to promote peace in the world.

In considering the requirements for the rehabilitation of Europe the physical loss of life, the visible destruction of cities, factories, mines, and railroads was correctly estimated, but it has become obvious during recent months that this visible destruction was probably less serious than the dislocation of the entire fabric of European economy. For the past 10 years conditions have been highly abnormal. The feverish preparation for war and the more feverish maintenance of the war effort engulfed all aspects of national economies. Machinery has fallen into disrepair or is entirely obsolete. Under the arbitrary and destructive Nazi rule, virtually every possible enterprise was geared into the German war machine. Long-standing commercial ties, private institutions, banks, insurance companies and shipping companies disappeared through loss of capital, absorption through nationalization or by simple destruction. In many countries, confidence in the local currency has been severely shaken. The breakdown of the business structure of Europe during the war was complete. Recovery has been seriously retarded by the fact that 2 years after the close of hostilities a peace settlement with Germany and Austria has not been agreed upon. But even given a more prompt solution of these difficult problems, the rehabilitation of the economic structure of Europe quite evidently will require a much longer time and greater effort than had been foreseen.

There is a phase of this matter which is both interesting and serious. The farmer has always produced the foodstuffs to exchange with the city dweller for the other necessities of life. This division of labor is the basis of modern civilization. At the present time it is threatened with breakdown. The town and city industries are not producing adequate goods to exchange with the food-producing farmer. Raw materials and fuel are in short supply. Machinery is lacking or worn out. The farmer or the peasant cannot find the goods for sale which he desires to purchase. So the sale of his farm produce for money which he cannot use seems to him an unprofitable transaction. He, therefore, has withdrawn many fields from crop cultivation and is using them for grazing. He feeds more grain to stock and finds for himself and his family an ample supply of food, however short he may be on clothing and the other ordinary gadgets of civilization. Meanwhile people in the cities are short of food and fuel. So the governments are forced to use their foreign money and credits to procure these necessities abroad. This process exhausts funds which are urgently needed for reconstruction. Thus a very serious situation is rapidly developing which bodes no good for the world. The modern system of the division of labor upon which the exchange of products is based is in danger of breaking down.

The truth of the matter is that Europe's requirements for the next 3 or 4 years of foreign food and other essential products—principally from America—are so much greater than her present ability to pay that she must have substantial additional help, or face economic, social, and political deterioration of a very grave character.

The remedy lies in breaking the vicious circle and restoring the confidence of the European people in the economic future of their own countries and of Europe as a whole. The manufacturer and the farmer throughout wide areas must be able and willing to exchange their products for currencies the continuing value of which is not open to question.

Aside from the demoralizing effect on the world at large and the possibilities of disturbances arising as a result of the desperation of the people concerned, the consequences to the economy of the United States should be apparent to all. It is logical that the United States should do whatever it is able to do to assist in the return of normal economic health in the world, without which there can be no political stability and no assured peace. Our policy is directed not against any country or doctrine but against hunger, poverty, desperation, and chaos. Its purpose should be the revival of a working economy in the world so as to permit the emergence of political and social conditions in which free institutions can exist. Such assistance, I am convinced, must not be on a piecemeal basis as various crises develop. Any assistance that this Government may render in the future should provide a cure rather than a mere palliative. Any government that is willing to assist in the task of recovery will find full cooperation, I am sure, on the part of the United States Government. Any government which maneuvers to block the recovery of other countries cannot expect help from us. Furthermore, governments, political parties, or groups which seek to perpetuate human misery in order to profit therefrom politically or otherwise will encounter the opposition of the United States.

It is already evident that, before the United States Government can proceed much further in its efforts to alleviate the situation and help start the European world on its way to recovery, there must be some agreement among the countries of Europe as to the requirements of the situation and the part those countries themselves will take in order to give proper effect to whatever action might be undertaken by this Government. It would be neither fitting nor efficacious for this Government to undertake to draw up unilaterally a program designed to place Europe on its feet economically. This is the business of the Europeans. The initiative, I think, must come from Europe. The role of this country should consist of friendly aid in the drafting of a European program and of later support of such a program so far as it may be practical for us to do so. The program should be a joint one, agreed to by a number, if not all European nations.

An essential part of any successful action on the part of the United States is an understanding on the part of the people of America of the character of the problem and the remedies to be applied. Political passion and prejudice should have no part. With foresight, and a willingness on the part of our people to face up to the vast responsibility which history has clearly placed upon our country, the difficulties I have outlined can and will be overcome.

DOCUMENT 10

GEORGE F. KENNAN, "THE SOURCES OF SOVIET CONDUCT,"
JULY 1947

*The article excerpted here was unsigned when it first
appeared in the July 1947 issue of Foreign Affairs,
and was only later identified with its author.
George F. Kennan, then Counselor of the American
Embassy at Moscow, had long been a student of Russian affairs, and this article became the most influential statement of the doctrine of containment.*

Of the original [Soviet] ideology, nothing has been officially
junked. Belief is maintained in the basic badness of capitalism, in the inevitability of its destruction, in the obligation of the proletariat to assist in that destruction and to
take power into its own hands. But stress has come to be
laid primarily on those concepts which relate most
specifically to the Soviet regime itself: to its position as
the sole truly Socialist regime in a dark and misguided
world, and to the relationships of power within it.

The first of these concepts is that of the innate
antagonism between capitalism and Socialism. We have
seen how deeply that concept has become imbedded in
foundations of Soviet power. It has profound implications
for Russia's conduct as a member of international society.
It means that there can never be on Moscow's side any
sincere assumption of a community of aims between the
Soviet Union and powers which are regarded as capitalism.
It must invariably be assumed in Moscow that the aims of
the capitalist world are antagonistic to the Soviet regime,
and therefore, to the interests of the peoples it controls.
If the Soviet Government occasionally sets its signature
to documents which would indicate the contrary, this is
to be regarded as a tactical maneuver permissible in dealing with the enemy (who is without honor) and should
be taken in the spirit of *caveat emptor*. Basically, the antag-

onism remains. It is postulated. And from it flow many of the phenomena which we find disturbing in the Kremlin's conduct of foreign policy: the secretiveness, the lack of frankness, the duplicity, the wary suspiciousness, and the basic unfriendliness of purpose. These phenomena are there to stay, for the foreseeable future. There can be variations of degree and of emphasis. When there is something the Russians want from us, one or the other of these features of their policy may be thrust temporarily into the background; and when that happens there will always be Americans who will leap forward with gleeful announcements that "the Russians have changed," and some who will even try to take credit for having brought about such "changes." But we should not be misled by tactical maneuvers. These characteristics of Soviet policy, like the postulate from which they flow, are basic to the internal nature of Soviet power, and will be with us, whether in the foreground or the background, until the internal nature of Soviet power is changed.

This means that we are going to continue for a long time to find the Russians difficult to deal with. It does not mean that they should be considered as embarked upon a do-or-die program to overthrow our society by a given date. The theory of the inevitability of the eventual fall of capitalism has the fortunate connotation that there is no hurry about it. . . .

This brings us to the second of the concepts important to contemporary Soviet outlook. That is the infallibility of the Kremlin. The Soviet concept of power, which permits no focal points of organization outside the Party itself, requires that the Party leadership remain in theory the sole repository of truth. For if truth were to be found elsewhere, there would be justification for its expression in organized activity. But it is precisely that which the Kremlin cannot and will not permit.

The leadership of the Communist Party is therefore always right, and has been always right ever since in 1929 Stalin formalized his personal power by announcing that decisions of the Politburo were being taken unanimously. . . .

But we have seen that the Kremlin is under no ideological compulsion to accomplish its purposes in a hurry.

Like the Church, it is dealing in ideological concepts which are of long-term validity, and it can afford to be patient. It has no right to risk the existing achievements of the revolution for the sake of vain baubles of the future. The very teachings of Lenin himself require great caution and flexibility in the pursuit of Communist purposes. Again, these precepts are fortified by the lessons of Russian history: of centuries of obscure battles between nomadic forces over the stretches of a vast unfortified plain. Here caution, circumspection, flexibility and deception are the valuable qualities; and their value finds natural appreciation in the Russian or the oriental mind. Thus the Kremlin has no compunction about retreating in the face of superior force. And being under the compulsion of no timetable, it does not get panicky under the necessity for such retreat. . . .

These considerations make Soviet diplomacy at once easier and more difficult to deal with than the diplomacy of individual aggressive leaders like Napoleon and Hitler. On the one hand it is more sensitive to contrary force, more ready to yield on individual sectors of the diplomatic front when that force is felt to be too strong, and thus more rational in the logic and rhetoric of power. On the other hand it cannot be easily defeated or discouraged by a single victory on the part of its opponents. And the patient persistence by which it is animated means that it can be effectively countered not by sporadic acts which represent the momentary whims of democratic opinion but only by intelligent long-range policies on the part of Russia's adversaries—policies no less steady in their purpose, and no less variegated and resourceful in their application, than those of the Soviet Union itself.

In these circumstances it is clear that the main element of any United States policy toward the Soviet Union must be that of a long-term, patient but firm and vigilant containment of Russian expansive tendencies. It is important to note, however, that such a policy has nothing to do with outward histrionics: with threats or blustering or superfluous gestures of outward "toughness." While the Kremlin is basically flexible in its reaction to political realities, it is by no means unamenable to considerations of prestige. Like almost any other government, it can be placed by tactless and threatening gestures in a position where it cannot afford to yield even though this might be dictated by its sense of realism. The Russian leaders are keen judges of human psychology, and as such they are highly conscious that loss of temper and of self-control is never a source of strength in political affairs. They are quick to exploit such evidences of weakness. For these reasons, it is a *sine qua non* of successful dealing with Russia that the foreign government in question should remain at all times cool and collected and that its demands on Russian policy should be put forward in such a manner as to leave the way open for a compliance not too detrimental to Russian prestige.

In the light of the above, it will be clearly seen that the Soviet pressure against the free institutions of the Western world is something that can be contained by the adroit and vigilant application of counter-force at a series of constantly shifting geographical and political points, corresponding to the shifts and maneuvers of Soviet policy, but which cannot be charmed or talked out of existence. The Russians look forward to a duel of infinite duration, and they see that already they have scored great successes. It must be borne in mind that there was a time when the Communist Party represented far more of a minority in the sphere of Russian national life than Soviet power today represents in the world community.

But if ideology convinces the rulers of Russia that truth is on their side and that they can therefore afford to wait, those of us on whom that ideology has no claim are free to examine objectively the validity of that premise. The Soviet thesis not only implies complete lack of control by the West over its own economic destiny, it likewise assumes Russian unity, discipline and patience over an infinite period. Let us bring this apocalyptic vision down to earth, and suppose that the Western world finds the strength and resourcefulness to contain Soviet power over a period of ten to fifteen years. What does that spell for Russia itself? . . .

The Kremlin has also proved able to accomplish its purpose of building up in Russia, regardless of the interests of the inhabitants, an industrial foundation of heavy metallurgy, which is, to be sure, not yet complete but which is nevertheless continuing to grow and is approaching those of the other major industrial countries. All of this, however, both the maintenance of internal political security and the building of heavy industry, has been carried out at a terrible cost in human life and in human hopes and energies. It has necessitated the use of forced labor on a scale unprecedented in modern times under conditions of peace. It has involved the neglect or abuse of other phases of Soviet economic life, particularly agriculture, consumers' goods production, housing and transportation.

To all that, the war has added its tremendous toll. . . .

In these circumstances, there are limits to the physical and nervous strength of people themselves. These limits are absolute ones, and are binding even for the cruelest dictatorship, because beyond them people cannot be driven. . . .

In addition to this, we have the fact that Soviet economic development, while it can list certain formidable achievements, has been precariously spotty and uneven. . . .

Meanwhile, a great uncertainty hangs over the political life of the Soviet Union. That is the uncertainty involved in the transfer of power from one individual or group of individuals to others.

This is, of course, outstandingly the problem of the personal position of Stalin. We must remember that his succession to Lenin's pinnacle of preëminence in the Communist movement was the only such transfer of individual authority which the Soviet Union has experienced. That transfer took twelve years to consolidate. It cost the lives of millions of people and shook the state to its foundations. The attendant tremors were felt all through the international revolutionary movement, to the disadvantage of the Kremlin itself.

It is always possible that another transfer of preëminent power may take place quietly and inconspicuously, with no repercussions anywhere. But again, it is possible that the questions involved may unleash, to use some of Lenin's words, one of those "incredibly swift transitions" from "delicate deceit" to "wild violence" which characterize Russian history, and may shake Soviet power to its foundations.

But this is not only a question of Stalin himself. There has been, since 1938, a dangerous congealment of political life in the higher circles of Soviet power. . . .

Who can say whether, in these circumstances, the eventual rejuvenation of the higher spheres of authority (which can only be a matter of time) can take place smoothly and peacefully, or whether rivals in the quest for higher power will not eventually reach down into these politically immature and inexperienced masses in order to find support for their respective claims. If this were ever to happen, strange consequences could flow for the Communist Party: for the membership at large has been exercised only in the practices of iron discipline and obedience and not in the arts of compromise and accommodation. And if disunity were ever to seize and paralyze the Party, the chaos and weakness of Russian society would be revealed in forms beyond description. . . .

Thus the future of Soviet power may not be by any means as secure as Russian capacity for self-delusion would make it appear to the men in the Kremlin. . . . And who can say with assurance that the strong light still cast by the Kremlin on the dissatisfied peoples of the Western world is not the powerful afterglow of a constellation which is in actuality on the wane? This cannot be proved. And it cannot be disproved. But the possibility remains (and in the opinion of this writer it is a strong one) that Soviet power, like the capitalist world of its conception, bears within it the seeds of its own decay, and that the sprouting of these seeds is well advanced.

It is clear that the United States cannot expect in the foreseeable future to enjoy political intimacy with the Soviet regime. It must continue to regard the Soviet Union as a rival, not a partner, in the political arena. It must continue to expect that Soviet policies will reflect no abstract love of peace and stability, no real faith in the possibility of a permanent happy coexistence of the Socialist and capitalist worlds, but rather a cautious, persistent pressure toward the disruption and weakening of all rival influence and rival power.

Balanced against this are the facts that Russia, as opposed to the Western world in general, is still by far the weaker party, that Soviet policy is highly flexible, and that Soviet society may well contain deficiencies which will eventually weaken its own total potential. This would of itself warrant the United States entering with reasonable confidence upon a policy of firm containment, designed to confront the Russians with unalterable counter-force at every point where they show signs of encroaching upon the interests of a peaceful and stable world.

But in actuality the possibilities for American policy are by no means limited to holding the line and hoping for the best. It is entirely possible for the United States to influence by its actions the internal developments, both within Russia and throughout the international Communist movement, by which Russian policy is largely determined. This is not only a question of the modest measure of informational activity which this government can conduct in the Soviet Union and elsewhere, although that, too, is important. It is rather a question of the degree to which the United States can create among the peoples of the world generally the impression of a country which knows what it wants, which is coping successfully with the problems of its internal life and with the responsibilities of a World Power, and which has a spiritual vitality capable of holding its own among the major ideological currents of the time. To the extent that such an impression can be created and maintained, the aims of Russian Communism must appear sterile and quixotic, the hopes and enthusiasm of Moscow's supporters must wane, and added strain must be imposed on the Kremlin's foreign policies. For the palsied decrepitude of the capitalist world is the keystone of Communist philosophy. Even the failure of the United States to experience the early economic depression which the ravens of the Red Square have been predicting with such complacent confidence since hostilities ceased would have deep and important repercussions throughout the Communist world.

By the same token, exhibitions of indecision, disunity and internal disintegration within this country have an exhilarating effect on the whole Communist movement. At each evidence of these tendencies, a thrill of hope and

excitement goes through the Communist world; a new
jauntiness can be noted in the Moscow tread; new groups
of foreign supporters climb on to what they can only view
as the band wagon of international politics; and Russian
pressure increases all along the line in international affairs.

It would be an exaggeration to say that American behavior unassisted and alone could exercise a power of life
and death over the Communist movement and bring about
the early fall of Soviet power in Russia. But the United
States has it in its power to increase enormously the strains
under which Soviet policy must operate, to force upon the
Kremlin a far greater degree of moderation and circumspection than it has had to observe in recent years, and in
this way to promote tendencies which must eventually find
their outlet in either the break-up or the gradual mellow-
ing of Soviet power. For no mystical, Messianic movement—and particularly not that of the Kremlin—can face
frustration indefinitely without eventually adjusting itself
in one way or another to the logic of that state of affairs.

Thus the decision will really fall in large measure
in this country itself. The issue of Soviet-American relations is in essence a test of the over-all worth of the United
States as a nation among nations. To avoid destruction the
United States need only measure up to its own best traditions and prove itself worthy of preservation as a great
nation.

DOCUMENT 11

DEAN ACHESON, SPEECH FOR THE NORTH ATLANTIC TREATY,
MARCH 18, 1949

*In the excerpted portions of this radio address, the
recently appointed Secretary of State, Dean Acheson,
explained the purposes of the North Atlantic pact.*

The paramount purposes of the pact are peace and security. If peace and security can be achieved in the North
Atlantic area, we shall have gone a long way to assure
peace and security in other areas as well.

The achievement of peace and security means more than that in the final outcome we shall have prevented war and brought about the settlement of international disputes by peaceful means. There must be conviction of people everywhere that war will be prevented and that disputes will be settled peacefully. In the most practical terms, true international peace and security require a firm belief by the peoples of the world that they will not be subjected to unprovoked attack, to coercion and intimidation, to interference in their own affairs. Peace and security require confidence in the future, based on the assurance that the peoples of the world will be permitted to improve their conditions of life, free from fear that the fruits of their labor may be taken from them by alien hands. . . .

It is important to keep in mind that the really successful national and international institutions are those that recognize and express underlying realities. The North Atlantic community of nations is such a reality. It is based on the affinity and natural identity of interests of the North Atlantic powers.

The North Atlantic treaty which will formally unite them is the product of at least 350 years of history and perhaps more. There developed on our Atlantic Coast a community, which has spread across the continent, connected with Western Europe by common institutions and moral and ethical beliefs. Similarities of this kind are not superficial, but fundamental. They are the strongest kind of ties, because they are based on moral conviction, on acceptance of the same values in life.

The very basis of Western civilization, which we share with the other nations bordering on the North Atlantic, and which all of us share with many other nations, is the ingrained spirit of restraint and tolerance. This is the opposite of the Communist belief that coercion by force is a proper method of hastening the inevitable. Western civilization has lived by mutual restraint and tolerance. This civilization permits and stimulates free inquiry and bold experimentation. It creates the environment of freedom, from which flows the greatest amount of ingenuity, enterprise, and accomplishment. . . .

Now successful resistance to aggression in the modern world requires modern arms and trained military forces.

As a result of the recent war, the European countries joining in the pact are generally deficient in both requirements. The treaty does not bind the United States to any arms program. But we all know that the United States is now the only democratic nation with the resources and the productive capacity to help the free nations of Europe to recover their military strength.

Therefore, we expect to ask the Congress to supply our European partners some of the weapons and equipment they need to be able to resist aggression. We also expect to recommend military supplies for other free nations which will cooperate with us in safeguarding peace and security.

In the compact world of today the security of the United States cannot be defined in terms of boundaries and frontiers. A serious threat to international peace and security anywhere in the world is of direct concern to this country. Therefore it is our policy to help free peoples to maintain their integrity and independence, not only in Western Europe, not only in the Americas, but wherever the aid we are able to provide can be effective. . . .

Allegations that aggressive designs lie behind this country's signature of the Atlantic pact can rest only on a malicious misrepresentation or a fantastic misunderstanding of the nature and aims of American society. . . .

The United States is waging peace by throwing its full strength and energy into the struggle, and we shall continue to do so.

We sincerely hope that we can avoid strife, but we cannot avoid striving for what is right. We devoutly hope we can have genuine peace, but we cannot be complacent about the present uneasy and troubled peace.

A secure and stable peace is not a goal we can reach all at once and for all time. It is a dynamic state, produced by effort and faith, with courage and justice. The struggle is continuous and hard. The prize is never irrevocably ours.

To have this genuine peace we must constantly work for it. But we must do even more. We must make it clear that armed attack will be met by collective defense, prompt and effective.

That is the meaning of the North Atlantic pact.

DOCUMENT 12

ROBERT A. TAFT, SPEECH AGAINST THE NORTH ATLANTIC TREATY,

JULY 11, 1949

Senator Robert A. Taft of Ohio, perhaps the ablest and most articulate spokesman of American isolationism, stated in this speech in the Senate why he opposed the North Atlantic Treaty. After a long debate, however, the treaty was ratified on July 21, by a vote of 87 to 13 in the Senate.

I think the pact carries with it an obligation to assist in arming, at our expense, the nations of western Europe, because with that obligation I believe it will promote war in the world rather than peace, and because I think that with the arms plan it is wholly contrary to the spirit of the obligations we assumed in the United Nations Charter. I would vote for the pact if a reservation were adopted denying any legal or moral obligation to provide arms. . . .

The Atlantic Treaty as drawn is certainly no improvement over the United Nations, nor can it by any stretch of the imagination be regarded as a perfection of or supplement to that Charter. From the point of view of an international organization, it is a step backward. . . .

What is the nature of that treaty?

It is obviously . . . a defensive military alliance between certain nations, the essence of which is an obligation under article 5 to go to war if necessary with any nation which attacks any one of the signers of the treaty. . . . The obligation is completely binding for a period of 20 years. . . . By executing a treaty of this kind, we put ourselves at the mercy of the foreign policies of 11 other nations, and do so for a period of 20 years. The [treaty] is obviously aimed at possible Russian aggression against Western Europe, but the obligation assumed is far broader than that. I emphasize again that the obligation is much more unconditional, much less dependent on legal processes and much less dependent on joint action than the obligation of the United Nations Charter. . . .

Second. The pact standing by itself would clearly be a deterrent to war. If Russia knows that if it starts a war it wi'l immediately find itself at war with the United States, it is much less likely to start a war. . . . But if Russia sees itself ringed about gradually by so-called defensive arms, from Norway and Denmark to Turkey and Greece, it may form a different opinion. It may decide that the arming of western Europe, regardless of its present purpose, looks to an attack upon Russia. . . . They may well decide that if war is the certain result, that war might better occur now rather than after the arming of Europe is completed. . . .

Third. The pact with the arms obligation, I believe, violates our obligations under the United Nations. . . . I do not think article 51 extends the actual exercise of this right [of self-defense against armed attack] to the arming of other nations prior to the occurrence of such an attack. An undertaking by the most powerful nation in the world to arm half the world against the other half goes far beyond any "right of collective self-defense if an armed attack occurs." It violates the whole spirit of the United Nations Charter. . . .

Fourth. The obligation to furnish arms is either a mere token obligation, or it is one of vast extent. . . . We are entering on a new lend-lease. . . .

Fifth. The justification for the arms aid rests on the necessity of defense against Russia, but remember that once these arms are provided, they are completely within the control of the nation receiving them. They are subject to the orders of those who, at the time, control the government of the country. Those governors may be Communists or Fascists, they may be peace-loving, or they may be aggressors. . . .

Sixth. By approving this pact with the arms program, I believe we are committing ourselves to a particular course of action in war which may be unwise at the time when a war may actually develop. It is one thing to agree to go to war with Russia if it attacks western Europe. It is another to send American ground troops to defend Norway or Denmark or Holland or Italy or even France and England. . . .

Seventh. Finally . . . it is becoming increasingly apparent that England, at least, intends to trade extensively with Russia, and inevitably the same thing will be true of other western European nations. . . . The more we take off their shoulders the burden of providing for their own defense, the more free they will be to ship steel and heavy machinery to the east. . . . I do not think that the American people at this time desire to increase the overall aid we are giving to western Europe with its tremendous burden on the American taxpayer. . . .

My conclusion has been reached with the greatest discomfort. When so many disagree with that conclusion, I must admit that I may be completely wrong. . . . I would like to be able to vote for a policy that will commit us to war if Russia attacks western Europe. I would be glad to join in an agreement to occupy Germany indefinitely to guard against a third attack from that quarter. I would waive my other objections to the Atlantic Pact if I did not feel that it was inextricably involved with the arms program. But I cannot escape the logic of the situation as I see it, and therefore I cannot vote for a treaty which, in my opinion, will do far more to bring about a third world war than it will ever maintain the peace of the world.

DOCUMENT 13

DOUGLAS MacARTHUR, ADDRESS TO CONGRESS,

APRIL 19, 1951

When he returned from the Far East after his removal by President Truman, General MacArthur was greeted as a hero by a large section of the press and large numbers of people. His welcome provided an outlet for resentments about the Korean war. In a haughty and flamboyant speech to Congress, excerpted here,

he explained how he thought the Korean war should
be waged.

While I was not consulted prior to the President's decision
to intervene in support of the Republic of Korea, that decision from a military standpoint, proved a sound one.
As I say, it proved a sound one, as we hurled back the
invader and decimated his forces. Our victory was complete, and our objectives within reach, when Red China
intervened with numerically superior ground forces.

This created a new war and an entirely new situation,
a situation not contemplated when our forces were committed against the North Korean invaders; a situation
which called for new decisions in the diplomatic sphere to
permit the realistic adjustment of military strategy. Such
decisions have not been forthcoming.

While no man in his right mind would advocate sending our ground forces into continental China, and such was
never given a thought, the new situation did urgently demand a drastic revision of strategic planning if our political
aim was to defeat this new enemy as we had defeated the
old.

Apart from the military need, as I saw it, to neutralize
sanctuary protection given the enemy north of the Yalu,
I felt that military necessity in the conduct of the war
made necessary—

(1) The intensification of our economic blockade
against China.

(2) The imposition of a naval blockade against the
China coast.

(3) Removal of restrictions on air reconnaissance
of China's coastal areas and of Manchuria.

(4) Removal of restrictions on the forces of the Republic of China on Formosa, with logistical support to
contribute to their effective operations against the Chinese
mainland.

For entertaining these views, all professionally designed to support our forces committed to Korea and bring
hostilities to an end with the least possible delay and at
a saving of countless American and Allied lives, I have
been severely criticized in lay circles, principally abroad,
despite my understanding that from a military standpoint

the above views have been fully shared in the past by practically every military leader concerned with the Korean campaign, including our own Joint Chiefs of Staff.

I called for reinforcements, but was informed that reinforcements were not available. I made clear that if not permitted to destroy the enemy built-up bases north of the Yalu, if not permitted to utilize the friendly Chinese force of some 600,000 men on Formosa, if not permitted to blockade the China coast to prevent the Chinese Reds from getting succor from without, and if there were to be no hope of major reinforcements, the position of the command from the military standpoint forbade victory.

We could hold in Korea by constant maneuver and at an approximate area where our supply line advantages were in balance with the supply line disadvantages of the enemy, but we could hope at best for only an indecisive campaign with its terrible and constant attrition upon our forces if the enemy utilized his full military potential.

I have constantly called for the new political decisions essential to a solution.

Efforts have been made to distort my position. It has been said in effect that I was a warmonger. Nothing could be further from the truth.

I know war as few other men now living know it, and nothing to me is more revolting. I have long advocated its complete abolition, as its very destructiveness on both friend and foe has rendered it useless as a means of settling international disputes. . . .

But once [war] was forced upon us, there is no other alternative than to apply every available means to bring it to a swift end. War's very object is victory, not prolonged indecision.

In war there can be no substitute for victory.

There are some who for varying reasons would appease Red China. They are blind to history's clear lesson, for history teaches with unmistakable emphasis that appeasement but begets new and bloodier war. It points to no single instance where the end has justified that means, where appeasement has led to more than a sham peace.

Like blackmail, it lays the basis for new and successively greater demands until, as in blackmail, violence becomes the only other alternative. Why, my soldiers asked of me, surrender military advantages to an enemy in the field? I could not answer.

Some may say to avoid spread of the conflict into an all-out war with China. Others, to avoid Soviet intervention. Neither explanation seems valid, for China is already engaging with the maximum power it can commit, and the Soviet will not necessarily mesh its actions with our moves. Like a cobra, any new enemy will more likely strike whenever it feels that the relativity in military or other potential is in its favor on a world-wide basis.

The tragedy of Korea is further heightened by the fact that its military action is confined to its territorial limits. It condemns that nation, which it is our purpose to save, to suffer the devastating impact of full naval and air bombardment while the enemy's sanctuaries are fully protected from such attack and devastation.

Of the nations of the world, Korea alone, up to now, is the sole one which has risked its all against communism. The magnificence of the courage and fortitude of the Korean people defies description. They have chosen to risk death rather than slavery. Their last words to me were: "Don't scuttle the Pacific."

I have just left your fighting sons in Korea. They have met all tests there, and I can report to you without reservation that they are splendid in every way.

It was my constant effort to preserve them and end this savage conflict honorably and with the least loss of time and a minimum sacrifice of life. Its growing bloodshed has caused me the deepest anguish and anxiety. Those gallant men will remain often in my thoughts and in my prayers always.

DOCUMENT 14

DEAN ACHESON, TESTIMONY ON THE MILITARY SITUATION IN THE FAR EAST,
JUNE 1, 1951

In a statement to the Senate Committee on the Armed Services, excerpted here, Secretary Acheson articu-

> lately reviewed the case of the administration against
> the sort of aggressive policy in the Far East which
> MacArthur wanted.

I should like briefly to address myself to the alternative
course which was placed before this committee. This
course would seek to bring the conflict in Korea to an
end by enlarging the sphere of hostilities.

I will not try to review the military considerations
involved in this proposed course, since these have been
thoroughly discussed by the previous witnesses before
your committees.

It is enough to say that it is the judgment of the
President's military advisers that the proposed enlargement of our military action would not exercise a prompt
and decisive effect in bringing the hostilities to an end.
To this judgment there must be added a recognition of
the grave risks and other disadvantages of this alternative
course.

Against the dubious advantages of spreading the war
in an initially limited manner to the mainland of China,
there must be measured the risk of a general war with
China, the risk of Soviet intervention, and of world war
III, as well as the probable effects upon the solidarity of
the free world coalition.

The advocates of this program make two assumptions which require careful examination. They assume that
the Soviet Union will not necessarily respond to any action
on our part. They also assume that in the build-up of
strength relative to the Soviet Union and the Communist
sphere, time is not necessarily on our side.

As to Soviet reactions, no one can be sure he is fore-
casting accurately what they would be, but there are certain facts at hand that bear on this question.

We know of Soviet influence in North Korea, of
Soviet assistance to the North Koreans and to Communist
China, and we know that understandings must have accompanied this assistance. We also know that there is a
treaty between the Soviets and the Chinese Communists.

But even if the treaty did not exist, China is the
Soviet Union's largest and most important satellite. Rus-

sian self-interest in the Far East and the necessity of maintaining prestige in the Communist sphere make it difficult
to see how the Soviet Union could ignore a direct attack
upon the Chinese mainland.

I cannot accept the assumption that the Soviet Union
will go its way regardless of what we do. I do not think
that Russian policy is formed that way any more than our
own policy is formed that way. This view is certainly not
well enough grounded to justify a gamble with the essential
security of our Nation.

In response to the proposed course of action, there are
a number of courses of counteraction open to the Soviets.

They could turn over to the Chinese large numbers
of planes with "volunteer" crews for retaliatory action in
Korea and outside. They might participate with the Soviet Air Force and the submarine fleet.

The Kremlin could elect to parallel the action taken
by Peiping and intervene with a half-million or more
ground-force "volunteers"; or it could go the whole way
and launch an all-out war.

Singly, or in combination, these reactions contain
explosive possibilities, not only for the Far East, but
for the rest of the world as well.

We should also analyze the effect on our allies of our
taking steps to initiate the spread of war beyond Korea.
It would severely weaken their ties with us and in some instances it might sever them.

They are understandably reluctant to be drawn into
a general war in the Far East—one which holds the possibilities of becoming a world war—particularly if it developed out of an American impatience with the progress
of the effort to repel aggression, an effort which in their
belief offers an honorable and far less catastrophic solution.

If we followed the course proposed, we would be increasing our risks and commitments at the same time that
we diminished our strength by reducing the strength and
determination of our coalition.

We cannot expect that our collective-security system
will long survive if we take steps which unnecessarily and
dangerously expose the people who are in the system with

us. They would understandably hesitate to be tied to a partner who leads them to a highly dangerous short cut across a difficult crevasse.

In relation to the total world threat, our safety requires that we strengthen, not weaken, the bonds of our collective-security system.

The power of our coalition to deter an attack depends in part upon the will and the mutual confidence of our partners. If we, by the measures proposed, were to weaken that effect, particularly in the North Atlantic area, we would be jeopardizing the security of an area which is vital to our own national security.

What this adds up to, it seems to me, is that we are being asked to undertake a large risk of general war with China, risk of war with the Soviet Union, and a demonstrable weakening of our collective-security system—all this in return for what?

In return for measures whose effectiveness in bringing the conflict to an early conclusion are judged doubtful by our responsible military authorities.

DOCUMENT 15

JOHN FOSTER DULLES, TESTIMONY ON THE POLICY OF LIBERATION,
JANUARY 15, 1953

Appearing before the Senate Committee on Foreign Relations, John Foster Dulles, Eisenhower's designated Secretary of State, here attempted to clarify for Senator Alexander Wiley of Wisconsin what was meant by the much talked about policy of "liberation."

THE CHAIRMAN [Sen. Wiley]. I am particularly interested in something I read recently, to the effect that you stated you were not in favor of the policy of containment. I think you advocated a more dynamic or positive policy.

Can you tell us more specifically what you have in mind? This, of course, is subject always to your own objections, if you think the question goes beyond a matter of qualifications.

MR. DULLES. There are a number of policy matters which I would prefer to discuss with the committee in executive session, but I have no objection to saying in open session what I have said before: namely, that we shall never have a secure peace or a happy world so long as Soviet communism dominates one-third of all the peoples that there are, and is in the process of trying at least to extend its rule to many others. . . .

Therefore, we must always have in mind the liberation of these captive peoples. Now, liberation does not mean a war of liberation. Liberation can be accomplished by processes short of war. We have, as one example, not an ideal example, but it illustrates my point, the defection of Yugoslavia, under Tito from the domination of Soviet communism.

Well, that rule of Tito is not one which we admire, and it has many aspects of despotism, itself; but at least it illustrates that it is possible to disintegrate this present monolithic structure. . . .

The present tie between China and Moscow is an unholy arrangement which is contrary to the traditions, the hopes, the aspirations of the Chinese people. Certainly we cannot tolerate a continuance of that, or a welding of the 450 million people of China into the servile instrument of Soviet aggression.

Therefore, a policy which only aims at containing Russia where it now is, is, in itself, an unsound policy; but it is a policy which is bound to fail because a purely defensive policy never wins against an aggressive policy. If our only policy is to stay where we are, we will be driven back. It is only by keeping alive the hope of liberation, by taking advantage of that wherever opportunity arises, that we will end this terrible peril which dominates the world. . . . But all of this can be done and must be done in ways which will not provoke a general war, or in ways which will not provoke an insurrection which would be crushed with bloody violence. . . .

DOCUMENT 16

LEWIS MUMFORD, LETTER ON AMERICAN FOREIGN POLICY,
MARCH 28, 1954

Lewis Mumford, a provocative writer on American architecture and city planning, and a historian of American and European civilization, expressed in this letter to the editor of the New York Times *views which many troubled Americans shared.*

The power of the hydrogen bomb has, it is plain, given pause even to the leaders of our Government. Their very hesitation to give away the facts in itself gives away the facts. Under what mandate, then, do they continue to hold as secret the results we may expect from the use of weapons of extermination—not merely on our own cities and people but on all living organisms; not merely on our present lives but on the lives of countless generations to come?

Are our leaders afraid that when the truth is known our devotion to the perfection of scientific weapons of total destruction and extermination will turn out to be a profoundly irrational one: repulsive to morality, dangerous to national security, inimical to life?

Do they suspect that the American people are still sane enough to halt the blind automatism that continues, in the face of Soviet Russia's equal scientific powers, to produce these fatal weapons?

Do they fear that their fellow-countrymen may well doubt the usefulness of instruments which, under the guise of deterring an aggressor or insuring a cheap victory, might incidentally destroy the whole fabric of civilization and threaten the very existence of the human race?

Our secret weapons of extermination have been produced under conditions that have favored irresponsible censorship and short-sighted political and military judgments. Under the protection of secrecy a succession of fatal errors has been made, primarily as the result (since 1942) of our accepting total extermination as a method of warfare. These errors have been compounded by our counting upon such dehumanized methods to preserve peace and security.

In turn, our very need for secrecy in an abortive effort to monopolize technical and scientific knowledge, has produced pathological symptoms in the whole body politic: fear, suspicion, non-cooperation, hostility to critical judgment, above all delusions of power based on fantasies of unlimited extermination, as the only possible answer to the political threat of Soviet Russia. But demoralized men cannot be counted upon to control such automatic instruments of demoralization.

At a fatal moment our self-induced fears may produce the incalculable and irretrievable holocaust our own weapons have given us reason to dread. Only courage and intelligence of the highest order, backed by open discussion, will give us the strength to turn back from the suicidal path we have blindly followed since 1942.

Are there not enough Americans still possessed of their sanity to call a stop to these irrational decisions, which are automatically bringing us close to a total catastrophe?

There are many alternative courses to the policy to which we have committed ourselves, practically without debate. The worst of all these alternatives, submission to Communist totalitarianism, would still be far wiser than the final destruction of civilization.

As for the best of these alternatives, a policy of working firmly toward justice and cooperation, and free intercourse with all other peoples, in the faith that love begets love as surely as hatred begets hatred—would, in all probability, be the one instrument capable of piercing the strong political armor of our present enemies.

Once the facts of our policy of total extermination are publicly canvassed, and the final outcome, mass suicide, is faced, I believe that the American people are still sane enough to come to a wiser decision than our Government has yet made. They will realize that retaliation is not protection; that total extermination of both sides is not victory; that a constant state of morbid fear, suspicion and hatred is not security; that, in short, what seems like unlimited power has become impotence.

In the name of sanity let our Government now pause and seek the counsel of sane men: men who have not participated in the errors we have made and are not committed, out of pride, to defending them. Let us cease all further experiments with even more horrifying weapons of destruction, lest our own self-induced fears further upset our mental balance.

Let us all, as responsible citizens, not the cowed subjects of an all-wise state, weigh the alternatives and canvass new lines of approach to the problems of power and peace.

Let us deal with our own massive sins and errors as a step toward establishing firm relations of confidence with the rest of mankind. And let us, first of all, have the courage to speak up on behalf of humanity, on behalf of civilization, on behalf of life itself against the methodology of barbarism to which we are now committed.

If as a nation we have become mad it is time for the world to take note of that madness. If we are still humane and sane, then it is time for the powerful voice of sanity to be heard once more in our land.

DOCUMENT 17

DWIGHT D. EISENHOWER, REMARKS ON PEACEFUL CO-EXISTENCE,
JUNE 30, 1954

*This passage, from the transcript of a press confer-
ence, reports Eisenhower's endorsement of the idea
of "peaceful co-existence," short of appeasement.*

Question: Mr. President . . . What are the possibilities for peaceful co-existence between Soviet Russia and Communist China, on the one hand, and the non-communist nations on the other?

Eisenhower: Well, of course, that almost called for

a very long explanation, and he would try to limit his comments to a very few.

For a long, long time, everybody in the United States had urged that we attempt to reach a proper basis for peaceful co-existence.

We had found, though, an aggressive attitude on the part of the other side that had made such an accomplishment or consummation not easy to reach. In other words, there had to be good faith on both sides.

Moreover, we had to make certain that peaceful co-existence did not mean appeasement in the sense that we were willing to see any nation in the world, against its will, subordinated to an outside nation. . . .

So that he would say that within the limits he had just so briefly alluded to, why, he said the hope of the world would be that kind of an existence, because, certainly, we didn't expect to be eliminated, and certainly, he thought, it would be silly to say you could eliminate the other instantly. We have got to find ways of living together.

* PART VIII *

A Time of Troubles: The 1960's

INTRODUCTION

THE United States of the 1960's had to endure a double paradox: it had enormous affluence that could not be put to work to solve pressing social problems; and it had enormous power that could not be successfully brought to bear in its foreign policies.

Certainly this decade showed remarkable economic growth and general prosperity. Guided by the "new economics" derived from the theories of John Maynard Keynes, government and tax policies were skillfully used to sustain national economic growth. President John F. Kennedy, who had a keen understanding of the new economic principles, argued in 1962 that the technical problems of managing the economy had superseded old illusions and the clash of simple outworn ideologies (Document 3). The "new economics" was employed to good effect; and in 1969, when President Lyndon B. Johnson was about to leave office, he proudly recorded the success of the two Democratic administrations in maintaining the long economic boom of the decade (Document 20).

But while prosperity brought considerable affluence, pockets of acute poverty persisted and many social problems grew more acute—ghetto unemployment, the pollution of air and water, the rise of crime, ugly urban sprawl and overcrowding, the congestion of the cities, inferior education, the waste of natural and human resources (Documents 10, 11, 18). Among the major tasks of the future, it became clear, would be to reduce the substantial poverty that remained—there were about 35 million poor —and to arrest the deterioration in the quality of American life. The political stalemate that existed during Kennedy's Administration made a national attack on these problems exceedingly difficult, but after his assassination President Johnson launched such an attack with the call for a war on poverty (Document 10). He urged all Americans to join in efforts to create a Great Society (Document 11) which would address itself to improving the life of every citizen.

Many self-styled conservatives were profoundly skeptical of this undertaking, and Senator Barry Goldwater, campaigning against Johnson in 1964, argued that the developing welfare state was a threat to the liberty and moral fiber of the American people (Document 12). Indeed, he saw the dependency induced by the welfare state, rising crime and declining prestige, as symptoms of a loss of will, hardihood, and enterprise. However, his overwhelming defeat in the election of 1964 seemed to promise that the Johnson program would be vigorously carried on, and soon the strong Democratic Congress brought in by this election passed a large number of Johnson's Great Society measures—medicare, expanded federal aid to education, aid to poverty-stricken regions, an extension of the minimum-wage act, and a general anti-poverty program.

Troublesome questions continued to arise: In the light of its costly overseas commitments and aspirations, could the United States mobilize the resources and the political energy to attack successfully its domestic problems? Could urban America, shackled by political institutions inherited from an earlier agrarian age, find adequate ways to govern and improve itself? Most important: could progress in mitigating racial injustice be made at a sufficiently rapid pace? On this front, long forward steps seemed to be in the making in the summer of 1963 when a huge, peaceful bi-racial crowd of demonstrators gathered after a great March on Washington to listen to Martin Luther King's eloquent "I Have a Dream" speech (Document 13), which seemed to express the best aspirations of both whites and blacks, and again in 1965 when President Johnson, reacting to the events of "Bloody Sunday" in Selma, Alabama, made a powerful appeal for the voting rights of black people (Document 14), which led to the voting rights law of that year. However, the movement for civil rights and desegregation seemed to stall in the middle 1960's. Stung by the nation's failure to make rapid improvements in the condition of the black masses in the ghettos, an articulate and influential minority of black leaders began to spurn Martin Luther King's non-violence for still more militant modes of protest and to call for black power (Document 17). They rejected racial integration in favor of separation, independent political and economic action, and the search for black pride and black identity. Race riots in many cities in the summers of 1965, 1966, and 1967 heightened the sense of tension over national failure to heal this painful historic wound (Document 19). The disillusionment of blacks with the path of non-violence was both underlined and heightened by the horrifying murder of Martin Luther King in the spring of 1968; and the loss of the nation's most widely respected militant Negro leader was followed soon after by the assassination of Robert F. Kennedy, one of the nation's white politicians who had shown most concern for the condition of black Americans (Document 18).

Nonetheless, Negroes were making some economic gains and were beginning to win, and in increasing numbers to exercise, their civil rights, notably the right to vote. An equally consequential change in the character of American democracy seemed likely to result from a series of sweeping Supreme Court decisions in 1962 and 1964, the famous reapportionment decisions. The apportionment of both state legislatures and congressional districts, always heavily favoring rural and small-town voters against those of the cities, had filled legislative halls with small-town politicians averse to tackling the problems of the great metropolitan areas. In 1962, in the case of *Baker* v. *Carr* (Document 7), the Supreme Court, casting aside its own traditions, decided to intervene in the matter of legislative apportionment, ruling that citizens were deprived of the protection of their equal rights under the Fourteenth

Amendment by the unequal apportionment of districts in American legislatures. In a later decision (Document 8) it gave instructions to legislatures controlling the terms of reapportionment, and in another applied the "one man one vote" principle to Congressional districts as well. Both on and off the Court there was, of course, resistance to this sweeping change (Document 9). Critics argued both that the Court had stepped out of its purely judicial role to interfere in the political process and also that the fundamental difficulties of democratic representation were not really solved by the Court's formulae. Still, unless impaired by later cases or displaced by a constitutional amendment, the Court's decisions laid the groundwork for a drastic change in the representative basis of American legislatures, and promised to upgrade sharply the power of urban voters. The full impact of these decisions would not be felt until after the census of 1970, when further reapportionments would be made to reflect the current distribution of population.

In the 1960's even more decisively than in the 1950's, the United States was plagued by an unsuccessful foreign policy. Many Americans, still thinking in cold war terms, felt it necessary to maintain American influence both in Europe and in Asia, and to combat the spread of Communism in poverty-stricken Latin America and Asia. Also, since World War II and the Korean War, the influence of the military had grown enormously in the United States, and many people questioned how the nation could go on maintaining its many military commitments and its defense contracts and still keep its civilian character. On leaving office Dwight D. Eisenhower had warned against the dangers of a military-industrial complex (Document 1). John F. Kennedy in his Inaugural Address promised a vigorous pursuit of peace but also resolute world-wide opposition to Communism (Document 2). Could these two goals be successfully combined? Opposing what Americans defined as Communism often meant opposing the much more formidable force of nationalist revolutions in undeveloped or newly liberated countries. Kennedy's unsuccessful effort to help anti-Castro Cuban exiles in the Bay of Pigs episode (1961) underlined the difficulty of effective action against the leading revolutionary influence in Latin America.

But the greatest single challenge to Kennedy, and the greatest threat to the peace of the world, came in the terrifying showdown of October 1962 over the emplacement of Soviet missiles in Cuba (Documents 4 and 5), a crisis which brought the entire world to the brink of destruction. Yet the dangers of the Cuban crisis, once passed, were followed in less than a year by the promising Test Ban Treaty of 1963 (Document 6), in which the participating powers agreed to discontinue atmospheric nuclear testing. From this point onward tensions eased considerably, and evidence of internal disunion in the Soviets' empire in Eastern Europe persuaded many informed Americans that the situation that had produced the 1945-1962 cold war in Europe was changing markedly. Americans no longer believed that they were pitted against a unified world Communist force.

As relations with the Soviet Union improved, it was primarily the threat of Red China that began to trouble both the Soviets and the Americans. In large part because of the supposed dangers from Chinese expansion in Asia, and a fear of the general collapse of Western influence there, the United States became caught in the morass of an unmanageable commitment to South Vietnam which President Johnson continued to defend (Document 15). The war in Vietnam provoked the most intense debate of the decade, a debate that threatened to consume the entire body politic in acrimony. Radical critics considered it evidence of ruthless American imperialism. More conservative critics like Senator J. William Fulbright (Document 16) argued that the war, far from being necessary to American security, was a hazard to it, that it inflicted severe losses upon our reputation and safety abroad and upon our ability to cope with our problems at home. The war, Fulbright argued, betokened a dangerously arrogant and uncomprehending state of mind. More than any other issue, the failure of President Johnson's policy of escalation in Vietnam led to a sharp decline in his popularity; and in the spring of 1968, after he had been challenged first by Senator Eugene McCarthy and then by Senator Robert F. Kennedy, he announced his intention not to run for another term. Most American leaders had by now concluded that the United States must accept a negotiated peace rather than expect a military victory in Vietnam, and must be content to salvage what it could from the disaster. In the presidential election of 1968, both major-party candidates, taking their cue from Johnson's downfall, edged away from extravagant commitments to continuation of the war. Richard M. Nixon's Inaugural Address (Document 21) emphasized the importance of the search for peace not only with foreign powers but among divided Americans at home.

DOCUMENT 1

DWIGHT D. EISENHOWER, FAREWELL ADDRESS TO THE AMERICAN PEOPLE, JANUARY 17, 1961

A few days before his departure from office, Eisenhower delivered this radio and television address which attracted unusual attention because of his warning against the dangers of "the military-industrial complex." In the drafting Eisenhower was assisted by Presidential aide Malcolm Moos.

Throughout America's adventure in free government, our basic purposes have been to keep the peace; to foster progress in human achievement, and to enhance liberty, dignity and integrity among people and among nations. To strive for less would be unworthy of a free and religious people. Any failure traceable to arrogance, or our lack of comprehension or readiness to sacrifice would inflict upon us grievous hurt both at home and abroad.

Progress toward these noble goals is persistently threatened by the conflict now engulfing the world. . . .

A vital element in keeping the peace is our military establishment. Our arms must be mighty, ready for instant action, so that no potential aggressor may be tempted to risk his own destruction.

Our military organization today bears little relation to that known by any of my predecessors in peacetime, or indeed by the fighting men of World War II or Korea.

Until the latest of our world conflicts, the United

States had no armaments industry. American makers of plowshares could, with time and as required, make swords as well. But now we can no longer risk emergency improvisation of national defense; we have been compelled to create a permanent armaments industry of vast proportions. Added to this, three and a half million men and women are directly engaged in the defense establishment. We annually spend on military security more than the net income of all United States corporations.

This conjunction of an immense military establishment and a large arms industry is new in the American experience. The total influence—economic, political, even spiritual—is felt in every city, every State house, every office of the Federal government. We recognize the imperative need for the development. Yet we must not fail to comprehend its grave implications. Our toil, resources and livelihood are all involved; so is the very structure of our society.

In the councils of government, we must guard against the acquisition of unwarranted influence, whether sought or unsought, by the military-industrial complex. The potential for the disastrous rise of misplaced power exists and will persist.

We must never let the weight of this combination endanger our liberties or democratic processes. We should take nothing for granted. Only an alert and knowledgeable citizenry can compel the proper meshing of the huge industrial and military machinery of defense with our peaceful methods and goals, so that security and liberty may prosper together.

Akin to, and largely responsible for the sweeping changes in our industrial-military posture, has been the technological revolution during recent decades. In this revolution, research has become central; it also becomes more formalized, complex, and costly. A steadily increasing share is conducted for, by, or at the direction of, the Federal government.

Today, the solitary inventor, tinkering in his shop, has been overshadowed by task forces of scientists in laboratories and testing fields. In the same fashion, the free university, historically the fountainhead of free ideas and scientific discovery, has experienced a revolution in the conduct of research. Partly because of the huge costs involved, a government contract becomes virtually a substitute for intellectual curiosity. For every old blackboard there are now hundreds of new electronic computers.

The prospect of domination of the nation's scholars by Federal employment, project allocations, and the power of money is ever present—and is gravely to be regarded. Yet, in holding scientific research and discovery in respect, as we should, we must also be alert to the equal and opposite danger that public policy could itself become the captive of a scientific-technological elite.

It is the task of statesmanship to mold, to balance, and to integrate these and other forces, new and old, within the principles of our democratic system—ever aiming toward the supreme goals of our free society.

DOCUMENT 2

JOHN F. KENNEDY, INAUGURAL ADDRESS,
JANUARY 20, 1961

Kennedy spent his mornings during the week before his inauguration writing his address. His main assistant was Theodore C. Sorensen, though suggestions poured in from other advisers. It was the veteran journalist Walter Lippmann who suggested that the Soviet Union be described not as the "enemy" but as an "adversary," a term Kennedy continued to use. The famous "ask not" sentence had been hinted at in Kennedy's campaign speeches, but his concern with the idea may date from as early as 1945, when he made note of a quotation from Rousseau: "As soon as any man says of the affairs of state, What does it matter to me? the state may be given up as lost." The most extended account of the drafting of this address is in Theodore C. Sorensen, Kennedy (1965). But see also Arthur M. Schlesinger, Jr., A Thousand Days (1965).

We observe today not a victory of party but a celebration of freedom—symbolizing an end as well as a beginning—

signifying renewal as well as change. For I have sworn before you and Almighty God the same solemn oath our forebears prescribed nearly a century and three quarters ago.

The world is very different now. For man holds in his mortal hands the power to abolish all forms of human poverty and all forms of human life. And yet the same revolutionary beliefs for which our forebears fought are still at issue around the globe—the belief that the rights of man come not from the generosity of the state but from the hand of God.

We dare not forget today that we are the heirs of that first revolution. Let the word go forth from this time and place, to friend and foe alike, that the torch has been passed to a new generation of Americans—born in this century, tempered by war, disciplined by a hard and bitter peace, proud of our ancient heritage—and unwilling to witness or permit the slow undoing of those human rights to which this nation has always been committed, and to which we are committed today at home and around the world.

Let every nation know, whether it wishes us well or ill, that we shall pay any price, bear any burden, meet any hardship, support any friend, oppose any foe to assure the survival and the success of liberty.

This much we pledge—and more.

To those old allies whose cultural and spiritual origins we share, we pledge the loyalty of faithful friends. United, there is little we cannot do in a host of cooperative ventures. Divided, there is little we can do—for we dare not meet a powerful challenge at odds and split asunder.

To those new states whom we welcome to the ranks of the free, we pledge our word that one form of colonial control shall not have passed away merely to be replaced by a far more iron tyranny. We shall not always expect to find them supporting our view. But we shall always hope to find them strongly supporting their own freedom—and to remember that, in the past, those who foolishly sought power by riding the back of the tiger ended up inside.

To those peoples in the huts and villages of half the globe struggling to break the bonds of mass misery, we pledge our best efforts to help them help themselves, for whatever period is required—not because the communists may be doing it, not because we seek their votes, but because it is right. If a free society cannot help the many who are poor, it cannot save the few who are rich.

To our sister republics south of our border, we offer a special pledge—to convert our good words into good deeds—in a new alliance for progress—to assist free men and free governments in casting off the chains of poverty. But this peaceful revolution of hope cannot become the prey of hostile powers. Let all our neighbors know that we shall join with them to oppose aggression or subversion anywhere in the Americas. And let every other power know that this Hemisphere intends to remain the master of its own house.

To that world assembly of sovereign states, the United Nations, our last best hope in an age where the instruments of war have far outpaced the instruments of peace, we renew our pledge of support—to prevent it from becoming merely a forum for invective—to strengthen its shield of the new and the weak—and to enlarge the area in which its writ may run.

Finally, to those nations who would make themselves our adversary, we offer not a pledge but a request: that both sides begin anew the quest for peace, before the dark powers of destruction unleashed by science engulf all humanity in planned or accidental self-destruction.

We dare not tempt them with weakness. For only when our arms are sufficient beyond doubt can we be certain beyond doubt that they will never be employed.

But neither can two great and powerful groups of nations take comfort from our present course—both sides overburdened by the cost of modern weapons, both rightly alarmed by the steady spread of the deadly atom, yet both racing to alter that uncertain balance of terror that stays the hand of mankind's final war.

So let us begin anew—remembering on both sides that civility is not a sign of weakness, and sincerity is always subject to proof. Let us never negotiate out of fear. But let us never fear to negotiate.

Let both sides explore what problems unite us instead of belaboring those problems which divide us.

Let both sides, for the first time, formulate serious and precise proposals for the inspection and control of arms—and bring the absolute power to destroy other nations under the absolute control of all nations.

Let both sides seek to invoke the wonders of science instead of its terrors. Together let us explore the stars, conquer the deserts, eradicate disease, tap the ocean depths and encourage the arts and commerce.

Let both sides unite to heed in all corners of the earth the command of Isaiah—to "undo the heavy burdens . . . (and) let the oppressed go free."

And if a beach-head of cooperation may push back the jungle of suspicion, let both sides join in creating a new endeavor, not a new balance of power, but a new world of law, where the strong are just and the weak secure and the peace preserved.

All this will not be finished in the first one hundred days. Nor will it be finished in the first one thousand days, nor in the life of this Administration, nor even perhaps in our lifetime on this planet. But let us begin.

In your hands, my fellow citizens, more than mine, will rest the final success or failure of our course. Since this country was founded, each generation of Americans has been summoned to give testimony to its national loyalty. The graves of young Americans who answered the call to service surround the globe.

Now the trumpet summons us again—not as a call to bear arms, though arms we need—not as a call to battle, though embattled we are—but a call to bear the burden of a long twilight struggle, year in and year out, "rejoicing in hope, patient in tribulation"—a struggle against the common enemies of man: tyranny, poverty, disease and war itself.

Can we forge against these enemies a grand and global alliance, North and South, East and West, that can assure a more fruitful life for all mankind? Will you join in that historic effort?

In the long history of the world, only a few generations have been granted the role of defending freedom in its hour of maximum danger. I do not shrink from this responsibility—I welcome it. I do not believe that any of us would exchange places with any other people or any other generation. The energy, the faith, the devotion which we bring to this endeavor will light our country and all who serve it—and the glow from that fire can truly light the world.

And so, my fellow Americans: ask not what your country can do for you—ask what you can do for your country.

My fellow citizens of the world: ask not what America will do for you, but what together we can do for the freedom of man.

Finally, whether you are citizens of America or citizens of the world, ask of us here the same high standards of strength and sacrifice which we ask of you. With a good conscience our only sure reward, with history the final judge of our deeds, let us go forth to lead the land we love, asking His blessing and His help, but knowing that here on earth God's work must truly be our own.

DOCUMENT 3

JOHN F. KENNEDY, COMMENCEMENT ADDRESS AT YALE UNIVERSITY, JUNE 11, 1962

Kennedy became convinced of the difficulty of explaining complex economic policies to the public and to businessmen. Modern economic policy, he saw, was determined less by ideology and more by technical detail. In this address, notable as the first full and clear espousal of the "new economics" by a president, he gave voice to these views. A first draft was prepared by Arthur M. Schlesinger, Jr., and John Kenneth Galbraith. They were later helped by Theodore Sorensen, and McGeorge Bundy, and in the final draft Kennedy made his own changes.

As every past generation has had to disenthrall itself from an inheritance of truisms and stereotypes, so in our own time we must move on from the reassuring repetition of stale phrases to a new, difficult, but essential confrontation with reality.

For the great enemy of the truth is very often not the lie—deliberate, contrived, and dishonest—but the myth—persistent, persuasive, and unrealistic. Too often we hold fast to the cliches of our forebears. We subject all facts to a prefabricated set of interpretations. We enjoy the comfort of opinion without the discomfort of thought.

Mythology distracts us everywhere—in government as in business, in politics as in economics, in foreign affairs as in domestic affairs. But today I want to particularly consider the myth and reality in our national economy.

There are three great areas of our domestic affairs in which, today, there is a danger that illusion may prevent effective action. They are, first, the question of the size and the shape of government's responsibilities; second, the question of public fiscal policy; and third, the matter of confidence, business confidence or public confidence, or simply confidence in America. I want to talk about all three, and I want to talk about them carefully and dispassionately. . . .

Let us take first the question of the size and shape of government. The myth here is that government is big, and bad—and steadily getting bigger and worse. Obviously this myth has some excuse for existence. It is true that in recent history each new administration has spent much more money than its predecessor. . . .

But does it follow from this that big government is growing relatively bigger? It does not—for the fact is for the last 15 years, the Federal Government—and also the Federal debt—and also the Federal bureaucracy—have grown less rapidly than the economy as a whole. If we leave defense and space expenditures aside, the Federal Government since the Second World War has expanded less than any other major sector of our national life—less than industry, less than commerce, less than agriculture, less than higher education, and very much less than the noise about big government.

The truth about big government is the truth about any other great activity—it is complex. Certainly it is true that size brings dangers—but it is also true that size can bring benefits. . . . Few people realize that in 1961, in support of all university research in science and medicine, three dollars out of every four came from the Federal Government. I need hardly point out that this has taken place without undue enlargement of Government control—that American scientists remain second to none in their independence and in their individualism. . . .

Let me say a word about deficits. The myth persists that Federal deficits create inflation and budget surpluses prevent it. Yet sizeable budget surpluses after the war did not prevent inflation, and persistent deficits for the last several years have not upset our basic price stability. Obviously deficits are sometimes dangerous—and so are surpluses. But honest assessment plainly requires a more sophisticated view than the old and automatic cliche that deficits automatically bring inflation.

There are myths also about our public debt. It is widely supposed that this debt is growing at a dangerously rapid rate. In fact, both the debt per person and the debt as a proportion of our gross national product have declined sharply since the Second World War. In absolute terms the national debt since the end of World War II has increased only 8 percent, while private debt was increasing 305 percent, and the debts of State and local government—on whom people frequently suggest we should place additional burdens—the debts of State and local governments have increased 378 percent. Moreover, debts, public and private, are neither good nor bad, in and of themselves. Borrowing can lead to over-extension and collapse—but it can also lead to expansion and strength. There is no single, simple slogan in this field that we can trust.

Finally, I come to the problem of confidence. Confidence is a matter of myth and also a matter of truth—and this time let me take the truth of the matter first.

It is true—and of high importance—that the prosperity of this country depends on the assurance that all major elements within it will live up to their responsibilities. . . . This is the true issue of confidence.

But there is also the false issue—and its simplest form is the assertion that any and all unfavorable turns of the speculative wheel—however temporary and however plainly speculative in character—are the result of, and I quote, "a lack of confidence in the national administration." This I must tell you, while comforting, is not wholly true. Worse, it obscures the reality—which is also simple. The solid ground of mutual confidence is the necessary partnership of government with all of the sectors of our society in the steady quest for economic progress.

Corporate plans are not based on a political confidence in party leaders but on an economic confidence in the Nation's ability to invest and produce and consume. . . .

The stereotypes I have been discussing distract our attention and divide our effort. These stereotypes do our Nation a disservice, not just because they are exhausted and irrelevant, but above all because they are misleading— because they stand in the way of the solution of hard and complicated facts. . . .

The real issues of our time are rarely . . . dramatic. . . . The differences today are usually matters of degree. And we cannot understand and attack our contemporary problems in 1962 if we are bound by traditional labels and wornout slogans of an earlier era. But the unfortunate fact of the matter is that our rhetoric has not kept pace with the speed of social and economic change. Our political debates, our public discourse—on current domestic and economic issues—too often bear little or no relation to the actual problems the United States faces.

What is at stake in our economic decisions today is not some grand warfare of rival ideologies which will sweep the country with passion but the practical management of a modern economy. What we need is not labels and cliches but more basic discussion of the sophisticated and technical questions involved in keeping a great economic machinery moving ahead.

DOCUMENT 4

JOHN F. KENNEDY, REPORT TO THE AMERICAN PEOPLE ON SOVIET MISSILES IN CUBA,

OCTOBER 22, 1962

On October 15, 1962, American photoanalysts spotted on aerial reconaissance photos of Cuba some emplacements for ballistic missiles that had been supplied by the Soviet Union. On the following day the character of the weapons was confirmed. For several days Kennedy secretly studied the evidence with his aides and pondered what response to make. It was considered necessary to have a strategy worked out before reporting the missiles to the public. Several alternatives were carefully considered, ranging all the way from doing nothing to invading Cuba and knocking out the missile sites. Finally, it was decided to impose a blockade of Soviet and other military shipments to Cuba—though to soften the effects the word "quarantine" was used instead. The report of that decision, whose essentials are excerpted here, was then given to the public. The first draft was written by Theodore Sorensen, who significantly referred for background to the speeches of Woodrow Wilson and Franklin D. Roosevelt declaring war in 1917 and 1941. After several drafts, the text was subjected to a close review by the National Security Council, during which Kennedy made many changes and eliminated any suspicion that he intended to try to remove Castro. For the most complete account of the drafting see Sorensen, Kennedy (1965).

This Government, as promised, has maintained the closest surveillance of the Soviet military buildup on the island of Cuba. Within the past week, unmistakable evidence has established the fact that a series of offensive missile sites is now in preparation on that imprisoned island. The purpose of these bases can be none other than to provide a nuclear strike capability against the Western Hemisphere. . . .

This secret, swift, and extraordinary buildup of Communist missiles—in an area well known to have a special and historical relationship to the United States and the nations of the Western Hemisphere, in violation of Soviet assurances, and in defiance of American and hemispheric policy—this sudden, clandestine decision to station strategic weapons for the first time outside of Soviet soil—is a deliberately provocative and unjustified change in the status quo which cannot be accepted by this country, if our courage and our commitments are ever to be trusted again by either friend or foe.

The 1930's taught us a clear lesson: aggressive conduct, if allowed to go unchecked and unchallenged, ultimately leads to war. This nation is opposed to war. We are also true to our word. Our unswerving objective, therefore, must be to prevent the use of these missiles against this or any other country, and to secure their withdrawal or elimination from the Western Hemisphere. . . .

Acting, therefore, in the defense of our own security and of the entire Western Hemisphere, and under the authority entrusted to me by the Constitution as endorsed by the resolution of the Congress, I have directed that the following *initial* steps be taken immediately:

First: To halt this offensive buildup, a strict quarantine on all offensive military equipment under shipment to Cuba is being initiated. All ships of any kind bound for Cuba from whatever nation or port will, if found to contain cargoes of offensive weapons, be turned back. This quarantine will be extended, if needed, to other types of cargo and carriers. We are not at this time, however, denying the necessities of life as the Soviets attempted to do in their Berlin blockade of 1948.

Second: I have directed the continued and increased close surveillance of Cuba and its military buildup. The foreign ministers of the OAS, in their communique of October 6, rejected secrecy on such matters in this hemisphere. Should these offensive military preparations continue, thus increasing the threat to the hemisphere, further action will be justified. I have directed the Armed Forces to prepare for any eventualities; and I trust that in the interest of both the Cuban people and the Soviet technicians at the sites, the hazards to all concerned of continuing this threat will be recognized.

Third: It shall be the policy of this Nation to regard any nuclear missile launched from Cuba against any nation in the Western Hemisphere as an attack by the Soviet Union on the United States, requiring a full retaliatory response upon the Soviet Union.

Fourth: As a necessary military precaution, I have reinforced our base at Guantanamo, evacuated today the dependents of our personnel there, and ordered additional military units to be on a standby alert basis.

Fifth: We are calling tonight for an immediate meeting of the Organ of Consultation under the Organization of American States, to consider this threat to hemispheric security. . . . Our other allies around the world have also been alerted.

Sixth: Under the Charter of the United Nations, we are asking tonight that an emergency meeting of the Security Council be convoked without delay to take action against this latest Soviet threat to world peace. Our resolution will call for the prompt dismantling and withdrawal of all offensive weapons in Cuba, under the supervision of U.N. observers, before the quarantine can be lifted.

Seventh and finally: I call upon Chairman Khrushchev to halt and eliminate this clandestine, reckless, and provocative threat to world peace and to stable relations between our two nations. I call upon him further to abandon this course of world domination, and to join in an historic effort to end the perilous arms race and to transform the history of man. He has an opportunity now to move the world back from the abyss of destruction—by returning to his government's own words that it had no need to station missiles outside its own territory, and withdrawing these weapons from Cuba—by refraining from any action which will widen or deepen the present crisis—and then by participating in a search for peaceful and permanent solutions.

DOCUMENT 5

KENNEDY AND KHRUSHCHEV LETTERS DURING THE CUBAN MISSILES CRISIS, OCTOBER 27 AND 28, 1962

The decision to "quarantine" Cuba brought to a climax the terrifying confrontation between the two great nuclear powers, since Soviet ships were already en route to Havana. On October 26 Kennedy received a secret letter from Khrushchev which showed the Soviet leader's alarm over the crisis his own actions had precipitated, spoke of the horrors of war, and asked for an assurance that the United States would not invade Cuba. The message, though not offering to remove the missiles, gave the Administration reason for hope. But it was quickly followed by a second letter of October 27, which demanded the dismantling of American bases in Turkey in return for the removal of Russian weapons from Cuba. Kennedy had already concluded that the Turkish bases were of little military value to the United States, but he feared the consequences of yielding them under these circumstances. After much discussion, Attorney General Robert F. Kennedy suggested that Khrushchev's second letter be ignored and that the President respond only to the more promising one of October 26. With Theodore Sorensen, the President's brother prepared a first draft of Kennedy's response of October 27, which ignored the demands on the Turkish bases but did offer a pledge against a future invasion of Cuba. To the world's immense relief, Khrushchev seized the opening offered him and replied on October 28 that the missile bases would be dismantled. On the same day Kennedy issued a statement describing Khrushchev's action as a contribution to the cause of peace and sent him a letter indicating that the crisis could now be resolved and that the two nations should resume the search for peace, particularly for a nuclear test ban agreement. The texts of the letters exchanged between Khrushchev and Kennedy on October 27 and 28 are excerpted below.

A. KHRUSHCHEV TO KENNEDY, OCTOBER 27, 1962

You are worried over Cuba. You say that it worries you because it lies at a distance of 90 miles across the sea from the shores of the United States. However, Turkey lies next to us. Our sentinels are pacing up and down and watching each other. Do you believe that you have the right to demand security for your country, and the removal of such weapons that you qualify as offensive, while not recognizing this right for us?

You have stationed devastating rocket weapons, which you call offensive, in Turkey, literally right next to us. How then does recognition of our equal military possibilities tally with such unequal relations between our great states? This does not tally at all. . . .

This is why I make this proposal: we agree to remove those weapons from Cuba which you regard as offensive weapons. We agree to do this and to state this commitment in the United Nations. Your representatives will make a statement to the effect that the United States, on its part, bearing in mind the anxiety and concern of the Soviet state, will evacuate its analogous weapons from Turkey. Let us reach an understanding on what time you and we need to put this into effect.

After this, representatives of the U.N. Security Council could control on-the-spot the fulfillment of these commitments. . . .

B. KENNEDY TO KHRUSHCHEV, OCTOBER 27, 1962

I have read your letter of October 26th with great care and welcomed the statement of your desire to seek a prompt solution to the problem. The first thing that needs to be done, however, is for work to cease on offensive missile bases in Cuba and for all weapons systems in Cuba capable of offensive use to be rendered inoperable, under effective United Nations arrangements.

Assuming this is done promptly, I have given my representatives in New York instructions that will permit them to work out this week end—in cooperation with the Acting Secretary General and your representative—an arrangement for a permanent solution to the Cuban problem along the lines suggested in your letter of October 26th. As I read your letter, the key elements of your proposals— which seem generally acceptable as I understand them— are as follows:

    1. You would agree to remove these weapons systems from Cuba under appropriate United Nations observation and supervision; and undertake, with suitable safeguards, to halt the further introduction of such weapons systems into Cuba.

    2. We, on our part, would agree—upon the establishment of adequate arrangements through the United Nations to ensure the carrying out and continuation of these commitments—(a) to remove promptly the quarantine measures now in effect, and (b) to give assurances against an invasion of Cuba. I am confident that other nations of the Western Hemisphere would be prepared to do likewise.

    If you will give your representative similar instructions, there is no reason why we should not be able to complete these arrangements and announce them to the world within a couple of days. The effect of such a settlement on easing world tensions would enable us to work toward a more general arrangement regarding "other armaments," as proposed in your second letter, which you made public. I would like to say again that the United States is very much interested in reducing tensions and halting the arms race; and if your letter signifies that you are prepared to discuss a detente affecting NATO and the Warsaw Pact, we are quite prepared to consider with our allies any useful proposals.

    But the first ingredient, let me emphasize, is the cessation of work on missile sites in Cuba and measures to render such weapons inoperable, under effective international guarantees. The continuation of this threat, or a prolonging of this discussion concerning Cuba by linking these problems to the broader questions of European and world security, would surely lead to an intensification of the Cuban crisis and a grave risk to the peace of the world.

C. KHRUSHCHEV TO KENNEDY, OCTOBER 28, 1962

In order to eliminate as rapidly as possible the conflict which endangers the cause of peace, to give an assurance to all people who crave peace, and to reassure the American people who, I am certain, also want peace, as do the people of the Soviet Union, the Soviet Government, in addition to earlier instructions on the discontinuance of further work on weapons construction sites, has given a new order to dismantle the arms which you described as offensive, and to crate and return them to the Soviet Union. . . .

I regard with respect and trust the statement you made in your message of 27 October, 1962, that there would be no attack, no invasion of Cuba, and not only on the part of the United States, but also of other nations of the Western Hemisphere, as you said in your message. Then the motives which induced us to render assistance of such a kind to Cuba will disappear.

It is for this reason that we instructed our officers . . . to take appropriate measures to discontinue construction of the aforementioned facilities, to dismantle them, and to return them to the Soviet Union. As I had informed you in the letter of 27 October, we are prepared to reach agreement to enable the U.N. representatives to verify the dismantling of these means. Thus, in view of the assurances you have given and our instructions on dismantling, there is every condition for eliminating the present conflict.

D. KENNEDY TO KHRUSHCHEV, OCTOBER 28, 1962

I think that you and I, with our heavy responsibilities for the maintenance of peace, were aware that developments were reaching a point where events could have become unmanageable. . . . I consider my letter to you of October 27 and your reply of today as firm undertakings on the part of both our governments which should be promptly carried out. . . .

Mr. Chairman, both of our countries have great unfinished tasks and I know that your people as well as those of the United States can ask for nothing better than to pursue them free from the fear of war. . . .

I agree with you that we must devote urgent attention to the problem of disarmament, as it relates to the whole world and also to critical areas. Perhaps now, as we step back from danger, we can together make real progress in this vital field. I think we should give priority to questions relating to the proliferation of nuclear weapons on earth and in outer space, and to the great effort for a nuclear test ban.

DOCUMENT 6

JOHN F. KENNEDY, ADDRESS TO THE AMERICAN PEOPLE ON THE NUCLEAR TEST BAN TREATY
JULY 26, 1963

After the resolution of the missile crisis, Kennedy vigorously pursued a peace policy, and on June 10, 1963, he delivered a moving international appeal for peace in his American University address, which was published in full in the Soviet press. From this point, the governments moved rapidly to agreeing on a treaty banning further nuclear tests in the atmosphere, a limited but important move toward peace. Ratified by the Senate, 80–19, the treaty was regarded by Kennedy as the most satisfying of his accomplishments. The following is a portion of his first announcement of its terms to the public.

I speak to you tonight in a spirit of hope. Eighteen years ago the advent of nuclear weapons changed the course of the world as well as the war. Since that time, all mankind has been struggling to escape from the darkening prospect of mass destruction on earth. In an age when both sides have come to possess enough nuclear power to destroy the human race several times over, the world of communism and the world of free choice have been caught up in a vicious circle of conflicting ideology and interest. Each increase of tension has produced an increase of arms; each increase of arms has produced an increase of tension.

In these years, the United States and the Soviet Union have frequently communicated suspicion and warnings to each other, but very rarely hope. Our representatives have met at the summit and at the brink; they have met in Washington and in Moscow; in Geneva and at the United Nations. But too often these meetings have produced only darkness, discord, or disillusion.

Yesterday a shaft of light cut into the darkness. Negotiations were concluded in Moscow on a treaty to ban all nuclear tests in the atmosphere, in outer space, and under water. For the first time, an agreement has been reached on bringing the forces of nuclear destruction under international control. . . .

The treaty initialed yesterday . . . is a limited treaty which permits continued underground testing and prohibits only those tests that we ourselves can police. It requires no control posts, no onsite inspection, no international body.

We should also understand that it has other limits as well. Any nation which signs the treaty will have an opportunity to withdraw if it finds that extraordinary events related to the subject matter of the treaty have jeopardized its supreme interests; and no nation's right of self-defense will in any way be impaired. Nor does this treaty mean an end to the threat of nuclear war. It will not reduce nuclear stockpiles; it will not halt the production of nuclear weapons; it will not restrict their use in time of war.

Nevertheless, this limited treaty will radically reduce the nuclear testing which would otherwise be conducted on both sides; it will prohibit the United States, the United Kingdom, the Soviet Union, and all others who sign it, from engaging in the atmospheric tests which have so alarmed mankind; and it offers to all the world a welcome sign of hope.

This treaty is not the millennium. It will not resolve all conflicts, or cause the Communists to forego their ambitions, or eliminate the dangers of war. It will not reduce our need for arms or allies or programs of assistance to others. But it is an important first step—a step towards peace—a step towards reason—a step away from war.

Here is what this step can mean to you and to your children and your neighbors:

First, this treaty can be a step towards reduced world tension and broader areas of agreement. . . .

Second, this treaty can be a step towards freeing the

world from the fears and dangers of radioactive fallout.
Our own atmospheric tests last year were conducted under
conditions which restricted such fallout to an absolute
minimum. But over the years the number and the yield of
weapons tested have rapidly increased and so have the
radioactive hazards from such testing. Continued unrestricted testing by the nuclear powers, joined in time by
other nations which may be less adept in limiting pollution,
will increasingly contaminate the air that all of us must
breathe. . . .

Third, this treaty can be a step toward preventing the
spread of nuclear weapons to nations not now possessing
them.

I ask you to stop and think for a moment what it
would mean to have nuclear weapons in so many hands, in
the hands of countries large and small, stable and unstable,
responsible and irresponsible, scattered throughout the
world. There would be no rest for anyone then, no stability,
no real security, and no chance of effective disarmament.
There would only be the increased chance of accidental
war, and an increased necessity for the great powers to
involve themselves in what otherwise would be local conflicts. . . .

Neither the United States nor the Soviet Union nor
the United Kingdom nor France can look forward to that
day with equanimity. We have a great obligation, all four
nuclear powers have a great obligation, to use whatever
time remains to prevent the spread of nuclear weapons, to
persuade other countries not to test, transfer, acquire,
possess, or produce such weapons.

This treaty can be the opening wedge in that campaign. It provides that none of the parties will assist other
nations to test in the forbidden environments. It opens the
door for further agreements on the control of nuclear
weapons, and it is open for all nations to sign, for it is in
the interest of all nations, and already we have heard from
a number of countries who wish to join with us promptly.

Fourth and finally, this treaty can limit the nuclear
arms race in ways which, on balance, will strengthen our
Nation's security far more than the continuation of unrestricted testing. For in today's world, a nation's security
does not always increase as its arms increase, when its ad-

versary is doing the same, and unlimited competition in the testing and development of new types of destructive nuclear weapons will not make the world safer for either side. Under this limited treaty, on the other hand, the testing of other nations could never be sufficient to offset the ability of our strategic forces to deter or survive a nuclear attack and to penetrate and destroy an aggressor's homeland. . . .

But now, for the first time in many years, the path of peace may be open. No one can be certain what the future will bring. No one can say whether the time has come for an easing of the struggle. But history and our own conscience will judge us harsher if we do not now make every effort to test our hopes by action, and this is the place to begin. According to the ancient Chinese proverb, "A journey of a thousand miles must begin with a single step."

My fellow Americans, let us take that first step. Let us, if we can, step back from the shadows of war and seek out the way of peace. And if that journey is a thousand miles, or even more, let history record that we, in this land, at this time, took the first step.

DOCUMENT 7

LEGISLATIVE REAPPORTIONMENT: *BAKER* v. *CARR,* 1962

It has been said of this unprecedented case that it is "certain to be as historic in American constitutional history as Marbury v. Madison," *and its full implications are not yet known. The decision ended repeated judicial refusals to enter the "political thicket" of the reapportionment of legislatures. The political implications went far beyond the legal issue, for the whole meaning of representative democracy was at stake. The basic issue was put to the Court by a suit challenging the apportionment of the Tennessee Legislature on the ground that the inequity between districts deprived citizens of underrepresented districts of equal protection of the laws as guaranteed in the Fourteenth Amendment. The basic question before the Court was whether legislative apportionment is a "justiciable" question at all—that is, is it one that judges can hear and on which they can issue rulings? Previous precedents pointed to judicial restraint. In Colegrove v. Green (1946), for example, the court had dismissed a suit seeking to restrain further use of the existing Illinois congressional districts on the ground that inequality in their populations violated the Fourteenth Amendment. Now the Court, speaking through Justice William J. Brennan in a long and complex decision excerpted only very briefly here, moved aggressively into the political field. Ruling that the whole question was indeed justiciable, the Court based its decision on the clause guaranteeing equal protection of the laws in the Fourteenth Amendment, and then asserted the need for the Court to intervene to protect the democratic process by mandating substantial equality of representation. Sweeping implications were clarified by subsequent decisions, notably by the case of Reynolds v. Sims and its companion cases. See Documents 8 and 9; and for a review of the whole issue, Robert G. Dixon, Jr., Democratic Representation: Reapportionment in Law and Politics (1968).*

The complaint, alleging that by means of a 1901 statute of Tennessee apportioning the members of the General Assembly among the State's 95 counties, "these plaintiffs and others similarly situated, are denied the equal protection of the laws accorded them by the Fourteenth Amendment to the Constitution of the United States by virtue of the debasement of their votes," was dismissed by a three-judge court. . . . We hold that the dismissal was error, and remand the cause to the District Court for trial and further proceedings consistent with this opinion. . . .

Tennessee's standard for allocating legislative representation among her counties is the total number of qualified voters resident in the respective counties, subject only to minor qualifications. . . . In 1901 the General Assembly . . . passed the Apportionment Act here in controversy. In the more than 60 years since that action, all proposals in both Houses of the General Assembly for re-apportionment have failed to pass.

Between 1901 and 1961, Tennessee has experienced substantial growth and redistribution of her population. . . . It is primarily the continued application of the 1901 Apportionment Act to this shifted and enlarged voting population which gives rise to the present controversy. . . .

Our conclusion . . . infra, that this cause presents no nonjusticiable "political question" settles the only possible doubt that it is a case or controversy. Under the present heading of "Jurisdiction of the Subject Matter" we hold only that the matter set forth in the complaint does arise under the Constitution. . . .

The question here is the consistency of state action with the Federal Constitution. We have no question decided, or to be decided, by a political branch of government coequal with this Court. Nor do we risk embarrassment of our government abroad, or grave disturbance at home if we take issue with Tennessee as to the constitutionality of her action here challenged. Nor need the appellants, in order to succeed in this action, ask the Court to enter upon policy determinations for which judicially manageable standards are lacking. Judicial standards under the Equal Protection Clause are well developed and familiar, and it has been open to courts since the enactment of the Fourteenth Amendment to determine, if on the particular facts they must, that a discrimination reflects *no* policy, but simply arbitrary and capricious action. . . .

We conclude that the complaint's allegations of a denial of equal protection present a justiciable constitutional cause of action upon which appellants are entitled to a trial and a decision. The right asserted is within the reach of judicial protection under the Fourteenth Amendment.

DOCUMENT 8

LEGISLATIVE REAPPORTIONMENT:
REYNOLDS v. *SIMS,*
1964

In Baker *v.* Carr *the Court had not stated its view as
to the proper constitutional standards for evaluating
the validity of a state legislative apportionment
scheme. In this and associated cases the Court spelled
out its standards, and speaking through Chief Justice
Warren it made a more forceful statement of the
equal protection principle than can be found in* Baker
v. Carr. *The Court now called for "substantial equality of population among the various districts" represented in a state legislature, and districts "as nearly of
equal population as is practicable." In another 1964
decision,* Wesberry *v.* Sanders, *the Court also required
equal population districts within a state for elections
to the House of Representatives.*

Our problem . . . is to ascertain, in the instant cases,
whether there are any constitutionally cognizable principles
which would justify departures from the basic standard of
equality among voters in the apportionment of seats in
state legislatures. . . .

Legislators represent people, not trees or acres. Legislators are elected by voters, not farms or cities or economic interests. As long as ours is a representative form
of government, and our legislatures are those instruments
of government elected directly by and directly representative of the people, the right to elect legislators in a free and
unimpaired fashion is a bedrock of our political system.
It could hardly be gainsaid that a constitutional claim had
been asserted by an allegation that certain otherwise qualified voters had been entirely prohibited from voting for
members of their state legislature. . . . And it is inconceivable that a state law to the effect that, in counting votes
for legislators, the votes of citizens in one part of the State
would be multiplied by two, five, or 10, while the votes of
persons in another area would be counted only at face

value, could be constitutionally sustainable. Of course, the effect of state legislative districting schemes which give the same number of representatives to unequal numbers of constituents is identical. Overweighting and overvaluation of the votes of those living here has the certain effect of dilution and undervaluation of the votes of those living there. The resulting discrimination against those individual voters living in disfavored areas is demonstrable mathematically. Their right to vote is simply not the same right to vote as that of those living in a favored part of the State. Two, five, or 10 of them must vote before the effect of their voting is equivalent to that of their favored neighbor. Weighting the votes of citizens differently, by any method or means, merely because of where they happen to reside, hardly seems justifiable. . . .

Full and effective participation by all citizens in state government requires . . . that each citizen has an equally effective voice in the election of members of his state legislature. Modern and viable state government needs, and the Constitution demands, no less.

Logically, in a society ostensibly grounded on representative government, it would seem reasonable that a majority of the people of a State could elect a majority of that State's legislators. To conclude differently, and to sanction minority control of state legislative bodies, would appear to deny majority rights in a way that far surpasses any possible denial of minority rights that might otherwise be thought to result. Since legislatures are responsible for enacting laws by which all citizens are to be governed, they should be bodies which are collectively responsive to the popular will. And the concept of equal protection has been traditionally viewed as requiring the uniform treatment of persons standing in the same relation to the governmental action questioned or challenged. With respect to the allocation of legislative representation, all voters, as citizens of a State, stand in the same relation regardless of where they live. Any suggested criteria for the differentiation of citizens are insufficient to justify any discrimination, as to the weight of their votes, unless relevant to the permissible purposes of legislative apportionment. Since the achieving of fair and effective representation for all citizens is concededly the basic aim of legislative apportionment, we con-

clude that the Equal Protection Clause guarantees the
opportunity for equal participation by all voters in the
election of state legislators. Diluting the weight of votes
because of place of residence impairs basic constitutional
rights under the Fourteenth Amendment just as much as
invidious discriminations based upon factors such as
race . . . or economic status. . . . Our constitutional
system amply provides for the protection of minorities by
means other than giving them majority control of state
legislatures. And the democratic ideals of equality and
majority rule, which have served this Nation so well in the
past, are hardly of any less significance for the present and
the future.

    We are told that the matter of apportioning repre-
sentation in a state legislature is a complex and many-
faceted one. We are advised that States can rationally consider factors other than population in apportioning legislative representation. We are admonished not to restrict the
power of the States to impose differing views as to political
philosophy on their citizens. We are cautioned about the
dangers of entering into political thickets and mathematical
quagmires. Our answer is this: a denial of constitutionally
protected rights demands judicial protection; our oath and
our office require no less of us. . . . To the extent that
a citizen's right to vote is debased, he is that much less a
citizen. The fact that an individual lives here or there is not
a legitimate reason for overweighting or diluting the efficacy
of his vote. The complexions of societies and civilizations
change, often with amazing rapidity. . . . But the basic
principle of representative government remains, and must
remain, unchanged—the weight of a citizen's vote cannot
be made to depend on where he lives. Population is, of
necessity, the starting point for consideration and the controlling criterion for judgment in legislative apportionment controversies. A citizen, a qualified voter, is no more
nor no less so because he lives in the city or on the farm.
This is the clear and strong command of our Constitution's
Equal Protection Clause. This is an essential part of the
concept of a government of laws and not men. This is at
the heart of Lincoln's vision of "government of the people,
by the people, [and] for the people." The Equal Protection
Clause demands no less than substantially equal state leg-

islative representation for all citizens, of all places as well as of all races. . . .

We hold that, as a basic constitutional standard, the Equal Protection Clause requires that the seats in both houses of a bicameral state legislature must be apportioned on a population basis. Simply stated, an individual's right to vote for state legislators is unconstitutionally impaired when its weight is in a substantial fashion diluted when compared with votes of citizens living in other parts of the State.

DOCUMENT 9

JOHN MARSHALL HARLAN, DISSENTING OPINION IN *REYNOLDS* v. *SIMS*,
1964

The Court was divided in both reapportionment cases, and in Reynolds v. Sims *it split 6–3. A learned and forceful dissenting opinion was written by Justice John Marshall Harlan (a grandson of the John Marshall Harlan represented above in Part I and Part II). A portion of the dissenting opinion appears here.*

The history of the adoption of the Fourteenth Amendment provides conclusive evidence that neither those who proposed nor those who ratified the Amendment believed that the Equal Protection Clause limited the power of the States to apportion their legislatures as they saw fit. Moreover, the history demonstrates that the intention to leave this power undisturbed was deliberate and was widely believed to be essential to the adoption of the Amendment. . . .

In my judgment, today's decisions are refuted by the language of the Amendment which they construe and by the inference fairly to be drawn from subsequently enacted Amendments. They are unequivocally refuted by history and by consistent theory and practice from the time of the adoption of the Fourteenth Amendment until today.

Generalities cannot obscure the cold truth that cases

of this type are not amenable to the development of judicial standards. No set of standards can guide a court which has to decide how many legislative districts a State shall have, or what the shape of the districts shall be, or where to draw a particular district line. No judicially manageable standard can determine whether a State should have single-member districts or multimember districts or some combination of both. No such standard can control the balance between keeping up with population shifts and having stable districts. In all these respects, the courts will be called upon to make particular decisions with respect to which a principle of equally populated districts will be of no assistance whatsoever. Quite obviously, there are limitless possibilities for districting consistent with such a principle. Nor can these problems be avoided by judicial reliance on legislative judgments so far as possible. Reshaping or combining one or two districts, or modifying just a few district lines, is no less a matter of choosing among many possible solutions, with varying political consequences, than reapportionment broadside.

Although the Court . . . provides only generalities in elaboration of its main thesis, its opinion nevertheless fully demonstrates how far removed these problems are from fields of judicial competence. Recognizing that "indiscriminate districting" is an invitation to "partisan gerrymandering," . . . the Court nevertheless excludes virtually every basis for the formation of electoral districts other than "indiscriminate districting." In one or another of today's opinions, the Court declares it unconstitutional for a State to give effective consideration to any of the following in establishing legislative districts: (1) history; (2) "economic or other sorts of group interests"; (3) area; (4) geographical considerations; (5) a desire 'to insure effective representation for sparsely settled areas"; (6) "availability of access of citizens to their representatives"; (7) theories of bicameralism (except those approved by the Court); (8) occupation; (9) "an attempt to balance urban and rural power"; (10) the preference of a majority of voters in the State. So far as presently appears, the *only* factor which a State may consider, apart from numbers, is political subdivisions. But even "a clearly rational state policy" recognizing this factor is unconstitutional if "population is submerged as the controlling considera-tion. . . ."

I know of no principle of logic or practical or theo-retical politics, still less any constitutional principle, which establishes all or any of these exclusions. . . . So far as the Court says anything at all on this score, it says only that "legislators represent people, not trees or acres," . . . All this may be conceded. But it is surely equally obvious, and, in the context of elections, more meaningful to note that people are not ciphers and that legislators can represent their electors only by speaking for their interests —economic, social, political—many of which do reflect the place where the electors live. The Court does not estab-lish, or indeed even attempt to make a case for the propo-sition that conflicting interests within a State can only be adjusted by disregarding them when voters are grouped for purposes of representation.

With these cases the Court approaches the end of the third round set in motion by the complaint filed in *Baker v. Carr*. What is done today deepens my conviction that judicial entry into this realm is profoundly ill-advised and constitutionally impermissible.

DOCUMENT 10

LYNDON B. JOHNSON, SPEECH
TO CONGRESS CALLING
FOR A WAR ON POVERTY,
MARCH 16, 1964

In his State of the Union message of 1964 Johnson had asserted: "This Administration today, here and now, declares unconditional war on poverty in Amer-ica." Not many weeks afterward, in the Special Mes-sage excerpted here, he outlined to Congress his pro-gram for a many-faceted attack on poverty. The measure he was calling upon Congress to enact—the Economic Opportunity Act—was the first major legis-lation Johnson sent to Capitol Hill.

With the growth of our country has come opportunity for
our people—opportunity to educate our children, to use
our energies in productive work, to increase our leisure—
opportunity for almost every American to hope that
through work and talent he could create a better life for
himself and his family.

The path forward has not been an easy one. But we
have never lost sight of our goal: an America in which
every citizen shares all the opportunities of his society, in
which every man has a chance to advance his welfare to
the limit of his capacities. We have come a long way toward this goal. We still have a long way to go. The distance which remains is the measure of the great unfinished
work of our society. To finish that work I have called for
a national war on poverty. Our objective: total victory.

There are millions of Americans—one fifth of our
people—who have not shared in the abundance which has
been granted to most of us, and on whom the gates of opportunity have been closed.

What does this poverty mean to those who endure it?

It means a daily struggle to secure the necessities for
even a meager existence. It means that the abundance, the
comforts, the opportunities they see all around them are
beyond their grasp. Worst of all, it means hopelessness for
the young.

The young man or woman who grows up without a
decent education, in a broken home, in a hostile and
squalid environment, in ill health or in the face of racial
injustice—that young man or woman is often trapped in
a life of poverty.

He does not have the skills demanded by a complex
society. He does not know how to acquire those skills. He
faces a mounting sense of despair which drains initiative
and ambition and energy. . . .

Our fight against poverty will be an investment in the
most valuable of our resources—the skills and strength of
our people.

And in the future, as in the past, this investment will
return its cost many fold to our entire economy.

If we can raise the annual earnings of 10 million
among the poor by only $1,000 we will have added 14
billion dollars a year to our national output. In addition

we can make important reductions in public assistance payments which now cost us 4 billion dollars a year, and in the large costs of fighting crime and delinquency, disease and hunger. . . .

Our history has proved that each time we broaden the base of abundance, giving more people the chance to produce and consume, we create new industry, higher production, increased earnings and better income for all.

Giving new opportunity to those who have little will enrich the lives of all the rest.

Because it is right, because it is wise, and because, for the first time in our history, it is possible to conquer poverty, I submit, for the consideration of the Congress and the country, the Economic Opportunity Act of 1964.

DOCUMENT 11

LYNDON B. JOHNSON, GREAT SOCIETY SPEECH,
MAY 22, 1964

The phrase the Great Society, used in a Commencement address at the University of Michigan, became attached to the aspirations of the Johnson Administration, much as the New Frontier was for John F. Kennedy. The term Great Society dated from a book of that title (1914) by Graham Wallas, a Fabian Socialist who taught at the London School of Economics. On the drafting of this speech see Eric F. Goldman, The Tragedy of Lyndon Johnson *(1969).*

The challenge of the next half century is whether we have the wisdom to . . . enrich and elevate our national life, and to advance the quality of our American civilization.

Your imagination, your initiative, and your indignation will determine whether we build a society where progress is the servant of our needs, or a society where old values and new visions are buried under unbridled growth. For in your time we have the opportunity to move not only toward the rich society and the powerful society, but upward to the Great Society.

The Great Society rests on abundance and liberty for all. It demands an end to poverty and racial injustice, to which we are totally committed in our time. But that is just the beginning.

The Great Society is a place where every child can find knowledge to enrich his mind and to enlarge his talents. It is a place where leisure is a welcome change to build and reflect, not a feared cause of boredom and restlessness. It is a place where the city of man serves not only the needs of the body and the demands of commerce but the desire for beauty and the hunger for community.

It is a place where man can renew contact with nature. It is a place which honors creation for its own sake and for what it adds to the understanding of the race. It is a place where men are more concerned with the quality of their goals than the quantity of their goods.

But most of all, the Great Society is not a safe harbor, a resting place, a final objective, a finished work. It is a challenge constantly renewed, beckoning us toward a destiny where the meaning of our lives matches the marvelous products of our labor. . . .

The catalog of ills is long: there is the decay of the centers and the despoiling of the suburbs. There is not enough housing for our people or transportation for our traffic. Open land is vanishing and old landmarks are violated.

Worst of all expansion is eroding the precious and time honored values of community with neighbors and communion with nature. The loss of these values breeds loneliness and boredom and indifference.

Our society will never be great until our cities are great. Today the frontier of imagination and innovation is inside those cities and not beyond their borders. . . .

A second place where we begin to build the Great Society is in our countryside. We have always prided ourselves on being not only America the strong and America the free, but America the beautiful. Today that beauty is in danger. The water we drink, the food we eat, the very air that we breathe, are threatened with pollution. Our parks are overcrowded, our seashores overburdened. Green fields and dense forests are disappearing. . . . For once the battle is lost, once our natural splendor is destroyed, it can never be recaptured. . . . A third place to build the Great Society is in the classrooms of America. . . .

Today, 8 million adult Americans, more than the entire population of Michigan, have not finished 5 years of school. Nearly 20 million have not finished 8 years of school. Nearly 54 million—more than one-quarter of all America—have not even finished high school.

Each year more than 100,000 high school graduates, with proved ability, do not enter college because they cannot afford it. And if we cannot educate today's youth, what will we do in 1970 when elementary school enrollment will be 5 million greater than 1960? And high school enrollment will rise by 5 million. College enrollment will increase by more than 3 million.

In many places, classrooms are overcrowded and curricula are outdated. Most of our qualified teachers are underpaid, and many of our paid teachers are unqualified. So we must give every child a place to sit and a teacher to learn from. Poverty must not be a bar to learning, and learning must offer an escape from poverty. . . .

These are three of the central issues of the Great Society. While our Government has many programs directed at those issues, I do not pretend that we have the full answer to those problems.

But I do promise this: We are going to assemble the best thought and the broadest knowledge from all over the world to find those answers for America.

DOCUMENT 12

BARRY GOLDWATER, OPENING CAMPAIGN SPEECH AT PRESCOTT, ARIZONA,
SEPTEMBER 3, 1964

When President Johnson put his Economic Opportunity Act before Congress, Senator Barry Goldwater of Arizona called it "a dole for the poor, offered cyn-

*ically for votes." In this speech, which opened his
campaign for the Presidency in 1964, Goldwater developed two themes: the need for strength, will, and
relentless determination to oppose the international
threat of Communism, and the dangers of an over-
grown bureaucracy in Washington which he believed
the Johnson program threatened. His argument on
these domestic dangers is excerpted here.*

Today [this] free and orderly community faces the grave
danger of becoming merely another possession of the
White House, and we who live here face the grave danger
of becoming the servants of some Big Brother who lives
there.

We all sense this danger, not only those of us gathered in this square, but *all* of us across this land. There is
a stir in the land. There is a mood of uneasiness. We feel
adrift in an uncharted and stormy sea. We feel that we
have lost our way. . . .

Today, therefore . . . we also begin a great campaign to return the government of this nation to the people
of this nation. Today we take a first step toward ending
in our time the erosion of individual worth by a growing
Federal bureaucracy.

This time, in this election, we *have* a choice. It is
between far more than political personalities, far more
than political promises, far more than political programs.
It is a choice of what sort of people we want to be. It is
the choice of what sort of world we want to live in and
want to pass on to our children.

Choose the way of this present Administration and you
will have chosen the way of the regimented society, with
a number for every man, woman, and child, a pigeonhole
for every problem, and a bureaucrat for every decision.
Choose the way of this present Administration and you
have the way of mobs in the street, restrained only by the
plea that they wait until after election time to ignite violence once again. Choose the way of this present Administration and you chose the way of unilateral disarmament
and appeasement in foreign affairs. Choose the way of this
present Administration and you make real the prospect of

an America unarmed and aimless in the face of militant Communism around the world.

Instead, I ask that you join with me in providing that every American can stand on his own, make up his own mind, chart his own future, keep and control his own family, asking for help and getting help only when truly overwhelming problems, beyond his control, beset him. I ask you to join with me in finding Twentieth Century answers for Twentieth Century problems rather than relying on the old, disproved doctrine of turning our problems, our lives, and our liberties over to a supposed elite in an all-powerful central government. . . .

This country has grown great and strong and prosperous by placing major reliance on a free economy. What we have we owe to the ceaseless strivings of tens of millions of free men to better their own condition and to provide a better future for their children and their children's children.

Private property, free competition, hard work—these have been our greatest tools. Let us not discard them now!

This system has preserved and protected our freedom, our right to disagree, our diversity, our independence from arbitrary interference in our affairs. This system is the mighty engine of progress which enabled this country to develop from a small but independent citizenry to become a multitude spanning the Continent and living on a level that is the envy of the world.

Government-to-government aid from other countries did not do it for us. Hard work and freedom did it! Progress through freedom has been our heritage and must continue to be our goal.

Increasingly, however, government has been absorbing or controlling more and more of our resources, our energy, and our ambition. Today you work from January through April just to provide government with the money it spends. Until early February you are working to pay the expenses of local and state government. For twice as long thereafter you are working to pay the expenses of the Federal Government. Only then do you work for money that you yourself can use for what you yourself choose.

This cancerous growth of the Federal Government must and shall be stopped.

DOCUMENT 13

MARTIN LUTHER KING, JR., "I HAVE A DREAM" SPEECH BEFORE THE MARCH ON WASHINGTON,
AUGUST 28, 1963

Before an enormous crowd of blacks and whites stretched in front of the Lincoln Memorial, Martin Luther King delivered this moving statement of the aspirations of nonviolent civil rights protest.

Five score years ago, a great American, in whose symbolic shadow we stand, signed the Emancipation Proclamation. This momentous decree came as a great beacon light of hope to millions of Negro slaves who have been seared in the flames of withering injustice. It came as a joyous day-break to end the long night of captivity.

But one hundred years later, we must face the tragic fact that the Negro is still not free. One hundred years later, the life of the Negro is still sadly crippled by the manacles of segregation and the chains of discrimination. One hundred years later, the Negro lives on a lonely island of poverty in the midst of a vast ocean of material pros-perity. One hundred years later, the Negro is still languished in the corners of American society and finds himself an exile in his own land. So we have come here today to dramatize an appalling condition.

In a sense we have come to our nation's Capitol to cash a check. When the architects of our republic wrote the magnificent words of the Constitution and the Declaration of Independence, they were signing a promissory note to which every American was to fall heir. This note was a promise that all men would be guaranteed the unalienable rights of life, liberty, and the pursuit of happiness.

It is obvious today that America has defaulted on this promissory note insofar as her citizens of color are con-cerned. Instead of honoring this sacred obligation, America has given the Negro people a bad check; a check which has come back marked "insufficient funds." But we refuse to believe that the bank of justice is bankrupt. We refuse to believe that there are insufficient funds in the great vaults of opportunity of this nation. So we have come to cash this check—a check that will give us upon demand the riches of freedom and the security of justice. . . .

It would be fatal for the nation to overlook the urgency of the moment and to underestimate the determination of the Negro. This sweltering summer of the Negro's legitimate discontent will not pass until there is an invigorating autumn of freedom and equality. 1963 is not an end, but a beginning. Those who hope that the Negro needed to blow off steam and will now be content will have a rude awakening if the Nation returns to business as usual. There will be neither rest nor tranquility in America until the Negro is granted his citizenship rights. The whirlwinds of revolt will continue to shake the foundations of our Nation until the bright day of justice emerges.

But there is something that I must say to my people. . . . In the process of gaining our rightful place we must not be guilty of wrongful deeds. Let us not seek to satisfy our thirst for freedom by drinking from the cup of bitterness and hatred.

We must forever conduct our struggle on the high plane of dignity and discipline. We must not allow our creative protest to degenerate into physical violence. Again and again we must rise to the majestic heights of meeting physical force with soul force. The marvelous new militancy which has engulfed the Negro community must not lead us to a distrust of all white people, for many of our white brothers, as evidenced by their presence here today, have come to realize that their destiny is tied up with our destiny and their freedom is inextricably bound to our freedom. We cannot walk alone.

And as we walk, we must make the pledge that we shall march ahead. We cannot turn back. There are those who are asking the devotees of civil rights, "when will you be satisfied?" We can never be satisfied as long as the Negro is the victim of the unspeakable horrors of police brutality. We can never be satisfied as long as our bodies, heavy with the fatigue of travel, cannot gain lodging in the motels of the highways and the hotels of the cities. We cannot be satisfied as long as the Negro's basic mobility is from a smaller ghetto to a larger one. We can never be satisfied as long as a Negro in Mississippi cannot vote and a Negro in New York believes he has nothing for which to vote. No, no we are not satisfied, and we will not be satisfied until justice rolls down like waters and righteousness like a mighty stream.

I am not unmindful that some of you have come here out of great trials and tribulations. Some of you have come fresh from narrow jail cells. Some of you have come from areas where your quest for freedom left you battered by the storms of persecution and staggered by the winds of police brutality. You have been the veterans of creative suffering. Continue to work with the faith that unearned suffering is redemptive.

Go back to Mississippi, go back to Alabama, go back to South Carolina, go back to Georgia, go back to Louisiana, go back to the slums and ghettos of our northern cities, knowing that somehow this situation can and will be changed. Let us not wallow in the valley of despair.

I say to you today, my friends, that in spite of the difficulties and frustrations of the moment I still have a dream. It is a dream deeply rooted in the American dream.

I have a dream that one day this nation will rise up and live out the true meaning of its creed: "We hold these truths to be self-evident; that all men are created equal."

I have a dream that one day on the red hills of Georgia the sons of former slaves and the sons of former slaveowners will be able to sit down together at the table of brotherhood.

I have a dream that one day even the state of Mississippi, a desert state sweltering with the heat of injustice and oppression, will be transformed into an oasis of freedom and justice.

I have a dream that my four little children will one day live in a nation where they will not be judged by the color of their skin but by the content of their character.

I have a dream today.

I have a dream that one day the state of Alabama, whose governor's lips are presently dripping with the words of interposition and nullification, will be transformed into a situation where little black boys and black girls will be able to join hands with little white boys and white girls and walk together as sisters and brothers.

I have a dream today.

I have a dream that one day every valley shall be exalted, every hill and mountain shall be made low, the rough places will be made plains, and the crooked places will be made straight, and the glory of the Lord shall be revealed, and all flesh shall see it together.

This is our hope. This is the faith with which I return to the South. With this faith we will be able to hew out of the mountain of despair a stone of hope. With this faith we will be able to transform the jangling discords of our nation into a beautiful symphony of brotherhood. With this faith we will be able to work together, to pray together, to struggle together, to go to jail together, to stand up for freedom together, knowing that we will be free one day.

DOCUMENT 14

LYNDON B. JOHNSON, SPEECH ON THE VOTING RIGHTS ACT OF 1965,

MARCH 15, 1965

After the events of "Bloody Sunday" in Selma, Alabama, and the murder of the Reverend James Reeb, President Johnson prepared this appeal to Congress calling for voting rights legislation. Although several aides contributed suggestions and partial drafts, the final language was in large measure Lyndon Johnson's own. Washington learned by the grapevine that this would be a memorable speech, and Cabinet members, Supreme Court Justices, and Ambassadors entered the Chamber of the House of Representatives, filling every seat and jamming the aisles. The President then delivered the most emotional speech of his career, excerpted here.

I speak tonight for the dignity of man and the destiny of democracy.

I urge every member of both parties—Americans of
all religions and of all colors—from every section of this
country—to join me in that cause.

At times history and fate meet at a single time in a
single place to shape a turning point in man's unending
search for freedom. So it was at Lexington and Concord.
So it was a century ago at Appomattox. So it was last week
in Selma, Alabama.

There is no Negro problem. There is no southern
problem. There is no northern problem. There is only an
American problem.

And we are met here tonight as Americans—not as
Democrats or Republicans—we are met here as Americans
to solve that problem.

This was the first nation in the history of the world to
be founded with a purpose. The great phrases of that purpose still sound in every American heart, north and south:
"All men are created equal"—"Government by consent
of the governed"—"Give me liberty or give me death." . . .

Those words are a promise to every citizen that he
shall share in the dignity of man. This dignity cannot be
found in a man's possessions. It cannot be found in his
power or in his position. It really rests on his right to be
treated as a man equal in opportunity to all others. It says
that he shall share in freedom, he shall choose his leaders,
educate his children, provide for his family according to
his ability and his merits as a human being. . . .

Many of the issues of civil rights are very complex
and most difficult. But about this there can and should be
no argument. Every American citizen must have an equal
right to vote. There is no reason which can excuse the
denial of that right. There is no duty which weighs more
heavily on us than the duty we have to insure that right.

Yet the harsh fact is that in many places in this country men and women are kept from voting simply because
they are Negroes. . . .

Experience has clearly shown that the existing process
of law cannot overcome systematic and ingenious discrimination. No law that we now have on the books—and I
have helped to put three of them there—can insure the
right to vote when local officials are determined to deny it.

In such a case our duty must be clear to all of us. The

Constitution says that no person shall be kept from voting because of his race or his color. We have all sworn an oath before God to support and to defend that Constitution.

We must now act in obedience to that oath.

Wednesday I will send to Congress a law designed to eliminate illegal barriers to the right to vote. . . .

To those who seek to avoid action by their National Government in their home communities—who want to and who seek to maintain purely local control over elections—the answer is simple. Open your polling places to all your people. Allow men and women to register and vote whatever the color of their skin. Extend the rights of citizenship to every citizen of this land. There is no constitutional issue here. The command of the Constitution is plain. There is no moral issue. It is wrong—deadly wrong—to deny any of your fellow Americans the right to vote in this country. There is no issue of States rights or National rights. There is only the struggle for human rights.

I have not the slightest doubt what will be your answer. . . .

But even if we pass this bill, the battle will not be over. What happened in Selma is part of a far larger movement which reaches into every section and State of America. It is the effort of American Negroes to secure for themselves the full blessings of American life.

Their cause must be our cause too, because it is not just Negroes but really it is all of us, who must overcome the crippling legacy of bigotry and injustice. And we shall overcome. . . .

This great, rich, restless country can offer opportunity and education and hope to all—all black and white, all North and South, sharecropper and city dweller. These are the enemies—poverty, ignorance, disease—they are our enemies, not our fellow man, not our neighbor. And these enemies too—poverty, disease, and ignorance—we shall overcome.

DOCUMENT 15

LYNDON B. JOHNSON, AMERICAN POLICY IN VIETNAM,
APRIL 7, 1965

In the speech represented here President Johnson tried to justify the American presence in Vietnam, offered unconditional talks with the "governments concerned," thus omitting the Viet Cong, and at some length called for a concert of all Asian countries which, with American leadership and aid, would launch large-scale programs of economic and social improvement.

Over this war—and all Asia—is another reality: the deepening shadow of Communist China. The rulers in Hanoi are urged on by Peking. This is a regime which has destroyed freedom in Tibet, which has attacked India and has been condemned by the United Nations for aggression in Korea. It is a nation which is helping the forces of violence in almost every continent. The contest in Viet-Nam is part of a wider pattern of aggressive purposes.

Why are these realities our concern? Why are we in South Viet-Nam?

We are there because we have a promise to keep. Since 1954 every American President has offered support to the people of South Viet-Nam. We have helped to build, and we have helped to defend. Thus, over many years, we have made a national pledge to help South Viet-Nam defend its independence.

And I intend to keep that promise.

To dishonor that pledge, to abandon this small and brave nation to its enemies, and to the terror that must follow, would be an unforgivable wrong.

We are also there to strengthen world order. Around the globe from Berlin to Thailand are people whose well being rests in part on the belief that they can count on us if they are attacked. To leave Viet-Nam to its fate would shake the confidence of all these people in the value of an

American commitment and in the value of America's word. The result would be increased unrest and instability, and even wider war.

We are also there because there are great stakes in the balance. Let no one think for a moment that retreat from Viet-Nam would bring an end to conflict. The battle would be renewed in one country and then another. The central lesson of our time is that the appetite of aggression is never satisfied. To withdraw from one battlefield means only to prepare for the next. We must say in Southeast Asia—as we did in Europe—in the words of the Bible: "Hitherto shalt thou come, but no further."

There are those who say that all our effort there will be futile—that China's power is such that it is bound to dominate all Southeast Asia. But there is no end to that argument until all of the nations of Asia are swallowed up.

There are those who wonder why we have a responsibility there. Well, we have it there for the same reason that we have a responsibility for the defense of Europe. World War II was fought in both Europe and Asia and when it ended we found ourselves with continued responsibility for the defense of freedom.

Our objective is the independence of South Viet-Nam and its freedom from attack. We want nothing for ourselves—only that the people of South Viet-Nam be allowed to guide their own country in their own way.

We will do everything necessary to reach that objective and we will do only what is absolutely necessary.

In recent months attacks on South Viet-Nam were stepped up. Thus, it became necessary for us to increase our response and to make attacks by air. This is not a change of purpose. It is a change in what we believe that purpose requires.

We do this in order to slow down aggression. We do this to increase the confidence of the brave people of South Viet-Nam who have bravely borne this brutal battle for so many years with so many casualties. And we do this to convince the leaders of North Viet-Nam—and all who seek to share their conquest—of a simple fact: We will not be defeated. We will not grow tired. We will not withdraw, either openly or under the cloak of a meaningless agreement.

We know that air attacks alone will not accomplish all of these purposes. But it is our best and prayerful judgment that they are a necessary part of the surest road to peace.

We hope that peace will come swiftly. But that is in the hands of others besides ourselves. And we must be prepared for a long continued conflict. It will require patience as well as bravery—the will to endure as well as the will to resist.

I wish it were possible to convince others with words of what we now find it necessary to say with guns and planes: armed hostility is futile—our resources are equal to any challenge—because we fight for values and we fight for principle, rather than territory or colonies, our patience and our determination are unending.

Once this is clear, then it should also be clear that the only path for reasonable men is the path of peaceful settlement.

Such peace demands an independent South Viet-Nam —securely guaranteed and able to shape its own relationships to all others—free from outside interference—tied to no alliance—a military base for no other country.

These are the essentials of any final settlement.

We will never be second in the search for such a peaceful settlement in Viet-Nam.

There may be many ways to this kind of peace: in discussion or negotiation with the governments concerned; in large groups or in small ones; in the reaffirmation of old agreements or their strengthening with new ones.

We have stated this position over and over again fifty times and more to friend and foe alike. And we remain ready with this purpose for unconditional discussions.

And until that bright and necessary day of peace we will try to keep conflict from spreading. We have no desire to see thousands die in battle—Asians or Americans. We have no desire to devastate that which the people of North Viet-Nam have built with toil and sacrifice. We will use our power with restraint and with all the wisdom that we can command.

But we will use it.

DOCUMENT 16

SENATOR J. WILLIAM FULBRIGHT ON AMERICAN VIETNAM POLICY, 1966

In 1966 Senator J. William Fulbright, one of the most persistent critics of the Administration's course in Vietnam, published a book, The Arrogance of Power, *stating his criticisms of this and other American foreign policies. In the passage selected here, he argued that the war did not strengthen the American national interest and that it was having a fatal effect upon American efforts to solve problems at home.*

To an indeterminate but undoubtedly significant degree, the initial American involvement in Vietnam was influenced by two extraneous factors: Korea and McCarthy. After North Korea invaded South Korea in a direct and unambiguous act of aggression, the United States, understandably but inaccurately, came to regard the French war in Indochina as analogous to the war in Korea, overlooking extremely important considerations of nationalism and anti-colonialism. This view of the Indochinese war was reinforced by the McCarthy hysteria at home, which fostered undiscriminating attitudes of fear and hostility toward communism in all its forms. Not only were Americans disinclined in the late forties and early fifties to make distinctions among communist movements (with the notable exception of Yugoslavia), but at that time the communist world looked very much more like a monolith than it did a few years later. It was under these circumstances that the United States began indirect military assistance to the French in Indochina at the end of 1950. In September 1951 the United States signed an agreement for direct economic assistance to Vietnam and in October 1952 the two hundredth American ship carrying military aid arrived in Saigon.

The Eisenhower Administration went to the brink in

1954 but then decided against United States military intervention. . . .

The Geneva Agreements were signed in July 1954. They explicitly prohibited the introduction into Vietnam of additional military forces and explicitly provided that general elections would be held in Vietnam by July 1956. They also explicitly stated that the demarcation line between North and South Vietnam at the 17th Parallel was "provisional and should not in any way be interpreted as constituting a political or territorial boundary," a fact which is overlooked by those who maintain that North Vietnam is engaged in aggression against a *foreign* country rather than supporting a domestic insurrection. In its unilateral statement of July 21, 1954, the United States indicated, with respect to the Accords, that it would "refrain from the threat or use of force to disturb them," and further stated that the United States would "continue to seek to achieve unity through free elections, supervised by the U.N. to insure that they are conducted fairly."

It is not useful to try to assign degrees of guilt to each side for violations of the Geneva Accords. It suffices to note that there have been violations by all concerned, including the United States, which, in violation of its commitment of 1954, supported President Ngo Dinh Diem in his refusal to hold the elections provided for in the Geneva Accords, presumably because he feared that the communists would win. . . .

Through a series of small steps, none extremely important or irrevocable in itself, the United States gradually took over the French commitment in South Vietnam after the French withdrawal. The United States Military Assistance Advisory Group took over the training of the South Vietnamese Army in 1955 and thereafter the United States became increasingly committed to the Diem regime by means of economic and military support and public statements. In 1960 President Eisenhower increased the number of American military advisers from 327 to 685. Further increases followed and by February 1962 the number of United States military personnel in South Vietnam had reached four thousand. Step by step, as it became increasingly clear that the South Vietnamese Army was being defeated, the American commitment increased. The result has been that through a series of limited escalations, each one of which has been more or less compatible with the view that the war was not our war and would have to be won or lost by the South Vietnamese themselves, the war has indeed become our war. Gradually, almost imperceptibly, the commitment to support the South Vietnamese in a war which it was said *they* must either win or lose was supplanted by a commitment, as Secretary McNamara has put it, "to take all necessary measures within our capability to prevent a Communist victory."

The United States is now involved in a sizable and "open-ended" war against communism in the only country in the world which won freedom from colonial rule under communist leadership. In South Vietnam as in North Vietnam, the communists remain today the only solidly organized political force. That fact is both the measure of our failure and the key to its possible redemption. . . .

Our search for a solution to the Vietnamese war must begin with the general fact that nationalism is the strongest single political force in the world today and the specific fact, arising from the history to which I have referred, that in Vietnam the most effective nationalist movement is communist-controlled. We are compelled, therefore, once again to choose between opposition to communism and support of nationalism. I strongly recommend that for once we give priority to the latter. The dilemma is a cruel one, and one which we must hope to avoid in the future by timely and unstinting support of non-communist nationalist movements, but it is too late for that in Vietnam. I strongly recommend, therefore, that we seek to come to terms with both Hanoi and the Viet Cong, not, to be sure, by "turning tail and running," as the saying goes, but by conceding the Viet Cong a part in the government of South Vietnam. . . .

Present realities require a revision of priorities in American policy. The basis of my criticisms of American policy in Southeast Asia and Latin America is a belief that American interests are better served by supporting nationalism than by opposing communism, and that when the two are encountered in the same political movement it is in our interest to accept a communist role in the government of the country concerned rather than to undertake the cruel and all but impossible task of suppressing a genuinely nationalist revolution. In Vietnam we have allowed our fear of communism to make us once again the enemy of a nationalist revolution, and in that role we have wrought havoc. . . .

The war in Southeast Asia has affected the internal life of the United States in two important ways: it has diverted our energies from the Great Society program which began so promisingly, and it has generated the beginnings of a war fever in the minds of the American people and their leaders.

Despite brave talk about having both "guns and butter," the Vietnamese war has already had a destructive effect on the Great Society. The 89th Congress, which enacted so much important domestic legislation in 1965, enacted much less in 1966, partly, it is true, because of the unusual productivity of its first session but more because the Congress as a whole lost interest in the Great Society and became, politically and psychologically, a "war Congress."

There is a kind of Gresham's Law of public policy: fear drives out hope, security precedes welfare, and it is only to the extent that a country is successful in the prevention of bad things that it is set free to concentrate on those pursuits which renew the nation's strength and bring happiness into the lives of its people. . . .

My own view is that there is a kind of madness in the facile assumption that we can raise the many billions of dollars necessary to rebuild our schools and cities and public transport and eliminate the pollution of air and water while also spending tens of billions to finance an "open-ended" war in Asia. But even if the material resources can somehow be drawn from an expanding economy, I do not think that the spiritual resources will long be forthcoming from an angry and disappointed people.

DOCUMENT 17

STOKELY CARMICHAEL ON BLACK POWER, 1966

As the civil rights movement succumbed to disappointment and disillusionment and was in some degree replaced by the cry for black power, Stokely Carmichael, a leading activist in the Student Non-Violent Coordinating Committee, became one of the outstanding spokesmen for black power. The statement excerpted here was originally published as "What We Want" in the New York Review of Books, *September 22, 1966.*

For too many years, black Americans marched and had their heads broken and got shot. They were saying to the country, "Look, you guys are supposed to be nice guys and we are only going to do what we are supposed to do—why do you beat us up, why don't you give us what we ask, why don't you straighten yourselves out?" After years of this, we are at almost the same point—because we demonstrated from a position of weakness. We cannot be expected any longer to march and have our heads broken in order to say to whites: come on, you're nice guys. For you are not nice guys. We have found you out. . . .

Black power can be clearly defined for those who do not attach the fears of white America to their questions about it. We should begin with the basic fact that black Americans have two problems: they are poor and they are black. All other problems arise from this two-sided reality: lack of education, the so-called apathy of black men. Any program to end racism must address itself to that double reality.

Almost from its beginning, SNCC sought to address itself to both conditions with a program aimed at winning political power for impoverished Southern blacks. We had to begin with politics because black Americans are a propertyless people in a country where property is valued above all. We had to work for power, because this country does not function by morality, love, and non-violence, but by power. Thus we determined to win political power, with the idea of moving on from there into activity that would have economic effects. With power the masses could *make or participate in making* the decisions which govern their destinies, and thus create basic change in their day-to-day lives. . . .

Ultimately, the economic foundations of this country must be shaken if black people are to control their lives. The colonies of the United States—and this includes the black ghettoes within its borders, north and south—must be liberated. For a century, this nation has been like an octopus of exploitation, its tentacles stretching from Mississippi and Harlem to South America, the Middle East, southern Africa, and Vietnam; the form of exploitation varies from area to area but the essential result has been the same—a powerful few have been maintained and enriched at the expense of the poor and voiceless colored masses. This pattern must be broken. As its grip loosens here and there around the world, the hopes of black Americans become more realistic. For racism to die, a totally different America must be born.

This is what the white society does not wish to face; this is why that society prefers to talk about integration. But integration speaks not at all to the problem of poverty, only to the problem of blackness. Integration today means the man who "makes it," leaving his black brothers behind in the ghetto as fast as his new sports car will take him. It has no relevance to the Harlem wino or to the cottonpicker making three dollars a day. As a lady I know in Alabama once said, "the food that Ralph Bunche eats doesn't fill my stomach."

Integration, moreover, speaks to the problem of blackness in a despicable way. As a goal, it has been based on complete acceptance of the fact that *in order to have* a decent house or education, blacks must move into a white neighborhood or send their children to a white school. This reinforces, among both black and white, the idea that "white" is automatically better and "black" is by definition inferior. This is why integration is a subterfuge for the maintenance of white supremacy. It allows the nation to focus on a handful of Southern children who get into white schools, at great price, and to ignore the 94 per cent who are left behind in unimproved all-black schools. Such situations will not change until black people have power— to control their own school boards, in this case. Then Negroes become equal in a way that means something, and integration ceases to be a one-way street. Then integration doesn't mean draining skills and energies from the ghetto into white neighborhoods; then it can mean white people moving from Beverly Hills into Watts, white people joining the Lowndes County Freedom Organization. Then integration becomes relevant.

DOCUMENT 18

SENATOR ROBERT F. KENNEDY ON THE PROBLEMS OF THE CITIES,
AUGUST 15, 1966

In the years before his death Senator Kennedy became increasingly absorbed with the problems of the cities, and particularly of their most underprivileged citizens. The statement from which this passage is excerpted was given before the Subcommittee on Executive Reorganization of the Senate Committee on Government Operations.

What should we expect from our cities? A great historian of urban life, Lewis Mumford, has written: "What makes the city in fact one is the common interest in justice and the common aim, that of pursuing the good life." . . .

The city is not just housing and stores. It is not just education and employment, parks and theaters, banks and shops. It is a place where men should be able to live in dignity and security and harmony, where the great achievements of modern civilization and the ageless pleasures afforded by natural beauty should be available to all.

If this is what we want—and this is what we must

want if men are to be free for that "pursuit of happiness" which was the earliest promise of the American nation— we will need more than poverty programs, housing programs, and employment programs, although we will need all of these. We will need an outpouring of imagination, ingenuity, discipline, and hard work unmatched since the first adventurers set out to conquer the wilderness. For the problem is the largest we have ever known. And we confront an urban wilderness more formidable and resistant and in some ways more frightening than the wilderness faced by the pilgrims or the pioneers.

One great problem is sheer growth—growth which crowds people into slums, thrusts suburbs out over the countryside, burdens to the breaking point all our old ways of thought and action—our systems of transport and water supply and education, and our means of raising money to finance these vital services.

A second is destruction of the physical environment, stripping people of contact with sun and fresh air, clean rivers, grass, and trees—condemning them to a life among stone and concrete, neon lights and an endless flow of automobiles. This happens not only in the central city, but in the very suburbs where people once fled to find nature. "There is no police so effective," said Emerson, "as a good hill and a wide pasture . . . where the boys . . . can dispose of their superfluous strength and spirits." We cannot restore the pastures; but we must provide a chance to enjoy nature, a chance for recreation, for pleasure and for some restoration of that essential dimension of human existence which flows only from man's contact with the natural world around him.

A third is the increasing difficulty of transportation— adding concealed, unpaid hours to the workweek; removing men from the social and cultural amenities that are the heart of the city; sending destructive swarms of automobiles across the city, leaving behind them a band of concrete and a poisoned atmosphere. And sometimes— as in Watts—our surrender to the automobile has so crippled public transport that thousands literally cannot afford to go to work elsewhere in the city.

A fourth destructive force is the concentrated poverty and racial tension of the urban ghetto—a problem so vast that the barest recital of its symptoms is profoundly shocking:

> *Segregation* is becoming the governing rule: Washington is only the most prominent example of a city which has become overwhelmingly Negro as whites move to the suburbs; many other cities are moving along the same road—for example, Chicago, which, if present trends continue, will be over 50 percent Negro by 1975. The ghettoes of Harlem and Southside and Watts are cities in themselves, areas of as many as 350,000 people.

> *Poverty and Unemployment* are endemic: from ⅓ to ½ of the families in these areas live in poverty; in some, male unemployment may be as high as 40%. Unemployment of Negro youths nationally is over

> 25%.

> *Welfare and Dependency* are pervasive: ¼ of the children in these ghettoes, as in Harlem, may receive Federal Aid to Dependent Children; in New York City, ADC alone costs over $20 million a month; in our five largest cities, the ADC bill is over $500 million a year.

> *Housing* is overcrowded, unhealthy, and dilapidated: the last housing census found 43% of urban Negro housing to be substandard; in many of these ghettoes, ten thousand children may be injured or infected by rat bites every year.

> *Education* is segregated, unequal, and inadequate: the high school drop-out rate averages nearly 70%; there are academic high schools in which less than 3% of the entering students will graduate with an academic diploma.

> *Health* is poor and care inadequate: infant mortality in the ghettoes is more than twice the rate outside; mental retardation caused by inadequate prenatal care is more than seven times the white rate; ½ of all babies born in Manhattan last year will have had no

prenatal care at all; deaths from diseases like tuber-
culosis, influenza, and pneumonia are two to three
times as common as elsewhere.

Fifth is both cause and consequence of all the rest. It is
the destruction of the sense, and often the fact, of community, of human dialogue, the thousand invisible strands
of common experience and purpose, affection and respect
which tie men to their fellows. It is expressed in such
words as community, neighborhood, civic pride, friendship. It provides the life-sustaining force of human warmth,
of security among others, and a sense of one's own human
significance in the accepted association and companion-
ship of others. . . .

But of all our problems, the most immediate and
pressing, the one which threatens to paralyze our very
capacity to act, to obliterate our vision of the future is
the plight of the Negro of the center city. For this plight
—and the riots which are its product and symptom—
threaten to divide Americans for generations to come; to
add to the ever-present difficulties of race and class the
bitter legacy of violence and destruction and fear. . . .

It is therefore of the utmost importance that we go
beyond the temporary measures thus far adopted to deal
with riots—beyond the fire hoses and the billy-clubs; and
beyond even sprinklers on fire hydrants and new swimming pools as well. We must start . . . along the road
toward solutions to the underlying conditions which afflict
our cities, so that they may become the places of fulfillment and ease, comfort and joy, the communities they
were meant to be.

DOCUMENT 19

REPORT OF THE NATIONAL ADVISORY
COMMISSION ON CIVIL DISORDERS,
1968

*When in the summer of 1967 there were numbers of
serious riots in American cities President Johnson responded by establishing, July 28, 1967, the National*

Advisory Commission on Civil Disorders and directed it to answer three questions: What happened? Why did it happen? What can be done to prevent it from happening again? After months of investigation the Commission made a long report (often referred to as the Kerner Commission Report, after former Governor Kerner of Illinois, who headed the Commission) which opened with these words of warning.

This is our basic conclusion: Our nation is moving toward two societies, one black, one white—separate and unequal.

Reaction to last summer's disorders has quickened the movement and deepened the division. Discrimination and segregation have long permeated much of American life; they now threaten the future of every American.

This deepening racial division is not inevitable. The movement apart can be reversed. Choice is still possible. Our principal task is to define that choice and to press for a national resolution.

To pursue our present course will involve the continuing polarization of the American community and, ultimately, the destruction of basic democratic values.

The alternative is not blind repression or capitulation to lawlessness. It is the realization of common opportunities for all within a single society.

This alternative will require a commitment to national action—compassionate, massive and sustained, backed by the resorces of the most powerful and the richest nation on this earth. From every American it will require new attitudes, new understanding, and, above all, new will.

The vital needs of the nation must be met; hard choices must be made, and, if necessary, new taxes enacted.

Violence cannot build a better society. Disruption and disorder nourish repression, not justice. They strike at the freedom of every citizen. The community cannot—it will not—tolerate coercion and mob rule.

Violence and destruction must be ended—in the streets of the ghetto and in the lives of people.

Segregation and poverty have created in the racial ghetto a destructive environment totally unknown to most white Americans.

What white Americans have never fully understood—
but what the Negro can never forget—is that white society
is deeply implicated in the ghetto. White institutions created it, white institutions maintain it, and white society
condones it.

It is time now to turn with all the purpose at our
command to the major unfinished business of this nation.
It is time to adopt strategies for action that will produce
quick and visible progress. It is time to make good the
promises of American democracy to all citizens—urban
and rural, white and black, Spanish-surname, American
Indian, and every minority group.

Our recommendations embrace three basic principles:

To mount programs on a scale equal to the dimension
of the problems,

To aim these programs for high impact in the immediate future in order to close the gap between
promise and performance,

To undertake new initiatives and experiments that
can change the system of failure and frustration that
now dominates the ghetto and weakens our society.

These programs will require unprecedented levels of
funding and performance, but they neither probe deeper
nor demand more than the problems which called them
forth. There can be no higher priority for national action
and no higher claim on the nation's conscience.

DOCUMENT 20

LYNDON B. JOHNSON, ECONOMIC REPORT OF THE PRESIDENT,
JANUARY 16, 1969

*In the President's regular Annual Report excerpted
here, his last to the Congress, President Johnson
pointed with satisfaction to the achievements of the
long economic boom of the 1960's.*

The nation is now in its 95th month of continuous economic advance. Both in strength and length, this prosperity is without parallel in our history. We have steered clear of the business-cycle recessions which for generations derailed us repeatedly from the path of growth and progress.

This record demonstrates the vitality of a free economy and its capacity for steady growth. No longer do we view our economic life as a relentless tide of ups and downs. No longer do we fear that automation and technical progress will rob workers of jobs rather than help us to achieve greater abundance. No longer do we consider poverty and unemployment permanent landmarks on our economic scene.

Our progress did not just happen. It was created by American labor and business in effective partnership with the Government.

Ever since the historic passage of the Employment Act in 1946, economic policies have responded to the fire alarm of recession and boom. In the 1960's, we have adopted a new strategy aimed at fire prevention—sustaining prosperity and heading off recession or serious inflation before they could take hold.

In 1964 and 1965, tax reductions unleashed the vigor of private demand and brought the economy a giant step toward its full potential.

In 1966 and 1967, restrictive monetary and fiscal policies offset the strains of added defense spending. The adjustment was far from ideal, however, because of the delay in increasing taxes to pay the bills for the defense build-up and for continuing urgent civilian programs.

In 1968, our nation's finances were finally adjusted to the needs of a defense emergency. The Revenue and Expenditure Control Act strengthened the foundation of prosperity.

Aided by these policies in the past five years, the nation's total output of goods and services—our gross national product—has increased by more than $190-billion, after correcting for price changes. This is as large as the gain of the previous 11 years.

The prosperity of the last five years has been accompanied by benefits that extend into every corner of our national life.

—more than 8½ million additional workers found jobs,

—over-all unemployment declined from 5.7 per cent of our labor force to 3.3 per cent,

—unemployment of nonwhite adult males dropped particularly dramatically, from 9.7 per cent to 3.4 per cent,

—the number of persons in poverty declined by about 12½ million—progress greater than in the entire preceding 13 years,

—the average income of Americans (after taxes and after correction for price rises) increased by $535—more than one-fifth and again more than in the previous 13 years combined,

—corporate profits rose by about 50 per cent,

—wages and salaries also went up by 50 per cent,

—net income per farm advanced 36 per cent,

—the net financial assets of American families increased $460-billion—more than 50 per cent, and

—Federal revenues grew by $70-billion, helping to finance key social advances.

Meanwhile, a solid foundation has been built for continued growth in the years ahead.

Through Investment in Plant and Equipment. In the last five years, the stock of capital equipment has grown by nearly a third. Only 5 per cent of manufacturing corporations report that their capacity is in excess of currently foreseen needs.

Through Investment in Manpower. More than a million Americans have acquired skills in special training institutions or on the job—as a result of new Federal efforts.

Through Investment in Education. College enrollment has risen by 2¼ million since 1963. Expenditures on all public education have increased at an average of 10 per cent a year; Federal grants have almost quadrupled.

Through Investment in Our Neighborhoods. Our urban centers are beginning to be restored as decent places to live and initial steps have been taken to help ensure construction of 26 million new or rehabilitated housing units by 1978.

DOCUMENT 21

RICHARD M. NIXON, INAUGURAL ADDRESS,
JANUARY 20, 1969

In this Address, President Nixon continued with the appeal for peace among nations that has been a leading theme in recent Presidential statements. But in addition to calling for peace abroad, he called for peace at home and pointed to the lack of domestic unity as a major problem for his Administration.

Each moment in history is a fleeting time, precious and unique. But some stand out as moments of beginning, in which courses are set that shape decades or centuries. This can be such a moment. Forces now are converging that make possible for the first time the hope that many of man's deepest aspirations can at last be realized. The spiraling pace of change allows us to contemplate, within our own lifetime, advances that once would have taken centuries.

In throwing wide the horizons of space, we have discovered new horizons on earth.

For the first time, because the people of the world want peace and the leaders of the world are afraid of war, the times are on the side of peace. Eight years from now America will celebrate its 200th anniversary as a nation. And within the lifetime of most people now living, mankind will celebrate that great new year which comes only once in a thousand years—the beginning of the third millennium. What kind of a nation we will be, what kind of a world we will live in, whether we shape the future in the image of our hopes, is ours to determine by our actions and our choices.

The greatest honor history can bestow is the title of peacemaker. This honor now beckons America—the chance to help lead the world at last out of the valley of turmoil and on to that high ground of peace that man has dreamed of since the dawn of civilization. . . .

Standing in this same place a third of a century ago,

Franklin Delano Roosevelt addressed the nation ravaged
by depression gripped in fear. He could say in surveying
the nation's troubles: "They concern, thank God, only material things." Our crisis today is in reverse. We find ourselves rich in goods, but ragged in spirit, reaching with magnificent precision for the moon, but falling into raucous
discord on earth. We are caught in war, wanting peace.
We're torn by division, wanting unity. We see around us
empty lives, wanting fulfillment. We see tasks that need
doing, waiting for hands to do them.

To a crisis of the spirit, we need an answer of the
spirit. And to find that answer, we need only look within
ourselves. When we listen to the better angels of our nature,
we find that they celebrate the simple things, the basic
things—such as goodness, decency, love, kindness. Greatness comes in simple trappings.

The simple things are the ones most needed today if
we are to surmount what divides us and cement what
unites us. To lower our voices would be a simple thing. In
these difficult years, America has suffered from a fever of
words; from inflated rhetoric that promises more than it
can deliver; from angry rhetoric that fans discontents into
hatreds; from bombastic rhetoric that postures instead of
persuading. We cannot learn from one another until we
stop shouting at one another—until we speak quietly
enough so that our words can be heard as well as our
voices. For its part, government will listen.

We will strive to listen in new ways—to the voices of
quiet anguish, the voices that speak without words, the
voices of the heart—to the injured voices, the anxious
voices, the voices that have despaired of being heard.

Those who have been left out we will try to bring in.
Those left behind, we will help to catch up.

For all our people, we will set as our goal the decent
order that makes progress possible and our lives secure. As
we reach toward our hopes, our task is to build on what
has gone before—not turning away from the old, but
turning toward the new.

In this past third of a century, government has passed
more laws, spent more money, initiated more programs,
than in all our previous history. In pursuing our goals of
full employment, better housing, excellence in education;

in rebuilding our cities and improving our rural areas; in protecting our environment, enhancing the quality of life —in all these and more, we will and must press urgently forward.

We shall plan now for the day when our wealth can be transferred from the destruction of war abroad to the urgent needs of our people at home. The American dream does not come to those who fall asleep. But we are approaching the limits of what government alone can do. Our greatest need now is to reach beyond government, to enlist the legions of the concerned and the committed. What has to be done has to be done by government and people together or it will not be done at all. The lesson of past agony is that without the people we can do nothing; with the people we can do everything. . . .

Let us take as our goal: where peace is unknown, make it welcome; where peace is fragile, make it strong; where peace is temporary, make it permanent.

After a period of confrontation, we are entering an era of negotiation. Let all nations know that during this Administration our lines of communication will be open. We seek an open world—open to ideas, open to the exchange of goods and people, a world in which no people, great or small, will live in angry isolation. We cannot expect to make everyone our friend, but we can try to make no one our enemy. Those who would be our adversaries, we invite to a peaceful competition—not in conquering territory or extending dominion, but in enriching the life of man.

As we explore the reaches of space, let us go to the new worlds together—not as new worlds to be conquered, but as a new adventure to be shared. And with those who are willing to join, let us cooperate to reduce the burden of arms, to strengthen the structure of peace, to lift up the poor and the hungry. But to all those who would be tempted by weakness, let us leave no doubt that we will be as strong as we need to be for as long as we need to be. . . .

Let this message be heard by strong and weak alike. The peace we seek—the peace we seek to win—is not victory over any other people, but the peace that comes with healing in its wings; with compassion for those who have suffered; with understanding for those who have opposed us; with the opportunity for all the peoples of this earth to choose their own destiny. . . .

We have endured a long night of the American spirit. But as our eyes catch the dimness of the first rays of dawn, let us not curse the remaining dark. Let us gather the light.

Our destiny offers not the cup of despair, but the chalice of opportunity. So let us seize it, not in fear, but in gladness—and "riders on the earth together," let us go forward, firm in our faith, steadfast in our purpose, cautious of the dangers; but sustained by our confidence in the will of God and the promise of man.

*

Acknowledgments

THANKS are due to the following persons and publishers for permission to reprint material for which they hold the copyrights: to the Council on Foreign Relations and the editors of *Foreign Affairs* for a passage from "The Sources of Soviet Conduct," originally published in *Foreign Affairs*; to Harvard University Press for a passage from Elihu Root, *Addresses on Government and Citizenship*; to Henry Holt and Company for a passage from Walter Johnson, ed., *The Letters of William Allen White*; to Alfred A. Knopf, Inc., for a passage from W. L. Riordon, *Plunkitt of Tammany Hall*, Introd. by Roy V. Peel; to Mr. William L. White of Emporia, Kansas, for a passage from William Allen White, *The Old Order Changeth*.

Note on Sources

PART I. RECONSTRUCTION AND AFTER. 1. R. F. Basler ed., *Collected Works of Abraham Lincoln* (New Brunswick, N. J.), Vol. VII, pp. 433–4. 2. *New York Daily Tribune*, Aug. 5, 1864. 3. Basler, *op. cit.*, Vol. VIII, p. 400 ff. 4. W. L. Fleming ed., *Documentary History of Reconstruction* (Cleveland, 1906). Vol. I, pp. 147–9. 5. *Report of the Joint Committee on Reconstruction* (Washington, 1866), p. x ff. 6. *Proceedings of the Convention of the Colored People of Virginia, Held in the City of Alexandria, August 2, 3, 4, 5, 1865.* (Alexandria, 1865), pp. 21-2. 7. Fleming, *op. cit.*, Vol. I, pp. 195–6. 8. *Report of the Joint Committee on Reconstruction*, Part III, pp. 163 ff. 9. Fleming, *op. cit.*, pp. 223–6. 10. J. D. Richardson ed., *A Compilation of the Messages and Papers of the Presidents* (Washington, 1898), Vol. VI, p. 499 ff. 11. *Trial of Andrew Johnson* (Washington, 1868). Vol. III, p. 247 ff. 12. *Ibid.*, p. 331 ff. 13. Fleming, *op. cit.*, Vol. II, pp. 387–98. 14. *Congressional Record*, 44th Cong., 1st Sess., pp. 2100–5. 15. 16 Wallace, 36. 16. 109 U. S. 3 at 20. 17. *Ibid.*, at 26. 18. 163 U. S. 537. 19. *Ibid.*, at 554. 20. 347 U. S. 483. 21. *New York Times*, Mar. 12, 1956.

PART II. INDUSTRIALISM AND SOCIAL REFORM. 1. Henry George, *Progress and Poverty* (New York, 1883), p. 12 ff. 2. Edward Bellamy, *Looking Backward* (New York, 1889), p. 51 ff. 3. Andrew Carnegie, "Wealth," *North American Review*, Vol. 148 (June 1889), pp. 656–60. 4. A. G. Keller and M. R. Davie eds., *Essays of William Graham Sumner* (New Haven, 1940), Vol. I, p. 91 ff. 5. H. D. Lloyd, *Wealth Against Commonwealth* (New York, 1894), p. 1 ff. 6. *American Federationist*, Vol. I (Sept. 1894), pp. 150–2. 7. 158 U. S. 601. 8. *Ibid.*, at 664. 9. 156 U. S. 1. 10. *Ibid.*, at 36.

PART III. AGRARIAN PROTEST. 1. Jonathan Periam, *The Groundswell* (Chicago, 1874), p. 286 ff. 2. 94 U. S. 113. 3. *Ibid.*, at 138. 4. Edward McPherson, *A Hand-Book of Politics for 1892* (Washington, 1892), p. 269 ff. 5. Richardson, *op. cit.*, Vol. IX, p. 401 ff. 6. W. H. ("Coin") Harvey, *Coin's Financial School* (Chicago, 1894), p. 1 ff. 7. J. L. Laughlin, *Facts About Money*

515   *Note on Sources*

(Chicago, 1895), p. 223 ff. 8. W. J. Bryan, *The First Battle*
(Chicago, 1896), p. 199 ff. 9. W. A. White, *What's the Matter
With Kansas* (Emporia, Kansas, 1910).

PART IV. IMPERIALISM AND WAR. 1. Josiah Strong, *Our Country*
(New York, 1885), p. 161 ff. 2. H. C. Lodge, "Our Blundering
Foreign Policy," *The Forum*, Vol. 19 (March 1895), pp. 14–17.
3. Richardson, *op. cit.*, Vol. X, p. 139 ff. 4. W. H. Page, "The
War with Spain, and After," *Atlantic Monthly*, Vol. 81 (June
1898), pp. 725–7. 5. Carl Schurz, "The Policy of Imperialism,"
Liberty Tracts No. 4 (Chicago, 1899). 6. 63rd Cong., 2nd Sess.,
Senate Document No. 566. 7. 64th Cong., 2nd Sess., *Senate
Document* No. 685. 8. 65th Cong., 1st Sess., *Senate Document*
No. 5. 9. *Congressional Record*, 65th Cong., 1st Sess., pp.
213–14. 10. *Supplement to the Messages and Papers of the
Presidents Covering the Second Administration of Woodrow
Wilson*, Vol. 18, pp. 8423–6. 11. 65th Cong., 3rd Sess., *Senate
Document* No. 389, pp. 12–15. 12. *Congressional Record*, 65th
Cong., 1st Sess., p. 8781 ff.

PART V. PROGRESSIVISM. 1. Lincoln Steffens, *The Shame of the
Cities* (New York, 1904), p. 3 ff. 2. W. L. Riordon, *Plunkitt of
Tammany Hall* (New York, 1948), pp. 3–5, 6–7, 25–7. 3.
Walter Lippmann, *Drift and Mastery* (New York, 1914), p. 1 ff.
4. 198 U. S. 45. 5. *Ibid.*, at 75. 6. 208 U. S. 412. 7. 58th Cong.,
3rd Sess., *House Documents*, Vol. 100, p. 226 ff. 8. *Congressional Record*, 59th Cong., 1st Sess., p. 2252 ff. 9. W. A. White,
The Old Order Changeth (New York, 1910), p. 50 ff. 10.
Elihu Root, *Addresses on Government and Citizenship* (Cambridge, Mass., 1916), p. 83 ff. 11. *New York Times*, August 7,
1912. 12. Woodrow Wilson, *The New Freedom* (New York,
1913), p. 167 ff. 13. *Money Trust Investigation; Report of Subcommittee of the Committee on Banking and Currency* (Pujo
Committee) (Washington, 1913), Vol. 3, p. 55 ff. 14. *Supplement to Messages and Papers, op. cit.*, Vol. XVII, pp. 7868–71.

PART VI. PROSPERITY AND DEPRESSION. 1. 247 U. S. 251. 2.
Ibid., at 277. 3. 250 U. S. 616. 4. *Ibid.*, at 624. 5. H. W. Evans,
"The Klan's Fight for Americanism," *North American Review*
(March–April–May, 1926), Vol. 223, p. 38 ff. 6. Walter Johnson
ed., *Selected Letters of William Allen White* (New York, 1947),
pp 220–21. 7. "A New Declaration of Independence," *Statement and Platform* of Robert M. La Follette (Chicago, 1924),
pp. 18–24. 8. *New York Times*, October 23, 1928. 9. *Ibid.*,
September 24, 1932. 10. *Ibid.*, March 5, 1933. 11. *Ibid.*, October

31, 1936. 12. 297 U. S. 1. 13. *Ibid.*, at 78. 14. *New York Times*, March 10, 1937. 15. 75th Cong., 1st Sess., *Senate Report No. 711*, p. 3 ff.

PART VII. WORLD WAR II AND THE POST-WAR WORLD. 1. *New York Times*, October 6, 1937. 2. *New York Times*, December 18, 1940. 3. *New York Times*, January 7, 1941. 4. *Congressional Record*, 77th Cong., 1st Sess., Appendix, pp. 178–9. 5. *New York Times*, April 24, 1941. 6. *Ibid.*, August 15, 1941. 7. *Ibid.*, December 9, 1941. 8. *Congressional Record*, 80th Cong., 1st Sess., pp. 1980–1. 9. *Ibid.*, Appendix, p. 3248 ff. 10. "X" "Sources of Soviet Conduct," *Foreign Affairs*, Vol. XXV (July 1947), p. 571 ff. 11. *New York Times*, March 19, 1949. 12. *Congressional Record*, 81st Cong., 1st Sess., p. 9205 ff. 13. *New York Times*, April 20, 1951. 14. *Military Situation in the Far East: Hearings before the Committee on Armed Services and the Committee on Foreign Relations. United States Senate, Eighty-Second Congress, First Session.* (Washington, 1951), Part 3, pp. 1718–20. 15. *Hearings, United States Senate, Committee on Foreign Relations, On the Nomination of John Foster Dulles, Secretary of State-Designate.* 83rd Cong., 1st Sess. (Washington, 1953), p. 5 ff. 16. *New York Times*, March 28, 1954. 17. *Ibid.*, July 1, 1954. 18. *Ibid.*, January 21, 1957.

PART VIII: A TIME OF TROUBLES: THE 1960's. 1. *Public Papers of the Presidents, Dwight D. Eisenhower, 1960–61* (Washington, 1961), pp. 1036–9. 2. *Public Papers . . . John F. Kennedy, 1961* (Washington, 1961), pp. 1–3. 3. *Ibid.*, 1962, pp. 471–3. 4. *Ibid.*, pp. 806–8. 5. *New York Times*, October 28, 29, 1962. 6. *Public Papers . . . John F. Kennedy, 1963* (Washington, 1964), pp. 601–6. 7. 369 U.S. 186–9, 191–2, 198–9, 226, 237. 8. 377 U.S. 533, 561–3, 565, 566–8. 9. 377 U.S. 595, 614–15, 621–24. 10. *Public Papers . . . Lyndon B. Johnson, 1963–64* (Washington, 1965), I, pp. 375–7. 11. *Ibid.*, I, pp. 704–6. 12. Press Release, Republican National Committee, September 3, 1964. 13. Leon Friedman, ed., *The Civil Rights Reader* (New York, 1968), pp. 110–13. 14. *Public Papers . . . Lyndon B. Johnson, 1965* (Washington, 1966), I, pp. 281–7. 15. *Ibid.*, I pp. 394–9. 16. J. W. Fulbright, *The Arrogance of Power* (New York, 1966), pp. 115–19, 131, 133–4. 17. *New York Review of Books*, September 22, 1966. 18. *Pratt Planning Papers, IV* (1967), pp. 7–10. 19. *Report of National Advisory Commission on Civil Disorders* (New York, 1968), pp. 1–2. 20. *New York Times*, January 17, 1969. 21. *Ibid.*, January 21, 1969.

✳ INDEX ✳

A NOTE ABOUT THE AUTHOR

Richard Hofstadter, who died in October 1970, was DeWitt Clinton Professor of American History at Columbia University. He received his B.A. from the University of Buffalo and his M.A. and Ph.D. from Columbia University. He taught at the University of Maryland from 1942 until 1946, when he joined the History Department at Columbia. He also served as Pitt Professor of American History and Institutions at Cambridge University in 1958–9. The first of his books on American History was *Social Darwinism in American Thought,* published in 1944, followed by *The American Political Tradition,* in 1948. *The Age of Reform* (1955) won the Pulitzer Prize in history, and *Anti-intellectualism in American Life* (1963) received the Pulitzer Prize in general nonfiction, the Emerson Award of Phi Beta Kappa, and the Sidney Hillman Prize Award. Mr. Hofstadter's other books include *The Paranoid Style in American Politics* (1965), *The Progressive Historians* (1968), *The Idea of a Party System* (1969), and *America at 1750* (1971). He also edited, with Michael Wallace, *American Violence: A Documentary History* (1970).

VINTAGE HISTORY—AMERICAN